Germans as Victims in the Literary Fiction
of the Berlin Republic

Studies in German Literature, Linguistics, and Culture

Germans as Victims
in the Literary Fiction
of the Berlin Republic

Edited by
Stuart Taberner and Karina Berger

CAMDEN HOUSE
Rochester, New York

First published 2009 by Camden House
Transferred to digital printing 2011

Camden House is an imprint of Boydell & Brewer Inc.
668 Mt. Hope Avenue, Rochester, NY 14620, USA
www.camden-house.com
and of Boydell & Brewer Limited
PO Box 9, Woodbridge, Suffolk IP12 3DF, UK
www.boydellandbrewer.com

ISBN-13: 978-1-57113-393-9
ISBN-10: 1-57113-393-3

Library of Congress Cataloging-in-Publication Data

Germans as victims in the literary fiction of the Berlin Republic / edited by
Stuart Taberner and Karina Berger.
     p. cm.
Includes bibliographical references and index.
ISBN-13: 978-1-57113-393-9 (hardcover : alk. paper)
ISBN-10: 1-57113-393-3 (hardcover : alk. paper)
1. Victims in literature. 2. Germans in literature. 3. German literature
— 20th century — History and criticism. 4. World War, 1939–1945 —
Literature and the war. I. Taberner, Stuart. II. Berger, Karina, 1977–
III. Title.

PT405.G4585 2009
830.9'352931—dc22

                                                                 2008048070

This publication is printed on acid-free paper.

Contents

Acknowledgments

WITHOUT THE GENEROUS SUPPORT of the Arts and Humanities Research Council (UK), this book would have been a less coherent and less ambitious enterprise. The three-year project funded by the AHRC on "Representations of Germans as Victims" made possible a series of workshops and conferences which significantly improved the quality of our ruminations. This volume is joined by others on film, memorials, and international perspectives on "German suffering," and a wealth of articles and book chapters. We are grateful to all our collaborators on the project, particularly Professor Bill Niven, Professor Paul Cooke, Dr Helmut Schmitz and Dr Annette Seidel-Arpacı.

We are especially grateful, of course, to all the contributors to the volume for their hard work and forebearance with our editing. Finally, thanks are due to Ivor Taberner-Davies, whose arrival in the world two weeks later than anticipated gave his father just enough time to finish his work on this volume!

S. T. and K. B.
October 2008

Introduction

Karina Berger and Stuart Taberner

TWENTY YEARS AFTER THE FALL of the Berlin Wall in November 1989, how the Nazi past is discussed, represented, and commemorated in what has come to be known as the Berlin Republic now appears somewhat different from the "memory culture" of the "old" Federal Republic (FRG, or West Germany) and certainly distinct from the state-directed memorialization of the former East Germany. In place of a rather rigid opposition between a West German "official" culture of Holocaust remembrance, modesty in foreign affairs, and ritualized gestures of contrition — at least from the early 1970s — and an uneasiness on the part of many private citizens with repeated proclamations of German guilt and the "repression" of "German suffering,"[1] — most likely vocalized from the early 1980s by conservative challenges to the centrality of the Nazi past to public debate — we now see the emergence of a more fluid, less monolithic, and often more fragmented discourse on the years 1933 to 1945. This is a form of multifaceted engagement with a past that can never be grasped in its totality that accepts gaps in knowledge and understanding and explicitly attempts to capture the complexity of the period — above all, the reality that German perpetrators might also have been victims — as well as the bewilderingly contingent nature of individual motivations, personal circumstances, and the array of opportunities for both cowardice and courage. In a hitherto seldomly encountered fashion, then, much of today's debate on Nazism centers on the effort to reconcile empathy with "real" historical actors, their choices and limitations (individual choices and objectively "given"), with more abstract notions of historical justice, universal ethical imperatives, and personal responsibility.

Accompanying the emergence of the Berlin Republic as the most recent inscription of German statehood, a series of events, exhibitions, speeches, controversies, texts, and debates have marked the evolution of more textured perspectives on the Nazi period. These include the Crimes of the *Wehrmacht* exhibition of the mid to late 1990s; the appearance in German of Daniel Jonah Goldhagen's *Hitler's Willing Executioners* (1996); Martin Walser's 1998 speech on receipt of the Peace Prize of the German Book Trade Association during which he controversially called for an end to the "instrumentalization of Auschwitz" and the "permanent exhibition" of "our shame";[2] the publication in 1999 of W. G. Sebald's *Luftkrieg und Literatur* (On the Natural History of Destruction) and Günter Grass's *Im Krebsgang* (Crabwalk) in 2002, the second seeming to respond to the first's accusation that postwar writers had failed to document German suffering; and the furor caused by Jörg Friedrich's *Der Brand* (The Fire, 2002), a graphic history of the Allied bombing campaign, and by his collection of photographs *Brandstätten* (Sites of Fire, 2003). Other key instances include the sixtieth anniversary of the end of the war on 8 May 2005; the opening of the Berlin Holocaust memorial after years of heated debate in the same year; the 2006 *Erzwungene Wege* (Paths Unchosen) exhibition in Berlin and plans for a Center Against Expulsions; Grass's revelation in August 2006 that he had been a member of the *Waffen SS*; and the unmasking of prominent intellectuals who had been (perhaps without their knowledge) recruited into the Nazi Party.

Anne Fuchs and Mary Cosgrove have described such events, exhibitions, speeches, controversies, texts, and debates as "memory contests,"[3] a term that captures well both the discursive construction of public memory — the way in which versions of the past are negotiated and restated through the interaction of the media, "cultural bearers," scholars, politicians, and "ordinary" social actors — and the incendiary focus on what Jan Assmann terms "fixed points" such as anniversaries, historical figures, or key experiences.[4] To some extent, these memory contests arise more or less inevitably at the point at which "communicative memory" passes into "cultural memory," with the extent of contestation being, in the particular case of postwar Germany, directly proportional to the widespread perception that this or that group, most often the wartime generation or the "'68ers," has exercised a monopoly over representations of the period that must be challenged. The frequency of such memory contests, and their ferocity, moreover, attests to the continued centrality of the Nazi past to the German present and to the personal investment many feel they have in how the period is represented. Or, it may be that heated discussions of the past function as proxies for less overt disputes regarding ownership of the political present — that is, who has the right to define German culture and society, or even that such controversies are, to some extent at least, rather opportunistically staged as media spectacles or symbolic battles between generations or interest groups?

In any case, that Germany is now manifestly a "different" country — from Hitler's Reich, of course, but also from East and West Germany from 1949 to 1989, with their unavoidable biographical and historical roots in the catastrophe of Nazism — means that the debate has moved on. Indeed, this is best evidenced in that, unlike the early and mid-1990s, Germans no longer appear to be quite as obssessed with the pursuit of "normality" —

whatever that term means[5] — but are rather more concerned with mundane and less existential issues, such as unemployment, welfare provision, public sector strikes, and high energy costs. Germans are not neccesarily "unbefangen" (uninhibited) with regard to the Nazi past but they are certainly less viscerally affected, even threatened, by the notion that there are (inevitably) competing and frequently conflicting ways of interpreting and representing it.

The term "memory contests," although useful, may thus overstate the extent of real disagreement. Or, more accurately, it may understate the degree of acceptance of certain historical contradictions and epistemological insights that has emerged in the background, off-stage, less spectacularly, perhaps incrementally, and, indeed, most likely precisely as a result of the discursive spaces opened up by these selfsame memory contests. Dirk Moses, in his excellent book *German Intellectuals and the Nazi Past* (2007), argues in relation to the period from 1945 that "West German democracy was a *discursive* achievement," that is, that the development of common values was "an open process, a hermeneutical circle, a permanent debate."[6] This may be all the more the case for the post-1990 period, stripped of the inhibiting factors presented, for example, by Cold War rivalry between the two German states or temporal proximity and biographical connection to the Nazi past. Recent German memory contests, we suggest, are being conducted against the backdrop of a changed memory discourse. This changed discourse, above all, acknowledges both the complexity and fundamental unknowability of the past — of the individual's subjective perception of his or her "objective" reality — and the consequent, and perhaps even productive, tension between judgment and empathy.

Thus there may well be a great deal of controversy on the specific issue of the planned Center Against Expulsions in Berlin,[7] particularly concerning its purpose and ramifications (especially for German-Polish relations), but there is no longer a lack of general recognition that German wartime suffering was "absolute" (to the extent that suffering is always absolute for those on whom it is inflicted) but also simultaneously part of an overarching narrative of the global conflict instigated by Germany, the war against Germany, the Holocaust, and the emergence of a new world order following Germany's defeat. Equally, the outrage expressed by many commentators following Grass's revelation that he had been a member of the *Waffen SS* related, for the most part, to his perceived tardiness in making the information public — why had he not mentioned this during almost fifty years of campaigning for openness about the Nazi past? — rather than to the notion that it might be possible to be both complicit in the regime but also a victim of its brutalization, of circumstances at the time, or even of foolish self-deception, or that individuals might merit a degree of empathy even if they had made the "wrong" choices. The debate now, we argue, is largely about how different histories are juxtaposed — not about whether it is legitimate to juxtapose them — and about the limits to empathy, the relationship between individual life stories and the larger historical context, and the extent to what Bill Niven has called, in relation to individuals' actions, an "ongoing process of broadening understanding"[8] needs to be set within an ethical framework that wards against the risks of relativization and revisionism.

It will be clear from the examples above that one of the truly novel aspects of the changed manner in which the Nazi past is discussed in today's Germany is the integration of narratives of German wartime suffering. Much effort has been expended by scholars in recent years on examining the frequently made claim that the subject had been taboo in the FRG, with Aleida Assmann offering perhaps the most succinct description of the relationship between the telling and retelling of stories of German suffering in private circles and the "official" focus on German perpetration: "Such stories have been told continuously within German families," she claims, but "this communicative effect of family narratives [. . .] did not cross over into public discourse. It did not find a larger public resonance in the society as a whole. Thus the disconnection and divide between private memory and official remembrance, so characteristic for postwar German history, started already in the 1950s."[9] Harald Welzer, Sabine Moller, and Karoline Tschuggnall speak of the contrast between the "album" of family memories of bombing and expulsion and the public "lexicon" of factual knowledge about the Nazi period and the Holocaust.[10] Whatever the case, the bombing, mass rape, and expulsion endured by millions of Germans during the closing phase of the war are now very much part of public discourse. Yet, in contrast with previous periods, it is widely acknowledged that representations of such horrors are not per se "revisionist" but rather, in the main, an invitation to reflect on the sequencing of the "German" experience: Germans as aggressors, Germans as perpetrators (with occasional acts of moral righteousness), Germans as victims of the furious response provoked by their aggression, Germans as members of a vanquished nation. Again, the emphasis is typically on texture, the blurriness of the historical picture, and the intriguing tension between the desire to "understand" and the requirement to view the actions and omissions of historical actors within a larger moral and ethical framework.

"Germans as Victims" in the Literary Fiction of the Berlin Republic

Historical exhibitions, museums, diaries, autobiographies, films, and literature have been key cultural mechanisms in recent years for the integration of the story of German suffering into the larger wartime narrative, with varying degrees of complexity and attention to the causal link between German perpetration and German victimhood.[11] Examples of historical displays and personal accounts include the traveling exhibition *Flucht, Vertreibung und Integration* (Flight, Expulsion, and Integration), the Berlin museum *Gedenkstätte Deutscher Widerstand* (German Resistance Museum),[12] and the republication of *Eine Frau in Berlin* (A Woman in Berlin, 2003; first published in English in 1954 and in German in 1959), an anonymous account of a woman's multiple rape by Russian soldiers. In film, Sönke Wortmann's *Das Wunder von Bern* (The Miracle of Bern, 2003),[13] Oliver Hirschbiegel's *Der Untergang* (Downfall, 2004),[14] Marc Rothemund's *Sophie Scholl — Die letzten Tage* (Sophie Scholl — The Final Days, 2005),[15] and the TV film *Dresden* (2006)[16] have attracted a great deal of international interest and exploit the medium's ability to make vivid dramatic events from the past. In literature, Grass's *Im Krebsgang,* relating the story of the sinking of the *Wilhelm Gustloff,* similarly provoked intense discussion abroad as well as in Germany when it appeared in 2002 — many commentators expressed surprise that a left-leaning author such as Grass would tackle a theme previously associated with right-wing revisionists. Other literary works that have had less of an impact outside of the country but are nonetheless significant include Dieter Forte's *Der Junge mit den blutigen Schuhen* (The Boy with the Bloody Shoes, 1995), Walter Kempowski's five-volume *Das Echolot* (Soundings, 1999–2005), and Uwe Timm's *Am Beispiel meines Bruders* (In My Brother's Shadow, 2003).[17] There are also a large number of other texts, many of which are examined in this book, that contribute in important ways to the debate.

Literary representations of German wartime suffering in contemporary German culture — the subject of this volume — are, however, not simply part of a synchronic response to the reemergence of the topic in the media, political discourse, and culture of the Berlin Republic. They also form part of a long history of literary representations of expulsion and bombing in German writing stretching back to the immediate aftermath of defeat and the events themselves. The first wave of texts to portray German wartime suffering thus appeared already in the 1950s. Although the large number of publications from this period included a range of different styles and genres, it is possible to identify several key commonalities, most notably the strategies used to exculpate the German civilian population. In texts of the 1950s, then, Germans were more often than not denazified or even portrayed as anti-Nazi (although rarely actively so), and generally portrayed as "small people" caught up against their will in historical circumstances. Novels as diverse as Ruth Storm's *Das vorletzte Gericht* (The Penultimate Judgment, 1953), Hugo Hartung's *Gewiegt von Regen und Wind* (Swayed by Rain and Wind, 1954), and Hildegard Maria Rauchfuss's *Wem die Steine Antwort geben* (Who the Stones Answer, 1953) appear to transform Germans into "absolute" victims, first of the Nazis, then the Soviets and Allies, and, ultimately, fate. Indeed, many novels of the period embody what Robert Moeller has termed the "culture of victimhood," centering on German suffering, and most avoid issues of individual responsibility and ignore the principle of cause and effect.[18] Following the upheaval of the late 1960s, and perhaps contrary to expectations, we continue to see a steady number of literary reflections on German suffering — expulsion, for instance, is thematized in Christa Wolf's *Kindheitsmuster* (Childhood Patterns, 1976), Arno Surminski's *Jokehnen oder Wie lange fährt man von Ostpreußen nach Deutschland* (Jokehnen or How Long Is the Drive from East Prussia to Germany, 1974), Siegfried Lenz's *Heimatmuseum* (Heritage Museum, 1978), and Horst Bienek's *Erde und Feuer* (Earth and Fire, 1982), among many others — but the tone has changed noticeably. Thus texts of the 1970s and 1980s tend to be more muted and detached, and are often less emotionally involved. More critical and reflective, these narratives are often embedded in a wider historical framework, occasionally integrating original documents.

Bill Niven notes the "noticeable correlation" between constructions of victimhood in the past and the present.[19] Certainly, as far as literary representations of German suffering from the mid-1990s are concerned, there are clear comparisons to be drawn — in terms of style, with texts from the 1950s; insofar as they refer to a larger historical context, with novels of the 1970s and 1980s — and yet what is most striking is the degree to which these contemporary fictions effect a *synthesis* of earlier, apparently opposed modes of depicting the motives, behavior, and fates of "ordinary Germans" at the end of the war. Here, we return to the notion of a changed memory discourse: for the most part, recent literary texts concerned with German suffering, sometimes implictly rather than explicitly, derive their narrative tension from the question of the extent to which empathy with individuals can be reconciled with a more detached contextualization of their suffering within the overarching reality of German perpetration. This does not mean that there is no disagreement, or that there exists any absolute consensus — the balance between empathy and critical distance can vary considerably and imply quite diverse interpretations of the past — but it does mean that the tenor of the discussion is now somewhat different.

Recent literary representations of German wartime suffering, therefore, are often characterized by the following commonalities. First, we see a high degree of ethical and theoretical reflection on the limits of representation (of suffering per se, as a traumatic experience that aesthetic appropriation may, even unwittingly, violate) and the possibility that historical responsibility may be erased within a universalizing narrative of suffering as a recurring "given" of the human journey. Second, there is typically a proportion of historiographical rumination on the ways in which the "German story" has been told in the past and how such modes of representation intertwine with the modes of representing the experiences of Jews and other victims of Nazism. Occasionally, indeed, literary texts directly reference historical works, notably Christopher R. Browning's *Ordinary Men: Reserve Police Battalion 101* (English, 1993; German, 1998). Third, and combined with the above, rather abstract "narrative superstructure," we encounter time and again an emphasis on individuals and families: on how stories are transmitted between different generations, and how it feels to "live" the tension between bonds of familial intimacy — the desire to relate to the suffering experienced by a parent or grandparent — and acquired knowledge about the manner in which such suffering often followed complicity, whether direct or indirect. Texts as distinct from one another as Dieter Forte's *Der Junge mit den blutigen Schuhen,* Grass's *Im Krebsgang,* Reinhard Jirgl's *Die Unvollendeten* (The Unfinished, 2003), Dagmar Leupold's *Nach den Kriegen* (After the Wars, 2004), Timm's *Am Beispiel meines Bruders,* Thomas Medicus's *In den Augen meines Großvaters* (In My Grandfather's Eyes, 2004), or Wibke Bruhns's *Meines Vaters Land: Geschichte einer deutschen Familie* (My Father's Country: The Story of a German Family, 2004), by men and women writers, writers of different generations, and writers from both East and West Germany, incorporate at least two of these features (and all incorporate the third), and many include all three.

So why has literature emerged as such a key medium for the reflections on German wartime suffering, and why now? As the chapters of this volume demonstrate, literary fiction is well suited to engaging with the kinds of dilemmas and complexities that today's more differentiated, less ideological memory discourse generates. Indeed, deliberations on German writing since the early 1990s — for example, Ulrich Greiner's attack on postwar literature as "Gesinnungsästhetik" (aesthetics of conviction),[20] echoing Karl Heinz Bohrer's ongoing campaign against writers' unwillingness to explore "evil" for fear of undermining a post-'68 insistence on the necessary triumph of reason;[21] or the campaign for a "Neue Lesbarkeit" (new readability) in contemporary fiction[22] — have mirrored wider debates on the need for less rigid perspectives on the Nazi period. As previously discussed, however, the return of "narrative storytelling" (whether this means moving beyond an "aesthetics of conviction" or an emphasis on "readability") in German writing does not return us to the 1950s, to an era "unburdened" by the ferocious critical engagement with the past typical of the post-'68 period, but rather synthesizes a reconnecting with the novel's traditional focus on the fate of individuals with a more measured analytical detachment. In the contemporary German novel, it is possible to present contradictory perspectives simultaneously, to explore the individual's motives and conflicting behaviors, and to raise the possibility of empathy, even identification, with characters while sustaining narrative frameworks that probe the appropriateness of such "understanding" and the extent to which it may, perhaps unintentionally, exculpate perpetrators, fellow travelers, or bystanders who also happen to be "victims."

These questions seem particularly urgent today, not only in relation to how Germans view the Nazi past, but also in relation to the upsurge in genocide, ethnic cleansing, terrorism, and suicide bombings that has marked the period since the end of the Cold War: in Rwanda, Bosnia, Kosovo, Jerusalem, New York, Iraq, Madrid, London, Darfur, and many other locations besides. Issues of historical responsibility, "understanding" versus condemnation, and the relationship between perpetration and victimhood, are as much global concerns as they are narrow German preoccupations, and as much concerns of the present as they are of the past. As readers engage with the discussions of recent novels collated in this volume, we hope that something of the broader relevance of contemporary German literary representations of the nation's wartime suffering will become evident.

The Chapters

This volume emerges from the major research project funded by the UK Arts and Humanities Research Council, From Perpetrators to Victims?: Discourses of German "Wartime Suffering" from 1945 to the Present, based in the German Department at the University of Leeds, which ran from late 2005 to September 2008. Three further collections of essays, on film, perspectives from "outside," and memorials, are due to appear in 2010 and 2011, edited by other colleagues working within the project, Paul Cooke, Helmut Schmitz and Annette Seidel-Arpacı, and Bill Niven.

We begin the volume with a chapter by Stephen Brockmann on the fictional works of the author and critic W. G. Sebald, reflecting the importance of the "Sebald debate" of the late 1990s for the recent reemergence of the theme of German wartime suffering in public discourse. Sebald, as has been widely discussed,[23] famously criticized the "failure" of German postwar writers to portray the full horrors of the Allied bombing of German cities — and Geman wartime suffering more widely — and claimed that this "gap" had continued into the present.[24] In *Luftkrieg und Literatur* (On the Natural History of Destruction, 1999), Sebald postulated that the failure to represent the terrible destruction of German cities resulted from the complex postwar emotional landscape of guilt, denial, traumatization, and shame, and that those literary efforts that did exist merely replicated the "individual and collective amnesia" of the immediate postwar period.[25] In chapter 1, Brockmann examines the representation of suffering in a selection of Sebald's *literary* texts — namely his novel *Austerlitz* (2001), the collection of novellas *Die Ausgewanderten* (The Exiles, 1992), the travel book *Die Ringe des Saturn* (The Rings of Saturn, 1995), the collection of mixed travel and historical reflections *Schwindel: Gefühle* (Vertigo, 1990), and the poem *Nach der Natur* (After Nature, 1988) — and argues that, paradoxically, the author wrestles with the same traumatic blockages and aesthetic dilemmas that in *Luftkrieg und Literatur* he had identified as the cause of the lack of literary engagement with the air war in the fictional works of others.

In chapters 2 to 4 we return to the 1950s to explore how literary texts (or in the case of Heinrich Böll, autobiographical texts) of that period may be reread in the light of today's debates on how German wartime suffering is most "properly" to be represented. The inclusion of these chapters is intended to demonstrate the extent to which contemporary depictions of bombing and expulsion frequently invoke key motifs of the literature of the 1950s, in terms of plot and of affect, while — in the majority of cases — incorporating the critical attention to the larger historical context typically associated with the post-'68 era, albeit in a tempered fashion emphasizing investigation rather than accusation.

Colette Lawson's contribution on Gert Ledig's *Vergeltung* (Payback, 1956) in chapter 2 revisits Sebald's controversial argument that there had existed a taboo on representations of the devastation of German cities and critically examines the suggestion, put forward by Volker Hage in his *Zeugen der Zerstörung: Die Literaten und der Luftkrieg* (Witnesses to Destruction: Writers and the Air War, 2003), but also by others, that Ledig's novel — republished at Hage's instigation in the wake of the Sebald lectures — disproved this claim. Based on Sebald's broader conception of history, Lawson identifies what Sebald sees as the "ideal" form of literary representation of the bombings and shows that *Vergeltung* is a model of this form: Sebald's notion of a taboo, Lawson argues, relates not so much to the absence of literary representations of the bombings as to the marginalization in the 1950s of those literary representations that were so traumatic that they threatened to disrupt efforts in the postwar period to continue with "normal" life. In chapter 3, Karina Berger turns to literary representations of flight and expulsion from the immediate postwar period. Here, Berger argues that the suspicion with which these texts are typically viewed today may miss the point and that, if read sympathetically, some novels of the 1950s at least offer a more nuanced version of the closing months of the war and the immediate aftermath than might be expected. Berger examines three texts — Kurt Ihlenfeld's *Wintergewitter* (Winter Storm, 1951), Gertrud Fussenegger's *Das verschüttete Antlitz* (Buried Countenance, 1957), and Ruth Hoffmann's *Die schlesische Barmherzigkeit* (Silesian Mercy, 1950) — that attempt to position German victimization in the context of German perpetration, or include victims of the Holocaust in their representation of German suffering. In the final chapter to consider representations from the 1950s, Frank Finlay, in chapter 4, uncovers an unexpected dimension to Heinrich Böll's writings in the Nobel Prize–winning author's wartime letters, published in full (insofar as they are extant) in two volumes in 2002. Finlay draws particular attention to Böll's self-characterization as a victim of "the prison of the uniform" and explores exactly what the author meant by this, the extent to which such a claim might be seen as problematic, and how the letters relate to the debates on German wartime suffering taking place at the time of their publication. Finlay argues that in addition to constituting a unique historical document, Böll's subjective and immediate response to the aerial bombings during the war adds some important nuances and inflections to recent debates.

We next turn to literary representations of the 1990s. While each chapter examines aspects of particular texts, taken together they also give an indication of some of the major trends that mark literary representations of German wartime suffering of recent years. One major theme to emerge, reflected in chapters 5 to 7, is the generational aspect, that is, the passing down of memories, and trauma, which is becoming ever more significant as we move further and further in time from the actual events. In chapter 5, Helmut Schmitz investigates continuities of tradition and legacy across generations in four biographical and autobiographical "family" narratives — Stephan Wackwitz's *Ein unsichtbares Land* (An Invisible Country, 2003), Thomas Medicus's *In den Augen meines Großvaters* (In My Grandfather's Eyes, 2004), Dagmar Leupold's *Nach den Kriegen* (After the Wars, 2004), and Uwe Timm's *Am Beispiel meines Bruders* (In My Brother's Shadow, 2003). Schmitz examines the conflict between familial narratives of suffering and children's inheritance of collective responsibility for Nazism and thus, on a broader level, the friction between private family memories and public memory discourse. Similar to Schmitz's chapter but with a focus on the former German Democratic Republic (GDR), Elizabeth Boa looks at three generational novels in chapter 6 — Reinhard Jirgl's *Die Unvollendeten* (The Unfinished, 2003), Christoph Hein's *Landnahme* (Land Seizure, 2004), and Angelika Overath's *Nahe Tage: Roman in einer Nacht* (Near Days: Novel of One Night, 2005) — and discusses their portrayal of the traumatic loss of *Heimat,* the inheritance of trauma by the postwar generations, and the problematic integration into a new, socialist community allied with the Soviet Union. By viewing literature as the bridge between subjective experience of history and conventional historiography, Boa considers whether in these novels individual suffering can be represented without losing sight of the broader historical context.

Chapter 7 focuses on family memory from the perspective of women; Caroline Schaumann presents an overview of the wide range of recent women's literature on wartime suffering. Schaumann examines "memory contests" in accounts by German non-Jewish and Jewish women from the wartime and postwar generation and highlights men's and women's diverging memories of the Nazi period in three texts: Wibke Bruhns's *Meines Vaters Land: Geschichte einer deutschen Familie* (My Father's Country: The Story of a German Family, 2004), Ute Scheub's *Das falsche Leben: Eine Vatersuche* (A False Life: In Search of My Father, 2006), and Christina von Braun's *Stille Post: Eine andere Familiengeschichte* (Whispers Down the Lane: A Different Family Story, 2007).

Most of the texts that are discussed in this volume have been published in the past few years, and scholarly engagement with them is similarly new. Combined with the contentious nature of the subject, it thus comes as no surprise that the recent discourse has been marked by conflicting views, ongoing debate, and revisions of opinion. That the discourse surrounding German suffering is still evolving is reflected in the following three chapters, which all offer alternative readings to previous, established interpretations of key texts.

Hans-Ulrich Treichel's *Der Verlorene* (Lost, 1998), which relates the story of its protagonist's postwar alienation from parents who lost a child during the treks, has generally been read in the context of the contemporary reassessment of the student movement, its moral certainties, and harsh judgment of the wartime generation. David Clarke's analysis in chapter 8, however, reflects on a different aspect of the text — that is, Treichel's examination of the failed development of personal identity — which takes a familial experience of wartime suffering as its starting point but is not primarily concerned with the representation of such suffering in the context of a national cultural memory. In chapter 9, Katharina Hall offers a sympathetic rereading of Günter Grass's novella *Im Krebsgang* (Crabwalk, 2002), in which she draws attention to its intertextuality with the author's first four works. Hall demonstrates that for the informed reader the intersection between the texts encourages a collective reading of what she terms the "Danzig Quintet" and argues that the intertextual references provide an awareness of the complexities involved in remembering the Nazi past, which negate any possible tendencies toward relativization in the 2002 work. Likewise, in chapter 10, Rick Crownshaw rejects the critical consensus that suggests that *Der Vorleser* (The Reader, 1996) reconfigures the perpetrator generation into victims of Nazism and the second generation as victims of Nazism's legacy. Crownshaw argues for a more nuanced reading of Bernhard Schlink's novel as a text that problematizes the moral binaries of perpetrator and victim in a useful and productive fashion.

One of the key questions that has emerged in the contemporary discourse has been how best to represent German suffering in a balanced manner, that is, without relativizing the suffering of the Jews or sentimentalizing German victimhood. Three contributions, then, consider the ethical implications of representing German suffering in literature. Starting out from Sebald's claim that German postwar writers had failed to adequately portray the Allied bombings at the end of the war, Mary Cosgrove discusses the dilemma surrounding "authentic" narrative representations of trauma in portrayals of German wartime suffering. In chapter 11, Cosgrove questions trauma theory's insistence of the foundational incompatibility of language and trauma by way of an exploration of Dieter Forte's *Der Junge mit den blutigen Schuhen* (1995). In contrast, in chapter 12, Helen Finch critically examines the aesthetic and ethical pitfalls of the anecdotal approach in Grass's autobiography *Beim Häuten der Zwiebel* (Peeling the Onion, 2006), arguing that it conflicts with Grass's scrutiny of German wartime suffering and wartime culpability. Returning to the often unnoticed claim made by Sebald in the 1980s that Grass's ethics of representation were inadequate, Finch argues that the author's blending together of the two categories of "anecdotes" and "variable true stories" casts doubts on Grass's representation anew. The question of form is also central to Frank Finlay's examination of Uwe Timm's novel *Am Beispiel meines Bruders* (2003) in chapter 13. Finlay argues that Timm reinvigorates the "Father Books" of the 1970s by adopting a "polyphonic" form that allows him to achieve critical as well as empathetic aims by placing representations of German suffering within the larger context of German culpability.

On a metalevel, Stuart Taberner investigates a recent tendency to sentimentalize victimhood in literary representations by questioning the boundaries of empathetic identification — how far may writers go in empathizing with perpetrators who may also have been victims? By way of an analysis of three texts in chapter 14 — Walter Kempowski's *Alles umsonst* (All in Vain, 2006), Günter Grass's *Beim Häuten der Zwiebel,* and Thomas Medicus's *In den Augen meines Großvaters* (In My Grandfather's Eyes, 2004) — Taberner identifies degrees of empathy and critically assesses their implications.

Kathrin Schödel's contribution, which closes the volume, examines two short stories, Bernhard Schlink's "Die Beschneidung" (The Circumcision, 2000) and Maxim Biller's "Harlem Holocaust" (1990), as examples of what she argues is the construction of a seemingly simplistic construction of Jewish identity that has emerged as a counterpart to the increasing differentiation in German memory discourse. In chapter 15, Schödel identifies a recent tendency in German public memory toward the elaboration of a "secondary suffering" endured by Germans, that is, a German perception that they are "victims" of a burdened identity. Her analysis of Schlink's text in particular demonstrates how this perception of German secondary suffering frequently implies a contrast with an "un-burdened," and thereby "easier," Jewish identity.

This book is intended to appeal to both a specialist and student audience, as well as to the general reader. Its various chapters engage with a range of literary works that have been central to the public, political, and media discourse on German wartime suffering in recent years and to the integration of this topic into contemporary German cultural memory. Each contribution is self-contained, offering a nuanced reading of an individual text or series of texts, while the volume as a whole aims to offer both a comprehensive overview of the literary, cultural, and discursive landscape within which the Nazi past is debated in the Berlin Republic. We hope, in conclusion, that this volume will make its own contribution to a discussion that is likely to continue to remain lively for the foreseeable future.

Notes

[1] The quotation marks around "German suffering" indicate the controversial status of the term for many commentators and thus should be understood as such in all subsequent instances of its use.

[2]. Martin Walser, "Erfahrungen beim Verfassen einer Sonntagsrede," in *Die Walser-Bubis-Debatte,* ed. Frank Schirrmacher (Frankfurt am Main: Suhrkamp, 1999), 7–17, 15, and 13. See also Bill Niven, *Facing the Nazi Past: United Germany and the Legacy of the Third Reich* (London: Routledge, 2002), 175–93.

[3] See Anne Fuchs and Mary Cosgrove, eds., *Memory Contests,* special issue of *German Life and Letters* 59, no. 2 (2006): 163–68. See also *German Memory Contests: The Quest for Identity in Literature, Film and Discourse since 1990,* ed. Anne Fuchs, Mary Cosgrove, and Georg Grote (Rochester, NY: Camden House, 2006).

[4] See Jan Assmann, *Das kulturelle Gedächtnis: Schrift, Erinnerung und politische Identität in frühen Hochkulturen* (Munich: Beck, 1992).

[5] See *German Culture, Politics, and Literature into the Twenty-First Century: Beyond Normalization,* ed. Stuart Taberner and Paul Cooke (Rochester, NY: Camden House, 2006).

[6] A. Dirk Moses, *German Intellectuals and the Nazi Past* (Cambridge: CUP, 2007), 50.

[7] See Helmut Schmitz, "The Birth of the Collective from the Spirit of Empathy: From the 'Historians' Dispute' to German Suffering," in *Germans as Victims: Re-*

membering the Past in Contemporary Germany, ed. Bill Niven (Basingstoke, UK: Palgrave Macmillan, 2006), 93–108.

[8] Bill Niven, *Facing the Nazi Past* (London: Routledge, 2002), 5.

[9] Aleida Assmann, "On the (In)Compatibility of Guilt and Suffering in German Memory," *German Life and Letters* 59, no. 2 (2006): 189–90.

[10] Harald Welzer, Sabine Moller, and Karoline Tschuggnall, *Opa war kein Nazi: Nationalsozialismus und Holocaust im Familiengedächtnis* (Frankfurt am Main: Fischer, 2002).

[11] See Anne Fuchs, *Phantoms of War in Contemporary German Literature, Films and Discourse: The Politics of Memory* (New York: Palgrave Macmillan, 2008).

[12] See ibid., 116–22.

[13] See Stuart Taberner, "Philo-Semitism in Recent German Film: *Aimee and Jaguar, Rosenstraße,* and *Das Wunder von Bern,*" *German Life and Letters* 58, no. 3 (2005): 357–72.

[14] See Paul Cooke, "*Der Untergang* (2004): Victims, Perpetrators and the Continuing Fascination of Fascism," in *A Nation of Victims? Representation of Wartime Suffering from 1945 to the Present,* ed. Helmut Schmitz (Amsterdam: Rodopi, 2007), 247–61.

[15] See Fuchs, *Phantoms of War,* 147–52.

[16] See Paul Cooke, "*Dresden* (2006), Teamworx and *Titanic* (1997): German Wartime Suffering as Hollywood Disaster Movie," *German Life and Letters* 61, no. 2 (2008): 279–94.

[17] See Stuart Taberner, "Representations of German Wartime Suffering in Recent Fiction," in Niven, *Germans as Victims,* 164–80.

[18] See Robert Moeller, "Remembering the War in a Nation of Victims: West German Pasts in the 1950s," in *The Miracle Years: A Cultural History of West Germany, 1949–1968,* ed. Hanna Schissler (Princeton, NJ: Princeton UP, 2001), 83–109.

[19] Bill Niven, introduction to Niven, *Germans as Victims,* 12.

[20] Ulrich Greiner, "Die deutsche Gesinnungsästhetik," *Die Zeit,* 9 November 1990. Reprinted in *"Es geht nicht nur um Christa Wolf": Der Literaturstreit im vereinten Deutschland,* ed. Thomas Anz (Munich: Spangenberg, 1991), 208–16.

[21] See Karl Heinz Bohrer, "Die permanente Theodizee: Über das verfehlte Böse im deutschen Bewußtsein," in *Nach der Natur: Über Politik und Ästhetik* (Munich: Carl Hanser, 1988), 131–61.

[22] For discussion of these and other debates, see the chapter, "Literary Debates since Unification," in Stuart Taberner, *German Literature of the 1990s and Beyond: Normalization and the Berlin Republic* (Rochester, NY: Camden House, 2005), 1–32.

[23] See, e.g., Anne Fuchs, "A *Heimat* in Ruins and the Ruins as *Heimat:* W. G. Sebald's *Luftkrieg und Literatur,*" in Fuchs et al., *German Memory Contests,* 287–302.

[24] See W. G. Sebald, *On the Natural History of Destruction* (London: Penguin, 2004), 10, 30.

[25] Ibid., 9.

1: W. G. Sebald and German Wartime Suffering

Stephen Brockmann

SINCE W. G. SEBALD WAS LARGELY RESPONSIBLE for putting "German wartime suffering" back on Germany's intellectual agenda with his 1997 Zürich lectures about the air war and German literature — published in book form in Germany in 1999 under the title *Luftkrieg und Literatur* (Air War and Literature) — it is reasonable to inquire how he dealt with the problem of German suffering in his own literary works. After all, in *Luftkrieg und Literatur* Sebald argued that German writers, far from dwelling excessively on the problem of German suffering in the Second World War — and in particular on the air war that destroyed so many German cities — had actually avoided it, even treated it as a taboo subject. Seeing German writers as seismographs for the German intellectual and spiritual condition as a whole during and after the war, Sebald argued that writers' silence, reserve, and "instinctive looking away are the reasons why we know so little of what the Germans thought and observed in the five years between 1942 and 1947."[1] In other words, it was not just that Germans in general and German writers in particular largely avoided the problem of other people's suffering in the postwar years — the suffering of Jews, of Poles, of Russians, and so on — but that they largely avoided the problem of suffering in general, even (or especially) German suffering.

The validity of Sebald's observations about a taboo on German suffering in the immediate postwar period has been called into question in the years since 1999, and a general consensus has emerged that, at least in the first decades after the war, there was a good deal more consciousness and discussion of German suffering in Germany — in literature and in other media — than Sebald suggests.[2] Nevertheless, Sebald's claim that German pride about reconstruction fundamentally overshadowed German mourning has remained essentially uncontested. That claim largely confirmed the earlier findings of Alexander and Margarete Mitscherlich in their book *Die Unfähigkeit zu trauern* (The Inability to Mourn, 1967). The Mitscherlichs, not unlike Sebald, had argued that because of the negative connotations of Hitler specifically, and the so-called Third Reich generally, in the postwar period, large numbers of ordinary Germans were unable to acknowledge, let alone to mourn, their suffering and loss.

Sebald's argument about a taboo is also consonant with the arguments of another contemporary German intellectual, the literary critic Karl Heinz Bohrer, who, in the 1980s, argued that West German culture was characterized by what he called a "permanent theodicy," that is, by the inability to explore the problem of evil, and of the pain and suffering that evil causes. Bohrer argued that "real evil, fascism, created such favorable conditions for" Germany's inability to focus on pain and suffering "that, since 1945, the long established tabooization of literary evil has almost necessarily become the German method." Bohrer also claimed that "the contemporary diagnosis developed in Alexander Mitscherlich's concept of an 'inability to mourn' still characterizes, in one formulation, the state of consciousness of West German society in its majority and in its elites."[3]

Sebald's own analysis is caught on the horns of the same psychological and ethical dilemma that he identifies for German literary intellectuals in the immediate postwar period: how is it possible to acknowledge, let alone mourn, German suffering — the destruction of German cities, the deaths of German civilians — while also, simultaneously acknowledging that to a very large extent Germans brought this suffering on themselves? The more one emphasizes the former — German suffering, and mourning for German losses — the more one seems to call into question, at least implicitly, the justification for the Allied air war against Germany, that is, to call into question Germans' complicity in the very system (Nazism) that led to the German catastrophe. How is it possible, for instance, to mourn for the city of Dresden and the tens of thousands of German lives lost there on February 13, 1945 while acknowledging the justification for, or even the necessity of, the bombing of Dresden, or even contending that many Dresdeners deserved to be bombed? Sebald concludes that "to this day, any concern with the real scenes of horror during the catastrophe still has an aura of the forbidden about it, even of voyeurism, something that these notes of mine have not entirely been able to avoid" (*AW* 98).

Sebald thus admits that the problem he is writing about — Germany's destruction, together with how German writers have dealt (or not dealt) with that destruction — is more than just a challenge faced by other writers at another time; it is a problem that he himself, as both a writer and a scholar, faces. Paradoxically, Sebald ends his own essay on the destruction of German cities and literary intellectuals' failure to address that destruction with an invocation of the bombings of two non-German cities: London and Stalingrad. The problem of Germans as victims is thus, for Sebald, always accompanied by the problem of Germans as perpetrators. This consciousness of inadequacy, or of the inability to deal with one topic without dealing with the other — together with the consciousness that one topic necessarily has priority over the other, therefore almost necessarily overshadowing it, or rendering it, in Sebald's terminology, "forbidden" — runs through *Luftkrieg und Literatur* and much of Sebald's literary writing. Therefore Wilfried Wilms concludes that Sebald's "interpretive wings are clipped from the start by the political taboo with which he himself grew up."[4] In identifying the problem that German writers have in dealing with German suffering, then, Sebald was also identifying a problem that he himself had in dealing with German suffering.

Almost all of Sebald's literary writing — primarily his novel *Austerlitz* (2001), the collection of novellas *Die Ausgewanderten* (The Exiles, 1992), the travel book *Die Ringe des Saturn* (The Rings of Saturn, 1995), the collection of mixed travel and historical reflections *Schwindel: Gefühle* (Vertigo, 1990), and the poem *Nach der Natur* (After Nature, 1988) — deals with various kinds of suffering. For Sebald, history itself is a process of almost inevitable suffering, leading to decay, destruction, and death. As Anne Fuchs argues, Sebald's ideas constitute "a metaphysics of natural history that engulfs everybody," not just Germans.[5] This fundamentally pessimistic philosophy finds expression throughout Sebald's texts, perhaps most directly in *Die Ringe des Saturn,* a description of Sebald's hikes through the English county of Suffolk in 1992. This book contains many historical and philosophical reflections, including a consideration of the Chinese dowager empress Tz'u-hsi, who died in 1908 after having essentially ruled China for over four disastrous decades since the death of her husband, the emperor Hsien-feng, in 1861. Tz'u-hsi's reign represented the final decline of the Ch'ing dynasty, the last Chinese dynasty, and it was characterized by massive starvation and the domination of China by European colonial powers. Tz'u-hsi herself was skilled at court intrigue, capable of having her opponents murdered and of struggling for power against the deceased emperor's son T'ung-chih, who died in 1875, and against his pregnant widow, who died under suspicious circumstances several weeks after her husband. She also installed as emperor her nephew Kuang-hsü but ultimately kept him in virtual imprisonment for about a decade until his death in 1908, which occurred less than a day before her own death.

Sebald's reflections on this Chinese history are occasioned by a bridge over the river Blyth between Halesworth and Southwold that was originally built for a narrow-guage train intended for, but never delivered to, the court of a late nineteenth-century Chinese emperor. As Sebald describes his walk through the countryside of Suffolk, he also describes the bridge — and, characteristically, includes a picture of it in the book —

which leads him to a consideration of the train that once passed over it, and of Chinese history in the second half of the nineteenth century, which saw, Sebald writes, "the ritualization of imperial power . . . at its most elaborate" but also, simultaneously, the hollowing out of the emperor's power.[6] The ultimate insight into this Chinese history comes from Tz'u-hsi herself, whom Sebald describes as having come, at the end of her life, to the deathbed realization "that history consists of nothing but misfortune and the troubles that afflict us, wave upon wave as on the edge of the sea, so that in all our days on earth we never know one single moment that is genuinely free of fear" (R 153).[7] In other words, in 1908, on her deathbed, the Chinese dowager empress comes to a realization about history that is remarkably similar to Walter Benjamin's conception of history, articulated three decades later: that history is "one single catastrophe which keeps piling wreckage upon wreckage."[8] (It was with this often-quoted Benjaminian thesis that Sebald was later to close the second part of *Luftkrieg und Literatur; AW* 67–68.) Tz'u-hsi is herself anything but a mere victim of history, however; she is also a perpetrator. For Sebald this is also, necessarily, the position of Germany and of Germans: the country and its people are certainly the victims of a catastrophic history, but at the same time, because they themselves are implicated in the creation of this history, they are also perpetrators. History, in other words, is something that Germans have largely inflicted on themselves.

This bleak view of history finds expression again in Sebald's description of the "melancholy region" that he walks through in Suffolk, a landscape that he sees as the result of "the steady and advancing destruction, over a period of many centuries and indeed millennia, of the dense forests that extended over the entire British Isles after the last Ice Age." The destruction of this once thickly wooded landscape directly coincided, Sebald writes, with the region's settlement by human beings, who "burnt off the forests along those drier stretches of the eastern coast where the light soil could be tilled" (R 201). Human civilization is itself a massive, ongoing process of burning and destruction, Sebald believes. Indeed, "from the earliest times, human civilization has been no more than a strange luminescence growing more intense by the hour, of which no one can say when it will begin to wane and when it will fade away" (R 170).

The concept of world history as an ongoing process of destruction and suffering places Germany's own past — the history of both German suffering and German perpetration — into a vast context of suffering and perpetration that ultimately relativizes any national specificity. According to Sebald, German history is indeed a history of perpetration on the one hand and suffering on the other, but in the end this history, far from being unique in space or time, becomes one — admittedly extreme — example of more general suffering and perpetration in human history, a history that, far from being finished, continues into the present and the future. In the eighth chapter of *Die Ringe des Saturn,* Sebald describes a visit to a discontinued British military testing site on the peninsula of Orford Ness that contains "a number of buildings that" resemble "temples or pagodas, which seemed quite out of place in these military installations," and that, at least in the photograph that Sebald provides, look vaguely Chinese, seeming to connect the southeastern coast of Great Britain once again to Chinese cultural history (*R* 236–37). In the presence of these ruins, Sebald writes, "I imagined myself amidst the remains of our own civilization after its extinction in some future catastrophe," and he describes a feeling of alienation in the presence of the ruins of a culture of which he himself was and still is (at the time of the book's publication) a part: "to me too . . . the beings who had once lived and worked here were an enigma" (*R* 237). This feeling of alienation extends to German culture in the first half of the twentieth century, when Sebald himself was born. After walking around Orford Ness, Sebald pauses to look out over the North Sea in the direction of Germany: "There, I thought, I was once at home" (*R* 237). Germany is no longer a home, at least in the present, as seen by its former inhabitant from a great distance in both time and space.

Sebald makes the connection between Chinese and German cultural history clear in an exposition on the history of silk production in Germany, particularly Nazi Germany. Just as the Chinese dowager empress Tz'u-hsi had viewed silkworms as an ideal species, "diligent in service, ready to die, capable of multiplying vastly within a short span of time, and fixed on their one sole preordained aim, wholly unlike human beings, on whom there was basically no relying," so too the German Nazis had encouraged the raising of silkworms and the production of silk (*R* 151). Sebald cites an educational film made in Nazi Germany about the production of silk, as well as a booklet for teachers produced to accompany the film, which he says he found in an archive in the Bavarian town where he grew up. According to the author of this booklet, one Professor Dr. Friedrich Lange, the silkworm is not only economically useful in helping Germany to achieve autarky but is also "an almost ideal object lesson for the classroom," because "any number could be had for virtually nothing"; the insect is entirely tame and capable of being subjected to all sorts of useful experiments (*R* 294). Thus the Chinese ruler Tz'u-hsi and the German Nazis are connected by a silken thread, just as silkworms and human beings are connected to each other. As Sebald describes his wandering through Sufolk he also reflects on the unhappy history of China and Germany — the Asian "Middle Empire" and the nation at the core of Europe. In the Nazi era the so-called Reich Institute of Sericulture was located in Celle, and Sebald does not fail to note that he finishes writing *Die Ringe des Saturn* on April 13, 1995, Maundy Thursday, exactly fifty years after the city of Celle fell to Allied troops. Maundy Thursday, of course, is also the day that precedes Good Friday in the Christian calendar, and Good Friday, as the Bavarian-born Sebald well knew, commemorates what for Christians is the ultimate suffering: the crucifixion of Christ. History, for Sebald, is a never-ending path toward Good Friday, but without any hope for resurrection.

There are two parts of *Die Ringe des Saturn* that are directly connected not only to twentieth-century German history in general but to the problem of the air war and German victimization in particular. In the book's second chapter Sebald describes an encounter that he has with an English gardener named William Hazel in a glasshouse in a garden at Somerleyton, not far from Lowestoft, a manor house bought and rebuilt in a grand style by the nineteenth-century British industrialist and railway man Morton Peto. It is William Hazel who, according to Sebald, piques his interest in the Allied air war against Germany; Hazel tells him that most of the British sorties against Germany were carried out from air bases in East Anglia, the very area where Sebald lived and taught. In other words, even though Sebald himself grew up in a Germany full of cities destroyed in the air war, he claims not to have really reflected on what happened until a gardener drew his attention to the matter. Hazel views Germany as "a medieval and vastly enigmatic land," and he memorizes the names of German cities by learning about their destruction: he spells out the names of the cities whose destruction "had just been announced." Hazel thus becomes an expert on Germany and even learns the German language in order to read German accounts of the air war (*R* 39). Here Hazel's account of his experiences in Germany and with the German language begins to resemble the thesis that would later form the core of Sebald's *Luftkrieg und Literatur,* because Hazel asserts that his search for German accounts of the air war "invariably proved fruitless. No one at the time seemed to have written about their experiences or afterwards recorded their memories. Even if you asked people directly, it was as if everything had been erased from their minds" (*R* 39). If this account is accurate — which is possible, although one cannot be sure — then Sebald's central thesis in *Luftkrieg und Literatur* stems in part from a chance encounter with an English gardener at Somerleyton in the summer of 1992.[9] As Sebald taught German and Austrian literature at the University of East Anglia, and because his wanderings take him along the coast of what he sometimes refers to as the "German sea" (i.e., the North Sea, particularly between East Anglia and the mainland of Europe), his perspective on Germany is characterized by distance and displacement. He is both a German and an Englishman (in the sense that he spent almost all of his professional life living in England). And he views Germany from the perspective of both the Germans who were bombed and the English pilots who carried out the bombing.

The other part of *Die Ringe des Saturn* that directly deals with the problem of the destruction of German cities in the Second World War comes with Sebald's description of a stop that he makes in Middleton to visit the distinguished German-Jewish-English writer and translator Michael Hamburger (1924–2007), who left Germany with his mother and sisters in 1933, at age nine. Like Sebald, Hamburger was a German-born writer living and working in East Anglia. Sebald is particularly interested in Hamburger's account of his return to the city of his birth, Berlin, in 1947.[10] Berlin, once so familiar, is now uncanny to Sebald's Michael Hamburger, and he finds it impossible to climb the steps of his old building to knock on the door of the apartment where he once lived with his family. Leaving the site of his childhood home, Hamburger encounters a place where masses of bricks from bombed-out buildings are being stored: "If I now think back to that desolate place, I do not see a single human being, only bricks, millions of bricks, a rigorously perfected system of bricks reaching in serried ranks as far as the horizon, and above them the Berlin November sky from which presently the snow would come swirling down — a deathly silent image of the onset of winter" (*R* 179). In this passage, Sebald describes the ruins of a German city while distancing himself from it, as the memory is purportedly not his own but Hamburger's. One literary emigrant relives and reflects on the experiences and memories of another.

Sebald expresses his alienation from Germany more directly in the final part of *Schwindel: Gefühle,* which is entitled "Il ritorno in patria." The use of the Italian language here is a nod to Claudio Monteverdi's 1641 opera *Il ritorno d'Ulisse in patria,* an account of the triumphant homecoming of Odysseus to Ithaca after the Trojan War. Sebald's use of this title serves as a kind of ironic distanciation from the subject matter, which is Sebald's return, on foot, to Germany, to Bavaria, and to his own hometown not far from the Austrian border after an absence of more than three decades. (Odysseus had been gone from Ithaca for two decades.) The closer he gets to the town where he grew up, Sebald writes, the more uncomfortable he feels.[11] There is no place in the world that seems as foreign to him, he claims, as the place where he spent his childhood: "the village itself . . . was more remote from me than any other place I could conceive of" (*V* 185). When he checks into his hotel in W., Sebald declares himself to be a foreign reporter, confusing the hotel's receptionist, "for when and for what purpose had an English foreign correspondent ever come to W., on foot, in November, and unshaven to boot . . ." (Odysseus, of course, also returns to his homeland incognito; *V* 192). But Sebald is actually being more or less truthful, because his hometown really is a foreign country for him now, and he really does plan to write about it, if not for a newspaper, at least for his book. And whereas throughout Homer's epic Odysseus had wanted nothing more than to return to his homeland, Sebald has made it plain, in the course of *Schwindel: Gefühle,* that he is uncomfortable with his own Germanness. In Italy he finds his fellow Germans annoying: "How I wished during those sleepless hours that I belonged to a different nation, or, better still, to none at all" (*V* 93–94). Ironically enough, Sebald's wish is soon partially fulfilled, as his passport is lost, and he must ultimately go to the West German embassy in Milan to ask for official documentation of his German citizenship, documentation that is reproduced as a photograph in the book.

The first mention of Sebald's Bavarian hometown W. in *Schwindel: Gefühle* comes in a description of a visit that Sebald made to Venice at the end of October and beginning of November, 1980, around the time of All Saints Day and All Souls Day (November 1 and 2, respectively), a time when Catholics all over the world remember and pray for the dead — in both Venice and, as Sebald recalls from his childhood, Bavaria. Characteristically, Sebald imagines himself to be dead on this day too: "I felt as if I had already been interred or laid out for burial" (*V* 65). Of course, this imagination of death, and communion with death, in Venice, has, as the Germanist Sebald undoubtedly knew, a rich connection with German literary history, particularly Thomas Mann's novella *Der Tod in Venedig* (Death in Venice, 1912). Around midnight on October 31, 1980 (All Hallows Eve), Sebald and an Italian acquaintance of his named Malachio had taken a boat out to an island off the coast of Venice, which houses the city crematorium. Here Malachio talks about the burning of organic life in a way that prefigures Sebald's own reflections about civilization as a process of burning in *Die Ringe des Saturn:* "The miracle of life born of carbon, I heard Malachio say, going up in flames" (*V* 61). Venice as a city of death is thus connected to Sebald's hometown of W. as a place of the dead, and in his own imagination he takes his place among the dead. The massive crematorium on the island off the coast of Venice is not far from a mill made from "millions of bricks" (*V* 61) that seem to point forward toward Sebald's later reference, in *Die Ringe des Saturn,* to Michael Hamburger's purported recollection of a "deathly silent image of the onset of winter" in Berlin featuring "millions of bricks" (*R* 179). The visit to the crematorium island thus prefigures Sebald's "ritorno in patria" (return home), aligning Germany itself with a massive crematorium. The boat trip to the island off the coast of Venice also prefigures Sebald's boat trip, in *Die Ringe des Saturn,* to the East Anglian peninsula of Orford Ness, which Sebald was to refer to as an "isle of the dead" (*R* 237) — probably in reference to Arnold Böcklin's painting *Die Toteninsel* (The Island of the Dead). In both of these travel descriptions — the visit to the island off the coast of Venice and the visit to Orford Ness in the "German sea" —

Sebald imagines himself as a passenger on a boat taking him into the realm of the dead, a realm characterized by a lack of living, breathing human beings, and by silence. This is the way that Thomas Mann's Gustav von Aschenbach had arrived in Venice as well.

It is precisely as such a land of the dead that Sebald describes Germany. When he leaves W. to return to England, he travels through "the German countryside, which has always been alien to me, straightened out and tidied up as it is to the last square inch and corner. Everything appeared to be appeased and numbed in some sinister way, and this sense of numbness soon came over me also" (*V* 253). What particularly disturbs Sebald when he looks out the train window is the lack of people (*V* 277). Whether he was aware of it or not, Sebald's description of postwar Germany resembles Hermann Kasack's *Die Stadt hinter dem Strom* (The City beyond the River, 1947), an allegorical novel whose writer protagonist Robert Lindhoff becomes the chronicler of the city of the dead, and who travels to and from the city by train.[12] Ironically, in *Luftkrieg und Literatur* Sebald was later highly critical of Kasack's novel, accusing it of "the artifice of abstraction and metaphysical fraudulence" (*AW* 50).[13] Yet both Kasack and Sebald treat postwar Germany as a land of the dead.

Sebald's negative description of a too-clean and too-orderly postwar Germany resonates with both *Luftkrieg und Literatur* (in which Sebald condemns Germany's postwar emphasis on reconstruction rather than mourning) and Sebald's other literary writings. Max Aurach, the German-born Jewish protagonist of the fourth story in *Die Ausgewanderten*, proclaims to the story's Sebald-like first-person narrator: "Probably the reason why I have never been to Germany again is that I am afraid to find that this insanity really exists. To me, you see, Germany is a country frozen in the past, destroyed, a curiously extraterritorial place, inhabited by people whose faces are both lovely and dreadful."[14] In Germany, the narrator of the Aurach story complains about "the mental impoverishment and lack of memory that marked the Germans, and the efficiency with which they had cleaned everything up" (*E* 225). Jacques Austerlitz, the Czech-born Jewish protagonist of the novel *Austerlitz*, declares to the novel's first-person narrator (again, like Sebald) that when, for the first time, he travels to Germany, he is alienated not by its destruction but by its rebuilding. Germany, Austerlitz declares, is "probably more unfamiliar to me than any other country in the world, more foreign even than Afghanistan or Paraguay" (*A* 222).[15] This description of Germany as fundamentally strange and foreign resonates with Sebald's own oft-stated alienation from Germany: here Sebald is using the fictional figure of a Czech-born Jew to express his own feelings of discomfort with postwar Germany.

Sebald's alienation from West Germany also resonates with many West German writers' alienation from East Germany, and it is noteworthy that even though Sebald emerged as a major writer in the immediate aftermath of German reunification, he never talks about reunification or the German Democratic Republic (GDR).[16] The absence of the GDR from Sebald's writing is all the more remarkable because it is precisely in East Germany that Sebald would have found the run-down buildings and historical ruins that he claimed to miss in an all-too-neatly restored postwar West Germany. Nuremberg, the city of the Nazis' party rallies that Austerlitz's father had once visited, now in some ways resembles the places of the dead in Sebald's other writing: Austerlitz tells the novel's narrator, "Looking up at the façades on both sides of the street, even those of the older buildings which, judging by their style, must date from the sixteenth or fifteenth century, I was troubled to realize that I could not see a crooked line anywhere, not at the corners of the houses or on the gables, the window frames or the sills, nor was there any other trace of past history" (*A* 223). In other words, what is problematic about Germany is not just that it seems to resemble a city of the dead (the silence, the lack of human feeling) but that, even worse, it seems to be trying to hide its ruined status behind orderliness and cleanliness. The problem with Germany, for Sebald, is not so much that it is a land of the dead (because for him all places are lands of the dead), but rather that it is a land of the undead, of zombies.[17]

In *Schwindel: Gefühle* Sebald writes that as a child he imagined cities as naturally being composed of ruins, probably because the only cities he ever saw as a child were full of them. Two years later, in *Die Ausgewanderten,* Sebald declares that as a child he was happy to move from W. to the larger town of S., precisely because of the ruins in the city, which appear to him to be "particularly auspicious . . ., for ever since I had once visited Munich I had felt nothing to be so unambiguously linked to the word *city* as the presence of heaps of rubble, fire-scorched walls, and the gaps of windows through which one could see the vacant air" (*E* 30). Sebald returns to this topic in *Luftkrieg und Literatur,* where he writes, "In one of my narratives I have described how in 1952, when I moved with my parents and siblings from my birthplace of Wertach to Sonthofen, nineteen kilometers away, nothing seemed as fascinating as the presence of areas of waste land here and there among the rows of houses, for ever since I had been to Munich, as I said in that passage, few things were so clearly linked in my mind with the word 'city' as mounds of rubble, cracked walls, and empty windows through which you saw the empty air" (*AW* 74).

These passages are consistent with each other: Sebald's childhood association of large cities with ruins on the one hand and the lack of any kind of ascription of causation for the ruined condition of major German cities on the other. That condition seems to the young Sebald to be natural, not manmade. The word "vielversprechend" (translated more accurately as "auspicious" in one passage and less accurately as "fascinating" in the other) in the last two passages is noteworthy, because it associates the ruined condition of Germany's cities not with any negative feelings but rather with positive ones: as a child Sebald actually seems to have *liked* ruins and to have felt comfortable with them. Sebald confirms the positive emotional association he has with ruins in *Luftkrieg und Literatur,* where he writes that it is not the beauties of rural Bavaria that conjure up associations of having a home for him but rather images of destruction (*AW* 71). In the third part of his long poem *Nach der Natur,* Sebald writes that he was born (perhaps not unlike Walter Benjamin) under the melancholy sign of Saturn, but "without an idea of destruction," that is, without any kind of intellectual concept of what human actions cause or result in destruction.[18] Even as a child, however, he claims to have been filled with the imagination of "a silent catastrophe that occurs / almost unperceived." As an adult he admits, he still subscribes to this vision of destruction: "What I thought up at the time / [. . .] I have never got over" (*AN* 89). It is characteristic of Sebald's writing that much of what he describes throughout his literary works are ruins or destruction — from ruined beach resorts in England or France to an abandoned insane asylum in Ithaca, New York. When, in the fourth part of *Die Ausgewanderten,* Sebald describes his arrival in Manchester in 1966, he writes, "One might have supposed that the city had long since been deserted, and was left now as a necropolis or mausoleum" (*E* 151). Much of what appeals to Sebald about England appears to be its deteriorated, run-down condition prior to the advent of New Labour and "Cool Britannia." These run-down environs seem to be more congenial to Sebald than postwar West Germany, which has eliminated so many traces of destruction and decay.

What Sebald finds so disturbing about postwar Germany, in both his literary writing and his essay *Luftkrieg und Literatur,* is that, as a nation, it seems to be straying from its assignations with the past and hiding any connection to what went before. The destruction of Germany in the Second World War was bad enough, Sebald suggests, but what was even worse was the postwar denial of that destruction, in which the Germans — victims of a history that they themselves largely caused — allegedly proceeded to eliminate all traces of even their own traumas. Sebald's protagonist Austerlitz deplores what a French acquaintance of his calls the "increasingly importunate urge to break with everything which still has some living connection to the past" (*A* 286). For Sebald, Germany seems far more advanced than any other country in promoting the dissolution of the past. What has occurred in Germany are two kinds of ruination: first, the destruction of Germany itself, and then, in a sense, the destruction of the destruction, so that now contemporary Germany seems to exist without any kind of connection to its own history *even as a ruin.* In *Luftkrieg und Literatur* Sebald calls this a "second liquidation [. . .] of the nation's own past history" (*AW* 7).

There is, of course, something perverse in all of this, as Sebald seems to prefer ruins, dirt, and destruction (i.e., the dead), to rebuilding and cleanup (which Sebald sees as the undead). However, for a writer who freely admits to his own melancholy nature and acknowledges the perversity of his preference for ruins, and who, in his poem *Nach der Natur,* places his own history and the history of Germany into a direct connection with the German painter Albrecht Altdorfer's image of the burning city of Sodom, such preferences should not be surprising.[19] After all, Sebald himself admitted, in *Luftkrieg und Literatur,* that there was still "an aura of the forbidden . . . even of voyeurism" in his own project of ruin recovery (*AW* 98). In the second part of *Nach der Natur,* Sebald describes his own coming into the world as being intimately connected with his mother's experience of the bombing of Nuremberg on August 27, 1943: "During the night of the 28th / 582 aircraft flew in / to attack Nürnberg. Mother, / who on the next day planned / to return to her parents' / home in the Alps, / got no further than / Fürth. From there she / saw Nürnberg in flames, / but cannot recall now / what the burning town looked like / or what her feelings were / at this sight. / On the same day, she told me recently, / from Fürth she had travelled on / to Windsheim and an acquaintance / at whose house she waited until / the worst was over, and realized / that she was with child" (*AN* 86). Sebald thus connects the empty image of the burning Nuremberg (empty because his mother does not remember what it looked like) with Altdorfer's 1537 painting *Lot and his Daughters,* which shows the burning city of Sodom in the background: "On the horizon / a terrible conflagration blazes / devouring a large city. / Smoke ascends from the site, / the flames rise to the sky and / in the blood-red reflection / one sees the blackened / façades of the houses" (*AN* 87). Sebald writes that when he first saw this painting by Altdorfer "I had the strange feeling / of having seen all of it / before, and a little later, / crossing to Floridsdorf / on the Bridge of Peace, / I nearly went out of my mind" (*AN* 87). The implication is clear: the shock comes from Sebald's recognition that he himself emerged from a burning Germany that had already been prefigured in Altdorfer's painting of a city destroyed by God for its wickedness.

Altdorfer returns in the final pages of *Nach der Natur,* when Sebald describes a dream in which he flies (not unlike Allied bomber pilots in the Second World War) from England to Germany to see an image of war and destruction: Altdorfer's 1529 *Alexanderschlacht* (Alexander's Victory at Issus) in Munich's Alte Pinakotek, a painting that depicts the battle between Alexander the Great and Darius III of Persia in 333 B.C. For Sebald, Altdorfer's image of a titanic battle between the West and the

East is a depiction not just of the past but of the future: "Since then I have / read in another teacher's writings / that we have death in front of us / rather like a picture of Alexander's battle / on our schoolroom wall" (*AN* 115). Since, in his dream, Sebald has flown over Germany itself, with its "cities phosphorescent / on the riverbank, industry's / glowing piles waiting / beneath the smoke trails" and "the towers of Frankfurt," Altdorfer's image appears to be directly connected to Germany itself and to its titanic struggles in both the past and, Sebald probably suspects, the future (*AN* 113). Such future struggles will certainly produce more victims, but it is doubtful that for Sebald those victims will be innocent of their own undoing.

Notes

[1] W. G. Sebald, "Air War and Literature: Zürich Lectures," in Sebald, *On the Natural History of Destruction,* trans. Anthea Bell (New York: Random House, 2003), 31. Subsequent references to this work are cited in the text using the abbreviation *AW* and page number.

[2] See Bill Niven, ed., *Germans as Victims: Remembering the Past in Contemporary Germany* (Basingstoke, UK: Palgrave Macmillan, 2006).

[3] Karl Heinz Bohrer, "Die permanente Theodizee: Über das verfehlte Böse im deutschen Bewußtsein," in Bohrer, *Nach der Natur: Über Politik und Ästhetik* (Munich: Carl Hanser, 1988), 144 and 156.

[4] Wilfried Wilms, "Taboo and Repression in W. G. Sebald's *On the Natural History of Destruction,*" in *W. G. Sebald — A Critical Companion,* ed. J. J. Long and Anne Whitehead (Seattle: U of Washington P, 2004), 188.

[5] Anne Fuchs, "A *Heimat* in Ruins and the Ruins as *Heimat:* W. G. Sebald's *Luftkrieg und Literatur,*" in *German Memory Contests: The Quest for Identity in Literature, Film, and Discourse since 1990,* ed. Anne Fuchs, Mary Cosgrove, and Georg Grote (Rochester, NY: Camden House, 2006), 296.

[6] W. G. Sebald, *The Rings of Saturn,* trans. Michael Hulse (New York: New Directions, 1998), 139, 140. Subsequent references to this work are cited in the text using the abbreviation *R* and page number.

[7] I have added the words "wave upon wave as on the edge of the sea," which correspond to Sebald's original: "Welle um Welle wie über das Ufer des Meers." These words are left out of the English-language translation. Original German: Sebald, *Die Ringe des Saturn* (Frankfurt: Fischer, 1997), 185.

[8] Walter Benjamin, *Illuminations: Essays and Reflections,* ed. Hannah Arendt (New York: Schocken, 1968), 257.

[9] Susanne Vees-Gulani notes that "Sebald, through the words of the gardener, already formulates in a fictional framework part of his thesis" in *Luftkrieg und Literatur.* See Vees-Gulani, *Trauma and Guilt: Literature of Wartime Bombing in Germany* (Berlin: Walter de Gruyter, 2003), 128. At any rate, Sebald had already been reflecting on the problem for at least a decade; in 1982 he had published an article

on the topic. See Sebald, "Zwischen Geschichte und Naturgeschichte: Versuch über die literarische Beschreibung totaler Zerstörung mit Anmerkungen zu Kasack, Nossack und Kluge," in Sebald, *Campo Santo,* ed. Sven Meyer (Munich: Carl Hanser, 2003), 69–100. First pub. in *Orbis Litterarum* 37, no. 4 (1982): 345–66.

[10] Sebald's account of Hamburger's return to Berlin is not identical with Hamburger's, although there are similarities. See Michael Hamburger, *String of Beginnings: Intermittent Memoirs 1924–1954* (London: Skoob Books, 1991), originally pub. as *A Mug's Game: Intermittent Memoirs 1924–1954* (London: Carcanet Press, 1973), 10–12 and 184–85.

[11] W. G. Sebald, *Vertigo,* trans. Michael Hulse (New York: New Directions, 1999), 178. Subsequent references to this work are cited in the text using the abbreviation *V* and page number.

[12] See my *German Literary Culture at the Zero Hour* (Rochester, NY: Camden House, 2004), 144–46.

[13] Anne Fuchs points out that even in *Luftkrieg und Literatur* Sebald's view of human history as falling back into natural history "is characterized by the very allegorization of destruction that he accused Nossack of a few pages before" (*"Heimat* in Ruins," 296).

[14] W. G. Sebald, *The Emigrants,* trans. Michael Hulse (New York: New Directions, 1997), 181. Subsequent references to this work are cited in the text using the abbreviation *E* and page number. In the English version of this story, Aurach is called Max Ferber to respect the identity of the real-life Frank Auerbach.

[15] W. G. Sebald, *Austerlitz,* trans. Anthea Bell (New York: Random House, 2001), 222. Subsequent references to this work are cited in the text using the abbreviation *A* and page number.

[16] Anne Fuchs notes this fact for *Luftkrieg und Literatur,* but it also holds for Sebald's literary writing. See Fuchs, *"Heimat* in Ruins," 291. On West German writers' alienated reactions to East Germany, see my *Literature and German Reunification* (Cambridge: CUP, 1999), 163–64.

[17] For Karl Heinz Bohrer, too, Germany is a land of zombies. See Bohrer, *Nach der Natur,* 39–46.

[18] W. G. Sebald, *After Nature,* trans. Michael Hamburger (New York: Random House, 2002), 89. Subsequent references to this work are cited in the text using the abbreviation *AN* and page number. Susan Sontag titled her essay on Walter Benjamin "Under the Sign of Saturn." See Sontag, *Under the Sign of Saturn* (New York: Farrar, Straus and Giroux), 107–34.

[19] In *Luftkrieg und Literatur,* Sebald refers to his preference for ruins as perverse. The word "perverserweise" is rendered as "oddly enough" in the English version (*"Air War and Literature,"* 71).

2: The Natural History of Destruction: W. G. Sebald, Gert Ledig, and the Allied Bombings

Colette Lawson

FIRST PUBLISHED IN 1956, Gert Ledig's novel *Vergeltung* (Payback)[1] is an unremittingly brutal account of sixty-nine minutes of an Allied air raid on a German city toward the end of the war. Following the success of his first novel, *Stalinorgel* (The Stalin Organ, 1955),[2] a similarly stark narration of warfare on the Eastern front, Ledig had been celebrated and invited to meetings of the Group 47. The novel *Vergeltung*, by contrast, was uniformly dismissed by critics as everything from unrealistic and sensationalist to badly written and ungrammatical. It achieved none of the commercial success of the first novel and sank, along with Ledig's literary career, into obscurity.

The novel was rediscovered and republished in 1999 in response to the debate surrounding W. G. Sebald's *Luftkrieg und Literatur* (Airwar and Literature, published in English as On the Natural History of Destruction) of the same year.[3] The critical response to Sebald's thesis — that the bombings and their aftermath had been poorly represented in German literature — centered on the notion of a taboo on representing German suffering.[4] Contributors to the debate either praised Sebald for bringing forgotten suffering into the public realm, or rejected his taboo theory by pointing to the existence of many postwar texts in which the bombs and the ruins were featured. Volker Hage championed Ledig's *Vergeltung* as a forgotten masterpiece that went some way to disproving Sebald's argument.[5]

In this chapter, I argue that the existence of these texts does not disprove Sebald's thesis, that is, if we read *Luftkrieg und Literatur* closely and as part of Sebald's wider prose oeuvre. The taboo he identifies relates to a specific form of literary narrative that he sets out in the text as a "natural history of destruction." Furthermore, the wider critical rejection of Ledig's novel serves to support Sebald's theory. As an example of this natural history of destruction, I argue, it was subject to a taboo on any memory that threatened to disrupt efforts in the postwar period to continue with "normal" life.

Sebald's Taboo Thesis

Luftkrieg und Literatur investigates how West Germany remembered the bombings in the postwar period and how it was represented in literature. Sebald finds that, thanks to a taboo motivated by the shame of living in the ruins, the experience of this unprecedented destruction left "scarcely a trace of pain" (*NHD* 4) on the emerging consciousness of West Germany. Instead, the shattering reality of a degraded and broken society was distorted into a narrative of rebirth and redemption that sought to extract metaphysical meaning from the violence, driven by a desire to cling to an illusion of "normality" that could offer a sense of continuity. Sebald's accusation against West German literature is not that it avoided the subject of bombing at all, but that in the main it colluded in the effort to distort memory, sparing the Germans from the horror and violence of the catastrophe they unleashed, and building a new state founded on old values with "corpses built into the foundations" (*NHD* 13). Sebald uses his own descriptive passages and literary criticism as a search for a viable narrative form that can avoid this pitfall.

Luftkrieg und Literatur is the published form of Sebald's 1997 Zurich Poetry Lectures, in which his ideas about the bombings were elucidated by passages from his prose oeuvre. A nuanced reading of Sebald's taboo thesis depends on maintaining this link and reading the text as a part of, rather than separate from, his other work. Helmut Schmitz writes that

> all of Sebald's work is a sensitive exploration of the remnants of the prolonged history of inhumanity that characterises European modernity and which has the Holocaust as its point of culmination. . . . [It is] concerned with wresting away the individual fate from the immunity and abstraction that public discourse on "the Holocaust" confers on the victims.[6]

On a different, but identically focused level, *Luftkrieg und Literatur* is concerned with finding an appropriate language that can wrest the catastrophe that was borne of National Socialism from the immunity and abstraction that the perpetrators have imposed on their own experience and which ultimately spares them from absorbing the full horror of the history they imposed on Europe.

Sebald's concern with the memory of the Allied bombings is motivated by the same historical philosophy and critique of European modernity that informs all his writing. It is a critique that is influenced both by the historical messianism of Walter Benjamin and the later philosophy of Adorno and Horkheimer.[7] Benjamin's historical messianism, which found its zenith in his final work, "Theses on the Philosophy of History,"[8] called for a form of historical representation that, instead of telling the story of the victors of history, recognized that for the oppressed violence is the norm. A history of defeats rather than of victories could exert messianic power by allowing the past and the future to converge in the present at the "moment of danger" (danger for the oppressed), dispelling the lazy notion of history as uninterrupted progress.[9] For Benjamin, writing in the late 1930s, the rise of National Socialism was the ultimate moment of danger.

After the war, Adorno and Horkheimer, influenced by Benjamin's critique of progress and frozen into a traumatized pessimism by their confrontation with fascism, came to see mankind as a whole, propelled by its giant technological apparatus, heading toward an inferno. In the resulting work they set out to explain "why humanity, instead of entering into a truly human state, is sinking into a new kind of barbarism."[10] Their *Dialectic of Enlightenment,* first published in 1947, proposed that enlightenment, in its effort to demystify the world, is driven by an impulse to dominate nature and the self. This, however, becomes a limitation and liquidates all true knowledge of the object. The course of irresistible progress is therefore irresistible regression. Rationality becomes instrumental rationality, that is, rationality that progresses unthinkingly regardless of its object. As part of this process, nature must be demystified and becomes manipulable material. Any natural residues in man must also be eliminated and nature is therefore overcome at the expense of violence both to the world and to the self.[11]

Like Adorno and Horkheimer, Sebald perceives modern humankind as evolving inexorably toward the infernos of the war and, like Benjamin, he feels the heat of those fires burning in the present moment:

> As a whole, it appears, if you look at it from a very long way away as a phenomenon of evolution, the way we have developed is one great aberration, some kind of calculating error in the evolutionary matrix, somehow. And of course, increasingly, we know this and the great fires of the Second World War were only the first of the kinds of fires that are lit now. This is almost like an amoral perspective, when you think of the burning cities and the burning bodies of the 1940s, and then somehow link it up, as I quite often do, with the images of the burning forests of Borneo or of the Amazon. It would be false piety to look back upon 1940 to 1945 and say, "what horrible times these were!" We're still living in the middle of them, I feel.[12]

Sebald's criticism of the Germans in the text is that they, with the version of memory that they have chosen, have foreclosed any possibility of messianic redemption of history at precisely the moment when it might have been possible. The reality of a society that was "morally almost entirely discredited" (*NHD* ix) could have been the point at which the illusion of mastery over nature and history was dispelled, but instead, "the true state of material and moral ruin in which the country found itself was not to be described" (*NHD* 10). By making themselves the heroes of a rebuilt state, they continued a history of victories, when in fact it is one of defeats:

> They make it look as if the image of total destruction were not the horrifying end of a collective aberration, but something more like the first stage of a brave new world. (*NHD* 5–6)

The darkest aspects of society's downfall remained a shameful secret. Instead, even among the ruins of their former lives, the Germans try desperately to cling to normality, to the values of a "healthy human reason" (*NHD* 42). The consequences of this appropriation of the history of the bombings are grave, for if the storm of progress continues unhindered by the catastrophes of the past, only further catastrophes can follow. Sebald feels this storm in postwar Germany blowing behind the unfeasibly speedy rebuilding of German cities during the "economic miracle" of the 1950s. The consequence for the new Germany, he fears, is "that we are incorrigible and will continue along the beaten tracks that bear some slight relation to the old road network" (*NHD* 68).

Undoubtedly, to his mind, Germany is treading the old roads still. To conclude his essay Sebald includes an account of a letter he received in response to his original Zurich lectures, which propounds the theory that the Allies waged the war in the air with the aim of cutting the Germans off from their origins and inheritance by destroying their cities. This strategy was, according to the letter, devised by Jews living abroad, exploiting the special knowledge of the human psyche, foreign cultures, and foreign mentalities that they are known to have acquired during their wanderings (*NHD* 99). Sebald warns us not to dismiss this theory of a Jewish conspiracy as the musings of a crank. It is, perhaps, symptomatic of the fact that we stand, after reunification, at what Benjamin might term a moment of danger:

> Perhaps we ought to remind ourselves of that context now, when the project of creating a greater Europe that has already failed twice, is entering a new phase, and the sphere of influence of the Deutschmark . . . seems to extend almost precisely to the confines of the area occupied by the Wehrmacht in the year 1941. (*NHD* 13)

With this in mind, it is appropriate that Sebald invokes Benjamin's "Angel of History" (*NHD* 38). While we see the teleological progress of time, the angel sees the inseparability of past and present. For him, history is not governed by empty, homogenous time, but rather by time filled with the presence of the now, or *Jetztzeit*. The Angel would like to stand still in this moment to tend to the victims of the violent past, but he is irresistibly propelled forward by the storm of progress toward ever more destructive catastrophes. What the Angel sees is a fleeting glimpse of the redemption of history, but it does not last because the storm is too strong. For Sebald, the ruins of the German cities are just like those piled up at the feet of the Angel. Now, in this present moment of danger, Sebald, like the angel, can see the convolution of the past and the present in a disruptive account of history. However, like the Angel's, his glimpse is all too fleeting, because the storm has been allowed to keep blowing as strongly as ever before.

Writing a Natural History of Destruction: Gert Ledig's *Vergeltung*

In his "Theses on the Philosophy of History," Benjamin writes:

> There is no document of culture which is not at the same time a document of barbarism. And just as such a document is never free from barbarism, so barbarism taints the manner in which it was transmitted from one hand to the other.[13]

This could be the central tenet of *Luftkrieg und Literatur*. Sebald's engagement with the literature of the air war is based on the charge that the writers of postwar Germany continued to collude in the production of documents of barbarism. The accusation is not that they have avoided the theme, but rather that the form in which, for the most part, they have addressed it is inadequate: "I do not doubt that there were and are memories of those nights of destruction; I simply do not trust the form — including the literary form — in which they are expressed (*NHD* 87). This form is one which is designed to "sanitize or eliminate a kind of knowledge incompatible with any sense of normality" (*NHD* 11) and in so doing invalidates literature's purpose (*NHD* 53), a process for which "only a steadfast gaze bent on reality can compensate" (*NHD* 51).

Sebald is engaged in the search for a viable form of representation that can maintain this steadfast gaze and thus produce a document that is not one of barbarism. The term he applies to this form is "Naturgeschichte der Zerstörung" (natural history of destruction). It is a history that is natural in the sense that it is "of nature," displacing man as the subject and instead allowing the world (or, in this case, the destruction) to be the subject of history; it is also natural in its process of observing and documenting, allowing the events to come to the fore free of preconceived cultural paradigms and political manipulations.

It might seem pertinent here to ask why it is solely in literary fiction that Sebald places his hopes of finding such a narrative, rather than, perhaps, in eyewitness accounts or historiographical documentation. The answer lies in his belief in the creative ability of literary narrative to employ a "synoptic and artificial" narrative viewpoint (*NHD* 26). Eyewitness accounts will inevitably be replete with clichés, unable to break out of the "bounds of verbal convention" as they struggle to "make sense" of the experience (*NHD* 25). Historical documentation, in contrast, will tend to conceal the horror behind the language of the "victors" of history: technical breakdowns, military strategy, facts and figures. For the natural history of destruction to transcend these restrictions, it will require the freedom that literature can provide in which to shed traditional paradigms of conventional narration. To explore how a synoptic, artificial view might achieve this, I will now turn to Gert Ledig's *Vergeltung,* which, closely resembling Sebald's own narrative strategy in *Luftkrieg und Literatur,* is a model of the natural history of destruction at work and, in its public rejection, is a demonstration of the taboo identified by Sebald.

Gert Ledig experienced the war as a young *Wehrmacht* soldier in Stalingrad, then later, when wounded, in Munich in the midst of the bombing raids. His novel of the bombings was almost entirely absent from the postwar canon until 1999 and Sebald therefore made no mention of it in his original lectures, but gave it brief yet strong praise in his postscript to the published version as a "book that attacks the final illusions" (*NHD* 95) and that threatened to break through the "*cordon sanitaire* cast by society around the death zones of the dystopian incursions that actually occurred" (*NHD* 97).

The novel describes sixty-nine minutes of a bombing raid in an unnamed German city in 1944. The narrative shifts frequently between simultaneous episodes occurring in different parts of the city, in the air and underground. It features a disparate group of largely unnamed people, identified usually only by military rank or social position. The reader is given only scant detail about these people which, coupled with the speed of the narrative shifts, precludes any real empathetic identification with them. The detail with which the scenes of destruction are described is sharp and unremitting and the narrative voice restricts itself to raw sensory description. It is this peculiarly constructed narrative voice, his synoptic, artificial gaze, that is Ledig's most powerful tool and that makes *Vergeltung* a viable example of a natural history of destruction.

To better understand the nature of the narrative voice both Ledig and Sebald use to write about the bombings, it is helpful to appropriate some of the terms of phenomenology. When employing the phenomenological gaze toward an object, we are required to suspend our intentionalities, that is, the conscious relationship we have with that object.[14] By doing this, we suspend our "default attitude" to the object, and can move into the "phenomenological attitude," from which we can focus reflectively on everything in the default attitude. The aim is to avoid all misconstructions and impositions placed on experience in advance, such as those drawn from cultural and religious traditions and protocols, even common sense, to allow the world to appear to us as it "really is."[15] When we move into this attitude, we become "like detached observers of a passing scene or like spectators at a game" and contemplate the involvements we have with the world as well as the world in its human involvement.[16]

A natural history of destruction would require any narrator to contemplate the violence in this way and this is the value of Ledig's narrative voice, resulting in what Gregor Streim has called a "distant proximity,"[17] which is precisely the goal of the phenomenological gaze: the suspension of conscious involvement with the world allows us to become datives of truth *to whom* the world can appear, enabling us to get closer to the object we are contemplating. It is the empathetic distance from the scene in Ledig that enables the "truth" of the violence and the state to which the world has been brought to emerge from the behind the smokescreen.

The language of this phenomenology is accordingly stripped of extraneous embellishment and reference to external categories, giving the violence the space to become the subject of the scene:

> Next to the mother stood a woman burning like a torch. She was screaming. The mother looked on helpless, then she too was on fire. It raced up her legs, up her thighs, to her body . . . a shock wave exploded along the graveyard wall and in that moment the road burned too. Asphalt, stones, air. That was what happened in the graveyard. (*P* 2)

Here, as throughout the novel, the bodies of the women are equal components of the destruction as the road, the wall, even the air. The people featured, like all objects of the narrative, become nothing more than datives of the destruction, which is, rather than the people, the subject of the narrative. Both before and after death, humans feature as nothing more than bodies *to whom* violence is done:

> The butt of the machine gun slipped from the turret-gunner's shoulder, smashing into his jaw. Almost painlessly he lost thirty teeth. An explosive round ripped through his chest and shredded his lung through his ribs. The wound gaped from his right collar-bone to his left nipple. Half a gallon of blood gushed out. (*P* 20)

The separation of parts of the body from its whole is a recurrent theme, making abstract objects out of previously living beings: "He clutched warm flesh. He was holding a piece of windpipe between his fingers" (*P* 21). Such sensory experiences are not given further context, as it is to these that the world is reduced. It is only with sight, smell, taste, and sensation, rather than with reason, that the destruction is represented.

Despite this, the narrative voice is what would traditionally be classified as omniscient. The book has a narrative structure that is spatial rather than temporal, relying on the omniscience of the narrative voice, which can move freely around simultaneously occurring events. Nevertheless, this omniscience is a limited one. While it is privy to some of the thoughts of the people featured, it never takes us into their heads, always keeping its distance by reporting isolated thoughts: "He thought: My grandfather picked cotton" (*P* 7). Although it is made certain that the narration is of a past event, these events appear to the reader in real time, or even in slow motion. What we witness as readers is only of the now, restricted to the current moment, with little in the way of temporal context. The narrative does not employ flashbacks or quicken the pace, as would usually be the strategy of the all-knowing narrator.

This limited omniscience provides the crucial synoptic element of the natural-historical narrative Sebald demands. Only a narrator who is all-powerful in the sense of being able to see more than a normal human being will be able to tell the "true" story of the bombings, which is not of life and survival, but of death and violence. The majority of the people featured in *Vergeltung* do not live past the end of the narrative and, because it is their deaths rather than their lives that are the subject of the novel, only a narrator of this kind could fulfill the task. Furthermore, it is only from this position that the aim of a natural history of destruction, as Sebald dictates, can be achieved; if the Germans are to be written as object rather than subject of history, the narrative voice must be able to transcend the confines of human concerns. That Ledig sets out to do just that is made clear in the very opening scene of the novel, which describes a bomb falling on a graveyard and blowing up a pile of child corpses. This, as in other episodes, is an incident that is not witnessed by any living person in the text. The narration is thus from the outset placed outside of human memory and is able to make the violence itself the subject of the narrative: as Susanne Vees-Gulani has put it, "the true hero of the novel is not one of the characters but destruction itself."[18] The occasional autobiographical excerpts that permeate the text represent the attempt by a "human" narrative to break through and impose itself. However, amid the narrative of violence, the scant, disjointed details about their lives that the characters offer from beyond the grave now sound hollow and inconsequential, ultimately failing to regain control of the narrative and extract empathy from the reader.

Ledig's narrative strategy foretells Sebald's own in the narrative passages of *Luftkrieg und Literatur*. Compare, for instance: "Horribly disfigured corpses lay everywhere. Bluish little phosphorous flames flickered around them; others had been roasted blue or purple and reduced to a third of their size" (*NHD* 28); or "the glass in the tramcar windows melted; stocks of sugar boiled in the bakery cellars. Those who had fled their shelters sank, in grotesque contortions, in the thick bubbles thrown up by the melting asphalt" (*NHD* 27–28). It is a form that opens the way for a lifting of the taboo Sebald identifies, as Ledig's "distant proximity" exposes the evidence of the futility of the effort to dominate nature: Adorno and Horkheimer argue that the effort to demystify the world drives enlightened thought to pull everything inside into a condition of "pure immanence" and that anything that cannot be brought inside of thought is mere fiction. To demystify the world outside of thought, the subjective must be projected onto it. By reducing the world to physicality, Ledig shows us how the violence of the bombings is exemplary of the futility of this endeavor: experience is wrenched out of thought and the world is mediated solely through the body. The body is the mediating force between man and nature that cannot be mastered. It is repeatedly shown to be vulnerable, fallible, and totally subject to the demands of the physical environment. Whether by a rotting, severed hand (*P* 2), or spilt blood seeping back into the earth or evaporating into the air (*P* 78), the body is shown continuously to be a component of the natural world. While death is often depicted as painful but swift, ongoing suffering is a result of the physical demands of the body for air, water, or defecation. Even emotions are expressed purely physically: shame, guilt, and horror are not described explicitly, but are signaled by vomiting (*P* 11); fear is not a reasoned reaction to danger, but merely a complex system of actions in the brain (*P* 45). Even without the incursions of violence such as this, we are reminded that the body is always slowly decaying by Dessy Cheovski's worries about looking old (*P* 19). Ultimately, despite the efforts to the contrary, people are shown to have no control even over their own death: a man who sinks into burning tar does not die "any manner of death that was ever invented. He was grilled" (*P* 125).

In this remystified, pre-enlightened world, people are returned to just the archaic state that they most fear. Excrement and urine permeate the burning city (*P* 161) in which people are losing the battle to retain human dignity: "A gunner stood in the trench, legs splayed. With his trousers open he reached between his legs. His hand fished out shit and smeared it on the wall of the trench" (*P* 154). The gunner is called a "pig" by his officer in just one of numerous incidences of people "becoming" animals. Similarly, Sebald's descriptions show a regressed people, for whom the distinctions between animal and human, natural and manmade, interior and exterior have become blurred. Life in the ruins is mere existence governed by the struggle to survive in the natural world. They are nomadic gatherers, thrust back to an unrecognizable state outside of civilization: "This is the necropolis of a foreign, mysterious people, torn from its civil existence and its history, thrown back to the evolutionary stage of nomadic gatherers" (*NHD* 36). Eventually, nature begins to reclaim the charred earth, forcing the people out of the shelters that once protected them from it: "elsewhere trees were already growing, pretty little trees springing up in bedrooms and kitchens" (*NHD* 39).

In this exposed world all civilized and moral structures that might otherwise give comfort are shown to be illusory. Like Sebald, Ledig recognizes the absurdity of the supposed German need for order in the face of the downfall of the familiar. Sebald mentions, with some disgust, the tendency for orchestras to hold concerts in the ruined halls immediately after bombings so that the population might continue to uphold "higher cultural rituals" (*NHD* 44). In *Vergeltung,* the Cheovski couple, awaiting death wearing their best clothes in their newly cleaned apartment, is exemplary of this tendency, even discussing where best they should wait (*P* 17). Instrumental logic, as well as the desperate attempt to hold onto it, is showcased as having become absurd: "'You shouldn't eat before an air raid.' He added: 'My dad said it was in case you got hit in the belly'" (*P* 14). Categories that are usually clearly defined melt away into an indistinct amalgam of human behavior. Innocence and guilt, for example, are not mutually exclusive, as many of the people featured repeatedly cross the boundaries of victim and perpetrator: Maria Weinert, for instance, has drunk champagne sent from the conquered France, and is implicated in the murder of an invalid woman to save herself, but is later subject to a rape while buried under rubble (*P* 5, 10, 95). Uniforms, medals, or marks of rank prove meaningless or motivated by empty values, such as the iron cross that is bartered for a case of wine (*P* 111). Trusted structures of society betray those who still have faith in them: the American pilot Strenehen thinks he has finally found safety in the care of a doctor only for that doctor to commit an archaic act of retribution and violence (*P* 188).

Even the most universal constructions break down. In desperate attempts to retain control of their world, people repeatedly seek out ways to tell the time and keep track of its passage, but always in vain. Temporality is repeatedly used as a potent symbol of the illusion of control that is rapidly being dispelled: "It was moving slowly, or at breakneck speed, they couldn't tell" (*P* 54). Even when attempts to tell the time are successful, the illusion of being in control of it has been lifted: "The big hand and the little hand pointed at numbers. Nobody saw them" (*P* 46). Time, a potentially comforting sign of the familiar that everyone craves, becomes the enemy that no one can control: "Without looking at the clock, he knew that the hand was moving. Time was running out. It had come too suddenly" (*P* 19). Sebald's ruined city is also a place where the conventional markers of enlightenment have become worthless, even absurd. Sebald devotes three pages to the destruction of the Berlin Zoo, an especially poignant example of this loss, since, as he puts it, they "owe their existence to a desire to demonstrate princely power [and] are at the same time supposed to be a kind of imitation of the Garden of Eden" (*NHD* 93). This manmade Eden now lies in ruins, its animals suffocated or charred in their cages. Those that survive make for a carnevalesque scene in which exotic animals roam the streets. (*NHD* 92). The city-dwellers are now more like jungle tribes, hunted by big cats and themselves resorting to killing and eating wild beasts: "'the crocodile tails, cooked in large pans, tasted like fat chicken,' and later, he continues, 'we regarded bear hams and bear sausage as delicacies'" (*NHD* 93).

In contrast to the writers that Sebald criticizes in *Luftkrieg und Literatur,* then, Ledig's narrative deliberately avoids the strategies of abstraction that might be employed to subsume the reality of the bombings into a progressive, teleological history. One of the most common of these strategies is the inception of a universal, biblical model of retribution, redemption, and rebirth from the ashes. In *Vergeltung,* by contrast, this model is turned on its head as the possibility of Christian redemption and continuing faith in God is precluded.[19] In the course of the narrative, numerous people lose their faith in God as they die, not least of whom a priest, who in the last throes of death makes a final plea to God for salvation but is betrayed (*P* 81). The American pilot, who tried to sabotage the dropping of his bombs, suffers a death that resembles the passion of the Christ as he is lynched, though unarmed, by the waiting mob. Yet his martyrdom is pointless, as those who might be redeemed by his death are themselves seconds later blown to pieces (*P* 188).

By unsettling the most universal of cultural paradigms and civilized structures, Ledig is consciously reinforcing the process that occurs naturally in war and to which Sebald wishes to draw our attention, namely, to the shattering of blind faith in instrumental progress. In *Luftkrieg und Literatur,* the bombing campaigns are an example of enlightened man being led into the inferno by his blind faith in technological and economic progress. He describes how the campaign acquires a momentum of its own regardless of the human cost and marvels at the technological fervor with which bombing strategies were pursued, and reminds us again of the continuing threat by noting that this eventually led to the production of the atomic bomb (*NHD* 16). Ledig too sees the destructive tendencies at the heart of technological progress: "Technology shattered technology. It bent masts, tore apart machines, opened up craters, demolished walls, and life was just so much rubbish" (*P* 39). The archaic, violent heart that is veiled by enlightened values is best represented by the figure of the doctor, that most potent of symbols of the enlightenment, who indulges in torturing the American pilot: "as far as I'm concerned . . . war is the father of all things" (*P* 197).

Like Sebald, Ledig recognizes that without the interjection of a disruptive history, the future will be founded on the same belief: "An hour was all it took for terror to triumph. Afterwards, some people wanted to forget that fact. Others claimed not to have known it" (*P* 200). The result is that "progress destroyed both past and future" (*P* 199).

In conclusion, then, Ledig's rejection by a Germany in the throes of the economic miracle makes him the exception that proves Sebald's thesis. His refusal to allow the memory of the bombings to form a platform for any positive message of rebirth made him inaccessible to an audience wishing to carry on as before. Ledig therefore suffered the fate of the doomed messenger Sebald describes, who is compelled to speak of what he has seen in Hamburg, but whose audience then kills him. In contrast, "those who can salvage some metaphysical meaning from the destruction are usually spared such a wretched fate; their trade is less dangerous than dealing in concrete memory" (*NHD* 59). In the debate that broke out in 1998, Sebald too suffered the fate of the messenger as commentators leapt either to denounce his historical relativism or, conversely, to commit the exact crimes he described, by declaring it high time that Germans be recognized as victims.

Notes

[1] Gert Ledig, *Vergeltung* (Frankfurt am Main: Suhrkamp, 1999), trans. Shaun Whiteside as *Payback* (London: Granta, 2003). Quotations are from the translation; subsequent references to this work are cited in the text using the abbreviation *P* and page number.

[2] Gert Ledig, *Die Stalinorgel* (Frankfurt am Main: Suhrkamp, 2003).

[3] W. G. Sebald, *Luftkrieg und Literatur: Mit einem Essay zu Alfred Andersch* (Munich: Carl Hanser, 1999), trans. Anthea Bell as *On the Natural History of Destruction* (London: Penguin, 2003). Quotations are from the translation; subsequent references to this work are cited in the text using the abbreviation *NHD* and page number.

[4] The critical debate is compiled in Volker Hage et al., eds., *Deutsche Literatur 1998: Jahresüberblick* (Ditzingen: Reklam, 1999).

[5] See Volker Hage, *Zeugen der Zerstörung: Die Literaten und der Luftkrieg: Essays und Gespräche* (Frankfurt am Main: Suhrkamp, 2003).

[6] Helmut Schmitz, *On Their Own Terms: The Legacy of National Socialism in Post-1990 German Fiction* (Birmingham, UK: U of Birmingham P, 2004), 291.

[7] The influence of both Benjamin and Adorno and Horkheimer on *Luftkrieg und Literatur* is further explored in Graham Jackman, "Gebranntes Kind? W. G. Sebald's 'Metaphysik der Geschichte,'" *German Life and Letters* 57, no. 4 (2004): 456–71 and Rick Crownshaw, "German Suffering or 'Narrative Fetishism'?: W. G. Sebald's 'Air War and Literature: Zurich Lectures,'" in *Searching for Sebald: Photography after W. G. Sebald*, ed. Lise Patt (Los Angeles: ICI Press, 2007), 558–83.

[8] Walter Benjamin, "Theses on the Philosophy of History," in *Illuminations* (London: Random House, 1999), 245–55.

[9] See Michael Löwy, *Fire Alarm: Reading Walter Benjamin's "On the Concept of History,"* trans. Chris Turner (London: Verso, 2005).

[10] Theodor W. Adorno and Max Horkheimer, *Dialectic of Enlightenment: Philosophical Fragments* (Stanford, CA: Stanford UP, 2002), xiv.

[11] See Paul Connerton, *The Tragedy of Enlightenment: An Essay on the Frankfurt School* (Cambridge: CUP, 1980), 60–91; Simon Jarvis, *Adorno: A Critical Introduction* (Cambridge: CUP, 1998); Zoltan Tar, *The Frankfurt School: The Critical Theories of Max Horkheimer and Theodor W. Adorno* (London: John Wiley, 1977).

[12] W. G. Sebald and Gordon Turner, "Introduction and Transcript of an Interview given by Max Sebald (Interviewer: Michael Zeeman)," in *W. G. Sebald: History-Memory-Trauma,* ed. Scott Denham (Berlin: Walter de Gruyter, 2006), 28.

[13] Benjamin, "Philosophy of History," 248.

[14] This is not be confused with "intention" as in the purpose we have in mind when we act. The phenomenological notion of intentionality refers to knowledge rather than action. See Robert Sokolowski, *Introduction to Phenomenology* (Cambridge: CUP, 2000), 8.

[15] See Dermot Moran, *Introduction to Phenomenology* (London: Routledge, 2000), 4.

[16] Sokolowski, *Introduction to Phenomenology,* 48.

[17] See Gregor Streim, "Der Bombenkrieg als Sensation und als Dokumentation: Gert Ledigs Roman *Vergeltung* und die Debatte um W. G. Sebalds *Luftkrieg und Literatur,*" in *Krieg in den Medien,* ed. Heinz-Peter Preusser (Amsterdam: Rodopi, 2005), 308.

[18] Susanne Vees-Gulani, *Trauma and Guilt: Literature of Wartime Bombing in Germany* (Berlin: Walter de Gruyter, 2003), 90.

[19] For a full treatment of the Christian narrative in *Vergeltung,* see Florian Radvan, "Religiöse Bildlichkeit und transtextuelle Bezüge in Gert Ledigs Luftkriegsroman *Vergeltung,*" in *Bombs Away! Representing the Airwar over Europe and Japan,* ed. Wilfried Wilms and William Rasch (Amsterdam: Rodopi, 2006), 165–79.

3: Expulsion Novels of the 1950s: More than Meets the Eye?

Karina Berger

AT THE END OF THE 1950s, critic Karl Heinz Gehrmann spoke of the "unmanageable abundance" of literary works dealing with expulsion.[1] Indeed, the decade produced a vast amount of texts — novels, diaries, and autobiographies — often written by expellees themselves to document or come to terms with their experience. Many of these stories retell the harrowing ordeal of being expelled, while others concentrate on the beauty and virtues of their lost *Heimat*. Tarnished perhaps by the sometimes aggressive calls by *Vertriebenenverbände* (expellee organizations) in the postwar years to reinstate the borders of 1937 and reclaim lost territories, expulsion texts from the 1950s have largely been viewed with suspicion. From the 1960s onward, expulsion literature has had to contend with the widespread assumption among critics and academics that it is revisionist or even revanchist, that it focuses exclusively on German suffering, and that it fails to engage with issues such as guilt and responsibility, and especially the victims of Nazism and the Holocaust.[2] Thus, the Polish literary historian Ludmila Slugocka claimed in 1964 that these books were written "in the name of revanchism" and with a "readiness to fight for reacquisition,"[3] while Germanist Jost Hermand, writing in 1979, criticized that, when reading these texts, one got the impression that Germans from the eastern provinces had been the primary victims of the Second World War, rather than Russians, Poles, or Jews.[4] Indeed, Gertrud Fussenegger, one of the authors to be examined in this chapter, also noted that those thematizing expulsion in literature were generally regarded as "suspicious."[5]

In reality, however, only a small minority of texts can be seen as genuinely revisionist or revanchist. In his comprehensive study Louis F. Helbig classes only four of the seventy-four works cited as problematic, notably the nationalistic Edwin Erich Dwinger's *Wenn die Dämme brechen* (When the Dams Burst, 1950) and Olga Barényi's sensationalist *Prager Totentanz* (Death Dance in Prague, 1958).[6] Most of the texts do not fall into this category, though it is true that many reflect prevalent mentalities of the immediate postwar years, which are very different from contemporary ones, and therefore may now appear inappropriate, or even unacceptable. For instance, in the 1950s, the Second World War was frequently de-politicized and de-ideologized, which inevitably led to a reduction, or evasion, into existential, religious, private, or mythical views of the past. Such attempts often relied on notions of mass responsibility, giving short shrift to closer scrutiny of individual guilt. In religious interpretations, the war — and suffering in general — was seen as a form of redemption and absolution from guilt. National Socialism was often depicted as a sickness or madness that had overwhelmed the German people, or as a demonic force, under which Germany had suffered.[7] Indeed, literary critic Judith Ryan speaks of the widespread perception of "a totally passive citizenry trampled underfoot by the inevitable march of history."[8] Nazism, then, was not seen as a political and social evil with a specific historical cause, but rather as an inescapable and inevitable fate, or the reincarnation of evil, which negated any form of causality between historical events and German suffering.[9] Such reactions may have had a valuable consolatory function, yet the omission of questions surrounding personal responsibility and guilt are problematic. Moreover, the Second World War and the Holocaust were often not viewed as one unique and horrific event, but rather as part of a much greater story of suffering and martyrdom in the continuum of human history which, again, not only relieved the German population from guilt, but also relativized the Nazi victims' suffering.[10]

However, some of the texts *do* address questions of guilt and imply historical responsibility, or complicity. In this chapter I argue that a number of expulsion novels of the 1950s go beyond conventional expectations by drawing a link between expulsion and German aggression and including victims of the Holocaust in their representation of German suffering. In the remainder of this chapter I examine three texts in more detail, all of which, within the limitations posed by the postwar context, go beyond conventional expectations in their treatment of the subject of expulsion: *Wintergewitter* (Winter Storm, 1951) by Kurt Ihlenfeld, *Das verschüttete Antlitz* (Buried Countenance, 1957) by Gertrud Fussenegger, and *Die schlesische Barmherzigkeit* (Silesian Mercy, 1950) by Ruth Hoffmann.[11] Between them, these texts represent the wide range of styles that can be found in expulsion literature of the 1950s: one has a religious leaning, one is highly symbolic, and the last text is an example of popular literature dealing with the theme.

Wintergewitter

Wintergewitter was Kurt Ihlenfeld's first novel and one of the earliest texts to deal with expulsion. Although it brought the author success and won him the *Berliner Literaturpreis* and prestigious *Fontane Preis* in 1952, and though some of his works were republished into the late 1980s, he is virtually unheard of today. Ihlenfeld, a theologian, was one of the leading figures of Protestant literature after 1945, a movement that constituted one of the primary intellectual phenomena in the first postwar years, but its rapid decline in the following decades meant that the author soon sank into oblivion. Ihlenfeld was part of an older generation, along with authors such as Ernst Wiechert and Marie Luise Kaschnitz, who rejected any idea of a new start, but wished to regenerate what they saw as the traditional German qualities of kindness, wisdom, tolerance, and humanity. Ihlenfeld rejected National Socialism; as editor of the Christian literary magazine *Eckart,* he founded the "Eckart circle," bringing together a group of like-minded "inner emigrant" writers, such as Ricarda Huch, Reinhold Schneider, Rudolf Alexander Schröder, Jochen Klepper, and Werner Bergengruen. In 1943, the magazine fell victim to Nazi censorship and was forced to close.

In 1945, he and his family moved to Lower Silesia, where Ihlenfeld looked after a parish, and where he witnessed the Germans' flight and expulsion, which he later addressed in his epic work *Wintergewitter.* The main part of the sizeable eight-hundred page novel describes the events of one day in a village in lower Silesia. The date is 3 February 1945; the Red Army has reached the nearby Oder River. It is on this day that the villagers first hear the sounds of the artillery — the winter storm (the "Wintergewitter") — and are confronted with the reality of war. Their intial reaction is denial, then helplessness. The reader follows the central character, the parish priest, through the day's events, which include the arrival of a tank on its way to the Eastern front, the arrival of expellees from areas further east and a group of women from a concentration camp that is led through the village. The novel concludes before the actual catastrophe, but it is clear that the end of Silesia is nigh and that the villagers will have to leave their homes to escape the Russian army.

Wintergewitter exhibits many of the characteristics typical of the "religiously inflected" 1950s novel, with its existentialist terminology, the mythologization and demonization of Nazism, and the Christian notion of redemption through suffering, a key theme in the text. Thus, the language is at times reminiscent of religious sermons, and the narrative includes numerous Christian motifs and symbols, such as the biblical flood. Also representative are the vague, sometimes even cryptic, references to the war and National Socialism: Hitler is described as "the villain" (*W* 248), while fascism is referred to as "the other world" (*W* 444).

Typically, the narrative also places the war and its atrocities in the larger context of human history: the battle over Silesia is seen as the latest in a long chain of conflicts in the region, beginning with the Battle of Wahlstatt (1241; *W* 696), and followed by the Thirty Years' War (1618–1648; *W* 576), the Seven Year War (also known as the Third Silesian War,

1756–1763; *W* 707–8) and the First World War (*W* 121).[12] Similarly, the expellees' fate is portrayed as part of a long line of expulsions throughout history: there are references to the expulsion of the Helvetians (*W* 89), the flight of "Israel's children" (*W* 739), and the banishment from Paradise (*W* 71, 778), a common metaphor in early expulsion texts. When observing the first expellees' arrival in the village, the priest makes the almost cynical observation that expellees "always look like that" (*W* 94).

Comparable to many other expulsion novels of the period, the portrayal of foreigners is occasionally problematic, notably of the Russians, who are portrayed as terrifying, brutal, and primitive (*W* 701, 735–36). This is particularly evident in one passage in which a lieutenant, who is also a theologian, tries to "cure" a raving Tartar. He and his fellow POWs are patronizingly described in the diminutive as "gutmütiges Völkchen" (good-natured folk; *W* 36), while the description of their physical appearance is unfavorable and based entirely on stereotypes: they are short but of broad build, with round heads that jut out, and with a "glum Mongolian expression" on their faces (*W* 36).

However, the text goes beyond the characteristic traits of early expulsion novels by addressing issues such as guilt, the fate of Jewish victims, and German responsibility for their own suffering, although much of the engagement with the past, and guilt in particular, remains on a religious level. Most notable in *Wintergewitter* are the references to Jewish suffering. Firstly, there is the Jewish Herr von Schindel who lives among the villagers and has managed to remain undiscovered for more than a decade. Just months before the end of the war, he and his family are discovered and deported by the Gestapo. Although the word "Jew" is never spelled out in the novel, von Schindel's background is described in unambiguous terms when the narrator realizes that Schindel "comes from Israel" (*W* 415–16). Here, Jewish persecution is addressed, although the choice of words may reveal prejudices: by describing Herr von Schindel as coming "from Israel," he is marked as "foreign" or "un-German," and it may also be seen to echo the Nazi law that Jewish men adopt "Israel" as their second name.[13]

The most concrete depiction of the crimes of the Holocaust is a group of female concentration camp prisoners that is led through the village. Typically, many of the expressions describing the women are of metaphysical nature or vague, but hints that they are coming from the East, that they are escorted by women in uniform, that they are wearing inadequate clothing and no shoes, and that they are Polish or Czech, leave little doubt about their identiy — and not just with the benefit of hindsight. Importantly, the villagers seem to know who these women are, implying that if even the inhabitants of this small and remote village, which was spared by the war until the very last few months, know about concentration camps, then this must have been widely known across Germany, signaling perhaps implicit criticism at the common excuse of "not having known." As though to emphasize this further, the narrator notes: "They were seen by everyone. Now everyone knows. There are no excuses anymore" (*W* 239). However, the narrative does not provide specific, or more explicit, details of the Holocaust.

Lastly, the fate of the Jews is addressed by reference to Jochen Klepper, a protestant Silesian poet and close friend of Ihlenfeld's, who was married to a Jew and committed suicide with his entire family in 1942. Again, Klepper's name is not directly mentioned, but Ihlenfeld drops several hints in the passage describing the family's (unmarked) grave, for instance, referring to the family's cause of death and the impossibility to openly mourn their death because they were "victims of persecution" (*W* 498). The narrative also quotes verses from Klepper's church hymns, and the poet is named in the dedication of the book. However, that Klepper himself was not Jewish, but Protestant, could be construed as what Stuart Taberner has more recently termed "sentimentalised victimhood." Reminiscent of the film *Aimée und Jaguar* (1998), empathy here is largely evoked for the non-Jewish man, rather than his Jewish wife and children.[14]

Notwithstanding such problematic aspects, Jewish suffering is addressed on several levels in *Wintergewitter,* countering the claim that expulsion novels of the 1950s focus exclusively on the Germans' plight. Significantly, Jewish suffering is also brought into direct connection with expulsion: the narrative emphasizes that what is being inflicted on Germans is a direct result of, and punishment for, what the Germans inflicted on others.[15] Here, the wording is more explicit: the protagonist declares, after seeing first the refugee trek, and then the concentration camp prisoners: "They belong together. One will never be able to separate them" (*W* 238).

However, although the notion of German guilt is addressed, the engagement with guilt remains largely on a religious level. Although National Socialist crimes are shown to be the cause of expulsion, events are ultimately portrayed as part of something "much more general" (*W* 238). Expulsion is framed as God's judgment: for German crimes, but also as punishment for the decline of Christian faith more generally. In this interpretation, guilt is simply one component of God's plan for mankind (*W* 790), regardless of individual beliefs or circumstances: all are guilty, without exception (*W* 791), though no one is personally responsible. Moreover, suffering is presented as a form of redemption and salvation, and as the way to a better future (*W* 790). In *Wintergewitter,* then, the notion of German culpability is confronted, and historical responsibility implied, but the events of the Second World War are ultimately portrayed as inevitable, and the individual as powerless, leading to the moral and political exoneration of ordinary Germans. Despite such limitations, the religious pattern of guilt and redemption did lend the first viable framework to address the Nazi past, including, to some extent, the psychological problems of guilt and atonement, even though such belief frameworks may appear less accessible, or even alienating, today.

Principally, the message of *Wintergewitter* can be described as conciliatory. In keeping with its religious leaning, it calls for greater humanity and for peaceful relations between nations in general, but also refers more specifically to previously good relations between Poles and Germans as an example of a time in which borders and nationalities are not of primary importance (*W* 257).[16] Ihlenfeld distances himself from National Socialism in his narrative, though apart from one or two passages this is, again, implied rather than concrete. More important, and refuting the claim that early expulsion texts were often revanchist, the narrative is clear on the subject of expulsion: it is clearly portrayed as a consequence of German crimes, and emphasizes that expulsion is irreversible (*W* 219) and that there is no hope for return (*W* 90).

Das verschüttete Antlitz

Das verschüttete Antlitz, by the controversial Austrian author Gertrud Fussenegger, is very different in tone and style, although the overall message — that humanity will prevail even in adverse conditions — is similar. A prolific writer since the 1930s, Fussenegger had been criticized for publishing anti-Semitic texts in the Nazi Party newspaper *Völkischer Beobachter* during the Nazi regime. Not one to deny her enthusiasm for National Socialism at the time, since the end of the war she repeatedly used literature, guided by her return to Catholicism, to address the question of German guilt, including her own, although her genuineness has been questioned by some.

Guilt, in its many guises, is also central to her novel *Das verschüttete Antlitz,* which is set in Bohemia between about 1900 and 1945 and forms the final part of a large-scale trilogy about the region. Prague and Pilsen and two small neighboring Czech-German villages, between which the border is drawn toward the end of the narrative, provide the symbolic frame for the plot. Like the location, the central character symbolizes the border between Czechs and Germans: born to a German mother and a Czech father, doctor Victorin Zeman embodies the tensions between the two nations. The borderland theme is further emphasized by the friendship between the Zemans and a bourgeois German family, Elisabeth and Leonhard Jering, who live in the neighboring village, which later becomes annexed to Germany. The doctor's decline begins after he is falsely suspected of the murder of a prostitute. Although he is released free of charge, he is deserted by his patients and left by his wife. He is then sought out by shady guests with dubious medical requests from the nearby health resorts. It is only now that Zeman crosses into immoral territory by accepting their money. His wife Pussy, a Jewish, playful, naïve, and corrupt woman, returns when she learns of his new success, but Zeman ends the unhappy marriage by turning into an actual murderer and drowning her. He turns himself in and is released seven years later, in 1941 — not as a German into the "Reich," but as a Czech into the protectorate. It is at this point that Zeman is able to redeem his sins: he saves Elisabeth and her children before the collapse and arranges for their escape to Germany. Finally, he also saves Elisabeth's husband, whom he has always despised, and smuggles him across the border. Thus, the guilty Zeman atones for his sins by his good deed — offering help, not revenge, to his enemy — and recovers his "buried countenance" as a human being.

Although this brief synopsis barely captures the reach and complexity of the plot, I hope to have shown that in Fussenegger's novel Germans, Czechs, and Jews are connected by multiple interdependencies, and the concepts of guilt and responsibility are addressed on several levels. For instance, there are several allusions to German complicity: both Elisabeth's father and husband are portrayed as staunchly nationalistic, and Leonhard is drafted in to fight on the Eastern front. Elisabeth, who embodies many positive "German" virtues, is at the same time shown to be ignorant and passive, representative perhaps of many "fellow travelers." Furthermore, *Das verschüttete Antlitz* points to the overwhelming pro-Nazi sentiment that pervaded the region in the 1930s by acknowledging that, in September 1938, there had been no resistance but instead widespread acceptance (*VA* 329–30) — a reference to the enthusiastically welcomed Munich Agreement, according to which the border regions of Bohemia inhabited predominantly by ethnic Germans (the so-called Sudetenland) were annexed to Germany.

The narrative also draws attention to Jewish suffering and, by implication, to German crimes. Beginning with hints to the anti-Semitic Nazi policies in the prewar years, the text explicitly refers to the ghettoization of Jews and the poor conditions therein (*VA* 322), as well as mass killings (*VA* 310) and mass graves (*VA* 308). A comment by Elisabeth's maid further emphasizes the brutality of the Holocaust, yet her cold and unemotional language reveals little or no empathy for the victims:

> Haben Sie schon gehört: die Juden kommen nach Polen, samt und sonders. Dort werden sie abgemacht. [. . .] Sie schaufeln [. . .] ihre Gräber selbst und dann tack tack tack, ein Maschinengewehr. [. . .] Mit den Juden kennen die Unsern einfach gar kein Pardon. Männer, Weiber, Kinder, alle kommen in die Gruben. (*VA* 310)

[Have you heard: the Jews are sent to Poland, all of them. There they are got rid of. They dig their own graves and then tack tack tack, a machine gun. Our lot just have no mercy for the Jews. Males, females, children, all go into the pits.]

The choice of the brutal word "abgemacht" (got rid of) is striking here, and is reminiscent of rough soldier-speak in the trenches, while the word "Weiber" has derogatory connotations. Moreover, the use of the onomatopoeic "tack tack tack," a short, sharp sound, brings to mind the brutality of the victims' death, and is delivered devoid of any pity, or judgment, or even disapproval: "our lot" have "no mercy" for the Jews — this is delivered as simple fact, with no indication that this may be considered wrong, even despicable. Passages like this may serve to illustrate how banal such crimes appeared to many Germans, and to what extent they were indoctrinated by Nazi propaganda, seeing the Jews as unworthy of pity. It also highlights the blind acceptance of the Nazi regime's actions among large parts of the population, and the unquestioning, uncritical attitude that was commonplace. Passages like this are uncomfortable, even disconcerting, for the present-day reader, but in the 1950s it may have been intended as a mirror, intended to prompt self-questioning, and shock readers out of what some perceived to be postwar complacency.

The question of guilt is addressed more clearly a few pages later when Elisabeth witnesses a packed train transporting Jews eastward (prompted by the now-Czech Zeman). Here, the language is more emotive and carries a moral judgment, marking all Germans, including passive fellow travelers — and thus, herself — as guilty. Thus, references to "the murderers" and "guilty peoples" who "witnessed" what was happening (*VA* 322–23) clearly point to complicity and responsibility among all ethnic Germans in Bohemia.

Although the narrative emphasizes Jewish suffering before and during the war, the representation of Jews in the novel itself can on the whole be described as unfavorable, leading to claims in the past that the text was anti-Semitic. A Jewish paper rejected this charge, but nonetheless deemed it "tactless" and "tasteless."[17] Indeed, the representation of Jewish characters is steeped in negative stereotypes: the Jew Ehrlicher, for instance, Pussy's stepfather, is old, fat, and rich, and is shown to benefit from the war financially at first (*VA* 164), making him appear as a ruthless opportunist, and also mirroring Nazi propaganda concerning the Jews' business ethics. Similarly, Zeman's wife Pussy's negative traits seem to outweigh any positive aspects: she is portrayed as calculating, unthoughtful, perfidious, and selfish.

The representation of Czechs, too, is not overly sympathetic. Zeman is a cynical, obsessive, and often pathetic character, while his Czech father is described as primitive and crippled. It is to the novel's credit that German characters are also flawed — for example, Leonhard is portrayed as a nationalistic and self-satisfied bourgeois — yet on the whole it is possible to identify a bias in the narrative. Individual characters aside, the Czechs are depicted as a brutal, revengeful people, who revel in the gratuitous killings of defenseless Germans in the aftermath of the war (*VA* 337). Such descriptions stand in uneasy relation to references to German crimes, which focus primarily on Jews, not Czechs, making Germans appear as unprovoked victims of their callous neighbors. Equally problematic is the explicit charge of anti-Semitism among Czechs, according to which the Jews' persecution had been watched with a hint of *Schadenfreude* (*VA* 331). Such representations may be seen to relativize German crimes against the Jews, or mark them as somehow "less objectionable." Moreover, by pitting the Czechs against both the Germans and the Jews, the latter implicitly form a victim collective, while the Czechs emerge as the "real" perpetrators (*VA* 205).[18] The notion of Bohemians as victims is further reinforced by the implication that the region is somehow separate from Germany, a common notion in early expulsion novels. While German crimes are acknowledged, Bohemians are excluded from this as they are, essentially, "not part of" Germany. As a result, they perceive themselves to be not among the perpetrators, but among the victims of the Nazi regime, as well as of the Czechs, making them "absolute victims."

Nonetheless, the inclusion of non-German perspectives provides the narrative with some sort of balance, and certainly avoids an exclusively German viewpoint, which makes it an exception among expulsion novels of its time. It also serves as a platform to illustrate the influence of the war, and German occupation, on different levels of the mixed population. Moreover, although the representation of Czechs is problematic in places, it is limited to only a few pages and avoids sensationalism, unlike, for instance, Olga Barényi's *Prager Totentanz,* which throughout the novel describes the Czechs as bloodthirsty, out-of-control barbarians, often by means of horrendously graphic imagery.

Yet ultimately, and again reflecting the common tendency of the 1950s, *Das verschüttete Antlitz* does not address the theme on a political level, but rather on an existential one. Thus, the focus of the book, inherent in the title, is not so much on Bohemia, but rather on the "countenance" of the individual, and the nobility and virtue of the human being, which will always struggle to the surface in the end (*VA* 331). By portraying war, racial tensions, and expulsion as an ethical and psychological interplay between human beings, the narrative may appear to relativize German crimes and complicity and, again, universalize German guilt. In addition, and similar to *Wintergewitter,* suffering and punishment are framed as salvation. Zeman suffers with humility and atones his sins by overcoming his hatred and helping his enemy. The implication is that beyond the hatred and violence lies reconciliation and peace between nations, symbolized by the handshake between the two former foes — the Czech Zeman and the German Jering — at the end of the novel (*VA* 343). While this may offer hope, it also lacks credibility — indeed, Fussenegger has been criticized in the past for her tendency to "harmonize" her fiction.[19] The ending also throws up questions regarding *Vergangenheitsbewältigung:* only the Czech character goes through a period of coming to terms with the past, while the German character appears to be suddenly, and instantly, "converted." This not only implicitly places the onus on the non-German participants of the war, but also appears to take for granted the widespread conviction around the time of the novel's publication that 1945 had been a "zero hour," that is, that postwar (West) Germany had emerged out of nowhere, without a past and therefore unburdended by the problems of that past.

Die schlesische Barmherzigkeit

Subtle symbolism is not to be found in *Die schlesische Barmherzigkeit* (1950) by Ruth Hoffmann. The Silesian author, whose Jewish husband was killed in Auschwitz, and who was banned from publishing between 1936 and 1945, has made both her lost homeland and Jewish suffering the focus of her writing. *Die schlesische Barmherzigkeit* can be described as little more than a light popular or even trashy novel, but nonetheless — or maybe because of this — it appears to have enjoyed considerable success, being republished in 1953, 1974, and 1983. The novel tells the story of Emma Mühlen, the eldest daughter of a working-class family, who grows up in Breslau and later settles in a nearby Silesian village, where she remains until she is forced to leave in 1945, by now in her mid-fifties. The village is largely unaffected by the war until the very end; indeed, it is presented as a "safe haven" (*SB* 308). The arrival of the Poles and Russians disrupts the idyll and confronts the inhabitants with the reality of war for the first time. Although many had been Nazi supporters, they feel unjustly treated by the occupation and discrimination they experience. Soon after, all Germans are forced to leave. The novel concludes with the inhabitants' temporary stay in refugee camps, and so stops short of portraying the integration in West Germany.

For the first three hundred pages the text appears to be little more than a pleasant popular novel: the style is friendly and intimate, and the unpleasant aspects of war are marginal at most. Like many expulsion novels, the narrative dwells on the beauty of Silesia and emphasizes its people's deep-rooted connectedness with their *Heimat.* Later, during the occupation by Russians and Poles, *Die schlesische Barmherzigkeit* focuses primarily

on the villagers' hardship and suffering: the strange-sounding Polish street and place names that had replaced their own, having to hand over much of their properties to the occupiers, as well as hunger, discrimination, rape, and looting. Finally, when the Germans are forced to leave, the narrative dedicates several pages to the harrowing train journey, describing the trauma of being severed from the treasured homeland, often with excruciating pathos and self-pity.

Yet despite this ostensible focus on German suffering, *Die schlesische Barmherzigkeit* is more than a one-sided account. Importantly, Hoffmann draws a clear causal connection between German suffering and German crimes in her narrative. When the villagers complain about the imminent expulsion, Emma, the protagonist, points back to the first National Socialist "misdeeds" (*SB* 315) — significantly, she dates these to 1933, when the National Socialists first came to power, not 1939 or the early 1940s, implying historical complicity for a time long before the war began, a time that witnessed high levels of support for the Nazi party by ethnic Germans living in the eastern provinces. Similar to *Das verschüttete Antlitz*, then, Hoffman's text draws attention to the prewar years, holding almost everyone — those who cheered, those who accepted, and the majority who chose to silently ignore the political developments (*SB* 315) — responsible for what is now taking place in Silesia. Indeed, the novel implies that, due to the many crimes committed by Germans since 1933, the discrimination, violence, and, ultimately, expulsion, should come as no surprise but should be seen as the "least penance" enjoined on Germans (*SB* 324).

With the onset of the war, the tone of the narrative changes noticeably: it is now straightforward and critical, displaying a strong anti-Nazi and antiwar tendency, which is evident primarily in the references to Jewish suffering. Unlike in *Wintergewitter*, these are not indirect or cryptic, but explicit and unambiguous. They are also frequent: we find references to Jews (*SB* 280), burning synagogues (*SB* 275), Auschwitz, gas chambers, and ovens (*SB* 294). Moreover, the white armbands that became compulsory for Germans once the Poles took over are likened to the Star of David the Jews were forced to wear — a connection that is often not made in other novels: "Die weiße Binde war nichts anderes als ein zwangsweiser Trauerflor für den Millionenfachen Auschwitzer Tod" (*SB* 342). [The white armband was nothing else than a compulsory ribbon of mourning for the millions killed at Auschwitz.] Here, the author explicitly acknowledges the Holocaust, rather than referring to Jewish suffering in general, while the word "zwangsweise" implies a clear causal connection between the Holocaust and German crime. It may also be seen as implicit criticism at the lack of remembrance or mourning for Jewish victims by Germans — the mourning here is compulsory, not voluntary. This is later underlined by an exclamation by Emma's protégé Hans Hildebrandt, which not only condemns the often lenient treatment of Nazis after the war, but also claims that Germans had a "talent" to forget, especially that what "happened to the Jews" (*SB* 407).

Moreover, while some texts of the 1950s appear to imply that German suffering was at least as great, if not greater than Jewish suffering, *Die schlesische Barmherzigkeit* emphasizes that Jewish suffering must take precedence over German suffering and that, ultimately, the two are simply "incomparable" (*SB* 359). The distinction between German and Jewish suffering is also reflected in the language: while descriptions of German suffering are occasionally almost lighthearted or flippant — the narrative refers to the time during the occupation as "topsy-turvy," which brought with it "all types of visitors" (*SB* 313) — references to Jewish suffering are clear, concise, and to the point, describing the way Jews were "dragged, pushed, kicked" (*SB* 280) or "charred, murdered and martyred" (*SB* 313).

Of the three texts, *Die schlesische Barmherzigkeit* most explicitly refers to German crimes, Jewish suffering, and the Holocaust, and the Germans' lack of remorse. This may be expected, given that the author's Jewish husband was a victim of persecution. Yet Hoffmann's novel, too, ultimately appeals to the "higher," giving the impression that human beings are dependent on larger, mysterious powers, and at the mercy of fate: thus, Emma, like everyone else, is "a plaything in fate's palm of hand" (*SB* 289). This notion, and the implied inevitability and uncontrollability of fate, once again appears to relieve the individual of personal responsibility. On a more concrete level, too, the treatment of personal responsibility is ambiguous and could be construed as apologetic. For instance, the narrative implies at several points that most people were not aware of what was going on (*SB* 294, 302, 315), seemingly justifying the common postwar claim of ignorance. Moreover, the novel appears to excuse the Germans' general lack of resistance by offering a convenient motive for their passivity: the will to survive, which is stronger than outrage at injustice (*SB* 280). This also includes the protagonist herself; although Emma secretly supports Jews and Poles during the war years — supplying a Jewish doctor and a concentration camp prisoner with food — she stops short of open, active resistance against the regime, or even voicing her opinion in public. Protest would have meant death, and Emma "wanted to survive, under all circumstances" (*SB* 281). Thus, while the novel draws attention to the Germans' lack of resistance, it does not force the reader to examine their own behavior.

In its final moments, *Die schlesische Barmherzigkeit* largely returns to the genre of popular literature by presenting the reader with a happy ending: by coincidence, Emma finds Hans again, whom she looked after when he was a boy, and he takes her in as household help once more. Bordering on corny, and seemingly in contradiction with large parts of the narrative, this ending naïvely seems to imply that, ultimately, everything will turn out all right. Of course, as a trivial or popular novel, the text is bound by certain genre convention; a happy ending is one of them. Yet overall, *Die schlesische Barmherzigkeit* can be seen to break with such conventions, demonstrating that even popular literature dealing with expulsion can be critical and politically minded. To be sure, the novel's literary quality is questionable; its prose is often turgid and, occasionally, unpolished in its desire to make a point. Nonetheless, its overt denunciation of the Germans' crimes against the Jews, and the clear causal connection it draws between these crimes and German suffering, including expulsion, makes it stand out among novels of its kind. Finally, and similar to *Wintergewitter, Die schlesische Barmherzigkeit* also explicitly states the finality and irreversibility of the Germans' expulsion by accepting the new border between Poland and Germany — the Neiße River — as "Grenze und Niemalswieder" (border and never-again, *SB* 364).

Conclusion

In conclusion, then, at least some texts of the 1950s dealing with expulsion present a more differentiated and broader range than conventional expectations might have suggested. We have seen three examples that — to varying extents and by different means — have linked expulsion with German crimes and have emphasized the plight of non-German victims. We have also seen the more problematic aspects in the treatment of expulsion and the war in general, notably the representation of Jews, Russians, and Czechs, as well as the existentialist response to the war. Moreover, the inclusion of non-German perspectives is rare and the exploration of personal responsibility often lacking or missing entirely. Yet overall, and although by today's standards these texts may seem outdated or wrongheaded, some expulsion novels of the 1950s at least exhibit a more nuanced and critical approach than this much maligned form of early postwar German fiction has generally been credited with.

Notes

[1] Karl Heinz Gehrmann, "Versuche der literarischen Bewältigung" in *Die Vertriebenen in Westdeutschland: Ihre Eingliederung und ihr Einfluss auf Gesellschaft, Wirtschaft, Politik und Geistesleben,* ed. Eugen Lemberg and Friedrich Edding (Kiel: Ferdinand Hirt, 1959), 276.

[2] For a comprehensive discussion of the prejudices toward expulsion literature, see Louis F. Helbig, *Der ungeheure Verlust: Flucht und Vertreibung in der deutschsprachigen Belletristik der Nachkriegszeit* (Wiesbaden: Harrassowitz, 1996), 33–43.

[3] Ludmila Slugocka, *Die deutsche Polenliteratur auf dem Gebiet der Deutschen Demokratischen Republik in der Zeit von 1945–1960* (Poznan, Poland: PWN, 1964), 122–23.

[4] Jost Hermand, "Darstellungen des Zweiten Weltkrieges," in *Literatur nach 1945 (I): Politische und Regionale Aspekte,* ed. Jost Hermand (Wiesbaden: Athenaion, 1979), 32.

[5] See Frank-Lothar Kroll, ed., *Flucht und Vertreibung in der Literatur nach 1945* (Berlin: Gebr. Mann, 1977), 21. Of note is that the volume was published on behalf of the "Kulturstiftung der deutschen Vertriebenen" (arts council of German expellees).

[6] Helbig, *Der ungeheure Verlust,* 92.

[7] Keith Bullivant, *Beyond 1989: Re-reading German Literary History since 1945* (Providence, RI: Berghahn Books, 1997), 3.

[8] Judith Ryan, *The Uncompleted Past: Postwar German Novels and the Third Reich* (Detroit, MI: Wayne State UP, 1983), 15.

[9] Ibid., 23.

[10] Stephen Brockmann, *German Literary Culture at the Zero Hour* (Rochester, NY: Camden House, 2004), 7–8.

[11] Kurt Ihlenfeld, *Wintergewitter* (Berlin: Eckart, 1951); Gertrud Fussenegger, *Das verschüttete Antlitz* (Darmstadt: DVA, 1957); Ruth Hoffmann, *Die schlesische Barmherzigkeit* (Munich: Aufstieg, 1974; 1st ed., 1950). Subsequent page references to these works are cited in the text preceeded by the letters *W, VA,* and *SB,* respectively. Translations of excerpts are my own.

[12] See also Wolfgang Schneiß, *Flucht, Vertreibung und verlorene Heimat im früheren Ostdeutschland: Beispiele literarischer Bearbeitung* (Frankfurt am Main: Peter Lang, 1996), 93.

[13] See §2 of "Zweite Verordnung zur Durchführung des Gesetzes über die Änderung von Familiennamen und Vornamen" (Law regarding the change of surnames and first names) of 17 August 1938, Reichsgesetzblatt, 1938, 1044.

[14] See Stuart Taberner, "Hans-Ulrich Treichel's *Der Verlorene* and the Problem of German Wartime Suffering," *Modern Language Review* 97 (2002): 125.

[15] See also Schneiß, *Flucht,* 94.

[16] See also ibid., 101–2.

[17] *Allgemeine Wochenzeitung der Juden in Deutschland,* 27 December 1963.

[18] This is reminiscent of Dieter Forte's *Ein Junge mit den blutigen Schuhen* (1995), where civilian Germans, Jews, and forced laborers are linked into a victim collective. See also Bill Niven, *Germans as Victims: Remembering the Past in Contemporary Germany* (Basingstoke, UK: Palgrave Macmillan, 2006), 13.

[19] *Die Welt,* 7 May 1992, 22.

4: "In this prison of the guard room": Heinrich Böll's *Briefe aus dem Krieg 1939–1945* in the Context of Contemporary Debates

Frank Finlay

Introduction

HEINRICH BÖLL (1917–1985), THE FIRST CITIZEN of the old Federal Republic of Germany to be awarded the Nobel Prize for literature, established his literary reputation with the antiwar novels *Der Zug war pünktlich* (The Train Was on Time, 1949), *Wo warst Du Adam* (Adam, Where Art Thou?, 1951), and the anthology of short stories, *Wanderer, kommst Du nach Spa . . .* (Traveler, If You Come to Spa, 1950). The title story of the latter volume, a satire on military heroism, remains required reading in German schools and the enduring impact of war surfaces to a greater or lesser extent as a theme in Böll's entire oeuvre. The firsthand experience of war also influenced the writer's often impassioned interventions as a critical intellectual in the period after 1945, earning him epithets such as the "Conscience of the Nation," and the "Good Person of Cologne," which he found particularly irksome. Of the many political causes he was to embrace, perhaps the most relevant in the present context were his opposition to German rearmament in the 1950s; to the ethical evasions, omissions, and compromises of official attempts to deal with the legacy of the National Socialist past (*Vergangenheitsbewältigung*) and, in his later years, his support for the Peace Movement's campaign against NATO's deployment of Cruise and Pershing missiles on German soil.

A short time after Böll's death, a small sample of the one thousand letters he wrote as a German infantryman during the war years appeared in a biography and a collection of his travel writing.[1] The very limited attention they attracted at the time focused primarily on their evocative description of places and on their expressive quality, with one critic identifying similarities with the *Zerissenheit* (inner conflict) of the early Goethe and the *Weltschmerz* (world-weariness) of Georg Büchner.[2] These publications were to serve as a prelude to a major edition of the correspondence scheduled to appear a few years later. However, the project encountered many problems. Böll's deliberately illegible handwriting, for example, could only be laboriously deciphered by his wife, Annemarie, and publication was repeatedly delayed. The two volumes of *Briefe aus dem Krieg 1939–1945* (Wartime Letters), assiduously annotated and with a magisterial "Afterword,"[3] finally appeared in 2002, ten years later than planned and backed by the considerable promotional weight of the publisher Kiepenheuer and Witsch, which, in the blurb, invited comparisons with the German-Jewish survivor Victor Klemperer's *Diaries* (1995). For Böll scholars there is the opportunity to chart the emotional and intellectual maturation in extremis of a surprisingly self-centered, prejudiced, occasionally xenophobic "angry young man," to a more open, tolerant, and mature individual. It was the letters as "a novel of the development of an individual"[4] that dominated their prominent reception in the cultural pages of Germany's serious press, with one leading critic going as far as to claim that they constituted "nothing less than a new [literary] work."[5] The two volumes also offer much in the way of new insights into an underresearched phase of the writer's life, correcting simple matters of fact, overturning certain misapprehensions, and challenging some of the writer's own previously inaccurate autobiographical recollections. My concern here, however, is of broader interest and arises for two main reasons.

First, Böll's record of his wartime career is quite simply a unique historical document, as a few statistics reveal. It is conservatively estimated that some 40,000 million letters and packages were sent between, to, and from the many distant fronts at which the rapacious German *Wehrmacht* operated in the years from 1939 to 1945, running as high as 520 million a month. As early as 1938, Army Regulation Number 84 defined the German forces' *Feldpostwesen* (postal service) as an essential military support service that aimed to provide the link between units of the army in the field with the homeland. Promoted by free or subsidized postal rates, facilitated inter alia by first motorized and later airborne postal units and carefully monitored by rigorous censors, the *Feldpost* functioned until the closing weeks of the war. However, of this enormous quantity, the bulk is thought not to have survived, and certainly only a tiny proportion of the 120,000 letters stored in public archives have found their way into anthologies and edited collections. Containing 878 letters that Böll wrote to his family and his fiancée and later wife Annemarie, *Briefe aus dem Krieg* are thus the largest collection of *Feldpostbriefe* (army postal service letters) from a single hand. As the letters make abundantly clear, they were composed typically in hurried moments of privacy that Böll was able to snatch, frequently against a background of the coarse "noises off" barrack-room talk and blaring propaganda broadcasts. A very few emanate from frantic scribblings during brief lulls in fire on the Russian front. As a consequence, and with their almost daily frequency lending them some of the qualities of a diary, these are immediate and unvarnished accounts of wartime that paint a portrait of events — as they happened. Thus, there are none of the convenient benefits of hindsight or the linking of personal experience to landmark events in history that are often the hallmarks of autobiography, as a comparison of Böll's letters with, say, Günter Grass's recent *Beim Häuten der Zwiebel* (Peeling the Onion, 2006), or even with his own autobiographical interviews and conversations of the 1970s and 1980s, would amply demonstrate. Similarly, the wartime letters contrast with existing anthologies, which tend to focus on the experience of life in the line of fire, often covering only short periods of time and arranged in a tendentious order to reflect the concerns of the respective editors.[6] Moreover, owing to the astonishing trajectory of Böll's military service that, as we shall see, was punctuated by only the briefest of encounters with actual fighting, they have the additional benefit of providing a practical, direct, and unblinking look at the often banal and tedious realities of daily life for soldiers in the *Wehrmacht* and the conditions faced by noncombatants on the home front.

My second reason arises, as with all the other contributions to the present volume, from the current obsession in German sociocultural and political discourse with German wartime suffering. In this chapter I concentrate on two aspects of that suffering that are directly relevant: the first is the suffering caused by the Allied Strategic Bombing Campaign, which devastated 131 cities, claimed between 400,000 and 600,000 mostly civilian lives, left 7.5 million homeless, and subjected millions more to the psychological terror of bombing. This by now well-documented debate was triggered by a literary dispute around the writer W. G. Sebald's contention, in a series of lectures in 1997 on "Air War and Literature," that there had been a neglect by writers of the German experience of bombing.[7] The most controversial of recent publications in this regard are, of course, Jörg Friedrich's provocative questioning of the moral basis of the bombing and emphasis on German victimhood in *Der Brand* (The Fire, 2002), in which he borrowed liberally from the discourse of the Holocaust,[8] and the follow-up publication, *Brandstätten* (Sites of Fire, 2003). The stir caused by Friedrich has brought into particularly sharp focus the precarious balancing act facing a post–Cold War Germany when it seeks to find an objective and nuanced means of acknowledging the pain visited on its own people without vitiating its complicity, by way of excessive empathy, in a barbaric war of its own making;[9] a phenomenon repeated in relation to the second main area of German suffering, which has featured prominently in recent years, namely, the expulsion of ethnic Germans from the eastern provinces at the end of the war.

A second focus of the postunification discourse on the Third Reich has fallen on the question as to why the Germans supported Hitler in such large numbers to the bitter end of the war and why there was never a popular revolt against his regime. This is, of course, hardly a new question. In the immediate aftermath of the conflict, for example, liberal historians looked to stereotypical aspects of the German national character to find their answers in a love of militarism, an exaggerated respect for authority, and a civil society unbuttressed by a strong democratic tradition, the result of an alleged aberrant "Special Path" that Germany had taken in the eighteenth and nineteenth centuries away from the democratic evolution of France and Great Britain. Others have focused on Germans seduced by charismatic leadership, with early foreign policy and military successes interpreted as a balm to a national pride wounded in the wake of the First World War; or on a nation brainwashed by propaganda and held in obedient thrall by the coercion and terror of a police state. More recent — and germane to the context in which I set Böll's letters — has been the accentuation of the role of "ordinary" Germans as "willing executioners" and co-conspirators, which was given such public prominence by Daniel Goldhagen's now widely criticized thesis that the vast majority of Germans were eliminationist anti-Semites. Similarly, and less academically controversial, Hannes Heer's traveling exhibition Crimes of the *Wehrmacht* foregrounded the crimes of regular German army units — the "ordinary men" (see Christopher Browning's *Ordinary Men*) — as opposed to the long-demonized SS. One contentious debate, which has hitherto attracted less attention in recent Anglo-American accounts of the discourse of German suffering, features in my discussion, as Böll's letters are cited as witness in the altogether different case prosecuted by the maverick historian Götz Aly, in his highly controversial *Hitlers Volksstaat: Raub, Rassenkrieg und nationaler Sozialismus* (Hitler's Beneficiaries: Plunder, Racial War and the Nazi Welfare State, 2005; English translation, 2007). As we shall see, Aly deploys impressive archive sources to argue that the compliance, enthusiasm, and loyalty of ordinary Germans was quite simply bought and paid for by a vast campaign of systematic plunder: by the looting of the occupied territories, "Ayrianization," and a system of welfare benefits. Thus, so-called ordinary Germans became, by means of a raised standard of living, willing beneficiaries with a vested interest in the regime that provided them with goods they could otherwise never have afforded.

Böll's Wartime Letters

Böll first donned uniform when he was conscripted into the *Reichsarbeitsdienst* (Reich Labor Service) in 1938. In retrospect, he regarded the five months of harsh discipline, hard work, and primitive living conditions in this "Nazi criminal organization"[10] as a precursor to the six full years of military service, which, with the exception of a brief sojourn at the University of Cologne, followed on seamlessly. The chances of survival for Böll's cohort, born in 1917, were by his own reckoning one in three,[11] and it was only a mixture of ill health, outrageous good fortune, and his own native cunning and resourcefulness that quite remarkably restricted his exposure to active combat to little more than a month. Thus the invasion of Poland in September 1939 coincided with his basic training. In his own words one of the "most unmilitary" members of his company (*KB* 21), he was left behind when units of his infantry regiment moved east in October. By the time he had arrived in Poland, in Bromberg (West Prussia) in June 1940, the country had been subjugated and the *Blitzkrieg* campaigns in the west against Holland and France were already under way. Not mentioned in the letters, presumably for fear of the censor, is his witnessing of the criminal activities of the SS in Bromberg, which he was to describe much later in an interview (*I* 618).

Böll was posted to France only after the capitulation, when he joined the forces massing for the subsequently postponed Operation Sea Lion, the invasion of Britain. His good luck held when he succumbed to an acute case of dysentery, which again kept him out of the firing line. After a brief convalescence in Amiens, the highly infectious nature of the disease debarred Böll from active service, and from September 1940 until May 1942 he joined the ranks of the *Landesschutz* (protectors of the home front), which comprised other invalids and aged soldiers involved in a range of generally mundane duties. Böll was particularly fortunate to spend much of this time within easy reach of his friends and loved ones, with a full sixteen months in his native city of Cologne itself, during which time his relationship with Annemarie blossomed. His duties consisted of various types of manual labor — street-sweeping, picking up litter, peeling potatoes, gathering fuel and, at one point, even filling holes on the racecourse in Mühlheim/Ruhr — and guard duty, including supervising German soldiers sentenced to hard labor and keeping watch over military installations. After his illness was cured, he was not commandeered to the Russian Front, as he might have expected, but was again extremely lucky to rejoin the army of occupation in France, now building the massive defensive positions of the so-called Atlantic Wall to repulse an expected Allied landing on the European mainland. Spent mostly on the Channel coast between the small towns of St. Valéry-sur-Somme and le Tréport, this was to be Böll's longest posting (July 1942 to October 1943). Accordingly, it is from France that the greatest number of letters was written. The remainder of the war finally brought brief but traumatic experiences of ferocious frontline battle in the Crimea in the autumn of

1943, in Rumania in May 1944, and on the collapsing Western front in the spring of 1945, where he was taken prisoner by the Americans one month before the official cessation of hostilities. The fifteen letters from the Crimean front in particular bear eloquent witness to his terrifying experiences, which are shorn of the quest for meaning and transcendence that typifies the fictional transposition of them. Moreover, far from blunting his sensitivity to moral and ethical issues, as was the case with many German soldiers,[12] the physical hardship of life in the trenches (sleep deprivation, infestation with lice, hunger, and thirst), together with the psychological strain and emotional loss of a close comrade, sharpened his reflections on them. Firsthand exposure to the "true face of the war" revealed it to be "cruel and terrible, really hellish," "evil," "bestial," and "mad murder," convincing Böll that "there is nothing more criminal than war" (*KB* 948). Similar sentiments emerge following his next frontline encounter in Romania in May 1944, on an Eastern front now in an even greater state of chaos and several hundreds of miles closer to Germany. Böll's brief but intense baptism of fire over a six-month period were epiphanies; the memories etched "indelibly and eternally" on his mind, acting as a benchmark to judge the future (*KB* 950), turning him into an "absolute anti-militarist" (*KB* 1035).

Even though Böll was wounded four times, not only did the peculiar evolution of his career in the army spare him prolonged exposure to combat, but that he spent the bulk of his time in the "forbidden zone" guarding western coastal defenses, and that when he was eventually posted eastward, the German armies had made hasty retreat, very likely account for his having no direct experience of the apparatus and prosecution of the Holocaust. Certainly, there is no mention of the deportation of French Jews in the letters, nor do any atrocities of the *Wehrmacht*, which have attracted so much recent attention, feature. As a consequence, the letters root firmly in his own biography some familiar tropes and rightly criticized weaknesses of his fictional representations of life as a soldier: war as idiocy, as senseless, brutalizing bureaucracy dominated by boredom, inactivity, and passivity.[13]

Böll's letters have, as we have seen, two sets of addressees: his family and his (future) wife Annemarie. The early letters to the former make up the minority and are of little real interest, unlike those to his wife, which are markedly different in both content and tone. Often repetitive, Böll's letters "home" were written for open consumption within a wide circle, to provide information and reassurances about his well-being. They typically sketch the rigors, banalities, discomforts, and frustrations of everyday barrack life, with the unremitting tedium punctuated only by the equally unwelcome physical exertions of drill and exercises. Similarly prevalent are requests for creature comforts to be sent from home to alleviate his "suffering," including cigarettes and the amphetamine Pervetin, which was then freely available and to which Böll appears to have been addicted. Notable, too, are some ironic comments, such as on the guidelines soldiers receive on what to write home (*KB* 32) and deliberately evasive and ambiguous remarks designed to entertain his family by hoodwinking the censor (*KB* 69).

It is important to recall in reading this material that all *Feldpostbriefe* were subjected to censorship, which given the vast volume of correspondence, however, could only be carried out on a sample basis. Nevertheless, anyone who was found to have revealed military secrets or to have made remarks critical either of the army or the political leadership faced draconian punishments for defeatism and subversion, with an estimated 15,000 death sentences carried out. Thus there are constant reminders of the possibility of censorship in Böll's correspondence and there is documentary evidence that at least one of his letters was examined. An early example is a joke he tells at Hitler's expense on the pretext of keeping his parents informed of the "irresponsible attitudes of certain members of the national community" (*KB* 45). Together with such mischievous comments there are also repeated exhortations to read between the lines. In addition to the military censorship there is, of course, an element of self-censorship in all personal communication and the *Briefe aus dem Krieg* are no exception, with Böll particularly keen not to alarm his loved ones. Moreover, the letters have undergone a third level of censorship in that Böll's wife has elided various intimacies in her transcriptions and has only published seventy-five percent of his epistles and none of her own responses. To this extent, the two volumes are not a *Briefwechsel* (exchange of letters) in the accepted sense, but rather a monologue.

In the context of the recent preoccupation with wartime suffering, the account of Böll's experience of Allied bombing is of particular interest. Böll's first exposure to modern aerial warfare was during his return from Poland to his posting in France, in the summer of 1940, and it is significant that it was German acts to which he bears witness. The sight of the aftermath of the *Luftwaffe*'s notorious destruction of the unprotected city of Rotterdam (14 May 1940), when 8,000 civilians lost their lives, appears to have had an affect so profound that he struggles to put it adequately into words and tells Annemarie that it is best discussed in person. His first epistolary judgment on it is that war is "utter madness," and "the embodiment of horror" (*KB* 90). Concluding that the devastation of the Dutch city far outweighs the havoc wreaked by his comrades on French cities and towns, he avers that there is nothing more terrible than war (*KB* 94). Similar comments occur when he sees the destruction of Amiens (*KB* 109), which had been the scene of heavy fighting in June, with high civilian casualties. Thereafter, a longing for a swift cessation of hostilities and a disgust of war are leitmotifs of the correspondence.

It is in Amiens that there is the first mention of Allied bombing; Böll hears Royal Air Force (RAF) squadrons on their way to Germany, referring to them as "the English planes that . . . are pestering you" (*KB* 117). That the bombing raids should only "pester" his family at this stage of the conflict (September 1940) testifies that the deliberate saturation targeting of civilian centers was still some time in the future. Böll was not to have firsthand experience of being under aerial assault until July 1941. In a letter of 9 July, he refers to what British records show to have been the year's heaviest raid on Cologne, when 114 Wellington bombers attacked districts close to the main railway station and famous Gothic cathedral, leaving 45 dead, 14 injured, and 5,450 bombed out. Some notable civic buildings were destroyed in the process, including the city's military headquarters and, before Böll's own eyes, the Church of the Assumption of the Virgin Mary.[14]

Böll's lengthy account of this event is remarkable for a number of reasons. First, there is an unmistakable sense of awe that imbues his evocative recollection of the "unforgettable" fire with a distinctly literary quality. Thus the "wonderfully fantastic and elemental" flames brightly illuminate the cathedral, "sparks fly wildly through the night," and the cacophony of burning wooden beams and the howling of the flames heighten the drama (*KB* 212). More remarkable still is what Böll deems "equally unforgettable": the appearance on the scene of a clanking "bright-red, ugly" vehicle delivering the Nazi newspaper, the *Westdeuscher Beobachter* (*KB* 212). Far from the political decontextualization that characterizes some recent narratives of German suffering,[15] or an analytical void in relation to cause and effect, it is worth underscoring how Böll, with memories of Rotterdam still fresh, uses a sharply observed detail to point up the causal link between the scene of conflagration and Nazi responsibility for unleashing the war, concluding pithily that "one ought also to recognize the symbols and interpret them, whenever they appear all too clearly" (*KB* 212). Indicative of the relatively low level of damage inflicted by bombing during this stage of the war and the swift return to normality, Böll notes the clear blue of the sky (the pall of subsequent, heavier raids was to hang over the city for days), and with a sigh of self-pity he envies the civilians able to amuse themselves on the terrace of the luxurious *Dom Hotel* while he must remain "in this prison of the guard room" and the "dungeon of this thick grey uniform" (*KB* 212). Of greatest significance here is the self-presentation of the soldier's life as a victim of circumstance, of imprisonment against one's will and the infringement of personal liberty that is the dominant tenor of the entire correspondence.

By the time Böll was to return to ruminations on the Allied bombings, there had been a marked change in policy by military planners, most notably with the accession to the head of the RAF's Bomber Command of Sir Arthur "Bomber" Harris in early 1942. With the aid of more advanced machinery capable of delivering increased bomb tonnage, and sophisticated new navigational and targeting aids, so-called area bombing became the primary type of operation. Böll's hometown, where all of his family resided, was to be the target of the notorious Operation Millennium, the first thousand-bomber raid in history during the night of 31 May 1942. Ninety percent of damage was caused by fire, the death toll was a new record for the RAF (486, with 5,027 injured), as was the number of buildings and dwellings destroyed (12,840). These included the total destruction of Annemarie's flat. Böll's letters show that since the escalation in the air war, new military regulations were introduced to enable personnel to take "special leave" to visit family members who were "victims of the bombing," the duration of which was contingent on the scale of destruction, which was to be attested to by the local police and was divided into three categories. With Annemarie's flat classified as "totally destroyed," Böll was able to spend several days in Cologne. The bombing brought first shock and relief, followed by the joy of unscheduled reunion with a loved one, and then sadness at witnessing such domestic destruction, a pattern that was to be repeated on two further occasions. Thus Annemarie was temporarily bombed out in February 1943, and Böll was on regular leave when Cologne was hit by three major assaults in the space of one week in the early summer of 1943. The first of these at the end of June features in his autobiographical *Brief an meine Söhne* (Letter to My Sons) when mention is made of the night of 29 June "in which Cologne was bombed into virtual ruin,"[16] the city's worst raid of the war, with around 22,000 buildings destroyed or damaged, 4,377 people killed, 10,000 injured, and 230,000 forced to leave their homes.[17] The carnage and trauma of the bombing is a recurring theme in his subsequent letters. Thus, a mere matter of days after returning to his unit in France, Böll describes the lack of empathy and incomprehension of his comrades who have no direct personal experience of the bombing: "None of these people really understand what it means to experience a city like Cologne being totally wiped out; there is also no point in telling them, indeed, it does seem that one has to experience such things directly, at least that is the case for the average person" (*KB* 818). The war on the home front would touch his family on several more occasions: his wife was bombed out yet again in March 1944 and evacuated with Böll's parents and sister to a rural retreat, where his mother died of a heart attack during a raid six months later (*FT* 208). Released a matter of months after the war's end from a POW camp (a further marker of his good fortune) and well before any postwar cleanup, Böll also witnessed the hand-to-mouth existence of life among the ruins of his beloved Cologne. If Böll's lived experience of wartime bombing is one he shared with literally millions of his contemporaries, his commitment to portraying it in his fiction does set him apart from many, as even Sebald conceded.[18] What Sebald fails to mention is that wartime destruction — whether physical, material, or emotional — dominates Böll's entire oeuvre from the "rubble literature" of his early work to the posthumously published *Frauen vor Flusslandschaft* (Women in a River Landscape, 1985) with its central presence of a bombed-out building on the banks of the Rhine, which, as one of the characters makes clear, should be left to remain as an unofficial "monument to shame." Little wonder that an "Aesthetics of Ruins" is a constant in Böll's literary achievement.[19]

Unmistakable in the letters are expressions of guilt. Hence Böll's response to Operation Millennium is significant in identifying — in terms that recall Brecht's *Mother Courage* — a central paradox of his and his family's situation. For it must be a "completely incredibly strange war," Böll avers, in which "we soldiers are sitting here almost as if in peace-time, we're sun-tanned and healthy while you are starving at home [experiencing] the horrors of war" in air-raid shelters and "the cellar" (*KB* 359). A year later, listening once more to the bombers bound for his homeland, anxiety at which city is to be "eradicated" soon transmutes again into audible feelings of guilt at the "madness" of civilians being so directly in the front line: "It really is a crazy war; we're living, as it were, in complete peace while in Germany the most brutal war rages" (*KB* 839).

It is in Böll's detailed depiction of this "complete peace" that was largely the fate of soldiers occupying "La douce France" (*KB* 97) that his wartime letters shed further differentiated light on recent debates of German suffering. In particular, they bring into even sharper relief the stark, paradoxical contrast at certain stages of the war between the plight of the German civilian population and those fortunate to do service away from the front line as soldiers of the occupation across Hitler's far-flung empire. In sharp distinction to Germany between the wars, France was a rich country that offered ordinary German soldiers unimagined luxuries and the opportunity to live off the fat of the land at the expense of the local population. With more than a smattering of schoolboy French, Böll had good access to the local population and witnessed all manner of large-scale corruption, embezzlement, theft, and shady deals of various hues, although one has to look to his postwar essays and interviews for anything more than the oblique references that the letters contain.

Of particular interest in the context of the present volume is that Böll's letters are adduced as evidence by historian Götz Aly to support his contention that the Nazi regime enabled German families to live better in the early years of the war than in peacetime by way of a systematic range of measures to encourage German soldiers to buy up everything they could find and send the loot home. Aly documents how soldiers were equipped with devalued local currencies, and how regulations on the flow of reichs-marks sent from home and the size of packages allowed back from the front were relaxed over time to encourage a sustained shopping spree. Thus Böll constantly requests money to be sent to him and is able to dispatch con-sumer goods in short supply at home: everyday comestibles such as eggs, coffee, butter, cigarettes; necessities such as soap and shoes; and luxury items purchased in Paris such as an etching, fine textiles, and chocolates. Similarly, whenever he came home on leave, he was laden with all manner of treats, including on one occasion in 1940 half a suckling pig. His brief sojourn on the Eastern front exposed him to a veritable cornucopia that the authorities certainly would not have sanctioned, not least because of the evidence it provides of a corrupt trade in German army issue. With the ob-servation that with a "thick wallet" one could purchase "everything, liter-ally everything," Böll prefaces a richly evocative description of the "bazaar" in the Crimean town of Odessa, among whose wares displayed were "the most beautiful south Russian women [. . .] coats, pullovers, shirts, socks [. . .], wedding rings, watches, pocket torches [. . .], army tunics" (KB 987–88). However, with the censor perhaps in mind, there is no mention of the trade in official documentation that one had been wounded, or the sale of military hardware, including complete flak batteries to the parti-sans, which he later claimed to have witnessed (I 629–30).

Aly's book, which was timed to appear in advance of the various com-memorative ceremonies for the sixtieth anniversary of the end of the war, caused a considerable stir, as it clearly challenges some of the central tenets of the debate that Germans suffered too. The unedifying picture that emerges from his book is of a nation of vultures that enthusiastically embraced a "feel-good dictator" who not only restored their sense of national pride but also made sure they were well cared for by the state. Moreover, avarice ensured their acquiescence in the plunder, murder, and genocide that financed the largesse. It must be said that the book as a whole has been criticized as fundamentally flawed by many leading histo-rians on several counts. For example, its one-dimensional focus on material factors is at the expense of ideology and belief; there are basic errors in claims about redistribution of wealth, the calculation of the true costs of the war, and the burden on the German population that undermine the central thesis; it willfully ignores a great deal of existing, particularly Anglo-American, scholarship; it underplays the central support lent to the regime by German big business; and it disregards the real privations of the German civilian population in the wake of the bombing campaign and military dis-asters on a variety of fronts.[20] Where the same historians do agree, however, is that the chapter that deploys Böll's letters is a promising line of re-search, and a timely intervention in the current debate.

Postscript

In closing this chapter, I offer a few thoughts on what a reading of Böll's letters from the war might contribute to the contemporary fixation on wartime suffering in the public consciousness of the Federal Republic of Germany. The first important point to rehearse is that the letters were never written with publication in mind and, allowing for the three levels of censorship I have indentified, they give an account only of what one person (and his close family) experienced in the war. As a consequence, and unlike autobiographical and fictional accounts of wartime experience, particularly those that have proliferated in recent years, the perspective offered is immediate and unalloyed, free of the manipulations, ideological or otherwise, that the benefits of hindsight can provide. Moreover, there is no question of any claims to being representative. The special quality of the letters resides, therefore, in that Böll relates *his* subjective experiences and *his* responses to them mostly within hours of their occurrence, and over a period that encompasses the entire period of the conflict, rendering the letters an important historical document. Allowing for these considerable caveats, the letters do add some important nuances and inflections to recent debates. Thus the suffering of German civilians in the aerial war is not decontextualized, with an awareness of cause and effect heightened by Böll's prior witnessing of the devastation visited on undefended Dutch and French cities by the *Luftwaffe*. Moreover, Böll's letters bring into sharp definition his experience of the inversion of the role of the combatant and the noncombatant. Further, they offer insights into everyday realities on the home front and the important role that the German army played in maintaining the living standards of "ordinary" German civilians, which is only now starting to feature in historical accounts.

Finally, Böll's highly untypical career trajectory (more relevant than his very real fears of the censor) means that the letters relate nothing at all about the Crimes of the *Wehrmacht* or any awareness of being a small cog in its murderous rampages. What does emerge is a critique of the by no means comparable, and morally altogether different, category of "crime" that *is* the Werhmacht; an institution of control that robs this particular individual of his youth, liberty, and higher calling, separates him from his loved ones, and subjugates him to harsh physical labor, a coarse, deadeningly tedious routine, the capricious power of authority, and, ultimately, the horrors of combat. Böll's years in "the prison of the guard room" taught him a lesson for life, which he put into the words of a returning soldier in one of his first published short stories and which, in light of the recent highly charged debates, has an astonishing prescience: "I knew that the war would never be over, never, as long as somewhere a wound was bleeding that it had inflicted."[21]

Notes

[1] Gabriele Hoffmann, *Heinrich Böll, erweiterte Ausgabe* (Bornheim-Merten: Lamuv, 1985); Heinrich Böll, *Rom auf den ersten Blick: Lanschaften Städte Reisen* (Bornheim-Merten: Lamuv, 1987).

[2] Michael Butler, "Wir wollen abschwören allem Irrsinn vergangener Jahre . . .": The Early Letters of Heinrich Böll," *University of Dayton Review* 24, no. 3 (Summer 1997): 10.

[3] Heinrich Böll, *Briefe aus dem Krieg 1939–1945, Mit einem Vorwort von Annemarie Böll und einem Nachwort von Hamish Reid, Herausgegeben und kommentiert von Jochen Schubert* (Cologne: Kiepenheuer and Witsch, 2001). All subsequent references are in parentheses in the text and use the abbreviation *KB* followed by the page number.

[4] Reid, "Nachwort," in ibid., n.p.

[5] Hans Wollschläger, "Nur eines Menschen Stimme, gewaltig zu hören," *Frankfurter Allgemeine Zeitung,* 9 October 2001.

[6] Reid, "Nachwort," in Böll, *Briefe aus dem Krieg,* 1512.

[7] Published version in *On the Natural History of Destruction,* trans. Anthea Bell (London: Penguin, 2004). Sebald had made similar claims many years before in his "Zwischen Geschichte und Naturgeschichte: Versuch über die literarische Beschreibung totaler Zerstörung mit Anmerkungen zu Kasack, Nossack und Kluge," *Orbis Litterarum* 37 (1982): 345–66. A more nuanced view is provided by Volker Hage in his *Zeugen der Zerstörung: Die Literaten und der Luftkrieg: Essays und Gespräche* (Frankfurt am Main: Suhrkamp, 2003).

[8] See Aleida Assmann, "On the (In)Compatibility of Guilt and Suffering in German Memory," *German Life and Letters* 59 (2006): 195.

[9] For a collection of some of the important contributions to the debate, see Lothar Kettenacker, ed., *Ein Volk von Opfern? Die neue Debatte um den Bombenkrieg 1940–1945* (Berlin: Rowolth, 2003).

[10] Heinrich Böll, *Interviews I,* ed. Bernd Balzer (Cologne: Kiepenheuer and Witsch, n.d. [1979]), 619. Subsequent references are in parentheses in the text and use the abbreviation *I* followed by the page number.

[11] Heinrich Böll, "An einen Bischof, einen General und einen Minister des Jahrgangs 1917," in *Essayistische Schriften und Reden 2,* ed. Bernd Balzer (Cologne: Kiepenheuer and Witsch, 1977), 234. Government statistics reveal that the chances of survival were actually slightly worse, namely 1 to 2.5.

[12] Omer Bartov, *The Eastern Front 1941–1945, German Troops and the Barbarisation of Warfare,* 2nd ed. (Basingstoke, UK: Palgrave, 2001), 35.

[13] See, e.g., Alan Bance, "Heinrich Böll's 'Wo Warst Du, Adam?': National Identity and German War Writing — Reunification as the Return of the Repressed," *Forum for Modern Language Studies* 29, no. 4 (1993): 311–22 and Ernestine Schlant, *The Language of Silence: West German Literature and the Holocaust* (New York: Routledge, 1999), particularly 25–36.

[14] Martin Middlebrook and Chris Everitt, *The Bomber Command War Diaries: An Operational Reference Book 1939–1945* (London: Penguin, 1990), 176.

[15] See Bill Niven's insightful discussion in the introduction to his edited collection *Germans as Victims: Remembering the Past in Contemporary Germany* (Basingstoke, UK: Palgrave Macmillan, 2006), 1–25.

[16] Heinrich Böll, *Die Fähigkeit zu trauern* (Munich: DTV, 1985), 214. Subsequent references are in parentheses in the text and use the abbreviation *FT* followed by the page number.

[17] Middlebrook and Everitt, *Bomber Command War Diaries,* 404.

[18] W. G. Sebald, *Luftkrieg und Literatur* (Munich: Carl Hanser, 1999), 18–19.

[19] J. H. Reid, "From 'Bekenntnis zur Trümmerliteratur' to *Frauen vor Flußlandschaft:* Art, Power and the Aesthetics of Ruins," *University of Dayton Review* 24, no. 3 (1997): 43.

[20] See, e.g., Richard J. Evan's review of Götz Aly's book, *Hitlers Volksstaat (Hitler's Beneficiaries), The Nation,* 8 January 2007 and Adam Tooze, *The Wages of Destruction: The Making and Breaking of the Nazi Economy* (London: Allen Lane, 2006). Tooze was particularly outspoken in his critique of Aly, as an exchange of articles in the left-wing *taz* demonstrate. See, e.g., Tooze's "Einfach verkalkuliert," *Zeit Online,* http://www.taz.de/index.php?id=archivseite&dig=2005/03/12/a0289 (accessed 15 September 2008).

[21] Heinrich Böll, "Die Botschaft," in *Werke Band 3,* ed. Frank Finlay and Jochen Schubart (Cologne: Kiepenheuer and Witsch, 2003), 156.

5: Family, Heritage, and German Wartime Suffering in Hanns-Josef Ortheil, Stephan Wackwitz, Thomas Medicus, Dagmar Leupold, and Uwe Timm

Helmut Schmitz

FROM AROUND THE MID-1990s, there has been a veritable renaissance of the family novel in German-language literature. A strikingly large number of texts address issues of German twentieth-century history through the medium of family stories by way of fictional, biographical, and autobiographical narratives. In contrast to the condemnatory tone of a first wave of family narratives in the late 1970s and early 1980s, with their often explicit dissociation from family and tradition,[1] recent family novels investigate continuities of tradition and legacy between wartime and postwar generations.

According to Sigrid Weigel, these intergenerational texts substitute the previously dominant model of generation as experiential community, as developed by Karl Mannheim, for a genealogical model. Weigel argues that Mannheim's model with its concept of synchronicity of experience and implicit forgetting of genealogy implies the "rejection or denial of one's own parentage," a model that after the Second World War animates the "Gruppe 47" (Group 47, the loose collection of oppositional West German writers in the postwar period), with their idea of a guilt-free, new generation, and the notion of a zero hour. This fantasy of a virgin birth is repeated by the student movement in 1968 in their rejection of the "perpetrator-fathers." It is only the reawakened interest in the family history in recent years, Weigel argues, that has overcome this model that animated the so-called father-novels of the 1970s and 1980s, which, with their focus on the perpetrator-fathers, obscured the issue of a transgenerational transfer of trauma.[2]

However, most of the recent generational texts implicitly incorporate a synchronic concept of generation, as writers or narrators frequently originate in the wider environment of the student movement and texts feature old "68ers" with parents or grandparents as representative, generational First World War and/or Second World War participants. Even as these texts reevaluate the political and mental history of postwar West Germany, their genealogical model confirms rather than challenges the prevalent periodization of twentieth-century German history by generation.

The renaissance of the intergenerational novel is thus related to the reassessment of the role of the '68 student movement in postwar German memory discourse. The reawakened interest in family history is part of a larger shift in the memory discourse of the Berlin Republic toward a pluralization of memories, following the "institutionalization" of the legacy of National Socialism under the concept of historical responsibility in the 1990s. This has been frequently commented on;[3] for the purpose of this chapter, I wish to highlight only two points. First, the concept of responsibility under which National Socialism and the Holocaust is integrated into the prehistory of the Berlin Republic implicitly contains the idea of heritage.[4] This logic is clearly expressed by the daughter in Ulla Hahn's novel *Unscharfe Bilder* (Blurred Images, 2003). Hahn's protagonist Katharina, biographically a member of the so-called second generation, believes that she has identified her father in one of the photographs in the controversial Crimes of the *Wehrmacht* 1941–44 exhibition and confronts her father with the catalogue. However, instead of exposing her father as a perpetrator, she is confronted with his deep-seated traumatization. This increasingly erodes her moralizing postwar perspective, making way for an attitude of understanding and listening. She muses:

> If we want to be the inheritors of our fathers' and mothers' entanglement in the Nazi years, if we honestly want to take on responsibility for this history, then we must also become the inheritors of the suffering, the pain, of all the destroyed life-plans of the Germans of these years.[5]

What this conditional sentence expresses is an intention to "complete" the one-dimensional public image of Nazi history that, Hahn's novel asserts, focuses solely on perpetration, crime, and guilt, by also acknowledging the traumatic wartime experiences of the Germans, in this case the German soldier who fought on the Eastern front.

The genealogical model thus appears to imply a reconciliation with history through the medium of the family and an end to the "discourse of guilt and attrition."[6] This frequently works through a de-legitimization of the morally charged contemporary perspective that is said to have originated in the student movement and a relegitimization of a seemingly authentic perspective of suffering through the traumatized war participants. In other words, there is a transition from a juristic to a therapeutic discourse, substituting the judgmental attitude of '68 for a position of listening and understanding.[7]

However, what does it mean to inherit the suffering, the pain, and the damaged lives of these years? Ideally speaking, it would mean an understanding of the inextricable intertwining of Nazism *and* suffering, of historical responsibility, guilt, shame, *and* traumatic experience in the Nazi generations and of their continuity in the following generations. Hence, the act of inheriting would imply the recognition of oneself as inheritor of both historical guilt and repression and trauma through intergenerational transmission, and thus as damaged oneself.

The German term "Erbe" (heritage) in this context takes on a rather ambiguous meaning, referring both to the legacy of remembrance of Nazi crimes and to the unconscious transmission of trauma and of mental structures from the Third Reich onto the next generations. The transgenerative transmission of both unconscious Nazi legacy and parental wartime trauma has been described by Sigrid Weigel as "telescopage," a phenomenon in which the unconscious of the first generation returns in displaced fashion in the second generation.[8] This issue has attracted increased attention in recent years, both in psychoanalysis and cultural studies and as a result of the inflationary use of trauma concepts and the above-mentioned shift from a judgmental to a therapeutic attitude to the past. Both have been severely criticized for a tendency to de-historicize and de-contextualize the specificity of traumatic historical events.[9] I would add that the increasing institutionalization of psychoanalytical approaches and their focus on the traumatization of the individual not only disregards the difference between political and therapeutic discourse, but also implicitly produces integration. It is thus analogous to integrative historization.[10] Moreover, there is the danger of blurring the distinction between secondary trauma and transgenerative Nazi legacy. Both phenomena can only with difficulty be narrated as *one* story, as a number of the recent family texts show. For instance, in Hahn's novel, the image of the father as perpetrator is increasingly overwritten with an image of him as traumatized victim, while the daughter assumes the role of a passive listener; both images prove ultimately incompatible.[11]

Second, I discuss the issue of the conflict between public and private memories of the National Socialist past and its legacies, something that has become increasingly visible since the controversial Walser-Bubis Affair of 1998. Harald Welzer and others have argued that public and family memory operate according to different principles: while the "lexicon" of public memory archives images of Nazi crimes, the "album" of family memory functions by way of narratives of "war and heroism, suffering, self-denial and sacrifice, fascination and fantasies of grandeur."[12] In contrast to the discourse within "real" families, however, which is defined by the incompatibility of lexicon and album, the conflict between public and private memory can be traced in almost any fictional exploration of family history in contemporary German-language literature.

Indeed, this staging of the conflict between lexicon and album can be said to define a specific German form of "postmemory." By postmemory, Marianne Hirsch understands a form of second-generation memory that "characterizes the experience of those who grow up with narratives that preceded their birth, whose own belated stories are evacuated by the stories of the previous generation shaped by traumatic events that can be neither understood nor recreated." The power of postmemory is determined not by recollection but by "imaginative investment and creation."[13] Elsewhere, Hirsch characterizes postmemory as defining "familial inheritance and transmission of cultural trauma," and as *retrospective witnessing by adoption.*" Hirsch's concept, which was developed with respect to the second generation of Holocaust survivors, has recently been adopted by many scholars with respect to German second-generation narratives.[14] J. J. Long, however, has sharply criticized Hirsch's concept of postmemory as "radically overdetermined," arguing that it ascribes a privileged epistemological position to the children as inheritors and interpreters of their parents' suffering, which threatens to undermine the ethical claims of postmemory. Furthermore, he asserts, the extension of memory from a particular context to public culture as a whole is problematic as it does not sufficiently distinguish between individual psychosocial disposition and collective forms of representation.[15] In addition, Hirsch's concept does not sufficiently distinguish between the unwitting inheritance of parental trauma narratives and their imaginative appropriation: while postmemory is on one level an interfamilial *condition,* on another it is a conscious *product* shaped by the inheritor of trauma in a process of engagement with family photographs, letters, diaries, and other sources. The interface and friction between private family memories and public memory discourses are precisely what is reflected in all recent family novels, most of which are marked by "epistemological anxieties" both with respect to the truth value of the family stories as well as to their own process of narrating these stories.[16] The "metacritical narrative perspective" that characterizes these family narratives marks them as a self-conscious contribution to a public memory discourse.[17]

With this in mind I discuss four biographical and autobiographical family narratives that explicitly address the issue of mediated legacies and heritage with respect to the family history of Nazism and wartime trauma. Stephan Wackwitz's *Ein unsichtbares Land* (An Invisible Country, 2003), Thomas Medicus's *In den Augen meines Großvaters* (In My Grandfather's Eyes, 2004), Dagmar Leupold's *Nach den Kriegen* (After the Wars, 2004), and Uwe Timm's *Am Beispiel meines Bruders* (In My Brother's Shadow, 2003) all, in different ways, depict the process of becoming "the inheritors of the suffering, the pain, of all the destroyed life-plans of the Germans of these years" (Hahn 145).[18] As the issue of heritage in each of these texts individually is receiving increasing critical attention, I focus here on a series of similarities between them.[19] I begin, however, with a brief sketch of Hanns-Josef Ortheil's parental novels *Hecke* (Hedge, 1983) and *Abschied von den Kriegsteilnehmern* (Farewell to the War Participants, 1992), as Ortheil's novels may be seen to mark a paradigm shift from the "father-literature" of the late 1970s to a literary exploration of transgenerational trauma, preempting the contemporary focus on intergenerational transmission by more than a decade.

From Trauma Legacy to Heritage: Hanns-Josef Ortheil

Ortheil's novels *Hecke* and *Abschied von den Kriegsteilnehmern* explore the traumatic wartime experiences of the narrator's parents and the damage to the narrator as the only surviving child. In both novels, the narrator's investigation of his parents' experiences in the war leads him back to reassess his own childhood as overshadowed by the destroyed desires of his traumatized parents. The narrator, the only survivor in a series of miscarriages and early childhood deaths as a result of the war, grows up with the feeling of having to "replace" his dead siblings and subsequently struggles to develop his own identity. In their assessment of the intergenerational transmission of trauma, Ortheil's novels are an attempt to historicize German wartime experiences as the origin of the insecure mental state of a subsequent, postwar generation. In retrospect, it can be seen that Ortheil preempts the recent paradigm shift from a "victim-centered" to a "perpetrator-centered" memory in various aspects.[20]

Ortheil's novels introduce the perspective shift from a moralizing postwar perspective to an a priori perspective that actively reconstructs the experiential viewpoint of the parents through documents, interviews, and photographs. This act of appropriation, shared by the authors of all texts discussed below, is a precondition for the narrator's ability to recognize his own implication in his parents' trauma and the long-term impact of this trauma on himself. This belated empathy with the parents' wartime suffering produces what I call the healing of the historical and geographical continuum that had been ruptured by the postwar generation's belated focus on the Holocaust. As a child of the postwar era, the narrator's life is dominated by the irresolvable conflict between a family narrative of suffering, victimhood, and survival and the historical rupture of the Holocaust. The ensuing incompatibility of the father's view of himself as victim and the son's focus on Auschwitz leaves the son literally displaced from genealogical and historical time.

Reading his family history as a history of collective trauma results in an acceptance of the parents' traumatic history that the son takes up as legacy, finally decoupling the signifier "Germany" from the signified "war." Ortheil's narrator imaginatively integrates himself into the "symbolic geography of the fathers"[21] by transforming unconscious traumatic legacy into heritage: "I am the sole, the single inheritor, [. . .] I vouch for the inheritance."[22]

Displacements I: Victims of History?

Genealogical and sometimes geographical displacement and the active construction of family history as a site of heritage also characterizes the books of Wackwitz, Medicus, Leupold and Timm. All four authors read their father's lives as having been displaced by the defeat of Wilhelmine Germany in the First World War, which appears as the twentieth century's original catastrophe, representing the humiliation of national fantasies of grandeur. Their masculine ancestors emerge as latently depressed, essentially damaged characters; Medicus comments on the "melancholic eyes" (*AG* 237) of his grandfather, while Wackwitz refers to the "out and out depression of the First World War veteran" (*UL* 133).

In the eyes of these authors, fathers and grandfathers attain somewhat paradigmatic roles as representatives of a historical humiliation for which the hegemonic and supremacist fantasies of Nazism represent some form of compensation. Medicus's grandfather, General Wilhelm Crisolli, was involved in war crimes as an army commandant in northern Italy before he was killed by partisans in 1944. Wackwitz's grandfather, a protestant priest and First World War veteran, who participated in the Kapp Putsch of 1920 (an early right-wing attempt to overthrow the Weimar Republic), was stationed ten kilometers from Auschwitz in the 1930s before being posted to Windhuk/Namibia, and finished his career in Luckenwalde, the birthplace of student movement leader Rudi Dutschke. Timm's father was a First World War veteran, was close to a right-wing terrorist organization during the early Weimar Republic, and an airforce officer in the Second World War. Leupold's father, who grew up as part of the German-speaking minority in Poland, began his career as member of the ultranationalist Young German Party in 1935 before joining the Nazi administration of occupied Poland under Hans Frank.

This historical displacement and the "damage" (*NK* 7) resulting from a series of defeats and narcissistic injuries continues to affect the surviving fathers and grandfather into the postwar period as their value systems become progressively outdated as a result of the economic miracle and West Germany's growing liberalization, democratization, and integration into the West. Wackwitz, Leupold, and Timm portray their forefathers as incapable of making their peace with the changed world after the Second World War. They are living embodiments of the "inability to mourn."

Displacements II: Continuities — Secrets, Phantoms, and Stories

The fathers' and grandfathers' displacement is continued into the children's generation who inherit their ancestors' historical damage in the form of either family secrets or stories that invade their own life story and prevent the development of an independent existence. Wackwitz and Medicus specifically are concerned with the transgenerational transmission of "family phantoms" that resurface uncannily in the following generations and animate their unconscious.[23] Both texts employ the metaphor of the phantom, the specter, and the undead as an interpretational category in their intertextual, highly literate family novels that trace the specter of heritage back to their Prussian grandfathers' generation, seeking to redefine their authors' relationship to both family and German tradition, particularly to the geographical space of the "German East."

Medicus's family history appears as a paradigmatic case of family phantoms. After 1945, his grandmother actively "forgets" her dead husband, suspecting his involvement in the civilian massacres his superiors committed in northern Italy. The shameful war as well as the flight from Silesia and the loss of social status are never spoken of in the family and communicated to Medicus only through metonymic acts, such as the childhood gift of St. Exupéry's *Flight to Arras* (1942). Medicus grows up in a "wealth of secrets" (*AG* 17), an aura that simultaneously shields him from the past and sediments the lost geographical space of the German East in his unconscious from where it resurfaces as nostalgic longing. Medicus's text represents an attempt to clear up both the family secret and the tension between his postwar consciousness and the inherited geographical unconscious; it is a form of necromancy for the purpose of exorcism, the laying to rest of the familial "undead" (*AG* 38) in the transformation of unconscious heritage into family memory.

Wackwitz is not just concerned with one but with several specters and phantoms. Similar to Ortheil, Wackwitz draws a parallel between a post–Second World War mentality and geography; the ghostly political pathology of the young Federal Republic and its nonrecognition of the loss of the eastern territories is interpreted by Wackwitz as a form of phantom pain that uncannily mirrors his grandfather's refusal to accept the changes to German territory after 1918. The psychological life of the young postwar generation is thus determined by a double absence, the loss of the German hegemonic fantasies embodied by Adolf Hitler and the repressed guilt of the Nazi crimes. Both return, telescoped into each other as spec-

ter, in 1968. Taking his cue from Freud's "Family Romances," Wackwitz
reads his family novel as a representative and compressed psychohistory of
the postwar era in which the Nazi past returns in the form of Hamlet's
ghost, leaving the student movement with the delegated task to put the
world right.[24] The student movement appears as a collective Freudian family
romance, where an entire generation selects a set of substitutive fathers in
surviving Jewish philosophers (e.g., Adorno and Marcuse) out of a feeling
of shame and inability to come to terms with the history of country and
family.

Ein unsichtbares Land synthesizes the history of German exception-
alism, idealism, nationalism, and colonialism from the eighteenth century
to the student movement through the prism of Wackwitz's grandfather's
life story and memoirs. Wackwitz, who was politically active on the fringes
of the second *Rote Armee Fraktion* (RAF) generation (West German terrorist group that emerged in the 1970s), describes his own political radicalization in direct opposition to the values embodied by his grandfather.
He reads the student movement and the RAF as unconsciously inheriting
and reembodying totalitarian fantasies, the origins of which he locates in a
particular German Protestant tradition of "inflamed speech," a tradition
he pursues from Prussian pietism, by way of Fichte's 1808 *Speeches to the
German Nation*, Wilhelmine Imperialism, and Nazism. Wackwitz sees this
tradition, which conceives of its own position as absolute and nonnego-
tiable, alive in his grandfather as well as in student leader Rudi Dutschke's
"redemptive and victim fantasies" (*UL* 258) and the self-destructive ex-
terminatory fantasies of the RAF.

In contrast, Leupold's and Timm's lives are dominated and invaded
by their parents' excessive victim narratives. The power of Leupold's father's repetitive wartime narratives overshadows the daughter's life, deval-
uing her own experience. Equating narratable life with war, the daughter
sees her own existence invalidated by the constant hypervalidation of the
father's lost life in the east and his disregard for the present. Timm's sense
of his own existence is similarly devalued by growing up in his dead
brother's shadow, a *Waffen SS* volunteer who was killed at the Eastern
front and who, even though he is dead, appears to be closer to his parents
because he experienced war, sacrifice, and suffering. Both Leupold's and
Timm's relations to their fathers are characterized by what Helm Stierlin
has described as "malignant deadlock," an emotional distance resulting
from the children's dissociation from their fathers due to an overbur-
dening in early childhood and an inheritance of the responsibility for Nazi
history avoided by their fathers. Something similar can also be found in
Ortheil's novels as well as Hans-Ulrich Treichel's *Der Verlorene* (Lost,
1998) and Grass's *Im Krebsgang* (Crabwalk, 2002).[25]

All four authors portray their own lives as determined by a double displacement, that is, the legacy of wartime trauma and its secrets and the legacy of Nazi atrocities. Like Ortheil, the texts by these authors characterize the belated encounter with the Holocaust as an expulsion from family genealogy. Medicus describes the "primal scene" of the belated recognition of ancestral crimes during a visit to the Holocaust memorial in Lidice in 1969 as a second expulsion from genealogy, after the first by grandmother and mother. Leupold feels uneasy with the idea of "lineage" (*NK* 19), having spent her life avoiding resembling her father, and Timm avoids the confrontation with his dead brother's wartime diary out of fear of the questions it will raise. The feeling that the lives of the fathers/ grandfathers constitute some kind of no-man's-land exemplifies what makes the emergence of a specifically German family postmemory difficult. The belated encounter with the specter of Auschwitz obscures the imaginative encounter with one's own family history. All four texts are therefore engaged in a historization of this specter and of the responsive position of the authors to enable a reencounter with the relative's life story.

Legacies and Heritage I: Transformations and Rewritings

All four authors are engaged in a self-reflexive act of active appropriation and rewriting of family legacies in which the "interfamilial co-production" (*NK* 33) of family legends is revisited and reinterpreted. Medicus's creation of his grandfather's "memory" (*AG* 75) results in a self-conscious exposure to the uncanny attraction of the grandfather's photographs from the Nazi period in which Medicus painstakingly registers his ambivalent response toward a masculine Prussian military tradition and his desire for an uncontaminated tradition, cleansed of the reflection of National Socialism. The photographs trigger a manic-melancholic search for the authentic traces of the dead, in the course of which Medicus increasingly incorporates his grandfather, while experiencing his inability to enter his grandfather's story. The obsessive search for the grandfather's ghost at authentic north Italian locations produces only "legends, rumors and half-truths" (*AG* 103), which, together with the photographs, create a "resonant space" (*AG* 110) in which the grandson threatens to disappear. Anne Fuchs has argued that Medicus's narrative examines the dangers of imaginatively reconstructing the lives of family relations involved in the Nazi system, a danger that consists in giving in to the fascination emanating from these photographs.[26] However, despite Medicus's increasing dislocation in the face of the rumors around his grandfather, his research and his imaginative "mercy" (*AG* 58) with the dead general do produce a concrete result. On the one hand, Medicus uncovers a death sentence for three partisans signed by his grandfather, while on the other, Crisolli emerges as a "fellow traveler." The grandmother's suspicion of Crisolli's participation in civilian massacres is exposed as misplaced, and the Prussian military tradition is cleansed, if not from its association with Nazism, then from its post-1968 odiousness, due to the grandfather having remained "relatively decent." Ultimately, the family secret goes up in smoke, together with Medicus's obsession; what remains is a sober look at the historical complexities that lead to the general's decision. What Medicus's research produces is thus the transformation of collective guilt by association into what he has referred to as "justiciable incidents of perpetration."[27] It is only the exorcism of the specter of Nazism from his grandfather's legacy that enables Medicus to read the grandfather's portrait photo as a document of depression reflecting his "lost life" (*AG* 237).

Medicus's narrative exemplifies the difference between a "German" and a Holocaust postmemory. According to Hirsch, the second Holocaust-survivor generation remains melancholically suspended in the diaspora, forever homeless, twice exiled from their origins, displaced both by the legacy of destruction and survival that it cannot inherit fully, and the total destruction of the geographical and social space of their origin.[28] In contrast, Medicus manages to escape the "resonant space" of his grandfather's past and arrives in a pure East Prussian present, at his newly acquired farm in Pommerania: "The secret was exposed, the post-war era was over" (*AG* 239). The narrative closes with a triumphant affirmation of survival, exiting from under the shadow of his grandfather into the genealogy of the future, in the location of his Pommeranian *Heimat:* "There stood my son, nearly three years old" (*AG* 248). Postmemory is transformed again, into family memory.

Similar to Medicus, Wackwitz is engaged with a sifting of German traditions for the purpose of appropriation, working through his grandfather's extensive memoirs in search of an uncontaminated tradition. Against a hegemonic German idealist tradition, his grandfather's towering influence, and the political absolutism of the radical German Left, Wackwitz invokes the ironic and playful liberal hermeneutics of Schleiermacher, Fichte's lifelong enemy, and of Habermas and Richard Rorty.[29] At the heart of Wackwitz's family novel is the renunciation of philosophical systems that claim access to absolute truth and representation in favor of an idea of language and thus representational truth as contingent. This constitutes an approach to writing and identity that takes into account the possibility that all origins are mere fiction, "every country an invented country, every people an accident and every tradition only a story that can end differently. That we can tell differently" (*UL* 179).

A large part of Wackwitz's text is dedicated to the investigation and description of his grandfather's lost universe, always aware that several his-

torical ruptures separate him from the historical reality. During a visit to
his grandfather's childhood residence in Lasskowitz in 2001, he finds the
area almost unchanged, as described in his grandfather's 1959 memoirs.
In contrast to Medicus, who discovers a nonironic, living connection to
Prussian traditions in his mother's cousin — "Prussia had never been lost
here" (*AG* 221) — Wackwitz's visit to his grandfather's childhood residence can only uncover traces of a lost world, without connection to the
present. The severance is expressed in the comparison of his grandfather's
manuscript to Kafka's parable "A Message from the Emperor," which never
reaches the addressee and thus requires imagination to be completed.[30]
Wackwitz's ironic and hermeneutic sifting of both national and family traditions results in a more relaxed approach toward them, noted in his tentative recognition of inheriting some of his grandfather's characteristics,
such as his literary sensibilities and his tendency to migrate.

Legacies and Heritage II:
The Post-War Family Revisited

In contrast to Ortheil's narrator who accepts the father's status as victim,
both Dagmar Leupold's *Nach den Kriegen* and Uwe Timm's *Am Beispiel
meines Bruders* are essentially engaged in a critical reassessment of the
victim narratives of their fathers and the family narratives they grew up
with. Where Wackwitz writes himself into a patrilinear masculine genealogy, Leupold and Timm undertake a critical revision of the masculine
(military) traditions and values that dominated their father's lives, and a
reorientation of traditions. Both texts investigate the transfer of authoritarian values from Nazism into the postwar family as a consequence of the
public humiliation of these values, portraying the postwar family as a site
of containment for the fathers' damaged selves, as well as a sphere of control, latent depression, and violence. Since both Leupold and Timm served
their fathers largely as receptacles for their failed desires, both narratives
serve the purpose of reestablishing the writer's identity in the face of the
parental history and cause each to investigate "which values, loyalties and
tasks determined my life?"[31] Both writers explicitly state their purpose of
"finding oneself anew" (*BB* 18) in the face of the "*established* memory"
(*BB* 33; italics in the original) and the "layer of protective myths" (*NK* 33),
marking the desire for a sense of ownership of this history, a shift from
mere listener and recipient to participant.

Leupold and Timm achieve this shift with a recontextualization of
family documents: Leupold with her father's diaries and manuscripts, and
Timm with his brother's wartime diary. These documents are placed into
context with other historical documents, such as official orders and Hans
Frank's diary in Leupold, and *Wehrmacht* orders and Holocaust survivors'

literature in Timm; both refer to Christopher Browning's *Ordinary Men* (1992). In the case of Leupold this leads, similar to Wackwitz, to an insight into the "biotope" (*NK* 195) in which nationalism, anti-Semitism, and hegemonic fantasies of power grew.

Timm and Leupold thus set the ever-present postwar family victim narratives of expulsions and bombings into a historical context — a context of Nazi history and prehistory, and of postwar silence, avoidance of responsibility, and stereotypical victim narratives. Both chart in detail the tasks that the psychodynamics of the postwar family left them with — in Leupold's case the "task" (*NK* 7) of fulfilling the father's aspirations as a writer, with Timm, the expectation to stand in for his brother's absence and to take over the family shop.

The result is a complex psychohistorical portrait of their fathers as defeated and damaged subjects, characterized by tentative empathy and a revision of their own histories. In stark contrast to Medicus and Wackwitz, who produce an "acceptable" image of their grandfathers, Timm's and Leupold's relationship to their fathers remains characterized by an insurmountable emotional distance. The irreparable emotional damage created by the psychodynamics of the postwar family is expressed in the lack of possessive pronouns when naming the parent, a stylistic device that also characterizes Treichel's *Der Verlorene* and Grass's *Im Krebsgang*.

Both Leupold and Timm are engaged in establishing a different tradition from within the family legacy. In Leupold this consists in subjecting her father's literary aspirations to a sensitive critique, situating his style as a writer in the proximity of Ernst Jünger's and Gottfried Benn's detached and cold observatory prose. Both writers' distance and indifference to Nazism and Nazi victims alike are exposed by Leupold as an aesthetic pose resulting from an avoidance of introspection in the face of a historical disappointment with civilization. Linking Jünger's and Benn's indifference to Nazi victims to the language of the Charta of expellee organizations, where her father was active, Leupold reads the writers' influential position in the cultural sphere of the early Federal Republic as a cultural reflection of a society's ethical failure to live up to its historical responsibility. Her father's lack of stylistic originality and his imitation of Jünger and Benn, the "formative influence" on his generation,[32] thus reflects his shortcomings as a political subject; the daughter's critique implicitly expresses her own idea of the task of a writer.

Timm likewise is anxious to reinscribe himself into a different tradition from that embodied by his father. It is Timm's mother who, in *Am Beispiel meines Bruders,* emerges as a positive model both in her successful process of mourning for her dead son and her tentative revision of her political convictions within the limits of her intellectual abilities. Furthermore, by his emphasis on her sense of humor and storytelling abilities

Timm has wishfully marked her out as the origin of his own concern with language and narrative. The values embodied by Timm's mother thus produce a different genealogy into which Timm, who in his father's eye is a "mummy's boy" (*BB* 18), inserts himself.

Conclusion: Stereoscopic Visions and Genealogy

The autobiographical texts discussed here exemplify why Hirsch's concept of postmemory cannot be easily transferred into a German context. As Medicus's and Wackwitz's texts make clear, postmemory is precisely what those who have grown up surrounded by shameful silence do not possess, as traumatic experiences in the previous generation were not communicated but were simply passed down on an unconscious level. Furthermore, the conflict between familial narratives of suffering and the children's inheritance of collective responsibility for Nazism make the formation of an uncontroversial family tradition impossible. While Wackwitz and Medicus wish to reconnect to a broken genealogy and tradition, Leupold and Timm seek to heal their damaged selves by investigating the legacy of the damaged selves of their fathers, producing a different genealogy. Friederike Eigler speaks of "two opposing trends" that characterize generational narratives, a focus on ruptures, and an attempt to produce continuities.[33] Indeed, the production of continuities only becomes possible through the revisitation of the ruptures of twentieth-century German (family) history. This continuity is visible in the children of the authors that explicitly figure in Wackwitz, Leupold, and Medicus as bearers of a different future.

These four authors discover a similar structure of political "negligence" (*UL* 126), of German nationalism, humiliated fantasies of grandeur, opportunism, and indifference to the suffering of those demarcated by Nazism as outside the people's community. This is a psychopolitical legacy that is passed on to the children in the form of unspoken tasks and family phantoms. Their texts thus read like an enactment of Derrida's *Hauntology*. In his *Specters of Marx*, Derrida discusses the work of inheritance in terms of an injunction, passed on to the following generation(s). Pointing out the hermeneutic work of inheritance, Derrida asserts that the readability of legacy is not simply given, but demands interpretation, the transformation of the spectral task through *reading*: "*one must* filter, sift, criticize, one must sort out several different possibles that inhabit the same injunction."[34] This includes a historicization of both the self-representation of the "perpetrator generation" (*BB* 99) as victims, as well as the position of Nazi crimes in post-1960s memory discourse as a barrier for the formation of genealogical memory.

However, unlike Wackwitz, who explicitly parallels his own youthful susceptibility to political indoctrination with his grandfather's susceptibility to Nazism, thus implicitly relativizing his own position, Leupold and Timm are at pains to preserve their right to judge their fathers' short-comings as political subjects. Leupold and Timm are engaged in what I call "stereoscopic vision." This preserves their own position while producing a complex image of their fathers' historical selves. Whereas Wackwitz's and Medicus's "exorcism" of the specter of Nazism from their grand-father's memory produces a form of historical integration for the authors that explicitly relativizes the moralizing position of the student movement, Leupold and Timm emerge from their texts without closure, but with an ownership of the continuity of historical damage.

Notes

[1] See Anne Fuchs, "The Tinderbox of Memory: Generation and Masculinity in *Väterliteratur* by Christoph Meckel, Uwe Timm, Ulla Hahn and Dagmar Leupold," in *German Memory Contests,* ed. Anne Fuchs, Mary Cosgrove, and Georg Grote (Rochester, NY: Camden House, 2006), 41–66, esp. 44.

[2] See Sigrid Weigel, "Families, Phantoms and the Discourse of 'Generations' as Politics of the Past: Rejection and Desire for Origins" (unpublished manuscript). See also Weigel, "'Generation' as Symbolic Form: On the Genealogical Discourse of Memory since 1945," *Germanic Review* 77 (2002): 264–77.

[3] See, e.g., Anne Fuchs, "From *Vergangenheitsbewältigung* to Generational Memory Contests in Günter Grass, Monika Maron and Uwe Timm," *German Life and Letters* 59, no. 2 (2006): 169–86 and Aleida Assmann, *Der lange Schatten der Vergangenheit: Erinnerungskultur und Geschichtspolitik* (Munich: Beck, 2006).

[4] See Bill Niven, *Facing the Nazi Past: United Germany and the Legacy of the Third Reich* (London: Routledge, 2002).

[5] Ulla Hahn, *Unscharfe Bilder* (Munich: DVA, 2003), 145. Subsequent references to this work are cited parenthetically in the text.

[6] See Harald Welzer's critique of generational novels, "Schön unscharf: Über die Konjunktur der Familien- und Generationenromane," *Mittelweg 36* (2004): 53–64.

[7] See Aleida Assmann, "Stabilisatoren der Erinnerung — Affekt, Symbol, Trauma," in *Die dunkle Spur der Vergangenheit: Psychoanalytische Zugänge zum Geschichtsbewusstsein,* ed. Jörn Rüsen and Jürgen Straub (Frankfurt am Main: Suhrkamp, 1998), 31–52.

[8] See Weigel, "Télescopage im Unbewussten: Zum Verhältnis von Trauma, Geschichtsbegriff und Literatur," in *Trauma: Zwischen Psychoanalyse und kulturellem Deutungsmuster,* ed. Elisabeth Bronfen, Birgit R. Erdle, and Sigrid Weigel (Cologne: Böhlau, 1999), 51–76. See also the contributions by Brigitte Rauschenbach, Werner Bohleber, and Michel B. Buchholz in Rüsen and Straub, *Die Dunkle Spur der Vergangenheit,* 242–55, 256–74, and 330–53.

[9] See, e.g., Weigel, "Telescopage im Unbewussten," esp. 52–57, and Susanne Vees-Gulani, *Trauma and Guilt: Literature of Wartime Bombing in Germany* (Berlin: Walter de Gruyter, 2003), 18–25.

[10] On this issue see Michael Roth, "Trauma, Repräsentation und historisches Bewusstsein" in Rüsen and Straub, *Die Dunkle Spur der Vergangenheit,* 153–73.

[11] For a detailed discussion of Hahn, see my "Reconciliation between the Generations: The Normalization of the Image of the Ordinary German Soldier in Dieter Wellershoff's *Der Ernstfall* and Ulla Hahn's *Unscharfe Bilder,*" in *German Culture, Politics, and Literature into the Twenty-First Century: Beyond Normalization,* ed. Stuart Taberner and Paul Cooke (Rochester, NY: Camden House, 2006), 151–65.

[12] See Harald Welzer, Sabine Moller, and Karoline Tschuggnall, *Opa war kein Nazi: Nationalsozialismus und Holocaust im Familiengedächtnis* (Frankfurt am Main: Fischer, 2002), 10.

[13] Marianne Hirsch, *Family Frames, Photography, Narrative and Postmemory* (Cambridge, MA: Harvard UP, 1997), 22.

[14] See Marianne Hirsch, "Surviving Images: Holocaust Photographs and the Work of Postmemory," *Yale Journal of Criticism* 14, no. 1 (2001): 9–10. See also in Hirsch, *Family Frames,* 22, where the cultural memory of the Holocaust is described as "postmemory," 50.

[15] See J. J. Long, "Monika Maron's *Pawels Briefe:* Photography, Narrative and the Claims of Postmemory," in Fuchs et al., *German Memory Contests,* 147–65, esp. 147–48.

[16] See Stuart Taberner, "Literary Representations in Contemporary German Fiction of the Expulsions of Germans from the East," in *A Nation of Victims? Representations of German Wartime Suffering from 1945 to the Present,* ed. Helmut Schmitz (Amsterdam: Rodopi, 2007), 225.

[17] See Anne Fuchs, "After-Images of History: Thomas Medicus's *In den Augen meines Großvaters,*" in *Jahrbuch Gegenwartsliteratur,* ed. Paul Michael Lützeler (Tübingen: Stauffenburg, 2006), 252–71.

[18] Stephan Wackwitz, *Ein unsichtbares Land: Familienroman* (Frankfurt am Main: Fischer, 2003); Thomas Medicus, *In den Augen meines Großvaters* (Munich: DVA, 2004); Dagmar Leupold, *Nach den Kriegen* (Munich: Beck, 2004); Uwe Timm, *Am Beispiel meines Bruders* (Cologne: Kiepenheuer and Witsch, 2003). Subsequent references to these works are cited in the text using the abbreviations *UL, AG, NK,* and *BB,* respectively, and page number.

[19] On Wackwitz, see Friederike Eigler, *Gedächtnis und Geschichte in Generationsromanen seit der Wende* (Berlin: Erich Schmidt, 2005), 185–225, on Medicus, see Fuchs, "After-Images of History." On Timm, see the essays in Friedhelm Marx, ed., *Erinnern, Vergessen, Erzählen* (Göttingen: Wallstein, 2007). On Leupold, see Fuchs, "Tinderbox of Memory." I only had the chance of reading Anne Fuchs's study on generational texts, *Family Narratives and the Politics of Memory in German Literature, Film and Discourse since Unification: Phantoms of War* (Houndsmills, UK: Palgrave Macmillan, 2008), after the completion of this chapter.

[20] See the chapter on Ortheil in my *On Their Own Terms: The Legacy of National Socialism in Post-1990 German Fiction* (Birmingham, UK: U of Birmingham P, 2004), 27–54.

[21] See Brian Jarvis, *Postmodern Cartography: The Geographical Imagination in Contemporary American Culture* (London: Pluto Press, 1998), 9.

[22] Hanns-Josef Ortheil, *Abschied von den Kriegsteilnehmern* (Munich: Piper, 1992), 184.

[23] On the issue of the "family phantom," see Nicholas Abraham, "Notes on the Phantom: A Complement to Freud's Metapsychology," in Nicholas Abraham and Maria Torok, *The Shell and the Kernel* (Chicago: U of Chicago P, 1994), 174. See also Bohleber in Rüsen and Straub, *Die Dunkle Spur der Vergangenheit.*

[24] "It was as if the ghosts of their fathers had suddenly appeared before them in Nazi uniforms, and their living fathers, with whom they had sat down at the supper table for twenty years, had been indicted of the most horrible collective crime committed by any generation during this century," in Michael Schneider, "Fathers and Sons, Retrospectively: The Damaged Relationship between the Generations," *New German Critique* (Winter 1984): 9.

[25] See Helm Stierlin, "The Dialogue between the Generations about the Nazi Era," in *The Collective Silence: German Identity and the Legacy of Shame,* ed. Barbara Heimannsberg and Christoph J. Schmidt (San Francisco: Jossey-Bass, 1993), 155.

[26] See Fuchs, "After-Images of History," 256–58.

[27] Medicus, "Im Archiv der Gefühle: Tätertöchter, der aktuelle 'Familienroman' und die deutsche Vergangenheit," *Mittelweg* 36 (2006): 6.

[28] Hirsch, *Family Frames,* 242–44.

[29] For a detailed discussion of Wackwitz's use of hermeneutics, see my "Zweierlei Allegorie: W. G. Sebald's *Austerlitz* und Stephan Wackwitz's *Ein unsichtbares Land,*" in *W. G. Sebald and Expatriate Writing,* ed. Gerhard Fischer (Amsterdam: Rodopi, forthcoming 2009).

[30] See Kafka, "Eine kaiserliche Botschaft," in *Gesammelte Werke in zwölf Bänden,* vol. 1 (Frankfurt am Main: Fischer, 1994), 1:221.

[31] Stierlin, "Dialogue between the Generations," 146.

[32] See Fuchs, "Tinderbox of Memory," 59. Fuchs points out that Jünger is mentioned also in Hahn, Timm, and Christoph Meckel's *Bildnis der Mutter als junge Frau.*

[33] Eigler, *Gedächtnis und Geschichte,* 26.

[34] Jacques Derrida, *Specters of Marx* (London: Routledge, 1994), 16. Italics in the original.

6: Lost *Heimat* in Generational Novels by Reinhard Jirgl, Christoph Hein, and Angelika Overath

Elizabeth Boa

Heimat Discourse and the Politics of Memory

IN ONE OF THE *UNTIMELY MEDITATIONS*, "On the Uses and Disadvantages of History for Life," Nietzsche warns that history may become a "hypertrophied virtue" or "consuming fever."[1] It can sometimes seem that Germany is afflicted by historical overload. Since unification, the political aspiration to build a common national identity has, if anything, intensified reflection on the meaning for the future of how the German past is perceived. Competing political and ethical perspectives fuel debate and different media shape different messages. As a recent study puts it, "memory contests are highly dynamic public engagements with the past that are triggered by an event that is perceived as a massive disturbance of a community's self-understanding."[2] The historians' dispute of the mid-1980s centered on the large-scale explanatory models of academic historiography. Over the last decade or so, however, the dwindling number of firsthand witnesses has added urgency to the wish to document personal experience. Goldhagen's *Hitler's Willing Executioners* (1996) and the Crimes of the *Wehrmacht* exhibition, touring major cities between 1995 and 1999, intensified the focus on ordinary Germans as perpetrators, but toward the end of the 1990s German suffering during the war and its aftermath also moved toward the center ground of debate.[3]

The pragmatic thrust of Nietzsche's argument — "We want to serve history only to the extent that history serves life" (*N* 59) — is still of interest in highlighting how historical enquiry may be driven by current agendas. Nietzsche distinguishes between monumental, antiquarian, and critical history. Monumental history looks at past greatness to encourage the present pursuit of future aims. Antiquarian history preserves and honors ancestral tradition. Critical history passes judgment: "For since we are the outcome of earlier generations, we are also the outcome of their aberrations, passions and errors, and indeed of their crimes; it is not possible wholly to free oneself of this chain" (*N* 76). After the Second World War, monumental history in the two Germanys sought through cultural icons to appropriate the heritage of a good Germany. Alternatively, it memorialized — literally through monuments — past crimes rather than greatness. Yet even such expressions of contrition tended to present National Socialism in terms designed to off-load greater guilt on the other Germany, through partially exculpating the antitotalitarian West, or the anticapitalist East. Monuments since unification, notably the Berlin Holocaust Memorial, have provoked the criticism that they operate as a moral cudgel preventing confident pursuit of future aims or that they are a substitute for genuine critical engagement.[4] My topic belongs in the equally controversial antiquarian category. According to Nietzsche, antiquarian history stabilizes identity and keeps the less favored social orders contented with their lot. Household goods passed down through generations house the soul of antiquarian man:

> The trivial, circumscribed, decaying and obsolete acquire their own dignity and inviolability through the fact that the preserving and revering soul of the antiquarian man has emigrated into them and there made its home. The history of his city becomes for him the history of himself. (*N* 73)

Nietzsche's antiquarian history anticipated the *Heimat* discourse that developed following German unification in 1871. The ideal of *Heimat* — that is, of attachment to a place of origin — mediated between new national and older regional loyalties: umbilical attachment to one's native heath infused blood into the more abstract identification with the fatherland, while the lost rural *Heimat* offered an urbanizing populace a store of mythic landscapes to intensify patriotic emotion. The aftermath of unification in 1990, too, has seen an upsurge of *Heimat* discourse as citizens of East Germany faced the ambivalent task of reconfiguring the past, often through balancing rejection of an authoritarian father-state with nostalgia for a maternal *Heimat,* as in the film *Goodbye Lenin.*[5]

Much current antiquarian history, however, addresses a more drastic loss of *Heimat.* Two recent documentary exhibitions provoked considerable argument over the politics of memorialization. Flight, Expulsion, Integration, which centered on German experience, opened in Bonn in November 2005, then moved to Berlin and Leipzig, closing in April 2007.[6] This had the word *Heimat* cutting vertically through the title, thus asserting the need to mourn loss, but with a view to moving on and settling in a new home. Accordingly, the exhibition documented where people had come from and their trek westward, but also resettlement in both East and West Germany. The emphasis on making a new *Heimat* sought to counter revanchist tendencies, while still remembering events that affected such huge numbers of people. A smaller comparative exhibition, Forced Migration: Flight and Expulsion in Twentieth Century Europe ran in Berlin from August to October 2006.[7] It was organized under nine headings, beginning with Armenians fleeing Turkey during the First World War, through to Bosnian refugees in the 1990s, and included prewar Jewish emigration, wartime expulsions in Eastern Europe to create German lebensraum, and expulsions of Germans at the end of the Second World War. Such a sequence makes German political responsibility plain, yet could also be seen to normalize German aggression as just one more horror in a catalogue of horrors. Whereas most of the exhibition consisted of text detailing facts and figures, a section devoted to *Heimat* displayed pathos-laden household items, folk costumes, and other mainly rural bric-a-brac. That millions of Jews did not flee but perished posed a dilemma for both exhibitions. The collective histories of the victims of genocide and of the perpetrators are different, yet "mutually implicated."[8] Flight, Expulsion, Integration opted for a symbolic installation in contrast to the documentary material otherwise on display; Forced Migrations included regional estimates of Jewish victims. The latter unleashed more controversy because it was a taster for a Center Against Expulsions, a project launched in 2000 by Erika Steinbach, president of the *Bund der Vertriebenen* (Union of Expellees) and viewed with great distrust in Poland, given earlier campaigns deploying emotive *Heimat* discourse for the restoration of lost territory.

Thus memorializing lost *Heimat* may merely keep old hostilities alive and wounds open. Yet individuals cannot be denied the right to remember. *Heimat* discourse is a prime locus of intersection between the private and the public, the personal and the political. Alongside journalistic polemics or museums, many recent novels have sought to bridge "the floating gap between the subjective experience of history and scholarly historical explanations."[9] As Elizabeth Dye argues, in its ability to combine different perspectives on complex experience, narrative fiction is well adapted to conveying individual suffering without losing sight of the broader historical context.[10] I consider here whether three generational novels depicting German suffering might be said to "serve life" in laying ghosts to rest by proper remembrance, so that, without denying the chain of connection to past crimes, the living may flourish, looking too at what their perspective on the past may portend for the future. Key motifs in Reinhard Jirgl's *Die Unvollendeten* (The Unfinished, 2003), Christoph Hein's *Landnahme* (Land Seizure, 2004), and Angelika Overath's *Nahe Tage: Roman in einer Nacht* (Near Days: Novel of One Night, 2005) are the traumatic loss of *Heimat;* the inheritance of trauma by children or grandchildren; and success or failure to integrate into the host community as a cure or a second wounding.[11] In Jirgl's and Overrath's novels the lost

Heimat is the Sudetenland; in Hein's it is Silesia. In Jirgl's and Hein's novels the new *Heimat* is the German Democratic Republic (GDR); in Overath's it is the West German Federal Republic (FRG). But all three novels are narrated from a standpoint in postunification Germany and end on open questions: Who feels at home and who cannot settle in what has now commonly come to be known as the Berlin Republic? Who is welcomed, who is shunned or excluded?

As Sigrid Weigel notes, the concept of generation may be diachronic, as in the vertical time line of family genealogy.[12] Or it may be synchronic, drawing horizontal connections to age cohorts defined relative to current events or social trends. The crisscrossing of horizontal and vertical connections makes generation a complex nodal point of identity construction. Jirgl and Overath shape their stories as "family novels": horizontal groupings also figure, but are secondary to family genealogy. Hein reverses these weightings: *Landnahme* does involve three, even four generations of a grandfather (mentioned only in one sentence), a father, his son (the main protagonist), and then his son, but the narrative centers relations within the protagonist's generation, stories about others in his age group being almost as important as the protagonist's story. The interplay between inheritance of trauma from earlier generations and wounds inflicted by peers in the host community raises questions. Does the inherited trauma block integration or even incite hostility in the hosts? Do wounds inflicted by the host community poison inherited trauma, thus setting in motion a life-threatening syndrome? In our mobile times children and grandchildren of migrants often seem more alienated than their elders whose lives on the face of it were more painfully disrupted. A vertical line of imaginary connection to the past may block horizontal connections in the present.

Like generation, *Heimat* too may be imagined as past or present. Commonly, *Heimat* designates a place of nostalgic childhood memory that may extend to encompass ancestral places; thus, urban children revisit the rural localities of parents and grandparents and migrants look to a homeland they may know only in imagination. But there is an equally strong sense of *Heimat* as a present place and habitus, created through investment of labor or cultural engagement, as in settler discourse or local patriotism. The covers marketing the novels appeal to one or other of these senses of *Heimat*. Jirgl's cover shows a woman in 1940s clothing, sitting by the roadside in a posture of weary despair. Dominick LaCapra comments on the dangers of confusing history with myth.[13] *Heimat* may be that past or future Eden we all mourn or long for: the trauma is the universal wound of expulsion from paradise, the longing the divine spark of discontent that fuels utopian dreams. Such mythic loss or longing stands in for what never was or will be and so cannot be made good or reached in this world. Historical loss of *Heimat,* by contrast, often could be made good in various ways. But when the mythic and the historical become entangled, the outcome may be an unending melancholia. Naked Adam and Eve offer a universal image of postlapsarian humanity. On Jirgl's cover, however, the woman's clothes mark out the historical victim. But a mixing of myth and history turns her shoes and headscarf into what Barthes, writing of photography, would term the punctum, the detail that pierces with an anguished sense of irreparable loss.[14] On Overrath's cover the woman's dress and hair also signal the 1940s, but her smile and the idyllic rural setting prompt not anguish but nostalgia. Alternatively, Hein's cover — a man in up-to-date black sweater and jeans and carrying a plank of wood — signals a do-it-yourself project of seizure of land to be built on here and now. Together the three covers suggest that women embody the lost *Heimat,* whether in melancholic or idyllic mood, whereas men make the new *Heimat.* In reading the texts at issue are: Does the emotional rhetoric borne by metonymic details and symbols evoking lost *Heimat* "serve life," or does the loss of *Heimat* become a running sore across generations, that is, LaCapra's "interminable melancholy"?[15] What do different responses portend for the future? Are pathos-laden gender stereotypes confirmed or subverted, and how far does antiquarian history mix with the larger perspectives of critical history?

Die Unvollendeten

Die Unvollendeten has three parts: the first tells of the flight of four women from Komotau, now Chumtow, in the Sudetenland; the second tells of early difficulties in the Soviet Zone, then in provincial GDR; the third interweaves the present in postunification Berlin with the later GDR years up to 1988. It emerges only in part three that the narrator is Reiner (*UV* 244), son of Anna and great-grandson, grandson, and grandnephew of three now dead women, Johanna, Hanna, and Maria whose story he tells, often in their own voices. The novel opens with a first wounding, or *Urtrauma,* an intensely vivid account of "wilde Vertreibung" (wild expulsions), when the rules set by the Allies for the regulated exchange of populations after the German defeat in 1945 were not observed and the German population was driven out without time to get ready: "30 MINUTES TIME — WITH A MAXIMUM OF 8 KILOS LUGGAGE PER PERSON" (*UV* 251). Suddenness is a key factor, inducing shock. The repetition of these words at the end enacts compulsive repetition, but by the narrator as a listener retelling an original telling: "listening to the voice and to the speech delivered by the other's wound," as Cathy Caruth puts it in her account of trauma.[16] The wounds speak with stunning vividness. But the voices are also filtered textually through Jirgl's eccentric typography of different fonts, use of italics and bold, and devices such as hyphenation.[17] These inflect the language tonally so that the voices of the dead and the living intertwine, sometimes in agreement, sometimes ironically distanced, sometimes in enraged struggle. The effect is a strange mixing of the performative with the vividly illusionistic, like the doubled voice of a medium in a séance. The dead speak through the narrator's mouth, yet he also resists their power in a mix of grief, guilt, and rage. Drawing on LaCapra's notion of "empathetic unsettlement," Anne Fuchs emphasizes the ethical need for balance between empathy and distance to avoid sentimentalizing or instrumentalizing the suffering of others.[18] The visual oddity of the printed page in Jirgl's text conveys less a balance than a battle, empathetic unsettlement with a vengeance.

The novel is structured around a sequence of locations, but the traumatic effects of the first loss block integration into a new *Heimat,* which local attitudes to refugees also hinder. The first book follows two strands: the older women's flight, followed by Anna's story. The lost *Heimat* is both the place and the ruptured family. That Anna got left behind and had to make her own way through nightmarish horrors causes lasting bitterness between mother and daughter. Anna witnesses SS men and local collaborators being beaten up and murdered in a football ground by Czech militia. The SS had shot all the slave workers at the nearby Mannesmann factory just before the capitulation. Besides suddenness, deflection from full realization is symptomatic of trauma. In Anna's memory the scene is a dissociated image, eerily silent, as if in a submarine world (*UV* 14). Writing of a similar experience, Günter Grass says it was like a jerky silent film.[19] Anna meets Erich, a young recent recruit who deserted from the *Waffen SS* following a massacre of concentration camp prisoners. Like Anna's submarine world or Grass's silent film, Erich remembers the event as if it had taken place in a theater or a dream, claiming not to know whether he had shot a prisoner or not. In the shadow of death, Anna's and Erich's lovemaking is frenzied. Pregnant by Erich, Anna is reunited with her family. Erich turns up again, but soon disappears finally. Although Anna knows of Hanna's agonized searching, her sense of abandonment is not assuaged. The separation is repeated in the estrangement between Anna and her son and his attachment to the older women.

In the immediate aftermath of the war the women move from a farm, to a village (where great-grandmother Johanna dies), to a small town; later, Hanna lodges in the provincial capital Magdeburg, while Anna moves to Berlin. Thus the novel enacts a phased shift from countryside to metropolis. The potential second *Heimat* is provincial Birkheim, where Hanna and Maria eventually remain, if not settle.[20] The novel conveys the strengths and weaknesses of official policies, as well as popular hostility to incomers. By speaking of *Umsiedler* (resettlers), rather than *Vertriebene* (expellees), officials emphasize integration and downplay the role of former enemies — the Soviet Union and Poland — who are now allies. But ordinary people were often less than welcoming: "Flüchtlinge u [*sic*] Dünnschiß kann eben niemand aufhalten" (There's no stopping refugees and diarrhea) (*UV* 91). This is how the widow with whom Hanna was billeted in bombed-out Magdeburg greeted her, an insult Hanna never forgets. Nietzsche urged the need to forget if the past is not to become "the gravedigger of the present" (*N* 62). But haunted by a promise to her dead husband and the illusory hope of return to the *Heimat,* Hanna refuses an offer of marriage from a work colleague, a refugee from Silesia. Yet the women do gradually give up on Komotau: "*the-Heimat*" becomes the "*Old Heimat*" (*UV* 220). But on retirement, getting older and lonelier, they are moved out of their homely flat in a prewar building into a new flat, well appointed but soulless. For the narrator this expulsion is a minitrek all over again.

The text constantly conveys the narrator's mix of anguished pity and impotent rage against mean-minded locals, but also horror at the cult of *Heimat.* Yet the narrator too is entangled. His nostalgic *Heimat* is Birkheim. He fails to connect with his mother or his own generation. Anna has defied Hanna's deathly cult in a countermove to make a living *Heimat.* But her son never feels at home in Berlin and hates his stepfather, a communist party official. He has no broader investment in the GDR, no horizontal connections, it seems, to his own age cohort. Nor has he any desire to flee west, for his anger spreads to former neighbors from Komotau now vulgarly prospering in West Germany. Nietzsche writes of *Urväter-Hausrath* (ancestral goods), of "the decaying and obsolete" (*N* 73) as the soul's dwelling place. Hanna had a best grey flannel costume for important occasions. But the people in the west eventually tell her that her old clothes stink and that the Birkheim cake she and Maria send every Christmas goes straight into the rubbish bin. Such insults to the decaying and obsolete (here Urmütter-Hausrath) fester in the narrator's memory. But his indignation scarcely masks guilt at his own neglect of Hanna and Maria. Empathetic identification with others' loss, anger at wounds inflicted by the host community, and guilt mix with a diffusely anguished sense of time, mortality, and horror of contemporary life to breed melancholia under the sign of Thanatos.

The narration proceeds from a cancer ward in the Berlin Charité hospital. At death's door himself, Reiner has set a trap for his estranged wife. They have been running a bookshop; if she goes to the shop as usual, and switches on the light, she will die in a gas explosion. But if she comes to the hospital and reads his letter (in effect the text of the novel), perhaps a salving if not closure of wounds may follow. The final words, "Es geht weiter" (*UV* 251) — literally, it is continuing — are ambiguous. They could mean the cancer is spreading: inherited trauma will continue to afflict the postunification Berlin generation. Less pessimistically, it could mean "to be continued." Either way, the ending suggests rejection of closure or normalization. The chain of connection to past suffering and crimes cannot simply be broken. But need memory turn antiquarian man into Nietzsche's "gravedigger of the present"? Reiner's family genealogy positions men as perpetrators and women as victims, but also complicates matters. In this case grandpa really wasn't a Nazi;[21] Reiner's maternal grandfather was Czech and dead before the outbreak of war, though according to Anna he was a domestic tyrant. Reiner's father Erich, indelibly marked by an SS tattoo, shows shock but not contrition in his account of the massacre of corpselike concentration camp prisoners. Nor does he shoulder other responsibilities, but disappears in the postwar chaos, leaving Reiner fatherless. Thus Jirgl clearly locates German suffering within the context of genocide and other war crimes, yet he also undoes to an extent the either/or of perpetrator/victim by showing that perpetrators can also be victims — for example, young men, recruited late on to a criminal military body — and that to acknowledge their suffering does not cancel out their crimes. Women appear as prime victims of modern warfare, which so devastates civilian populations, yet Hanna and Maria do move on, make a life, and care for a child. Where the generation of '68 dwelled on paternal crimes, Reiner dwells on grandmaternal suffering, but reponds, as did some of the '68 generation, with a terroristic impulse. The reader can see in Reiner a warning against too intense a dwelling on others' suffering, which may turn into destructive self-pity. The strange motif of the planned gas explosion recalls Fassbinder's *The Marriage of Maria Braun* (1979), in which the heroine, the allegorical embodiment of Germany, dies in a gas explosion, a motif also recalling Zyklon-B, the gas used in the concentration camps. We never hear the voices of Reiner's wife (the present) or his stepdaughter (the future); like the angel of history, Reiner's gaze is backward looking. Paradoxically, a fatherless man in mourning for dead women plans to murder a woman and orphan her daughter. Antiquarian history, it seems, does not serve, but threatens life. Or more precisely, antiquarian man is the threat. Erich recalls his education during the Third Reich to manly Germanic bravery; his son looks set to continue a destructive mode of masculinity. No welcome here for the Berlin Republic, then, and a warning of continuing chains of attachment to past crimes.[22]

Landnahme

In Hein's novel, *Heimat* is not just a theme. *Landnahme* is a *Heimat* novel in retro mode, with many motifs reminiscent of earlier work.[23] Hein's protagonist, Bernhard Haber, reinvents himself as antiquarian man: the history of his town becomes the history of himself. The novel starts and finishes with a third-person frame set in the present during Guldenberg's annual carnival. An erstwhile local, son of an eminent citizen, now returns as a stranger and bumps into a man who once arrived as a stranger and is now an eminent citizen. Thus, from the start, strangers and locals are positions open to reversal: *Heimat* is something you make, not where you originate. The frame encloses a sequence of first-person accounts by people who knew Bernhard at various stages, from the arrival of his family as refugees in 1950 onward. Asked where he comes from, Bernhard replies that he comes from Wrocław, but was born in Breslau (*LN* 19–20), thus curtly accepting the loss of his native city to Poland while asserting his German identity. We hear nothing more of lost Silesia. The narrative centers on the second *Heimat* in provincial East Germany where taciturn Bernhard becomes a prism mirroring Guldenberg and its inhabitants. Unlike Jirgl's Reiner, who moves to Berlin but mourns a provincial *Heimat* and the death of old women, Bernhard stays on to seize provincial land and father the future in the shape of a son and grandson.

Within the overarching *Heimat* mode, *Landnahme* ironically echoes two genres: the novel of development and the mystery story. The first charts Bernhard's horizontal connections within his own generation as he zigzags his way from outsider to insider. Phases of his life parallel developments in the GDR and place him in shifting positions vis-à-vis nation and locality: as refugee-stranger; party activist during the land reform; teenage delinquent; profiteer abetting flight to the West; small businessman on the make; post-unification property developer and paterfamilias. Running in parallel is the mystery of his father's suspicious death. Whereas for Jirgl's Reiner leaving Birkheim was a psychic amputation, Bernhard's father suffered the literal amputation of his arm in an accident in a Russian labor camp. This all-too-visible trauma incites hostility rather than compassion: for the townsfolk, the absent arm is like the lacking obelisk that would memorialize soldiers lost in the Second World War; the two absences are reminders of defeat and humiliation. Like Jirgl, Hein too touches on hostility to refugees in a hierarchy of enmity: the *Ausgebombte* (refugees bombed out from local cities) were less of a long-term threat to local interests. Have-nots from the east with their strange accents were much more resented and sneered at as gypsies or *Polacken* (Poles), even if the authorities called them *Umsiedler* (resettlers) and Germans "like us." Bernhard is furious that his family was treated scarcely any better than *Fremdarbeiter* (alien workers) during the war — victims of communal hostility do not, it seems, identify with other more drastically victimized groups. The father sets up as a carpenter, but is the victim of arson when his business does too well; then he is hit on the head by a plank, seemingly an accident; then he is found hanged, seemingly a suicide. As traumatic for Bernhard is the death of his dog Tinz, strangled by a wire noose. The sheer malice makes this loss especially traumatic. Hein vividly conveys the child's suffering and its remembrance in returning flashes of rage and pain. In the closing story, it comes out that Bernhard's father was murdered and that the town notabilities in the bowling club had colluded in the cover-up. Bernhard has avenged Tinz in various ways. But now, himself a member of the bowling club, he both wants and does not want to know the truth about his father, lest it all start up again and he find himself once more an alien stranger. It is as if Hein's Bernhard were answering Jirgl's Reiner: *Die Unvollendeten* ends on the compulsive repetition of trauma; Bernhard, by contrast, decides to serve history only to the extent that history serves life.

If Jirgl's novel suggests the impossibility of escaping from the past, Hein's suggests the necessity. *Landnahme* does not dwell on the lost *Heimat*. The father's missing arm, the *Urtrauma,* remains an empty signifier. The wounds at issue are those inflicted by German locals on German refugees. In a play on the double meaning of "Opfer" as both victim and sacrifice, Bernhard suggests that his innocent father's blood may have been the sacrifice that enabled his son to be accepted (*LN* 367). This deeply questionable suggestion disposes of a crime by sacralizing it, an accusation sometimes directed against Holocaust memorials that, it is claimed, substitute mystification for critical engagement. But because the victim in question is German, Bernhard's suggestion could also be seen as advice to groups such as the Union of Expellees to move on and get a life, as millions of German refugees so successfully did. Jirgl's bookseller antihero is totally hostile to postunification Germany and has a particular horror of young women authors whose readable books sell well. On the face of it, *Die Unvollendeten* eschews readability (though it is, despite the typographic eccentricities, an intensely vivid read). *Landnahme,* by contrast offers the readerly pleasures of the *Heimat* mode: the underdog triumphs and wrongs are righted, even if the central crime remains unavenged. If Jirgl's novel conveys the threat of unending melancholia, does Hein perhaps err in being too complacent? *Landnahme* could seem to advocate breaking the chain of connection to past crimes in the interests of economic prosperity in the new *Bundesländer* (federal states in the east of united Germany). A German father as innocent victim contrasts with Jirgl's ambiguous victim/perpetrator Erich. *Landnahme* does weave in passing allusions to German perpetration, albeit more to the treatment of Roma and Slav populations than to the genocide of the Jews. But in keeping with the foregrounding of German-German relations within the same generation, the novel centers around postwar racism, notably the episode concerning a baby of mixed black and white parentage. The man who thinks he is the father initially bonds with the child, but cannot stand his buddies' mockery when the baby's skin color indicates that he cannot be. In essence, the baby is cast out by the whole community. Right at the end, too, Bernhard's son Paul prevents a group of "Fidschis" — literally "Fijians," a slang term for Asian refugees such as Vietnamese — from joining in the carnival procession. Bernhard reminds him that his grandfather too had been a refugee, but Paul responds that his grandfather was a German with a right to live here. By bringing in the "Fidschis," Hein highlights current racist attitudes. Even so, Bernhard's pragmatic decision to let sleeping dogs lie offers a stark contrast to Reiner's melancholia turning into terror.

Nahe Tage

Heimat discourse in *Die Unvollendeten* is ambivalent: it evokes anguished longing yet warns against dwelling too deeply on others' loss. *Landnahme* ironizes *Heimat*: self-consciously retro in mode, it warns critically against current racism. Overath's *Nahe Tage* could be labeled an anti-*Heimat* novel: it unmasks the lost *Heimat* as a screen for dysfunctional family relations. The story centers on the daughter, Johanna, who is sorting through the contents of her dead mother's flat. As the title suggests, memories prompted by her mother's possessions return in close-up, threatening to banish the gap between past and present. The narration is in the third person, but focalized through Johanna: the narrow focus, the physical enclosure, and the temporal limitation to one night intensify the sense of sinking into memory. But the third person also distances what turns out to be a process of working through memories of an abused childhood: it renders the stream of memory, which threatens to overwhelm, into ordered narration.

The primary traumatized figure is the mother who then inflicts wounds on her daughter. The family — grandfather, grandmother, mother, and aunt — fled from the Sudetenland. Johanna's mother and father met after the flight, however, so the father was not from "Zuhaus" (home) — the word becomes a leitmotiv like "*die-Heimat*" in Jirgl's novel. Zuhaus was the river landscape where the Zwittau divides the provinces of Bohemia and Moravia, flowing between the villages of Böhmisch Wiesen and Böhmisch Mähren, situated 200 kilometers from Prague and 200 kilometers from Vienna (*NT* 76). The mother's mourning for the lost *Heimat* turns into a melancholic cult on the death of her father, Johanna's grandfather. Mother and daughter visit the grave every week. Unhappy in her marriage and without connections to her own generation, the mother draws Johanna into an ancestor cult. A sequence of bodily motifs takes on symbolic import. In a pun on the phrase "wunde Stelle" (sore point), the female genitalia — the mother's, then the grandmother's, then Johanna's

— are displayed as the locus of trauma. Driven from paradise, Eve gives birth in pain. Driven from Zuhaus, Johanna's mother is torn from vagina to rectum at her daughter's birth, as she often recounts, and tries to reincorporate the child into a "Mutterlegierung," a maternal alloy: Johanna is to be "in die Mutterlegierung eingeliebt" (*NT* 36), that is, to be loved into submission. The bed-bound grandmother's labia are a purple color like raw meat and nine-year-old Johanna still has her bottom wiped: Johanna is nightly laid out, splayed on the kitchen table as on the family altar, to be ritually cleansed by a priestess-mother, while her weakly collusive father looks on as ministrant (*NT* 21, 133). As in Ibsen's *Ghosts,* the genitalia are the running sore, passed down through the generations. But here the wounds are obscenely and blasphemously made sacred.

This motivic field combining child abuse and religious metaphor gradually emerges from a mass of realist metonymic details that cumulatively evoke an old-fashioned household. The "trivial, circumscribed, decaying and obsolete" become, so Nietzsche suggests, a homely nest for the antiquarian soul. The clearing of one's dead parent's dwelling is a quintessential work of filial piety. But this nest was never homely and is now "unheimlich," or uncanny. Instead of a home, the mother's household has been a minefield of "Zeitbomben" (time bombs), like the vase Johanna broke, only to be told that she could never make good the loss: the vase was from "Zuhaus" (*NT* 125). As Johanna collects dirty underwear, fluffy balls of hair, hankies crumpled in pockets, such abject traces of the maternal body become a ghostly haunting. Like Proustian taste, smell too is evocative. But where a loving child buries its head in the dead parent's clothes to bring them briefly back to life, for Johanna her mother's smell is a disgusting penetration, and she vomits, then flushes the loo to swirl it all down the drain. She launders a machine-load of clothes rather than just bagging them to be thrown out. Such details suggest something to be got rid of. Dents and knife marks in the oilcloth cover on the kitchen table awaken memories of a horrid secret. Gradually, the revelatory structure emerges: the dissociated memories knit together into a therapeutic working-through of an inherited trauma inflicted by an abusive mother who responded to her own suffering by scapegoating her daughter.

The novel sketches a cure. The enclosing flat is like the walls closing in on the mouse running toward the trap in the corner in Kafka's "A Little Fable": "'You only need to change your direction,' said the cat, and ate it up."[24] The cat, Johanna decides, is not an external threat, but an inner shame that she must face to escape entrapment. She is helped by an encounter with the woman who delivers a midnight pizza and stays to talk. Svetlana turns out to be a Russian–German. She had been a teacher in Aktau, now Shvevtshenko, situated an hour from Baku, Azerbaijan, and an hour from Krasnovdsk, Turkmenistan. She has come to Germany, bringing her father and her dead sister's daughter, to find a future away from ethnic conflict and the uranium mining that caused her sister's leukemia. Johanna decides to be like Svetlana, "a foreigner with a German pass" (*NT* 109). *Nahe Tage* proposes a change of direction toward a mobile world where nobody is "Zuhaus," and where children and old people are cared for, not sacrificed on the altar of nation, *Heimat,* or family. *Heimat* survives only in a prewar photograph: the abusive mother is just a baby, the ancient grandmother a young woman washing nappies in the Zwittau with a few geese in the background. *Nahe Tage* serves life by disentangling the historical from the mythic *Heimat,* which survives in the postmodern, nomadic world only as a fading photograph. There can be no return to the idyllic counterworld because the past never was like that. *Nahe Tage* could be seen to dispose of family memory too easily by taking such an extreme case of child abuse. And of the three novels it has the least to say about the larger political context of German war crimes, themes that *Die Unvollendeten* so vividly conveys. Yet like *Landnahme* it draws attention to current problems and is the most radical in disposing of *Heimat* ideology.

The grip of *Heimat* and memories of a war-torn past look set, however, to remain leading themes, as three final examples may suggest. Arno Geiger's *Es geht uns gut* (We're Doing Fine), winner of the 2005 German Book Prize, tells of a man clearing his dead parents' rotting house that becomes a metaphor, like the flat in *Nahe Tage,* for an antiquarian past that he eventually escapes in a change of direction, albeit in masculine careless, rather feminine caring mode.[25] Or there is Irene Dische's autobiographical novel, *Großmama packt aus* (The Empress of Weehawken), about a mixed German-Jewish family narrated by the monstrous yet lovable German grandmother who made a second *Heimat* in New York; this walks the tightrope of comic treatment of German-Jewish relations and engrained racism.[26] Or there is the documentary film *Söhne* (Sons) by the veteran East German filmmaker Volker Koepp.[27] This tells the story of four sons and their mother at the end of the war; the father had already died on the Eastern front. Advised she would have a better chance of getting through with just two children, the mother fled from the family farm in West Prussia, now in Poland, to West Germany, returning a year later to search for her other two children. She left again with, as she believed, her son Rainer who turned out, however, to have been substituted. The real Rainer turned up at the farm in 1959 and came west in 1977. The fourth son, virtually kidnapped by his foster mother, was brought up in Poland and chose, after a court case in 1955, to remain with his Polish family. The film interviews the now five brothers, including false and real Rainer and the Polish son. It documents current prosperity in Germany and now also in Poland, and a sentimental journey to a reunion at the farm that had been in the family for two hundred years. Toward the end, the five men, standing in a smiling if somewhat embarrassed row, are asked about where they think of as *Heimat:* is it the farm, is it Germany or Poland, or both? Each gives a slightly different answer; only the false Rainer, like Overath's heroine, rejects any notion of *Heimat.* As the title *Söhne,* rather than the equally possible *Brüder* (Brothers) implies, the absent center of the film is the mother, who died in 1998. By leaving the terrible anguish she must have suffered to the viewer's imagination and foregrounding the present amiable relations between the men and their families, the film both silently memorializes past suffering, yet offers hope for Polish-German fraternal relations in future.

Notes

[1] Friedrich Nietzsche, "On the Uses and Disadvantages of History for Life," in *Untimely Meditations,* ed. Daniel Breazeale, trans. R. J. Hollingdale (Cambridge: CUP, 1997), 59–60. Subsequent references are cited in the text using the abbreviation *N* and page number.

[2] Anne Fuchs, Mary Cosgrove, and Georg Grote, eds., *German Memory Contests: The Quest for Identity in Literature, Film and Discourse since 1990* (Rochester, NY: Camden House, 2006), 2.

[3] On phases in debate over Germans as perpetrators or victims, see Stuart Taberner, *German Literature of the 1990s and Beyond: Normalization and the Berlin Republic* (Rochester, NY: Camden House, 2005), chap. 5; see also Helmut Schmitz, "Introduction: The Return of Wartime Suffering in Contemporary German Memory Culture, Literature and Film," in *A Nation of Victims? Representations of German Wartime Suffering from 1945 to the Present,* ed. Helmut Schmitz (Amsterdam: Rodopi, 2007), 1–30.

[4] On memorialization, see Bill Niven, *Facing the Nazi Past: United Germany and the Legacy of the Third Reich* (London: Routledge, 2002), esp. chap. 8.

[5] On *Goodbye Lenin* as a *Heimat* film, see Elizabeth Boa, "Telling It How It Wasn't: Familial Allegories of Wish-Fulfillment in Postunification Germany," in Fuchs et al., *German Memory Contests,* 67–86. On provincial themes in East and West Germany, respectively, see Taberner, *German Literature,* 51–58 and 199–215.

[6] See the catalogue *Flucht Vertreibung Integration,* ed. Petra Rösgen, pub. Stiftung Haus der Geschichte der Bunderrepublik Deutschland (Bielefeld: Kerber, 2006).

[7] *Erzwungene Wege: Flucht und Vertreibung im Europa des 20 Jahrhunderts.* A German catalogue had still not appeared at the time of writing this essay. A slim English catalogue, with no ISBN number, was available during the exhibition.

[8] Helmut Schmitz, *On Their Own Terms: The Legacy of National Socialism in Post-1990 German Fiction* (Birmingham, UK: U of Birmingham P, 2004), 16.

[9] Anne Fuchs and Mary Cosgrove, "Introduction: Germany's Memory Contests and the Management of the Past," in Fuchs et al., *German Memory Contests,* 6.

[10] Elizabeth Dye, "Painful Memories: The Literary Representation of German Wartime Suffering" (PhD diss., University of Nottingham, 2006), 6. My essay is indebted to years of discussion with Elizabeth Dye.

[11] Reinhard Jirgl, *Die Unvollendeten* (Munich: Hanser, 2003); Christoph Hein, *Landnahme* (Frankfurt am Main: Suhrkamp, 2005); Angelika Overath, *Nahe Tage: Roman in einer Nacht* (Göttingen: Wallstein, 2005). Page references are cited in the text preceded by the abbreviations *UV, NT,* and *LN,* respectively. Translations of excerpts are my own.

[12] Sigrid Weigel, *Genea-Logik: Generation, Tradition und Evolution zwischen Kultur- und Naturwissenschaften* (Munich: Wilhelm Fink, 2006), 93–97.

[13] Dominick LaCapra, *Writing History, Writing Trauma* (Baltimore: Johns Hopkins UP, 2001), chap. 2.

[14] Roland Barthes, *La chambre claire* (Paris: Éditions du Seuil, 1980).

[15] LaCapra, *Writing History, Writing Trauma,* 69.

[16] Cathy Caruth, *Unclaimed Experience: Trauma, Narrative, and History* (Baltimore: Johns Hopkins UP, 1996), 8.

[17] For a full analysis of Jirgl's mannerisms, see Dye, *Painful Memories,* 286–99; for a useful summary, see Erk Grimm, "Die Lebensläufe Reinhard Jirgls: Techniken der melotraumatischen Inszenierungen," in *Reinhard Jirgl: Perspektiven, Lesarten, Kontexte,* ed. David Clarke and Arne De Winde (Amsterdam: Rodopi, 2007), 197–226.

[18] LaCapra, *Writing History, Writing Trauma,* 41; Anne Fuchs, *Die Schmerzensspuren der Geschichte: Zur Poetik der Erinnerung in W. G. Sebalds Prosa* (Cologne: Bohlau, 2004), 35. LaCapra and Fuchs both criticize Caruth's approach to trauma as lacking distance.

[19] Günter Grass, *Beim Häuten der Zwiebel* (Göttingen: Steidl, 2006), 170.

[20] Birkheim is based on Salzwedel where Jirgl lived with his grandmother until the age of ten.

[21] A much cited sociological study of defense mechanisms in family memory is titled *"Opa war kein Nazi": Nationalsozialismus und Holocaust im Familiengedächtnis,* by Harald Welzer, Sabine Moller, and Karoline Tschuggnall (Frankfurt am Main: Fischer, 2002).

[22] Clemens Kammler, "Unschärferelationen: Anmerkungen zu zwei problematischen Lesarten von Reinhard Jirgls Familienroman *Die Unvollendeten,*" in Clarke and De Winde, *Reinhard Jirgl,* 227–35, cites contrasting views as to whether Jirgl pays sufficient heed to German perpetration.

[23] Stealing tools from engineering works on a bridge recalls Marie Luise Fleisser's *Pioniere in Ingolstadt;* peasant cruelties recall Oskar Maria Graf; the local hero brings to mind figures in Clara Viebig's novels; a character called Marion is perhaps reminiscent of *Das Mädchen Marion,* a 1950s *Heimat* film; a comical episode of summer holidays and youthful sex is suggestive of the *Deutsche Filmakademie* (DEFA, German Film Academy) cult musical, *Heisser Sommer* (1968); communal scapegoating recalls Dürrenmatt's village in *Besuch der alten Dame* or Frisch's *Andorra.* There may even be a remote echo of *Hermann und Dorothea,* Goethe's small town epic, in the theme of the stranger-refugee.

[24] Franz Kafka, "A Little Fable," in *The Collected Short Stories of Franz Kafka,* ed. Nahum N. Glatzer (Harmondsworth, UK: Penguin, 1988), 445.

[25] Arno Geiger, *Es geht uns gut* (Munich: DTV, 2007; first pub. 2005).

[26] *Großmama packt aus,* trans. Reinhard Kaiser (Munich: DTV, 2006) appeared as *The Empress of Weehawken* in the American original only in 2007.

[27] *Söhne* won the Grand Prix at the 2007 Nyon documentary film festival in Switzerland.

7: "A Different Family Story": German Wartime Suffering in Women's Writing by Wibke Bruhns, Ute Scheub, and Christina von Braun

Caroline Schaumann

"WAR IS ALMOST ALWAYS AND EVERY WHERE the business of men,"[1] quotes Ute Scheub of Barbara Ehrenreich. It is a statement that recalls Ruth Klüger's well-known words in *weiter Leben: Eine Jugend* (Still Alive: A Holocaust Girlhood Remembered, 1992): "wars, and hence the memories of wars, are owned by the male of species."[2] Clearly these generalizations simplify the complexities of historical reality and omit women's roles as supporters, participants, and onlookers in wars and what leads up to them. Yet they lay bare the fact that men begin, wage, and justify wars, while women generally suffer from them. Even though German civilian women were among those first, and even foremost, affected by bombardment, displacement, occupation, and expulsion, a gendered perspective is often missing from the public discourse on "Germans as victims" of the Second World War. For instance, both Jörg Friedrich's seminal *Der Brand: Deutschland im Bombenkrieg 1940–45* (The Fire: The Bombing of Germany 1940–1945, 2002) and his later photo documentation *Brandstätten* (Fire Sites, 2003) display distraught women on their cover, yet neither text discusses women as a separate and distinct group of victims of war. Even though Günter Grass's protagonist Tulla Prokriefke in *Im Krebsgang* (Crabwalk, 2002) is a woman, she does not perceive the war and flight in ways much different from men. Her female experience, for the most part, consists of giving birth to the narrator. As women's suffering is not distinguished from men's but subsumed into a general (and thus, by default, male) category, knowledge of women's wartime experiences remains scant.

This chapter aims to present an overview of recent women's literature on wartime suffering, from accounts by eyewitnesses who met the advancing Soviet troops to novels by German-Jewish authors who depict survival and postwar life in Germany and Austria after 1945, to the autobiographical texts by non-Jewish authors who analyze in retrospect the family's suffering under authoritarian fathers during and after the Nazi years. Considering the texts by German non-Jewish and Jewish women of the war and postwar generation, I draw on Anne Fuchs's notion of "memory contests." According to Fuchs, the term, more accurately than *Vergangenheitsbewältigung* (coming to terms with the past), characterizes recent texts by the wartime and postwar generation that investigate and question prescriptive assumptions by previous generations, and that acknowledge fragmented and competing memories.[3] While Fuchs concentrates mainly on the generational conflict, this chapter focuses on men's and women's diverging memories of involvement in, and suffering under, the Nazi reign. I provide a close analysis of three texts: Wibke Bruhns's *Meines Vaters Land: Geschichte einer deutschen Familie* (My Father's Country: The Story of a German Family, 2004), Ute Scheub's *Das falsche Leben: Eine Vatersuche* (A False Life: In Search of My Father, 2006), and Christina von Braun's *Stille Post: Eine andere Familiengeschichte* (Whispers Down the Lane: A Different Family Story, 2007). In these texts, the autobiographical narrator considers her family history at large, examining parents' and grandparents' decisions in regard to collaboration, compliance, and resistance, as well as the entanglements of such categories. In this way, I suggest, the texts contribute to a negotiation of memory that challenges both the long-standing trope of Germans as perpetrators and the recent trope of Germans as victims.

Women's Accounts of Defeat, Occupation, and Rape

Having witnessed firsthand German war crimes and merciless acts of German perpetration, many Soviet troops turned the injustice they had suffered into acts of retaliation, raping women to strike against the very men from whom they sought vengeance. Estimates of the number of German women who were raped by the Red Army go as high as one and a half million,[4] though there are still few statistics, historical analyses, or literary representations. Helke Sanders's and Barbara Johr's book and two-part film *BeFreier und Befreite* (Liberators Take Liberties, 1991–1992) were among the first to document the mass rapes and their aftermath. In evocative and distressing interviews, women recount the sexual violence committed against them during April and May 1945 in Berlin, including the consequences of unwanted pregnancies, abortions, sexually transmitted diseases, the shame and blame placed on them by their husbands, and the lasting psychological aftereffects. While Sanders's film was lauded for publicly addressing the topic, it was also criticized for failing to provide a proper political framework in which Soviet mass rapes could be analyzed in the context of Hitler's war of extermination in Poland and Russia.[5]

More than a decade after *BeFreier und Befreite,* interest in women's wartime experiences was rekindled in the wake of the public discourse on Germans as victims. As a result, women's accounts of capitulation and its aftermath that were published in the 1950s and 1960s to little acclaim and visibility began to be republished in the new millennium with unprecedented success. The anonymous diary *Eine Frau in Berlin: Tagebuch-Aufzeichnungen vom 20 April bis 22 Juni 1945* (A Woman in Berlin, 2003), originally published in English in 1954 and in a small German edition with a Swiss publisher in 1959, became a bestseller when it was republished after the author's death in Hans Magnus Enzensberger's series *Die andere Bibliothek.*

In her unsentimental diary, the author describes in minute detail the struggle to sustain and rebuild her life in a defeated Berlin, revealing the daily challenges of finding a (safe and private) place to sleep, bartering for something to eat, restoring electricity, gas, and water, and obtaining news. The diary also bears witness to horrific, multiple rapes — and women's clever and desperate measures to endure, elude, and resist the threat. The book became the subject of heated debate when Jens Bisky, writing in the *Süddeutsche Zeitung,* questioned the authenticity of the document and identified the anonymous author as Marta Hiller.[6] While Enzensberger initially refuted these charges, the publisher has since confirmed Hiller as the writer. The authenticity of the subject matter, however, was vouchsafed after Walter Kempowski wrote a report on the matter for the Eichborn publisher in January 2004. In fall 2008, the film *Anonyma: Eine Frau in Berlin* (*A Woman in Berlin*), directed by Max Färberböck, was released.

Similar to *Eine Frau in Berlin,* Margret Boveri's *Tage des Überlebens: Berlin 1945* (Days of Survival: Berlin 1945, 2004) was republished posthumously to wide acclaim. Boveri (1900–1975), an esteemed journalist, established her career in Nazi Germany before she worked as a correspondent in Stockholm, New York, Lisbon, and Madrid, where she was able to elude severe Nazi censorship. In March 1944, however, Boveri decided to return to the devastated Berlin rather than remain safely abroad to chronicle Germany's capitulation. Her 1945 notes, written in letter form under Allied censorship, and (as Boveri later acknowledged) in the language of the perpetrators, strikingly detail bombardment, displacement, the threat of rape, and the hunt for food, heat, and shelter during the last months of the war and Russian occupation. Similar to the previous diary, however, Boveri's letters also reveal women's resourcefulness and how such resourcefulness enhanced their ability to survive and protect themselves. Though Boveri was initially hesitant to publish her letters for fear that they would be misconstrued as anti-Soviet propaganda, *Tage des Überlebens* was published in 1968 and republished in 1996. Once more, however, it was the 2004 edition that reached the largest readership.

Renate Meinhof's *Das Tagebuch der Maria Meinhof: April 1945 bis März 1946* (The Diary of Maria Meinhof: April 1945 to March 1946, 2005), finally, focuses on the terror of Russian occupation in the western Pomeranian village of Ducherow. Although Maria Meinhof initially wrote her diary to inform her six sons fighting at the front of what was happening at home, it is her granddaughter who rediscovered and decided to publish the text, complementing the accounts of starvation, violence, and rape with interviews of other surviving women witnesses.

Several anthologies and collections of interviews also delineate women's responses to the war and its aftermath, among them Gabriele Strecker's *Überleben ist nicht genug: Frauen 1945–60* (Survival Is Not Enough: Women 1945–60, 1984) and Sibylle Meyer and Eva Schulze's *Wie wir das alles geschafft haben: Alleinstehende Frauen berichten über ihr Leben nach 1945* (How We Managed All This: Single Women Describe Their Lives after 1945, 1984). More recently, Peter Süß's anthology *1945: Befreiung und Zusammenbruch: Erinnerungen aus sechs Jahrzehnten* (1945: Liberation and Collapse: Memories from Six Decades, 2005) compiles excerpts from twenty-two diverse texts by male and female witnesses and survivors (among them Hildegard Knef and Hannah Arendt) that recall the year 1945 as both a liberation and a breakdown, as an ending and a new beginning.

German-Jewish Family Novels

Different from these nonfictional accounts, German-Jewish women writers have frequently adopted the genre of fiction to delineate the Nazi persecution and its aftermath. Ilse Aichinger's esteemed novel *Die größere Hoffnung* (The Greater Hope, 1948) depicts the fate of a *Mischling* (mixed-race child) in Austria using poetic language and allegorical form (the text mentions neither Jews nor Nazis explicitly). The protagonist Ellen (with two "wrong," i.e., Jewish, grandparents) dies at the end of the novel when she is hit by a grenade; her friends (with four "wrong" grandparents) are deported to extermination camps. Thus, Aichinger considers both Jewish persecution and wartime suffering within a complex and troubling framework: even though Ellen escapes persecution, she nevertheless falls victim to the war.

Aichinger's perspective of a fifteen-year-old girl, who looks beyond the surface and is thus able to decipher the true evil of Nazism, is also espoused by the descendants of German and Austrian-Jewish Holocaust survivors. In several recent autobiographical novels, competing maternal and paternal histories cannot be united into one framework, but prompt protagonists to investigate, chronicle, and question their multifaceted family past. In Lena Kugler's *Wie viele Züge* (How Many Trains, 2001), the adolescent protagonist researches her father's past in the Ukraine, juxtaposing the fate of her Jewish father with that of her non-Jewish mother and her maternal grandfather who fought in the German *Wehrmacht*. In *So sind wir: Ein Familienroman* (That's the Way We Are: A Family Saga, 2005), Gila Lustiger traces the survival of her father, the Polish-Jewish historian Arno Lustiger, using imagination in the cases where memory fails.

In a similar vein, Viola Roggenkamp and Eva Menasse chronicle in their novels *Familienleben* (Family Life, 2004) and *Vienna* (2005) German and Austrian-Jewish family life before and after the war from the perspective of children born after. *Familienleben* takes place in the mid-1960s in Hamburg, where thirteen-year-old protagonist Fania and her older sister Vera negotiate Jewish, German, and German-Jewish identities in their relationships with parents, grandparents, and teachers. Fania's overly protective Jewish mother was saved by her gentile husband and keeps her Jewish heritage under wraps so that the children must turn to their grandmother and her Jewish friends of the "Theresienstadt coffee party" to find out more about her mother's past, her family roots, and Jewish tradition. In *Vienna,* the protagonist's identity is similarly complex: while her Jewish grandfather survived, thanks to his Catholic wife, her father escaped Nazi Germany on a *Kindertransport* to England and became a soccer player for the Austrian national team after the war. Rather than focus exclusively on survival and suffering, Roggenkamp and Menasse celebrate and continue the Jewish tradition of remembering and narration, from small detail to grand gesture. In this way, both novels affirm and portray Jewish life in Germany and Austria over multiple generations using humorous anecdotes, satirical portrayals, absurd occurrences, imaginary tales, and, above all, storytelling.

Non-Jewish German Writings after Unification

Whereas Roggenkamp and Menasse incorporate affectionate love stories in their depictions of family survival and suffering, the works of non-Jewish postwar women writers are dominated by conflict. In most of the following texts, children suffer primarily under (Nazi) fathers and grandfathers, and submissive mothers and grandmothers. Thus they suffer indirectly rather than directly from the war.

In Ulla Hahn's novel *Unscharfe Bilder* (Blurred Images, 2003), Katja Wild believes that she has recognized her father, Hans Musbach, shooting civilians in one of the photographs displayed in the Hamburg exhibition Crimes in the East. But when the daughter confronts her eighty-two-year-old father with the catalogue and demands a confession, Musbach instead speaks at length about his suffering on the Russian front. In the course of the novel, it is Katja who changes from mercilessly and self-righteously persecuting her father to accepting and even defending his elusive and far-fetched explanations. The novel concludes with a contrived reconciliation between father and daughter when Katja (and the reader) learns that the person in the photograph is not her father, and that Musbach purportedly not only refused to shoot prisoners of war but also knocked the commanding SS officer to the ground. After a brief struggle over the family's historiography, the daughter surrenders and follows not only her father's career as a teacher, but also his quiet conscience.

The protagonist in Tanja Dückers's novel *Himmelskörper* (Celestial Bodies, 2003) grows up listening to her grandparents' accounts of carpet bombings, burning cities, and their harrowing flight from Königsberg. Yet only later in life does Freia realize that her grandparents enthusiastically supported the expansionist and racist war for *Lebensraum* (living space) and retained many of their Nazi ideals after the war. As an expectant mother, Freia must reexamine and become involved in this ambiguous past to take responsibility for her child's future in Berlin. Like Günter Grass's *Im Krebsgang*, *Himmelskörper* depicts the sinking of the *Gustloff* refugee ship by Russian submarine in January 1945 with the loss of thousands of German lives. Dückers, however, charges Grass with giving only a partial view of Germans as victims, and in her novel depicts both the suffering and the collaboration of civilian refugees.

Dagmar Leupold's *Nach den Kriegen: Roman eines Lebens* (After the Wars: Novel of a Life, 2004) approaches her father Rudolf Leupold (1913–1986) by way of fiction, using his war diaries and her own research. For the narrator, Rudolf Leupold is a true opportunist: hoping to make a career in Nazi-occupied Poland, he became a Nazi follower, but turned into a liberal when it became convenient after the war. Yet even in the years of the *Wirtschaftswunder* (economic miracle) and beyond, her father became disappointed in his career as a physics and mathematics secondary school teacher and withdrew into depression, smoking incessantly, playing cards, watching television, and tormenting his family with angry fits.

Nonfictional works also fit with this theme. In Monika Jetter's *Mein Kriegsvater: Versuch einer Aussöhnung* (My War Father: Attempt at Reconciliation, 2004), the narrator suffers less from the war she experienced as a five-year-old but more when her father returns from the front in 1946 and seeks to raise the child according to (lost) Nazi ideals to be as tough as leather and as hard as steel. In *Schweigen tut weh: Eine deutsche Familiengeschichte* (Silence Hurts: A German Family Story, 2007), Alexandra Senfft investigates her mother's lifelong history of depression and alcoholism, culminating in her premature death at the age of sixty-four. Senfft's grandfather, Hanns Elard Ludin, was in charge of the deportation and killing of over 60,000 Slovakian Jews and the narrator makes the family's lack of confrontation with her grandfather's misdeeds responsible for her mother's suffering. Examining the mother–daughter relationship of her grandmother to her mother, and of her mother to herself, Senfft identifies distressing parallels and concludes that her family's long-standing tradition of silence and repression of the past contributes to the damage that is visible even in her own generation.

Wibke Bruhns's *Meines Vaters Land,* Ute Scheub's *Das falsche Leben,* and Christina von Braun's *Stille Post* also fit into this category, though all three works include both fictional and nonfictional elements. Using a first-person narrator and including family photographs (found both on the inside cover and in the texts themselves), letters, and outside sources, the texts guarantee a certain amount of authenticity and are the result of careful historical research. However, all three texts inevitably adopt an imaginative approach. Insisting that she does not know her father, Bruhns concedes: "I also don't know how the man who was my father spoke. That would be important now that I try to construe him."[7] With the term "construe" she indicates that her enterprise must remain fictional to the degree that it contains her fantasies and imaginations alongside the historical facts. Scheub's text documents her father's life by means of the extensive personal effects that the author discovered in the attic, yet she not only interweaves passages from Grass's novel on the 1969 election campaign *Aus dem Tagebuch einer Schnecke* (From the Diary of a Snail, 1972), in which her father appears as a minor character, but also keeps Grass's fictional name for her father, Manfred Augst. Von Braun similarly stretches the boundaries of fact and fiction when situating her work "somewhere in between a historical report and a novel,"[8] including not only diary entries, letters, and a wealth of other sources, but also a fictional letter exchange between the narrator and her deceased grandmother.

As indicated by her subtitle *Eine andere Familiengeschichte,* von Braun deliberately focuses on women's rather than men's history, drawing on her grandmothers' and mother's diaries. Conversely, Bruhns's and Scheub's narrators reexamine their fathers (as named in the titles), yet also reconsider the relationship to their mothers, seeking to reconstruct and give credit to women's activities and experiences. In what follows, I examine the works of Bruhns, Scheub, and von Braun as examples of narratives that contest a monolithic and one-dimensional representation of the Nazi past.

Wibke Bruhns's Meines Vaters Land:
Geschichte einer deutschen Familie (2004)

In *Meines Vaters Land,* Wibke Bruhns, born just before the war in 1938, painstakingly reconstructs her family past from the eighteenth century to the present, and in particular reexamines the life of her father, Hans Georg Klamroth (1898–1944), who was hanged in the aftermath of the failed Hitler assassination of 20 July 1944. Since she hardly knew her father — he rarely came home and apparently showed little interest in his youngest daughter — and since her mother withheld details about her husband after his death, the narrator vows to investigate retrospectively and to evaluate critically the life choices made by both parents.

Prepared for war from early childhood, Hans Georg enthusiastically welcomes the outbreak of hostilities in 1914, as does his father, Kurt Klamroth. While Kurt enlists at the first opportunity as cavalry captain in August 1914, his teenage son must complete school before he joins the Prussian army in the summer of 1916. Even though Hans Georg is successful, earning the Iron Cross Second Class on his second day in battle, the narrator more closely examines the instances that trouble the young soldier, for instance his shooting of a German infantry soldier in self-defense. This killing of a fellow countryman upsets Klamroth for decades and seems to foreshadow his subsequent wrestling with the Nazi regime. After the German defeat in the First World War, Klamroth begins a civilian career under the wing of his father, gets married, and establishes a family. However, the narrator explores the uneasiness within this pleasant picture, making tension a leitmotif throughout her text. In this way, she chronicles her parents' courtship, their 1922 wedding, and the birth of their children in 1923, 1924, 1925, 1933, and 1938, as well as her father's frequent extramarital relationships. She also reveals that her father's political beliefs were characterized by change and ambivalence: after his initial skepticism of the Nazis, Klamroth embraces the regime and joins the *Nationalsozialistische Deutsche Arbeiterpartei* (NSDAP) in 1933 and the SS in 1934, motivated by opportunism, careerism, and conviction. Swept away by their enthusiasm for the Nazis, the narrator shows her parents and grandparents paying no heed to antidemocratic and anti-Semitic measures such as the ban on other political parties, the murder of the "Sturm Abteilung" (SA, Storm Battalion) leadership, and the exclusion of Jews from public life, culminating in the open hostility and violence of the *Kristallnacht* (Night of the Broken Glass) in 1938. Indeed, as early as 1933 — two years before the Nuremberg laws — the Klamroths, following her father's expressed wish, add an "Aryan clause" to the family laws.

Yet at some point during his service in Poland, Denmark, and Russia during the Second World War, Klamroth befriends members of the resistance. The narrator is left to speculate about the specific reasons for his change of mind. Possibly, it is because he was forced to partake in the Nazi occupation of Denmark, the home of his in-laws, or that he witnessed the maltreatment of civilians in Poland, and the killing of Jews in Russia (though he never wrote about these events). While the narrator cannot determine her father's specific involvement in the resistance and the attempted assassination, she concludes that "he was a confidant, not a fellow perpetrator" (*MV* 354). Thanks to the narrator's persistent attention to the finer points and minute details, the reader begins to understand that Klamroth was both a loving and a deceitful husband, a man who ignored the suffering of Jews but who suffered himself at the hand of the Nazis; he was a collaborator with Wernher von Braun in the V-2 rocket (ballistic missile) production, which he witnessed at the Mittelbau-Dora concentration camp, and a coconspirator against Hitler.

Bruhns's *Meines Vaters Land,* however, offers more than a highly complex portrayal of Hans Georg Klamroth. Arguing that "only a woman can write such a book,"[9] the narrator embarks on a similar examination process of her mother, Else Podeus. She traces her mother's political beliefs, from her initial support for the communists to her acceptance of the Nazi regime (Podeus joined the NSDAP in 1937 and became a local leader of the Nazi Women's Organization), and illustrates her love for, and embitterment with, a husband who repeatedly betrays her, eroding all spousal trust. With the help of photographs, letters, documents, diary entries, family archives, songs, and poems, the text depicts in scrupulous detail women's challenges and responsibilities, juxtaposing men's and women's lives in Nazi Germany. While her husband is on assignment, Else gives birth to and raises five children, endures two abortions (performed by a Jewish doctor) and three miscarriages, goes shopping, supervises cooking, housecleaning, and laundering, and entertains guests on a nightly basis; the narrator comments wryly that "this woman has quite a bit on her plate!" (*MV* 259). During the war, these tasks become ever more challenging. Even though her mother still manages to organize a grand wedding feast for her daughter Ursula in 1942, the narrator suspects that alcoholism and addiction to sleeping pills are common responses to the meager circumstances. The narrator's relationship to her mother is likewise characterized by ambivalence; while she admires her savvy pluck — "Else delivers a logistical tour-de-force" (*MV* 325) — she critically evaluates Else's increasing resentment of her husband and her inability to relate to him in the critical years between 1942 and 1944.

Rather than recounting the 20 July assassination attempt and the hunt for the conspirators, the text deliberately focuses on women's experiences, providing unusual perspectives and less-known details. Hence the narrator describes her sister Ursula's difficult childbirth that occurs during an air raid. In an unsettling juxtaposition of life and death, love and betrayal, courage and cruelty, her husband Bernhard Klamroth has already been arrested by the time Ursula gives birth, and is hanged shortly thereafter. Likewise, the narrator recounts from a girl's point of view the firestorm on 8 April 1945, when Allied forces bombed Halberstadt and destroyed eighty-two percent of the old town. As a six-year-old, she experienced the bombing primarily as the destruction of her Easter eggs when a chandelier smashed into the Easter wreath on the dining room table. According to the narrator, her memory began with outrage over the wrecked eggs, a symbol of the war's unpredictable devastation that invaded her home on a Sunday afternoon, right at the dining room table, whereas the childhood memories of her town, home, and family, in particular of her father, remain buried deep in the rubble.

Ute Scheub's *Das falsche Leben: Eine Vatersuche* (2006)

In *Das falsche Leben,* Ute Scheub (born 1956), similar to Bruhns, reexamines her father's life story after his death but cannot arrive at an understanding of him. Scheub's father is known mostly for his infamous suicide: at the German Church Congress on 19 July 1969, after Günter Grass had read excerpts from his novel *Örtlich betäubt* (Local Anesthetic, 1969), her father took the microphone and launched into a convoluted, ludicrous speech that he concluded by greeting his comrades from the SS before drinking a small bottle of cyanide in front of two-thousand spectators. Grass later fictionalized the incident in his diary-novel *Aus dem Tagebuch einer Schnecke,* calling Scheub's father Manfred Augst, in explicit reference to *Angst,* the German word for fear. Scheub, thirteen at the time of her father's suicide, keeps the fictional rather than the actual name of her father when reconstructing his life thirty-five years later.

Similar to the narrator in *Meines Vaters Land* (who has no memories of her father speaking to her), the narrator in *Das falsche Leben* finds her father inaccessible during his lifetime (she can only recall two conversations with him) but is able to draw on a wealth of material aside from her memory. From her father's multiple suicide letters, notes to his children, and letters to his parents, as well as from documents and interviews with family members, she learns that both her father and grandfather were fervent Nazis. Her grandfather fought in the First World War, developed a deep hatred for the French, Jews, and communists in the Weimar Republic, voted for Adolf Hitler in 1933, and became a "housing block supervisor," denouncing anyone critical of the Nazi regime. With similar convictions but more violent zeal, her father, born in 1913, joined the NSDAP and the SA in 1931, marching with the Nazis even before they came to power. In 1933, he joined the SS, and in 1934 he began to study "racial science" in hopes of becoming a "breeding supervisor."[10] Though Augst's request for membership in the *Waffen SS* was rejected because he wore glasses, from 1939 he served in a special *Wehrmacht* battalion that protected Hermann Göring. The narrator never comes to know whether her father participated in the liquidation of the Warsaw ghetto or how many people he killed in the war.

However, it becomes clear over the course of the text that Augst is not exclusively a Nazi perpetrator. While it remains unclear whether he tried to desert from the German army in 1945, the narrator is certain that her father was deeply disturbed by his wartime experience, which explains his pacifist transformation in the 1960s. Contrasting her father's ruthless child-rearing methods with his participation at peace demonstrations and his depressive outbreaks that kept him in bed for days with his vindictiveness toward his wife who was dying of breast cancer and his son who tried to commit suicide, the narrator juxtaposes two imagined scenes: in one, her father marches in the SS in 1935, in the other, he confesses his war crimes to his family in the postwar years.

The narrator also reexamines her responses to her father. As a teenager, her intuitive impulse was to hate him along with everything connected with him, defining herself primarily in opposition to her father: "From now on, it was my life's goal to be the exact antonym of my father. As if he was the sand mold and I was its negative, the sand cake" (*DF* 34). Thirty-five years later, she also acknowledges some similarities: their love for nature and pacifism, but mainly what she calls being "locally anesthetized" (also the title of Grass's book) with respect to the past. In this way, the narrator diagnoses her symptoms — fear of fireworks, feelings of guilt and shame, nightmares, stomachaches — as responses to her father's (unacknowledged) acts of perpetration. While this self-analysis can sound a little deterministic (as, e.g., when she interprets her dreams of clogged "brown" [=Nazi] toilets as fear of becoming "soiled" [*DF* 145]), it is the result of her interaction with the children of perpetrators and bystanders, psychoanalysts and therapists, and offers a self-critical reevaluation of the 1968 student protest movement. The narrator never relinquishes her disapproval of her father's actions, yet throughout acknowledges her empathy with him. Both impulses are narrated as an inner dispute in which "the conciliator" has the last word: "Let him rest in peace, she says" (*DF* 250). In a play on words, she concludes "my father ceased to cause me Augst" (*DF* 261).

With expressions such as "wuuurghxx!" (*DF* 240), "uuuah!" (*DF* 207), "wrrrrr!" (*DF* 281), and "dirty swine" (*DF* 205), the narrator uses rather imprecise language even though she charges her father with not having the means to express himself. Yet the careful analysis of her father's (Nazi) language is one of the book's strengths. In reference to Victor Klemperer's analysis of the language of the Third Reich (*LTI: Lingua Tertii Imperii*), and several other studies (*DF* includes an extensive bibliography), the narrator traces the etymology of words such as "blood," "race," breed," and "victim" that provided her father with a grandiloquent vocabulary of power. This linguistic analysis enables her not only to decode her father's attempts to stage himself as a victim, and his suicide as a misplaced and misunderstood attempt at sacrificial death, but also to keep the victims of war and victims of National Socialism distinct from one another. In this way, she contrasts her father's perspective on the war with her own representation that recognizes the suffering of Polish, Russian, and Italian civilians, as well as the victims of the Holocaust. With a more careful attention to language, finally, the narrator is able to apply the word "reconcile" to her relationship with her father, translating it in its original meaning in Middle-High-German "to balance, to make good, to quiet" (*DF* 261).

Christina von Braun's *Stille Post:*
Eine andere Familiengeschichte (2007)

Different from the two works discussed above, von Braun's text privileges the memories of both grandmothers and her mother. The change is significant: the narrator explicitly focuses on what she calls "Chinese whispers," that is, women's memories that are easily overlooked and found in diaries rather than published memoirs or genealogies.

> I would like to retrieve some of what did not enter official historiography. There was always a specifically "female" kind of news chain that consisted of family secrets or the unutterable. Probably because women were barred from the official channels of history. In this way the subversive, the parallel intercession of news became a female specialty. (*SP* 14)

Here, rather than focusing on the leading rocket scientist of the twentieth century, her uncle Wernher von Braun (1912–1977),[11] Braun's primary interest lies in her maternal grandmother, Hildegard Margis (1887–1944), who died in a Berlin prison three months before the author was born.

After her husband died at the front in 1918, Margis was on her own, solely responsible for providing a living for her two children. Nevertheless, she quickly rose to success in the Weimar Republic. With women having just gained the right to vote, Margis founded her own company *Haushalt und Wirtschaft*, joined the administration of the *Deutsche Volks-*

partei (DVP, German People's Party) under Gustav Stresemann, became a leading member of several women's organizations, and published her own series of homemaking titles and cookbooks. When the Nazis gained control of the publishing market, however, Margis lost her job. She persuaded her son to study in England and, after 1937, mother and son helped Jewish friends to export money, jewelry, and gold from Germany. Margis also joined the communist resistance group *Freies Deutschland,* which cooperated with the *Kreisau Circle,* and apparently informed the resistance movement about the production of V-1 and V-2 rockets developed by her son-in-law's brother. After the failed attempt on Hitler's life in July 1944 and the following betrayal by Gestapo agent Ernst Rambow, Margis was arrested along with her friends. She died of heart failure at age fifty-seven in the women's prison in Berlin Barnimstraße, on 30 September 1944.

Von Braun not only reconstructs Margis's history as a victim of the Nazis but also the lives of her paternal grandparents and her parents who supported and benefited from the Nazis. Their documents — her grandmother's and her mother's diaries, as well as her grandfather's published memoirs — delineate her grandparents' expulsion from their Silesian farmhouse in 1946 and her parents' detention at the Vatican (1944–1949) following Italy's truce with the Allies. While her grandparents endured Russian and Polish occupation, cold, hunger, sickness, revenge, and the gradual loss of their assets and property, culminating in expulsion in July 1946, her parents existed in a "golden cage," not allowed to leave the Vatican but sheltered and protected from the war in Germany. The narrator's own childhood memories are shaped by a similar disproportion: she remembers the war and immediate postwar period as idyllic years in the Vatican, embodied by the sweet scent of mimosas.

Faced with the legacy of two families that made different if not opposing choices in the Nazi years (one of her uncles left Germany in 1936 and aided Jewish emigration, while another developed weapons for Nazi Germany), the narrator takes great care to represent the multifaceted and intersecting fates of victims, perpetrators, and bystanders in her family. Written in 2006 in the Cevennes Mountains in Southern France, she comments on and questions her grandmother's and mother's diary entries in fictional letters to her maternal grandmother. This framework allows her to elucidate civilian women's suffering during war and defeat while exposing continued racist and anti-Semitic thinking, as well as the deliberate ignorance of crimes committed by Germans. In other words, by evoking her maternal grandmother — "Since I occupy myself with you I find it easier to become interested in Emmy and Magnus's expulsion" (*SP* 283) — the narrator is able to recognize the suffering of Silesian refugees while pointing out the biased perspective and revisionist character of their narratives.

Stille Post is a conscious counternarrative to the memoir published by Magnus von Braun who appropriated, rewrote, and published his wife's diary in his own voice. Accusing her grandfather of deliberately silencing women's voices — "incidentally, the example of Magnus's memoirs shows pretty well how it comes about that 'women's history' time and again is made to disappear" (*SP* 244) — the narrator devotes herself to recovering women's stories, secrets, and anecdotes. In this vein, the text gives credit (as does *Meines Vaters Land*) to women's daily tasks and household chores while also including outside sources (both texts name Sebastian Haffner's *Geschichte eines Deutschen* from the year 2000, published in English in 2002 as *Defying Hitler: A Memoir*). Yet *Stille Post* avoids celebrating women's lives in an altogether soothing and affable tone. In excruciating detail the narrator lays bare her mother's unlikely love affair with a Catholic priest in the years between 1947 and 1949 as well as the fallout between her mother and grandmother and her mother's multiple suicide attempts. These "Chinese whispers" contradict her grandfather's coherent and harmonious narrative, enhancing instead the unpleasant specifics and inherent conflicts.

Conclusion

Meines Vaters Land, Das falsche Leben, and *Stille Post* complement our understanding of the diverse and complex experiences of German women before, during, and after the Second World War. The texts also elucidate men's experiences from a female perspective, hence evaluating both men's and women's choices and decisions, their achievements and lapses. Bruhns replaces her previous moralizing standpoint with an attempt to overcome the distance from her father, wrestling to understand rather than reproach him. In a similar vein, Scheub seeks to end, by way of writing, the fight with her father and his shadow even if she cannot arrive at an understanding of him. Von Braun, finally, strives to empathize with her paternal grandparents' experience of flight and expulsion while uncovering the fate of her maternal grandmother who defied the Nazis. With analytic and self-critical perspective and practice (all three authors include in their texts insights from their psychoanalysis), the texts negotiate competing memories in favor of an open-ended inquiry rather than a monolithic and one-dimensional representation of the Nazi past.

All three texts shun a representation that depicts Germans as either perpetrators or victims. Bruhns's narrator commits to a difficult balancing act that neither condemns nor glorifies Klamroth but depicts his transformation from an early Hitler supporter into a confidant in the attempted Hitler assassination of July 1944 to, finally, a victim of the Nazis in a complex, ambivalent, and decidedly unheroic fashion. Scheub's narrator, in contrast, unequivocally condemns her (Nazi) father, yet retrospectively comes to question and revise her identification as his mere opposite. Moreover, she investigates rather than glosses over the contradictions: Augst as an enthusiastic Nazi, a perpetrator, a shell-shocked victim of the war, a postwar pacifist, a Protestant, an abusive father, and finally, a man who commits suicide. Von Braun's text investigates the diverging war experiences of parents and paternal and maternal grandparents by way of juxtaposition: while the narrator's maternal grandmother worked for the German resistance until her death in a Berlin prison in 1944, her paternal grandmother supported the Nazis but suffered from defeat, occupation, and expulsion from Silesia. Focusing on the multifaceted lives of men, women, parents, and grandparents alike, and exploring the complexities within a given individual, all three texts contribute to the discourse on Germans as victims while refuting the narrow and revisionist character of such representation.

Notes

[1] Ute Scheub, *Das falsche Leben: Eine Vatersuche* (Munich: Piper, 2006), 243. Subsequent references are cited in the text using the abbreviation *DF* and page number.

[2] Ruth Kluger, *Still Alive: A Holocaust Girlhood Remembered* (New York: Feminist Press, 2001), 18.

[3] Anne Fuchs, "From *Vergangenheitsbewältigung* to Generational Memory Contests in Günter Grass, Monika Maron and Uwe Timm," *German Life and Letters* 59, no. 2 (2006): 179.

[4] Robert G. Moeller, "Germans as Victims? Thoughts on a Post-Cold War History of World War II's Legacies," *History and Memory* 17, no. 1 (2005): 151.

[5] See Eva-Elisabeth Fischer, "Vom Krieg der Männer gegen die Frauen: Helke Sanders Film *BeFreier und Befreite*," *Süddeutsche Zeitung*, 11 December 1992.

[6] Jens Bisky, "Wenn Jungen Weltgeschichte spielen, haben Mädchen stumme Rollen. Vielfach verändert, mehrfach überarbeitet, ohne Beweis der Echtheit: Das Buch der Anonyma. Wer war die Anonyma in Berlin?," *Süddeutsche Zeitung*, 3 September 2003.

[7] Wibke Bruhns, *Meines Vaters Land: Geschichte einer deutschen Familie* (Munich: Econ, 2004), 10. Subsequent references are cited in the text using the abbreviation *MV* and page number. My translation.

[8] Christina von Braun, *Stille Post: Eine andere Familiengeschichte* (Berlin: Propyläen, 2007), 22. Subsequent references are cited in the text using the abbreviation *SP* and page number. My translation.

[9] "So ein Buch kann nur eine Frau schreiben"; television interview with Wibke Bruhns, *Schümer und Dorn: Der Büchertalk*, *Südwestrundfunk*, 17 April 2004.

[10] The term is Augst's invention; he apparently suggested in a letter to the *Reichsernährungsministerium* (Ministry of Nutrition) that he might become a "Zuchtwart" (breeding supervisor) after his studies (Scheub, *Das falsche Leben*, 88–89).

[11] Wernher von Braun had a brilliant career under the Nazis and was personally promoted by Hitler to full professor at the age of thirty-one for his design of the A-4/V-2 (*Aggregat 4/Vergeltungswaffe* 2) ballistic missile during the Second World War. In May 1945, von Braun surrendered to the Americans and was recruited by the United States Army to continue his missile development in America. After the founding of NASA in 1958, he became instrumental in the space race. See Michael J. Neufeld, *Von Braun: Dreamer of Space, Engineer of War* (New York: Knopf, 2007).

8: The Place of German Wartime Suffering in Hans-Ulrich Treichel's Family Texts

David Clarke

T HE RENEWED PROMINENCE that has been given in recent German family novels to the suffering of Germans who fought in the Second World War, who were caught up as civilians in the bombing of German cities or in the expulsion of ethnic Germans from parts of Eastern and Central Europe, has, as Helmut Schmitz points out, often been linked to a sense of dissatisfaction with the political legacy of the so-called generation of 1968.[1] The work of Hans-Ulrich Treichel has also been understood in this context as a "contribution to the inner history of the post-war generations."[2] In a number of academic commentaries, Treichel's *Der Verlorene* (Lost, 1998) is read alongside Günter Grass's *Im Krebsgang* (Crabwalk, 2002), a text that explicitly highlights the alleged failure of both Grass's generation and that of 1968 to properly address the question of German wartime suffering. Stuart Taberner's detailed analysis operates within this framework and suggests, for instance, that Treichel's novel demonstrates the failure of the '68 generation to empathize with the suffering of the parental generation as normal adolescent rebellion becomes "channelled into the issue that seems most to separate the generations, that is, the Nazi past."[3] However, placed in the context of Treichel's more extensive writing based on his family's experiences at the end of the war, it is possible to observe in this author's work an examination of the failed development of personal identity. That examination takes as its starting point a familial experience of wartime suffering, yet, unlike Grass's text, is not primarily concerned with the proper representation of such suffering in the context of a national cultural memory.

Treichel was born in 1952 in a small town in Westphalia, where his parents, who had fled from Poland in 1944, ran a shop. Treichel's father, originally from the Ukraine, had been invalided out of the army during the war after the loss of his right arm in 1941, and had become a farmer in what was then the "Warthegau" between 1943 and 1944.[4] During their flight from Poland, the Treichels were stopped by Red Army soldiers and fled in fear for their lives, leaving their son, Günter, behind. They never saw their child again; after the war, they went on to have three more sons (*E*

24–25). In the late 1950s, the Treichels began to search for Günter through the Red Cross, although they never told their other children what they were doing. Günter's brothers believed that he had died during the trek from the east, and it was only shortly before their mother's death in 1991 that they found out what had actually happened.[5]

The consequences of these events for his own life have provided a rich seam of material for Treichel's writing. As well as *Der Verlorene,* a number of shorter texts contained in the volumes *Von Leib und Seele* (On Body and Soul, 1992) and *Heimatkunde oder Alles ist heiter und edel* (Local History or Everything Is Bright and Noble, 1996) also address his family's situation, and the volume of lectures *Der Entwurf des Autors* (The Author's Plan, 2000) and the novels *Menschenflug* (Human Flight, 2005) and *Anatolin* (2008) have returned to this dominant issue. In Treichel's "family texts," as I refer to them for the sake of convenience, the author has developed a number of motifs that reflect on the particular function of the parents' experience of expulsion from the east and their loss of a child in terms of the failed or problematic familial socialization of the younger sons he portrays. This failed socialization is expressed in different ways in the child's relationships to the individual parents, as the following discussion demonstrates.

The common element in Treichel's various fictionalized versions of his family's experience and of his own socialization is the notion of an insufficient recognition of the child protagonist by the parents. In the opening text of *Heimatkunde,* for example, the narrator relates an unlikely memory of his own birth, somewhat in the style of the opening of Grass's *Die Blechtrommel* (The Tin Drum, 1959). As the mother gives birth, the father interrupts to relay questions from the customers in the family's shop to his wife. Once born the child finds himself dangled upside down and staring into the eyes of the family dog, for whom he develops an immediate feeling of belonging (*H* 7–9; cf. also *A* 37). Another gaze of apparent recognition is provided by the film stars and celebrities in the magazines that the little boy is surrounded with as the son of a shopkeeper, whose faces are more familiar to the child than those of his busy, hard-working parents and who he imagines have adopted him (*H* 10). Although this short text begins by describing both parents as distant, it nevertheless concentrates mainly on the relationship with the father. The father keeps his distance, we are told (*H* 13), and the text ends with a brief account of the son's failure while helping his father to sell cigarettes at a local fête, which concludes with the father's declaration: "'You are no longer my son'" (*H* 15). Although the reasons for the parents' distance from their child are not elaborated on, apart from references to their excessive commitment to their business, this text does establish a basic pattern in relation to the figure of the father: he fails as the source of a gaze of recognition, ignoring the child, but then demands a display of filial loyalty, with the boy failing to meet these expectations. Here we see an alienating combination of nonrecognition, destabilizing the child's sense of identity, and a subsequent demand for obedience to paternal authority.

This pattern is repeated in relation to the symbolism of the photograph album in *Der Verlorene*. As Pierre Bourdieu notes, the family album exists to "supply pictures which permit recognition," securing the bonds of the family.[6] However, as Marianne Hirsch elaborates, the family album reinforces these bonds not merely by allowing the subject to recognize her belonging to the family, but also by allowing that subject to be recognized in her proper place in the hierarchy of the family unit.[7] Drawing on Lacanian psychoanalysis, Hirsch observes that the gaze in family photography is not just the subject's, who perceives her coherent identity in the mirror of the photograph, but also the gaze of the Other, or patriarchal authority, which fixes the subject within the familial frame provided by the album.

At the beginning of *Der Verlorene,* the narrator emphasizes his symbolic exclusion from the family album. In contrast to his lost brother, Arnold, whose whole body appears in a large photograph that takes pride of place at the front of the album, so that he appears to be a person of significance, the narrator is relegated to the back in photographs in which he is "only partly visible or sometimes not really visible at all" (*V* 2). For the narrator, the family album fulfills neither of the functions that Hirsch points to, which are to secure his sense of identity and to fix it within the context of the family. As in *Heimatkunde,* the narrator is not the object of the parental gaze and subsequently feels detached from the family unit. However, unlike in the earlier text, a concrete reason is identified for this overlooking of the younger child, namely, the fixation of the gaze of the parents on Arnold, who has "the leading role in the family" (*V* 9).

Ironically, it is the project of recovering Arnold that precipitates the full inclusion of the narrator in the family album. Yet the impetus for this inclusion does not come from the parents themselves, but rather from an external authority. The parents are required to make visible their biological relationship with the son they have to recover the son they have lost, with the consequence that the narrator is abruptly and violently submitted to the identifying gaze thus far denied him. As the father observes, the apparent visible resemblance of the lost child to the narrator is central to the identification of "Foundling 2307," a boy the mother is convinced is her son. The father goes on to comment that Foundling 2307 "looks as if he were carved out of your face" (*V* 41), accentuating the violence of this new paternal claim over the young narrator, and inspiring neurotic symptoms, including stomach pains and an "involuntary grin" (*V* 42). Whereas the narrator has thus far been denied an identity in the context of the family, he now suddenly has a family resemblance imposed on him that threatens whatever sense of self he has succeeded in establishing.

> I didn't want to look like anyone, particularly not my brother Arnold. The supposedly amazing likeness made me feel less and less like myself. Every look in the mirror grated on my nerves. I didn't see me, I saw Arnold, and he was getting less appealing all the time. (*V* 43)

The reinforcement of familial identity through photography is further emphasized when the narrator is finally sent to have his picture taken for the purposes of the investigation into Foundling 2307's parentage. The narrator fears that he will be included in the photographer's window display, which shows the town's inhabitants at various stages in their lives: "confirmation, boyfriend/girlfriend, bride and groom, parents with children" (*V* 49). These are again the kinds of photographs designed to reinforce the family unit's generational continuities, yet the display appears to the child as "a kind of pillory" for people destined to die (*V* 49). Also, before the narrator is photographed, he is given the short haircut of an "inmate of a camp" (*V* 50). Combined with photographing the child in such a way as to provide material to be analyzed by the anthropological institute investigating his lineage, while paradoxically denying his status as an individual (the photographs concentrate on the back of his head), this association of images (shaven heads, public humiliation, camps, pseudo-scientific anthropology) suggests a deathly patriarchal gaze, symbolically recalling the National Socialist state.

The techniques employed by anthropologist Professor Liebstedt further strengthen the link established here between the ideology of National Socialism, the making visible of identity and patriarchal authority. Liebstedt seems to have continued using spurious techniques of anthropological investigation typical under National Socialism. Yet, he also represents authority in a double sense: first, as a "baron" with roots, like the father, in Poland and thus as a man in a position of social authority in the eyes of the former peasant; second, in his official capacity as the scientist, empowered to verify or dismiss the father's claim to paternity, a claim that is therefore shown to rely on the social order that underwrites it.

This claim does not receive societal support: not only is Arnold found not to be the father's child, but the professor also absurdly throws doubt on the narrator's parentage (*V* 124–25). Under these circumstances, the father is forced to find other means of shoring up his position of authority and thus redoubles his efforts to build the family business. His sense of loss is experienced as a sense of shame, in which he accuses himself of having failed in the duties appropriate to his social position:

> A farmer from Rakowiec doesn't abandon his house of his own free will. He who abandons his house commits a sin. He who abandons his

house is ambushed by the Russians. He who abandons his house will
have his house plundered and destroyed. (*V* 99)

By fleeing from the Red Army, the father imagines that he has failed to
conform to the masculine role appropriate to his station in life, bringing
suffering on himself and his family. His answer to this predicament is to
build a new masculine persona for himself, one that makes good this failure, first by reinstating his material losses, and second by creating a public
image for himself as an affluent and hard-working male subject of the West
German economic miracle. For example, when he fails to establish parentage of Foundling 2307, he buys a more expensive car to drive his family
around in on Sundays.

At the same time, this new postwar masculine personality is experienced by the son as superficial and distant. During the examination of
the family by Professor Liebstedt's assistant, the narrator of *Der Verlorene*
is shocked to discover that the father is made of flesh and blood, rather
than of "starched shirts, a three-piece suit, and leather shoes" (*V* 70).
Similarly, in *Heimatkunde,* the narrator describes the father's morning
ritual of dressing, in which his various constraining items of clothing
transform him from an overweight, bent figure into a respectable and im-
posing businessman (*H* 18).

The fathers in Treichel's family texts are distant figures, who avoid
physical contact, are incommunicative, and hide their own degraded identity behind a hardened façade. They participate in a "culture of shame"
similar to that which Helmut Lethen observes in Germany after the First
World War. The catastrophe of the war, and the subsequent loss of face,
result not in guilt, but in a sense of failure and a psychology favoring
clearly delineated, de-complexified identity, expressed through surface ap-
pearances and self-control; a submission to the external pressures of social
expectations becomes a means of protecting a damaged inner self from
public humiliation.[8]

Clearly, the personality that the fathers in Treichel's family texts create is not suited to fostering an identification with him on the part of the
son, which in turn contributes to the son's own failure to achieve a satisfactory sense of identity. Since the sons in these texts are aware of the
father's underlying sense of shame, the failure of paternal authority also
disturbs the identity-giving mimetic process in which the father provides
an ego ideal. As Slavoj Žižek argues, the father in the bourgeois family
brings together two functions for the son: he is both the agent of integration into the social order and the ego ideal. If the father is perceived as a
failure in terms of his own relationship to the social order and its expectations, then this necessarily disturbs any such process of identification. In
addition, the more overt the father's oppressive role as disciplining inte-

grator appears, as in Treichel's family texts, the more likely it is that the son will perceive the gap between the father's demands and his own failures, the father becoming "utterly impotent and ridiculous."[9]

In *Anatolin,* the father figure, whose physical violence toward his three sons is emphasized, and who is referred to at one point as an evil and even dangerous figure (*A* 108), produces in the narrator an inability to identify with himself, particularly with his own mirror image and with photographs of himself: "I saw my enemy" (*A* 59). Here, the problem is not so much the son's inability to identify with the negatively connoted father, but more his having incorporated that negative father into his own problematic self-image so that he feels alienated from himself: "I could not be the good father to myself" (*A* 61).

Despite these difficulties, the sons in Treichel's family texts retain a strong attachment to the father and long for a successful identification with him, which becomes synonymous with full integration into the family line and thus with a more stable and rooted sense of personal identity. In the poem "Your Polish Curses," for example, the image of the photograph album is employed again to describe this longing. Here, the poet imagines the return of the dead father and an idealized scene of reconciliation:

> and if I had a photograph album,
> we would open it and cry out
> in pain and laughter: look
> how old we once were. (*G* 64)

The "I" of the poem here clearly states that he does not possess such a photograph album. He is therefore, by implication, also a figure not integrated into a family structure, literally, a man without a past. At the same time, he longs for that sense of belonging that such an album represents and also for that sense of belonging to be sanctioned by the paternal gaze, affirming a shared past, even if this shared past is not without pain.

Elsewhere in Treichel's writing, we find highly ironic episodes that highlight both the impossibility of repairing the father–son relationship and the strength of the desire for that reparation. In *Von Leib und Seele,* for example, the relationship of the narrator to his analyst Dr. Schilling, who he hopes will help him escape from the oppression of his childhood (*L* 57), is identified as symptomatic of his desire for a powerful and supportive father figure (*L* 66). Yet Dr. Schilling himself turns out to be as disturbed as his patients, and, forced to break off his analysis, the narrator feels a diffuse feeling of being lost (*L* 67). Elsewhere, Treichel describes a trip to Greece, during which he spends a number of days sitting listening to an old man on the beach. The narrator speaks no Greek himself, but feels that this talk is an act of recognition and fatherly or grandfatherly love (*E*

69). However, he soon feels increasingly trapped in this ridiculous situation and eventually walks away from the old man, whom he now perceives simply as rambling and senile (*E* 70). Here again the desire for identification with a paternal figure is frustrated by the realization of that figure's weakness.

This theme of "being spoken to" has a broader significance in relation to the fathers in Treichel's family texts. As Treichel observes in this context, he has always thought of himself as someone to whom nobody ever told anything (*E* 69). The absence of talk about the prewar past is a particular theme of *Der Entwurf des Autors,* in which the parents are presented as parents without a past (*E* 21), who never talk about their own childhoods, with the consequence that Treichel himself feels as if he has no past (*E* 21). This theme is echoed in *Menschenflug,* which relates the experiences of an author very much like Treichel himself after the publication of a novel about his parents' search for a lost child. Here, the parents' prewar past, and in particular that of the father, is only accessible by way of historical documents, since it was never discussed with the family's postwar offspring, and therefore remains incomprehensible (*M* 13–15, 51). The protagonist Stephan's engagement with these documents — for example, the homemade historical brochures produced by his distant relative Uncle Ernst — focuses on the paternal lineage and the father's birthplace in the German colony of Brychtsche. However, as the narrator notes, such information does not make Stephan feel any closer to his father (*M* 60). Here, the lack of access to the father's childhood results in a loss of the son's own sense of origin. Significantly enough, Stephan is also portrayed as a man who, although he has a strong desire to be the father of a loving family, is actually held at arm's length by his stepdaughters' daughters, who regard him as a stranger (*M* 97). He therefore appears, apart from the minimal familial contact maintained by his sisters, as a rootless, isolated figure, cut off from his family and its genealogy (*M* 81).

The search for a connection to the father's family line, which is foregrounded at the expense of the mother's family, is also a key theme of *Anatolin,* in which the narrator highlights similar patterns of noncommunication about the prewar past. Whereas in *Menschenflug* Stephan decides against a visit to his father's birthplace, the narrator of this novel undertakes such a journey, in the hope of reestablishing a familial narrative that includes the paternal grandparents he never knew. While he was still alive, the narrator's father not only failed to provide a figure of identification for his sons, but also to place himself within a genealogy that could serve as a source of identity. For example, the narrator describes rare moments of peace in the family on summer evenings when the father asked his sons to sit with him behind the house. However, instead of telling tales of Bryschtsche, his own parents, and the family's history, the father simply falls asleep (*A* 51).

For the sons of Treichel's family texts, then, it is clear that the flight from the east is a caesura in the father's life with far-reaching consequences. Primarily, by cutting the father off from his past, by humiliating him and undermining his own masculine identity, it produces patterns of behavior that favor silence, distance, violence, and the creation of a superficial personality based on the appearance of conformity and success, but which stands in the way of his son's identification with him as an ego ideal. This failed identification also means that the sons in these texts cannot see themselves as part of a patriarchal lineage stretching back beyond the father and founding their identity in a familial continuity.

Even in *Anatolin,* a novel whose narrative is framed by a trip to the titular Polish village that was the mother's birthplace, it is the father and his lineage that loom largest in the son's search for identity. However, the mother is not an insignificant figure in Treichel's fictionalization of his family history. In *Der Verlorene, Menschenflug,* and *Anatolin,* she represents a form of longing for origin that, however, does not ultimately offer a viable alternative to the failed paternal identification.

In *Der Verlorene,* the mother shows a similar disregard for the narrator, but is equally forced to pay more attention to him when he becomes important to the quest to establish the identity of Foundling 2307. Until this point, the mother withholds all physical expressions of affection from the narrator, engaging in an "endless contemplation" (*V* 3) of Arnold's photograph. The mother's gaze, denied to the narrator, not only functions to identify Arnold as part of the family, but is, as Lutz Koepnick suggests, a substitute for the physical contact the mother has lost.[10] Paradoxically, however, when the narrator is no longer denied physical affection by his mother, but rather has it imposed on him, the effect is disturbing. The narrator experiences her embraces as suffocating and, therefore, implicitly deadly. What begins as being squeezed against the mother (*V* 57) becomes a being squeezed "right into her stomach" (*V* 57), with the clear connotation of a reincorporation of the child into the maternal body, to a state before birth and thus before subjecthood, which is experienced as threatening. This link between the maternal body and the extinguishing of the subject is presaged in even more darkly comic form in *Heimatkunde,* in which the narrator takes a course on the work of Jungian cultural theorist Erich Neumann, becoming so obsessed with Neumann's book *Die Große Mutter* (The Great Mother, 1955) and its images of chasms, toothed openings in the ground, and consuming vaginas that he develops neurotic symptoms and literally has to fight for breath (*H* 59).

Neumann's theories, presented ironically here, place particular emphasis on the ambivalent character of the maternal, both as protective vessel and as destructively consuming.[11] In *Der Verlorene,* the latter image seems to dominate, yet at the same time the protective, enclosing maternal body is preserved in the image of a chamber in the old house owned by the father, into which the narrator imagines lowering himself on a rope (*V* 34), a metaphorical umbilical cord. This space, reminiscent of the enclosing maternal spaces that Gaston Bachelard associates with the childhood house,[12] provides an alternative point of origin, but does not survive the father's renovation of the property.

The engagement with the mother is more central to *Menschenflug,* not just in terms of its thematic importance, but also on a formal level, as the second of the book's three chapters, the centerpiece of the novel, is concerned precisely with this theme. Here, the protagonist Stephan, as Martina Ölke observes, replaces a journey to his father's birthplace, which he doubts will provide him with the sense of identity he seeks, with a journey to a maternal origin represented by Egypt.[13]

Stephan is sent on his way by his wife, a psychoanalyst, with a copy of Freud's *The Interpretation of Dreams,* in which she has highlighted a particular dream containing symbols of ancient Egypt. Before this point, Stephan has felt haunted by his mother, who appears to him in dreams as a destructive figure with a wide mouth full of sharp teeth (*M* 64). The interpretation that Stephan offers of the Egyptian anxiety dream described by Freud overlooks or represses certain aspects of Freud's own reading. The dream in question, which Freud remembers from his childhood, concerns his mother being carried into a room and being laid on a bed by figures with birds' heads. Stephan claims that Freud's interpretation of the dream is not included in *The Interpretation of Dreams,* even though it is, and prefers to see the figure of the sleeping mother as evidence that mothers can also be gentle creatures, who are not necessarily to be feared (*M* 107). In Freud's interpretation, however, the sexual content of the dream is foregrounded: the bird masks remind him of an illustration he was familiar with as a child from Philippson's bible, which featured bird-headed Egyptian figures. These in turn remind him of a boy called Philipp whom he knew as a child, and from whom he first heard the colloquial expression "vögeln," related to the noun "Vogel" (bird), but roughly translatable as "to screw."[14] Freud sees this dream in terms of the child's fear of losing the mother, yet also recognizes the presence of "an obscure and evidently sexual craving."[15] Stephan, however, overlooks the Oedipal content identified here, which may also be in his own dreams, in which the desire to be reincorporated into the mother's body can only find expression in repressed form through the fearful image of the cannibalistic mother.

Visits to a pyramid and the Sphinx further reflect Stephan's ambivalent relationship with the maternal. Once again, Treichel's protagonist seeks to enter a mysterious, enclosing space, this time in the form of a pyramid, yet no secret reveals itself (*M* 118): the pyramid, when he descends into its center, is empty (*M* 119). The Sphinx, a figure from the legend of Oedipus (*M* 121), also proves to be a disappointment, as the statue, which Stephan insists on gendering as a woman (*M* 120), seems dilapidated and harmless. Nevertheless, Stephan imagines that he is in danger of being eaten after all (*M* 121) and notes that the Sphinx's name comes from the verb "sphingo" (to strangle), recalling the suffocating presence of the maternal figures already discussed.

This Oedipal imagery continues when Stephan is rescued by Mercedes, a professor of archaeology, after an abortive attempt to cycle into the masculine Valley of the Kings, a journey that he abandons, just as he has abandoned that to his father's village. Stephan falls asleep and has a frightening dream of his mother with the body of a young girl in an Egyptian burial chamber: he immediately realizes that he is on dangerous ground in relation to the dream's sexual imagery of enclosed spaces and the opening of locked doors (*M* 141).

The chapter then concludes with Stephan sleeping with Mercedes. Although she is not too distant in age from him, the text again implies an Oedipal dimension, as Stephan imagines himself much younger than his own fifty years (*M* 148) and feels initially disturbed at going to bed with a sixty-year-old woman (*M* 147). Then, when Mercedes leaves, he experiences terrible feelings of abandonment (*M* 149), which echo his sense of having been neglected by his mother, whom he recalls as a stranger (*M* 68).

In Treichel's family texts, the maternal is clearly not a reassuring refuge from the failed project of establishing identity through the paternal identification. In some instances, the lost maternal origin merely proves illusory; in some cases the longing for a reunion with the mother is placed under an Oedipal taboo, and at other times that reunion endangers the subject by offering only a retreat into a presubjective realm, represented by the suffocating or cannibalistic mother. This latter aspect is also suggested in *Anatolin,* where the mother's birthplace proves just as disappointing as the father's village of Brychtsche. The narrator would like to have found paradise (*A* 187), he tells the reader as he surveys the village of Anatolin, yet the closest he can get to such a paradise is to follow a young Adam and Eve into the forest, where he lies "in the mother earth" (*A* 188) and falls asleep, dreaming himself back to the moment before his own conception (*A* 188). Here, he surrenders to that masochistic "regression" that Freud describes in his speculations on the death drive — an impulse to return to a nirvana before the organism came into being.[16]

I began this chapter by referring to those analyses of Treichel's *Der Verlorene* that relate this text to the generational conflict that emerged in West Germany in the late 1960s and 1970s. Broadly speaking, generational narratives are concerned with two axes: first, the succession of generations and their relationship to each other, and second, the establishment of relationships of solidarity between cogenerationalists, which exist in tension with intergenerational family loyalties. Cogenerationalists are markedly absent from Treichel's family texts, and particularly from *Der Verlorene*. Outside of the nuclear family, the narrator presents himself as an isolated child, sitting alone in the house on Sundays once he is finally released from the torture of family outings. While one might expect new solidarities with cogenerationalists to rush in to fill this void, particularly in the context of the radicalization of West Berlin students like Treichel himself in the wake of 1968, the '68 generation does not offer the sons of Treichel's family texts an alternative to their failed identity formation. His protagonists are typically isolated individuals, without friends or close social ties (e.g., *M* 157–58), and with political convictions that do not lead to collective action or identity: the narrator of *Anatolin*, for example, who was once a left-wing radical student, does not develop any stable ties to others with similar beliefs (*A* 56); rather than communal living and political engagement, he opts for a rented room in a flat owned by a Charlottenburg widow and feels lonelier than ever before in his life (A 56).

It is in the context of failed identification both with the father and with their cogenerationalists that the sons' longing to be reunited with the lost brother in Treichel's family texts can be best understood. The return of the brother represents the possibility of filling that "empty center" (*A* 153), which leaves the remaining brother bereft of a clear identity. The supposed brother in *Der Verlorene, Menschenflug,* and *Anatolin* bears a close physical resemblance to the putative younger brother. In *Der Verlorene,* this is first seen as a threat, yet the narrator's realization that Hermann, as Foundling 2307 becomes known, is a slightly older mirror image of himself (*V* 144) eventually produces a desire to be reunited with him, even though the mother appears to reject him (*V* 145). The use of the mirror metaphor suggests the possibility of an alternative identification with the older brother and of a more stable identity than that derived from parental sources.

In *Menschenflug* the unsuccessful attempt to return to a maternal origin in the central second chapter of the novel is followed by a final third chapter devoted to the protagonist's search for the lost brother. Unfortunately, a confrontation with the real Hermann reveals him to be an unpleasant old man (*M* 217), who offers no possible identification. In *Anatolin,* the unsuccessful search for a point of origin associated with the mother and the failure of the attempt to recover the brother are almost simultaneous. When the narrator wakes from his sleep in the woods, he immediately telephones to discover that a DNA test with his supposed brother is negative (*M* 189), so that the final path to the establishment of a satisfactory, rooted identity is closed off by the end of the novel.

The failure of familial strategies of identification that Treichel's family texts document is certainly not the end point of this search for identity. Indeed, the process of writing itself is discussed at length in Treichel's work as a substitute for that sense of identity that the family fails to provide.[17] However, in conclusion, the question of the relationship of Treichel's family texts to contemporary discourses on German victimhood, which are the subject of this volume, needs to be considered.

Although Treichel's family texts deal with the long-term effects of German suffering during the Second World War, those effects are individualized to a great extent, both for those who experienced them and their children. The parents are not presented as typical in their refusal to talk about the past: indeed, other expellees, for instance, Uncle Ernst or the organization of the expellee Germans from his father's homeland, whose annual congress Stephan visits in *Menschenflug* (*M* 221–29), maintain their sense of identity and connection with their past by discussing, documenting, and commemorating it. In *Anatolin*, the narrator states that he could have found other expellees from his father's birthplace, like their neighbor Ferdinand Popke, who would have been able to talk about the past more openly (*A* 126).

The individualization of the situation that Treichel's family texts describe also extends to the son's reaction to his parents' loss and their subsequent behavior toward him. In *Der Verlorene*, there are no other children in the family to share his sense of being without a satisfactory identity, and in *Menschenflug* and *Anatolin*, in which the son has, respectively, two sisters and two brothers, these figures either do not appear (as in *Anatolin*) or (in *Menschenflug*) seem largely indifferent to talk of the past (e.g., *M* 54). In this way, just as the sons at the center of Treichel's family texts seem to have little sense of connection with their historical generation, they also seem to be untypical of their biological generation within their own family.

Although Treichel's family texts take as their starting point a traumatic event in the life of a family that is the product of circumstances that belong to a collective or national history, they nevertheless repeatedly remind us of that necessary gap that Lutz Niethammer observes between a constructed collective memory and individual experience.[18] In this sense, if the recent reengagement with German wartime suffering in contemporary German literature can be regarded as part of an attempt to redefine the German national community around a sense of a shared inheritance of victimhood, rather than in terms of collective perpetration,[19] then Treichel's texts would appear to work against such a move, since they do not construct any collective experience at all, only an individual reaction that finally fails to achieve any identification, be it familial, generational, or national.

However, this inability to achieve a sense of collective identity is also potentially problematic in the context of the wartime experience of ordinary Germans. As Silke Horstkotte observes, by reducing the Second World War to the mere backdrop for a familial drama, which is presented as essentially private and unique, family texts run the risk of writing other victims of National Socialism out of the story, because their suffering does not have any function in the family drama portrayed.[20] Treichel's family texts have only recently acknowledged the context of the father's settling as a farmer in German-occupied Poland in the 1940s on what was probably land expropriated from Poles (*A* 122–24). Yet this fact is immediately relativized by the observation that the father can only have taken up this position some time after the expulsion of the original occupants, and therefore cannot be the object of his son's fantasies of him as a perpetrator (*A* 124). This obviously leaves open the question of a guilt of complicity as opposed to one of direct involvement in these crimes, even though Treichel shows how the father continues to hold racist views about Poles and Russians after the war, a fact that suggests the possibility of such complicity (e.g., *V* 88). Finally, however, Treichel's family texts pay scant attention to how "the victimhood of the expellees is *qualified*," as Bill Niven puts it,[21] because the moral assessment of their suffering is not shown as an issue relevant to the son's familial socialization and, therefore, to his own problematic identity. In this way it can be argued that Treichel's highly individualized approach to historical events stands in the way of a differentiated engagement with his parents' experiences in their historical context.

Notes

[1] Helmut Schmitz, "Representations of the Nazi Past II: German Wartime Suffering," in *Contemporary German Fiction: Writing in the Berlin Republic*, ed. Stuart Taberner (Cambridge: CUP, 2007), 144–45.

[2] Clemens Kammler and Matthias Krallmann, "'Ich wollte niemandem ähnlich sein . . .': Hans-Ulrich Treichel's Erzählung *Der Verlorene* als Beitrag zur inneren Geschichtsschreibung der Nachkriegsgeneration," *Deutschunterricht* 51, no. 4 (1999): 99–102.

[3] Stuart Taberner, "Hans-Ulrich Treichel's *Der Verlorene* and the Problem of German Wartime Suffering," *Modern Language Review* 97, no. 1 (2002): 133. See also Stephan Braese, "Tote zahlen keine Steuern: Flucht und Vertreibung in Günter Grass' *Im Krebsgang* und Hans-Ulrich Treichels *Der Verlorene*," *Gegenwartsliteratur* 2 (2003): 171–96; Martina Ölke, "'Flucht und Vertreibung' in Hans-Ulrich-Treichels *Der Verlorene* und *Menschenflug* und in Günter Grass' *Im Krebsgang*," *Seminar* 43, no. 2 (2007): 115–33. All of these texts draw different conclusions from the comparison, with Ölke in particular questioning the notion that Treichel's texts seek to represent the '68 generation.

[4] Hans-Ulrich Treichel, *Anatolin* (Frankfurt am Main: Suhrkamp, 2008), 117; 122–24. Subsequent references to this work are cited in the text using the abbreviation *A* and page number. Hans-Ulrich Treichel, *Der Entwurf des Autors: Frankfurter Poetikvorlesungen* (Frankfurt am Main: Suhrkamp, 2000), *Heimatkunde oder Alles ist heiter und edel* (Frankfurt am Main: Suhrkamp Taschenbuch, 2000), *Leib und Seele: Berichte* (Frankfurt am Main: Suhrkamp, 1998), *Menschenflug* (Frankfurt am Main: Suhrkamp, 2005). Page references are cited in the text preceded by the letters *E, H, L,* and *M,* respectively. Quotations from *Der Verlorene* are taken from the published English translation, *Lost,* trans. Carol Brown Janeway (London: Picador, 1999) and are referred to by the abbreviation *V* and page number. All other translations are my own.

[5] Rhys W. Willams, "'Mein Unbewusstes kannte . . . den Fall der Mauer und die deutsche Wiedervereinigung nicht": The Writer Hans-Ulrich Treichel," *German Life and Letters* 52, no. 2 (2002): 210.

[6] Pierre Bourdieu, *Photography: A Middle-brow Art,* trans. Shaun Whiteside (Cambridge: Polity, 1990), 31–32.

[7] Marianne Hirsch, *Family Frames: Photography, Narrative, and Postmemory* (Cambridge, MA: Harvard UP, 1997), 47.

[8] Helmut Lethen, *Verhaltenslehren der Kälte: Lebensversuche zwischen den Kriegen* (Frankfurt am Main: Suhrkamp, 1994), 33 and 53. See also my "Guilt and Shame in Hans-Ulrich Treichel's *Der Verlorene,"* in *Hans-Ulrich Treichel,* ed. David Basker (Cardiff, UK: U of Wales P, 2004), 61–78.

[9] Slavoj Žižek, *The Ticklish Subject: The Absent Centre of Political Ontology* (London: Verso, 2000), 316.

[10] Lutz Koepnick, "Photographs and Memories," *South Central Review* 21, no. 1 (Spring 2004): 103.

[11] Erich Neumann, *Die Große Mutter: Die weiblichen Gestaltungen des Unbewussten* (Düsseldorf: Patmos, 2003), 148.

[12] Gaston Bachelard, *The Poetics of Space,* trans. Maria Jolas (Boston: Beacon Press, 1994), 45–46.

[13] Ölke, "'Flucht und Vertreibung,'" 129.

[14] Sigmund Freud, *The Interpretation of Dreams,* in *The Complete Psychological Works of Sigmund Freud,* vols. 4–5 (London: Hogarth Press, 1953), 5:583.

[15] Ibid., 5:584.

[16] Sigmund Freud, *Beyond the Pleasure Principle,* in *The Complete Psychological Works of Sigmund Freud,* vol. 18 (London: Hogarth Press, 1953), 18:54–57.

[17] This issue is considered particularly in *Der Entwurf des Autors* and *Anatolin.* For an analysis of *Menschenflug* that addresses this theme, see Ölke "'Flucht und Vertreibung,'" 126–31.

[18] Lutz Niethammer, *Kollektive Identität: Heimliche Quellen einer unheimlichen Konjunktur* (Reinbek bei Hamburg: Rowohlt, 2000), 365.

[19] See Helmut Schmitz, "The Birth of the Collective from the Spirit of Empathy: From the 'Historians' Dispute' to German Suffering," in *Germans as Victims,* ed. Bill Niven (Basingstoke, UK: Palgrave Macmillan, 2006), 93–108.

[20] Silke Horstkotte, "'Ich bin ins Reich der Toten geraten': Stephan Wackwitz and the New German Family Novel," in *New German Literature: Life-Writing and Dialogue with the Arts,* ed. Julian Preece, Frank Finlay, and Ruth J. Owen (Oxford: Peter Lang, 2007), 325–42.

[21] Bill Niven, "Implicit Equations in Constructions of German Suffering," in *A Nation of Victims? Representations of German Wartime Suffering from 1945 to the Present,* ed. Helmut Schmitz (Amsterdam: Rodopi, 2007), 105–23, here 108. Emphasis in original.

9: "Why only now?": The Representation of German Wartime Suffering as a "Memory Taboo" in Günter Grass's Novella *Im Krebsgang*

Katharina Hall

THE PUBLICATION OF Günter Grass's novella *Im Krebsgang* (Crabwalk) in 2002 signaled the author's return, after thirty-three years, to the subject that had dominated his first four literary works from *Die Blechtrommel* (The Tin Drum, 1959), to *örtlich betäubt* (Local Anaesthetic, 1969): the German wartime past. However, whereas Grass's early works depict everyday life under National Socialism and the involvement of "ordinary" Germans in the regime, *Im Krebsgang* focuses on the sinking of the former *Kraft durch Freude* (Strength through Joy) ship the *Wilhelm Gustloff* on 30 January 1945, and, by extension, on the issue of German wartime suffering. The critic Günter Franzen of the newspaper *Die Zeit* was not alone in expressing his amazement that Grass, of all people, should address this subject in literary form: for Grass, a writer with impeccable left-wing intellectual credentials, to write on a subject often linked to right-wing discourses of German victimhood "was a surprise bordering on a miracle."[1]

In this chapter, I explore Grass's reasons for choosing to tell the story of the *Gustloff* in *Im Krebsgang,* interrogating his assertion that the memory of German wartime suffering was taboo in the postwar era, before going on to examine the wider representation of German wartime experience in the work. I argue that, while Grass's emphasis on German suffering as a "memory taboo" is misguided, other aspects of *Im Krebsgang*'s treatment of the topic remain nuanced and thought-provoking. At the same time, the chapter illustrates how the intersections between *Im Krebsgang* and Grass's first four works — *Die Blechtrommel, Katz und Maus* (Cat and Mouse, 1961), *Hundejahre* (Dog Years, 1963), and *örtlich betäubt* — encourage the reader to view them collectively as one overarching literary project, a "Danzig Quintet," which, by means of a series of "inferential walks,"[2] evinces a full awareness of the complexities of remembering the National Socialist past.

In many senses, *Im Krebsgang* is a case of unfinished business for Grass. This is indicated by Grass's alter ego within the text, a writer known as "the old man," who commissions a journalist, Paul Pokriefke, to write an account of the *Gustloff* tragedy:

> Properly speaking, any strand of the plot having to do with Danzig and its environs should be his concern. [. . .] Soon after the publication of that mighty tome, *Dog Years,* this material [about the *Gustloff*] had been dumped at his feet. He — who else? — should have been the one to dig through it, layer by layer. For there had been no shortage of references to the fate of the Pokriefkes, chief among them Tulla. [. . .] Unfortunately, he said, he hadn't been able to pull it off. A regrettable omission, or, to be quite frank, a failure on his part. But he wasn't trying to make excuses, only to admit that around the mid-sixties he'd had it with the past, that the voracious present with its incessant nownownow had kept him from producing the mere two hundred pages . . . [n]ow it was too late for him.[3]

Here the borders between reality and fiction are deliberately blurred: the old man's reference to *Hundejahre* invites the reader to identify him as Grass, while also implying that the Tulla of that novel was not fictional, but a real-life survivor of the *Gustloff*. This impression is reinforced when her son, the narrator Paul, is figured as "not invented, rather discovered, after a long search, on the list of survivors, like a piece of lost property" (80). This Chinese puzzle of a narrative allows Grass, the actual author, to articulate his regrets about not having fully explored the difficult experiences of Germans at the end of the war. The old man notes that, although he had the opportunity to write about the *Gustloff* after the publication of *Hundejahre,* his interest in contemporary issues prevented him from doing so, something he now views as a moral failure.

The reference to the city of Danzig also makes it clear that the old man regards *Im Krebsgang* as an important extension of the "Danzig" project that preoccupied him so greatly in his early writing career. This is reinforced within the narrative through Tulla's cantankerous presence, which allows Grass to link the postwar Germany of *Im Krebsgang* to the pre-1945 Danzig described in *Die Blechtrommel, Katz und Maus,* and *Hundejahre,* and to provide a rich backstory for the Pokriefke family over four generations. Numerous references to other characters from Grass's first four prose works underscore these historical and intertextual connections. In particular, Tulla's identification of Joachim Mahlke (*Katz und Maus*), Harry Liebenau, Walter Matern (*Hundejahre*), and Störtebeker (*Hundejahre* and *örtlich betäubt*) as the possible fathers of her son is used to figure Paul as the literal and literary offspring of earlier characters and texts. There are also striking thematic and structural continuities, most notably a common focus on the question of how to remember the wartime past in the postwar present, and the presence of first-person narrators and characters whose principal resource is memory. It is the cumulative impact of these shared features that invite the reader to view the texts as a "Danzig Quintet," an ambitious literary project that explores the evolution of Germany's relation to its Nazi past over a period of more than four decades.

The key respect in which *Im Krebsgang* differs from the other works of the quintet is in the kind of wartime memory the latter chooses to explore. While *Die Blechtrommel, Katz und Maus, Hundejahre,* and (to a lesser degree) *örtlich betäubt* all focus on the memory of German involvement in National Socialism, *Im Krebsgang* foregrounds the memory of German wartime suffering, and in particular, the memory of the nine thousand Germans who died when the *Gustloff* was torpedoed by a Soviet submarine. At first glance, and as Franzen's response in *Die Zeit* indicates, this emphasis on German suffering appeared to signal a major shift for the author, one that, in the crudest of terms, moved from a focus on the "German as perpetrator" to that of the "German as victim." However, Grass's own statements on the role of the writer suggest that his progression from the exploration of German guilt to that of German suffering had its own internal logic. In a 2000 talk to fellow PEN (International Writers Association) members in Moscow entitled "Nie wieder schweigen" (No more silence), Grass spoke, with obvious reference to Walter Benjamin's work, of admiring writers "who have brushed the course of history against the grain." For Grass, the writer's key role is to write against the dominant historical narrative, to provide a "counter-voice," "usually at odds with official historical discourses." The resulting literature "does not look away, it does not forget, it breaks the silence."[4] More specifically, Grass appeared to view his own authorial identity as synonymous with the act of writing against dominant historical memory, and in particular, of bringing memories to light that were deliberately repressed or considered taboo.

When commenting on his first three works, Grass has observed that his aim was to counter the amnesia of the 1950s and 1960s about the Nazi past, and to throw a spotlight on the crimes of the Holocaust.[5] In contrast, *Im Krebsgang* sought to dismantle the taboo that the author felt surrounded the memory of *Vertreibung,* the forced migration or expulsion of Germans from the eastern provinces at the end of the war.[6] "Subjects such as the flight and explusion of over ten million people from the lost provinces of the east have been extensively repressed," he argued, as had the memory of the sinking of the *Gustloff.*[7] Such statements suggest that *Im Krebsgang* can be viewed as a logical continuation of the literary project Grass had begun with *Die Blechtrommel,* not in spite of, but precisely because of, its focus on the memory of German wartime suffering. In his talk "Ich erinnere mich" (I remember) at the Future of Memory conference in Vilnius in 2000, Grass commented how he found it "strange and disturbing, how late and, even now, how hesitantly the suffering inflicted on Germans during the war is remembered."[8] By taking on this contemporary memory taboo, Grass replaced his earlier engagement with the marginalized memory of German wrongdoing in the Nazi era with the apparently marginalized memory of German wartime suffering. Grass's previous "Danzig" works are thereby linked to *Im Krebsgang* through the act of challenging prevailing discourses of memory, and Grass, like Tulla, is to be admired as the revealer of uncomfortable truths, as someone who dares to "say things other people don't wish to hear" (39), whether in relation to the horrors of concentration camps or to the theme of German wartime suffering.

The taboo surrounding the *Gustloff* and, by extension, the memory of German suffering, is a central theme within the novella. Its first words, "Why only now?" (1), immediately establish the idea that the memory of the *Gustloff* has been taboo, and several characters identify the contexts in which the articulation of this memory has been problematic. Tulla, speaking as a survivor of the ship who then settled in the German Democratic Republic (GDR), is bitter, "because for years and years 'you couldn't bring up the *Yustloff*. Over here in the East we sure as hell couldn't. And when you in the West talked about the past, it was always only about other bad stuff, like Auschwitz and such'" (50). Tulla implicitly attributes East Germany's silence on the sinking of the *Gustloff* to the fact that it was torpedoed by an enemy that is now its postwar ally, the USSR. By contrast, West Germany's engagement with the past focused "only" on the memory of the Holocaust. The sinking's status as a memory taboo is confirmed by her son Paul, who, it should be noted, does not often agree with his mother: "No one wanted to hear the story, not here in the West, and certainly not in the East. For decades the *Gustloff* and its awful fate were taboo, on a pan-German basis, so to speak" (29). This point of view is also underscored by the old man, who cites the urgent need to focus on issues of guilt in relation to the Holocaust as the reason for his generation's failure to address not just the sinking of the *Gustloff*, but the whole issue of German suffering at the end of the war (103).

What emerges in *Im Krebsgang*, then, is a narrative consensus that the memory and articulation of German wartime suffering in the postwar era was taboo (whether imposed by the individual, cultural norms, or the state). Grass has drawn considerable fire for holding this position, as the following comments from the historian Robert G. Moeller make clear:

When Germany's greatest living writer speaks, many people will listen. Nobel Prize–winning authors are, however, not necessarily good historians. The history that Grass gets wrong in *Im Krebsgang* is not the sinking of the *Gustloff* or the flight of the Germans from eastern Europe at the end of the Second World War. Rather, what he presents only incompletely is the history of how Germans have remembered and represented those events since 1945. In the 1950s, stories of German loss and suffering were central to the politics of memory in the Federal Republic, and even in the 1960s and 1970s, as many West Germans focused more on the victims of Germans than on German victims, they never entirely faded from view. In the 1980s, tales of the expulsion that dominated the "memory landscape" of the immediate post-war years once again defined a central point of reference in the public remembrance of the war's end.[9]

To a large extent, Moeller's criticism is justified. While the Soviet involvement in the expulsion of Germans from the east would have made it politically difficult for a GDR citizen like Tulla to talk of German wartime suffering, a much more complex picture emerges in the case of West Germany, where the old man and Paul were based, and the reunified Germany in which all the characters now live.

From the founding of West Germany, the subject of expulsion dominated the political agenda. Adenauer's First Government Policy Statement of 1949 refers sympathetically to the suffering of German expellees; the same year saw the formation of the Federal Ministry for Expellees, Refugees, and War-Wounded. By 1957, the 1952 *Lastenausgleichsgesetz* (Law for the Distribution of Burdens) had channeled more than seventeen million marks specifically to expellees.[10] These payments were not simply in response to the enormous tasks of resettlement and integration, but also due to the political pressure that the *Bund der Heimatvertriebenen und Entrechteten* (Union of Expellees and Dispossessed) and the *Zentralverband vertriebener Deutscher* (Central Association of German Expellees) were able to exert. Moeller argues that these measures "stressed that Germany was a nation of victims, an imagined community defined by the experience of loss and displacement during the Second World War."[11]

Between the 1950s and the present day at least two hundred and fifty studies have been published in Germany on the subject of the forced migration by mainstream publishers including Beck, DTV (Deutscher Taschenbuch Verlag), Fischer, Oldenbourg, Peter Lang, and Ullstein.[12] Collectively, these counter the idea that the discussion of German wartime suffering was taboo in the postwar era, or even, as is often suggested, that the memory of the expulsion could be articulated in the private, but not the public realm. Of particular note is the enormous documentation project initiated by the Federal Ministry for Expellees in 1951: the five volumes it produced between 1954 and 1961 detailed all aspects of the forced migration, and included over seven hundred refugee testimonies.[13] These volumes have become seminal works on the subject, and were re-published in 1984, 1992, and 2004.[14] Since the 1980s more books have been published on the subject than ever before, partly due to the sea change of German reunification, and partly due to the 40th, 50th and 60th anniversaries of the end of the war, which have refocused attention on the past.

Grass's claim that his generation failed to write about the issue of German wartime suffering also seems exaggerated. Louis Helbig, in his study *Der ungeheure Verlust: Flucht und Vertreibung in der deutsch-sprachigen Belletristik der Nachkriegszeit* (The Enormous Loss: Flight and Expulsion in German Literature of the Postwar Era), identifies thirty "novels of expulsion," many of which are written by well-known authors such as Ernst Wiechert, Siegfried Lenz, and Christa Wolf.[15] The sugges-tion in *Im Krebsgang* that the subject was ignored by writers such as Grass is all the more ironic given the numerous times he mentions it in his own works. A section of Helbig's study is entitled "Günter Grass: Oskar as the Tin-drummer of the Expulsion" and argues that Oskar's account of the chaotic journey westward from Danzig in 1945 captures "one of the typ-ical experiences that millions went through."[16] The *Blechtrommel* chapter "Disinfectant" also features a harrowing account by a doctor of how four thousand East Prussian children died in 1945 because they were unable to cross the River Vistula to safety. References to the experience of forced migration are also made in *Hundejahre, Die Rättin* (The Rat, 1986, in which Tulla is rumored to have perished on the *Gustloff*), and *Mein Jahr-hundert* (My Century, 1999), where the ship is seen by a reporter three days before its sinking. The aftereffects of these events are also depicted in Grass's 1992 novel *Unkenrufe* (Call of the Toad), in which the two main protagonists, one German and one Polish, set up a funeral collective to al-low the burial of expellees in Gdańsk/Danzig, a belated chance of return to the lost homeland.

One intriguing possibility is that Grass's insistence on the taboo of German wartime suffering masks a concern with a subtly different set of taboos: that of talking about German suffering without also mentioning the suffering of the victims of the Holocaust, and conversely, that of com-peting against the victims of the Holocaust within a hierarchy of suffering (a so-called *Opferkonkurrenz,* or competition among victim groups). Grass alludes to the latter taboo in his Vilnius speech: "One wrong superseded the other. It was forbidden to compare the one with the other."[17] When viewing Grass's earlier works through the prism of this second pair of ta-boos, it is interesting to note the very balanced approach Grass takes to the issue of suffering. In *Die Blechtrommel,* for example, the doctor's report of the tragic fate of the Prussian children is followed by Mariusz Fajngold's account of his horrific experiences in Treblinka, where fourteen members of his immediate family are killed. Grass is thus very careful to place German wartime suffering in the larger context of National Socialism and the Holocaust within the novel.

In *Im Krebsgang*, the narrative is undoubtedly weighted toward the issue of German suffering. Of all of Grass's literary works, it offers the most extended treatment of that theme, with chapter 6, in particular, depicting the horrors of the sinking in detail. The danger, of course, is that in doing so Grass opens himself up to the accusation of endorsing the transformation of perpetrators into victims, a cultural trend identified by critics such as Omer Bartov in relation to the popularity of works such as Bernhard Schlink's *Der Vorleser* (The Reader, 1995).[18] However, as I argue in the rest of this chapter, this would be to do *Im Krebsgang* a disservice, for the text is considerably more complex than such a judgment implies. While perhaps naïve in presenting German wartime suffering as a postwar memory taboo, the novella's examination of German war-memories at the end of the twentieth century also challenges a one-dimensional view of Germans as victims, and works, through repeated references back to the earlier parts of the quintet, to evoke as full a picture as possible of Germany's wartime past.

Paul Pokriefke, the last of the quintet's narrators, combines aspects of each of his six predecessors, while also taking the role in new directions. Like Oskar, Pilenz, Brauxel, Harry, Matern, and Starusch/Störtebeker before him, Paul looks back over the past from a point in the postwar present, this time the Germany following reunification. Like them he explores how his own life has been shaped by larger historical events: his birthday on 30 January is not only the day of the sinking, but also the birthday of Wilhelm Gustloff, the Nazi after whom the ship was named, and the date that Hitler took power in 1933. In particular, he is preoccupied by two disturbing events: first, the catastrophe of the *Gustloff*, and second, how distorted perceptions of National Socialism and the sinking led his teenage son Konny to shoot a Jewish boy, supposedly to avenge the murder of Wilhelm Gustloff by the Jewish student David Frankfurter in 1936. Paul investigates the causes of each event by zigzagging between different individual and historical strands within his narrative — the "crabwalk" of the title. These include Wilhelm Gustloff's assassination, the history of the *Gustloff* as a *Kraft durch Freude* liner, its sinking in 1945, and the impact of the latter on his own family over three generations.

Paul's status as a member of the "second generation" sets him apart from the other narrators of the quintet. Although technically present at the sinking of the *Gustloff*, he was too young to remember what took place, and has to rely on the memories of others to access the lived experience of that event. His own memories are thus not the main ones featured in the book: these belong to his mother Tulla, who was seventeen at the time of the sinking and remembers that night in vivid detail. Paul's role at times is therefore that of a secondary narrator, who is one step removed from the immediacy of the first-person account. This allows him to adopt the more objective approach of the writer of a "report" (129), which encourages a critically aware relation to different accounts of the past. This increased objectivity is of particular significance in the context of Tulla and Konny's distortions of German history, and is used by Grass to highlight the disjunctions between different recollections and representations of the past.

As in *Die Blechtrommel* and *Hundejahre*, the notion of memory as testimony is foregrounded in *Im Krebsgang*, here as a means of bearing witness to the German suffering on board the *Gustloff*. Tulla's moving first-hand descriptions of that night graphically communicate the horrors of the sinking:

> Everything started to slither. A thing like that you never forget. It never leaves you. It's not just in my dreams, that cry that spread over the water at the end there. And all them little children among the ice floes. . . . (57–58)

Tulla's traumatized state is undeniable: she loses both her parents in the sinking, witnesses the horror of thousands, many of them children, dying in the icy waters of the Baltic, while also giving birth to her son in extremely perilous conditions. The link between Tulla's memories and the trauma that she suffers is emphasized through the symbol of her hair, which turns white on the night of the sinking.

At the same time, *Im Krebsgang* explores how Tulla's memories of the sinking transmit that trauma from one generation to the next — from Tulla to her son Paul, and then to her grandson Konny. Paul is keenly aware of his mother's expectation, first articulated when he was a little boy, that he bear witness to the story of the *Gustloff* on her behalf: "'You've got to write about it. That much you owe us, seeing as how you were one of the lucky ones and survived. Someday I'll tell you the whole story, exactly what happened, and you'll write it all down'" (28). Helmut Schmitz convincingly draws on the work of Helm Stierlin to show how Paul is "overburdened" with his mother's memories and expectations, rebelling against her constant pressure to the extent that he denies the impact of the sinking on his own identity.[19] As a result, Tulla transfers her attentions to Konny, whom she starts seeing regularly following reunification when he is ten.

Konny proves much more receptive than Paul to Tulla's call to bear witness. After she buys him a computer as a fifteen-year-old, he sets up an Internet site devoted to the *Gustloff*, on which it becomes clear how many of her extreme views have shaped and inflamed his own. Over her lifetime

Tulla has acquired anti-Semitic views (under the Nazis), a hatred of Russians (from her experiences on the *Gustloff* at the end of the war), and an unwavering love of Stalin (from her time in the GDR) — this last something of a startling contradiction. She passes her prejudices on to Konny, along with a romanticized perception of the *Gustloff* (on which her parents once enjoyed a *Kraft durch Freude* cruise). Tulla is so driven by the need to have the story of the *Gustloff* told that she encourages Konny to accept the right-wing mythologies that have grown up around the sinking, mainly because this is the political arena in which German suffering is most sympathetically discussed. As Schmitz observes, Grass's narrative thus incorporates the principle of "the return of the repressed. In the manner of a pendulum swing, repressed German history manifests itself in the third generation."[20]

Konny's engagement with the memory of the *Gustloff* ends in tragedy when he shoots dead a young man who had challenged his views in an Internet chatroom. In an ironic twist, "David" (named after Gustloff's assassin) turns out not to be Jewish at all, but a philo-Semitic young man called Wolfgang Stremplin, whose father's indifference to the Holocaust causes him to adopt a Jewish persona. He is thus a mirror image of Konny, whose mother Gabi's "constant harping on Auschwitz" (210) is put forward as one of the reasons why he turns to the political right. Aside from "David" noone has tried to engage Konny in a dialogue about his views. When he elects to give a school presentation entitled "'The Positive Aspects of the Nazi Organization *Kraft durch Freude*'" (198), his teachers, all left-leaning, idealistic members of the '68 generation, are keen to avoid revisionist interpretations of history in the classroom. Rather than challenging his ideas, they simply forbid the presentation, thereby confirming Konny's conviction that free speech is only permissible as long as you toe the correct ideological line. When Konny eventually does find a public forum to bear witness for Tulla and to express his right-wing views — first on the Internet and then in the courtroom at his trial — the price is a young man's life.

Consequently, Paul writes the story of the *Gustloff*. He does so less for the old man, than for his mother and Konny, partly in response to his mother's calls to bear witness, but also to expose, in a very deliberate manner, the fallacy of the right-wing misrepresentations about the ship and its sinking. In effect, what Paul attempts to do through his narrative is to engage Konny in a belated dialogue and to challenge his views, something that he, Gabi, and Konny's teachers should all have done long before. Paul first dismantles the nostalgia that surrounds the memory of the *Gustloff* in its *Kraft durch Freude* days. The happy memories that Tulla's working-class parents August and Erna had of their *Gustloff* cruise are firmly embedded in Pokriefke family memory, and are used by both Tulla and Konny to claim the *Gustloff* as a model for a classless society. Paul, in contrast, uses his journalistic skills to trace the beginnings of the *Kraft durch Freude* movement, and to highlight the unpalatable fact that its leader Robert Ley appropriated funds from unions to finance the project, while, in the same historical moment, "the concentration camps were filling, batch after batch" (37). His investigations thus immediately stress the need for a full historical contextualization of the memory of the *Gustloff.*

Similarly, Paul challenges Konny's Internet account of the *Gustloff*'s sinking, which misrepresents the past in crucial ways. For example, it categorizes the ship as a "refugee ship only" (108), omitting to mention the one and a half thousand military personnel on board, whose presence turned the ship into a legitimate military target. Paul ponders the reason for Konny's silence about these crucial details:

> Why did Konny lie? Why did the boy deceive himself and others? Why, when he was otherwise such a stickler for detail, and knew each inch of the ship [. . .] did he refuse to admit that it was neither a Red Cross transport nor a cargo ship that lay tied up at the dock, loaded exclusively with refugees, but an armed passenger liner at the command of the navy, into which the most varied freight had been packed. Why did he deny facts available in print for years, facts that even the eternal has-beens hardly contested anymore? [. . .] I can only suspect what induced Konny to cheat: the desire for an unambiguous enemy. (109)

Konny is almost certainly aware of the ship's quasi-military status, but has chosen to omit details that might unsettle his own unambiguous account of events and his preferred reading of the sinking as a war crime. His selective use of facts to distort the past is reminiscent of other characters within the quintet, such as Oskar in *Die Blechtrommel* and Matern in *Hundejahre.* However, whereas their misrepresentations are used to obscure the guilt of their own actions in the past, Konny's aim is to misrepresent the larger historical memory of the *Gustloff.* Paul, in contrast to his son, is at pains to contextualize the sinking of the *Gustloff,* revealing it to be a complicated, multilayered story that contains a depressing measure of human cowardice, incompetence, and error: general mismanagement of the emergency, insufficient lifeboats, and iced-up ropes are all shown to have contributed considerably to the death toll.

With Konny serving a seven-year sentence, Paul finds himself at a loss as to how to move forward, and for the first time seeks advice on his relationship with his son. However, his appeals to Tulla, Gabi, and Rosi (Konny's girlfriend) fail: none are able to explain Konny's radicalization (primarily because they are unwilling to acknowledge their own contribution to that process), or to help him constructively with the future. In the end, Paul is shown turning to Konny himself, and begins the long overdue process of building a dialogue with his son. This positive break-through, which sees Konny relinquishing his obsession with the *Gustloff* through the symbolic smashing of a replica of the ship, is tempered at the end of the text, when Paul finds a new website that figures his son as a right-wing martyr. The message placed there for Konny — "'We believe in you, we will wait for you, we will follow you'" (234) — leaves Paul dejected, for even though his son may have let go of the past, the past now refuses to let him go: "It doesn't end. Never will it end" (234). As in each of the previous books in the quintet, there is no real closure to the past for the narrator or the reader, or any indication of what the future will hold, only an awkward moment of uncertainty that holds more questions than answers.

As the above reading of *Im Krebsgang* illustrates, the novella's discussion of the memory of German wartime suffering is often complex and nuanced. The work's openness in this respect is also underscored by the presence of numerous intertextual references to the other parts of the quintet. Just as Paul and the novella adopt a crablike style, moving to and fro between different strands of the past and present, so this movement is enacted in the larger literary context of all five works: readers are invited to take what the critical theorist Umberto Eco terms an "inferential walk" — "to 'walk' so to speak, outside the text, in order to gather intertextual support" — in this case from the other four works of the quintet.[21] As Eco emphasizes, these "walks" are "not mere whimsical initiatives on the part of the reader, but are elicited by discursive structures and foreseen by the whole textual strategy as indispensable components of the construction of the *fabula*."[22] In other words, they constitute a consciously thought-out design on Grass's part, and provide the informed reader with the means to properly contextualize the issues raised in *Im Krebsgang*.

Given the controversy surrounding the representation of German wartime suffering in *Im Krebsgang*, viewing the novella as a part of the quintet is particularly valuable, because it allows the breadth of Grass's treatment of the enormously complex postwar victim/perpetrator debates to become visible. When viewed collectively, it is clear that the quintet's works provide a full and extensive exploration of all aspects of German wartime experience. The myriad connections that are made between the different works on the levels of content, theme, and narrative structure also signal Grass's own awareness of the importance of viewing the works together. For example, in *Im Krebsgang*, causal links are made between Tulla's presence on the *Gustloff* and one of the central storylines in *Hundejahre*, the selection of Harras's puppy, Prinz, as a gift for Hitler. As a reward, the dog's owner, the carpenter Liebenau, is given a cruise on the *Gustloff*, which he donates to his assistant and brother-in-law August Pokriefke. But the result of the wonderful experiences that Tulla's parents have on the ship is Erna Pokriefke's later, fatal insistence that the family sail on the *Gustloff* as they flee to the west (114). These multiple connections make it impossible to separate the family's presence on the *Gustloff* from the preceding narrative of the Nazi years: one is shown to be inextricably bound to the other.

The constant references within *Im Krebsgang* to Tulla's complex history are also significant, because they allow the quintet's dual conceptualization of memory — as a form of testimony on the one hand, and as a representation open to distortion on the other — to be reiterated. Thus, in chapter 5, the old man recalls the episode from *Hundejahre,* in which Tulla has the courage to speak the truth about the Stutthof concentration camp and the Holocaust:

> After all, he says, it was the adolescent Tulla, who, in the middle of wartime and surrounded by people deliberately turning a blind eye, saw a whitish heap to one side of the Kaiserhafen flak battery, recognized it as human remains, and announced loudly, "That's a pile o' bones!" (104)

This passage, while reminding the reader of Tulla's boldness at a time when no one would speak of the camp, emphasizes the continued importance of bearing witness to the Holocaust. Then, a little later in *Im Krebsgang,* Tulla's connections to two key acts of persecution are also highlighted. The first, an incident that saw the half-Jewish Amsel driven from the carpenter's yard following repeated abuse with the derogatory term "Yid," Tulla blames on her father: "'And he said it out loud, too, before he kicked that Yid, Amsel was his name — out of our courtyard'" (111). This account highlights the tendency of postwar Germans to misrepresent their actions in the Nazi past, by inviting the reader to take an "inferential walk" within *Hundejahre,* where this episode is first related. When the reader returns to Harry Liebenau's memories of the event, a discrepancy in Tulla's later account immediately becomes clear: for while her father may have put her up to it, she is nonetheless identified as Amsel's chief persecutor, shouting the word "Yid" at him sixteen times. The contrast between these different sets of memories suggests that Tulla has now deliberately chosen to obscure her role in this event: her casual use of the term "Yid" (rather than the more neutral term of "Jew") as she recounts the story to Paul in *Im Krebsgang* betrays her lingering anti-Semitism and her guilt.

Subsequently, Jenny, Tulla's old childhood friend, alludes to the role that Tulla played in denouncing Jenny's adopted father, the teacher Oswald Brunies, thereby providing another crucial link back to *Hundejahre*'s examination of how ordinary people colluded in the operations of the Holocaust: "'It was pure mischief on her part. But it turned out badly. After the denunciation they came for Papa Brunies. . . . He was sent to Stutthof. . . . But in the end things turned out almost alright'" (229). Jenny, fully aware of Tulla's contribution to Brunies's death at Stutthof, shows a remarkable capacity for forgiveness, both here and at other points in the narrative: she and Tulla have somehow reached a mutual understanding about the events of that time. And yet, Jenny's inclusion of the word "almost" in that final sentence also stresses that Tulla's past actions, and their dreadful consequences, can never be entirely forgotten: everything has *almost* — but not *completely* — turned out alright. Such key, intertextual references take care to point the reader back to the earlier parts of the "Danzig Quintet," to the messy, complicated events that inform the postwar present of *Im Krebsgang*. As a consequence, the status of the "German as victim" in the text, as represented by the figure of Tulla, is significantly problematized, demonstrating Grass's continued awareness of the complexities involved in remembering the National Socialist past.

Notes

This essay is a modified version of Chapter 6, in my *Günter Grass's 'Danzig Quintet': Explorations in the Memory and History of the Nazi Era from* Die Blechtrommel *to* Im Krebsgang (Oxford: Peter Lang, 2007). The author gratefully acknowledges the permission of Peter Lang publishers to draw on material from this book.

[1] "Der alte Mann und sein Meer," *Die Zeit,* http://www.zeit.de/2002/07/200207_1-grass_xml?page=all (accessed 15 September 2008), my translation.

[2] Umberto Eco, *The Role of the Reader: Explorations in the Semiotics of Texts* (Bloomington: U of Indiana P, 1979), 32.

[3] Günter Grass, *Crabwalk,* trans. Krishna Winston (London: Faber and Faber, 2003), 79–80. All further page references are cited parenthetically in the text.

[4] http://www.radiobremen.de/online/grass/reden/schweigen.shtml (accessed 7 October 2008), my translation.

[5] See Günter Grass, "Writing after Auschwitz," in *Two States, One Nation?,* trans. Krishna Winston and Arthur S. Wensinger (London: Secker and Warburg, 1990). 94–123.

[6] *Vertreibung* is a very contentious term: I use both the translations mentioned as the context demands. The same applies to the term *Vertriebenen,* which can be translated as refugees or expellees.

[7] "Interview mit Günter Grass," *Steidl,* http://www.steidl.de/grass/ (accessed 15 September 2008), my translation.

[8] Günter Grass, "Ich erinnere mich," talk given at the Future of Memory conference, Vilnius, 2000, http://www.steidl.de/grass/a2_5_vilnius.html (accessed 15 September 2008), my translation.

[9] "Sinking Ships, the Lost *Heimat* and Broken Taboos: Günter Grass and the Politics of Memory in Contemporary Germany," *Contemporary European History* 12, no. 2 (2003): 151.

[10] Robert G. Moeller, *War Stories: The Search for a Useable Past in the Federal Republic of Germany* (Berkeley: U of California P, 2001), 45.

[11] Ibid., 6.

[12] Data from my own survey, carried out in the summer of 2005.

[13] See Moeller, *War Stories,* 54–74.

[14] *Dokumentation der Vertreibung der Deutschen aus Ost-Mitteleuropa, Gesamtausgabe in 8 Bänden* (Munich: DTV, 2004).

[15] Louis F. Helbig, *Die Ungeheure Verlust: Flucht und Vertreibung in der deutschsprachigen Belletristik der Nachkriegszeit* (Wiesbaden: Harrassowitz, 1988), 85.

[16] Ibid., 152, my translation.

[17] http://www.steidl.de/grass/a2_5_vilnius.html, my translation.

[18] Omer Bartov, "Germany as Victim," *New German Critique* 80 (2000): 29–40.

[19] Helmut Schmitz, *On Their Own Terms: The Legacy of National Socialism in Post-1990 German Fiction* (Birmingham, UK: U of Birmingham P, 2004), 270–71.

[20] Ibid., 271.

[21] Umberto Eco, *The Role of the Reader: Explorations in the Semiotics of Texts* (Bloomington: U of Indiana P, 1979), 32.

[22] Ibid.

10: Rereading *Der Vorleser*, Remembering the Perpetrator

Rick Crownshaw

BERNHARD SCHLINK'S 1995 NOVEL *Der Vorleser* (The Reader, 1996)[1] has attracted a critical consensus that deems it to have reconfigured the perpetrator generation as victims of Nazism and the second generation as victims of Nazism's legacy.[2] Such an appropriation of victim status is part of a wider discourse of German suffering, prevalent in the 1990s and 2000s, which has often sought to elide the memory of suffering caused by Germans. In this chapter, however, I argue that Schlink's novel actually attempts to intervene critically in these proclivities of German cultural memory. This intervention needs to be understood in relation to the binary thinking that governs the remembrance and construction of Germany's victims and perpetrators.

In 2006 Aleida Assmann perceived the persistence of a binary opposition in German cultural memory, in which Germans were remembered as either "victims" or "perpetrators," but never both. Memories of German suffering, according to Assmann, have been the stuff of private, familial, communicative memory, and have not been recognized at an official commemorative level, which is the preserve of a hegemonic Holocaust memory. Attempts after the immediate postwar period to elevate German suffering from the private and familial to the level of national and official commemoration, by way of, say, the *Bund der Vetriebenen* (Association of Expellees), were deemed by second-generation Germans in the 1960s to be revisionist attempts to subsume Holocaust memory by recourse to competing claims of victimization. Denunciations by the so-called '68ers left no room in the public sphere for empathy for the victims of Allied bombings, expulsions of ethnic Germans from the east, and of the Soviet army as it entered German territory.* As Assmann notes, it was not until the 1990s that the second generation was able, along with the third generation, to look back not in anger at what their parents and grandparents might have done during the war, but in empathy for what they might have suffered. The passing away of the first generation has intensified the memory work of the second and third generations as they anxiously reconstruct the experiences of the first. Despite their large-scale distribution by Germany's mass media, Assmann believes that these memories will be regulated and will remain, in essence, "private." At the level of national or state commemoration, a "normative framework of memory" safeguards Holocaust memory. She claims:

> The norm of German national memory, as established in the 1960s and reconfirmed in the 1980s, is the Holocaust, the recognition and working through of German guilt, involving the assumption of historical responsibility for the atrocities of the Nazi-regime. This is the normative framework into which all other memories have to be integrated.[3]

Integrated in this way, memories of German suffering and memories of suffering caused by Germans might exist "side by side" without "necessarily cancelling each other out."[4]

Assmann cites the campaign of Erika Steinbach, president of the *Bund der Vetriebenen,* as proof of how this regulatory framework works. Steinbach's personal and family memories of flight — she was born in 1940 — are essentially held in check by a hierarchy of memory. Assmann predicts that Steinbach's family memory, and those like it, will not be elevated to a national level of remembrance and institutionalized by, for example, Steinbach's proposed Center Against Expulsions. (In 2006, when Assmann made the prediction, the Center had not received state support.) In its design (based on the United States Holocaust Memorial Museum), exhibitionary contents and structure, and location in Berlin, the center would vie with the German Memorial to the Murdered Jews of Europe not just to constitute another national memorial, but to constitute *the* German national memorial.[5] Assmann's argument is that memories of German suffering are not and would not be institutionalized at a national level, but would remain at the level of the familial because a regulatory framework or hierarchy of memory was in operation that privileged Holocaust memory over memories of German suffering. However, as *Spiegel Online* reported on 19 March 2008, the German government approved plans for the museum for which Steinbach had been campaigning.[6] In other words, the hierarchy of memory has been inverted. As Helmut Schmitz noted, prior to the German government's decision, it is the very concept of a hierarchical framework that is problematic. Such a framework does not integrate memories of victimhood and perpetration — it does not allow them to exist side by side without canceling each other out, as Assmann would have it — but rather organizes them in terms of a binary opposition. This framework does not move beyond the conception of Germans as *either* victims *or* perpetrators, but rather reinstalls the dichotomy.[7] It was dichotomous or binary thinking that had organized how revisionary or competitive memories of German suffering sought to displace or dislodge the centrality of Holocaust memory in the first place, relegating the Holocaust to the private and familial and promoting German suffering to the national stage of remembrance. In sum, a hierarchy of memory is not integrative but prone to inversion.

The paradigm of a revisionary public-private binary was certainly evident in the 1990s' "memory culture," as in, for example, the controversy surrounding author Martin Walser's acceptance speech for the Peace Prize of the German Book Trade Fair in Frankfurt in 1998 and his literary work. Walser complained about a left-liberal instrumentalization in Germany of the memory of the Nazi past, forming a culture of contrition rather than national pride.[8] Such politically correct memories, he argued, could be traced back to the 1960s and the continuing influence of the second generation (the '68ers) that marginalized, if not excluded, all memory of German suffering. As well as suggesting the impossibility of mourning German loss, Bill Niven argues, Walser's accusation uncannily resonated with Nazi conspiracies that placed Jews (figured as perpetrators) at the center of plots against the nation.[9] Indeed, Schmitz argues that in the media debate that followed between Ignatz Bubis, then head of the Central Council of German Jews, and Walser, the position of conspiratorial "other" is allocated to a representative Bubis.

Synecdochically, Bubis stood for a victim's perspective that was perceived to be inauthentic and outside of the German *Volk*, or collective. Walser's accusations were predicated on the notion of the "privacy of conscience," an autonomous realm of authentic memory under siege from inauthentic public forms of address. As Schmitz interprets it, Walser's argument is that the "individual conscience" is privileged "because it is not representable . . . [is] not in danger of being instrumentalised."[10] This spurious isolation of private or individual historical conscience and consciousness separates memory into the authentic ("German") and inauthentic ("Jewish"). Such separation of memories is typical of Walser's literature. For example, his semiautobiographical novel set between 1932 and 1945, *Ein springender Brunnen* (A Springing Fountain, 1998) is conspicuous to the extent that it does not mention Auschwitz and is underpinned by an insistence that childhood memory cannot be deformed retrospectively by the political correctness of Holocaust remembrance. However, as Anne Fuchs puts it, "Insofar as it is inevitable that our memories are socially and linguistically constituted, they are never totally authored by the remembering self."[11]

The idea of a private, bracketed enclave of memory can be found quite widely in German culture, although its construction is not necessarily as revisionist as Walser's psychic topography of remembrance. For example, Fuchs, in commenting on Harald Welzer's interviews with three generations of 40 families, *Opa war kein Nazi* (Grandpa Wasn't a Nazi, 2003),[12] finds a "cumulative heroization" and romanticization of the perpetrator generation.[13] While the subsequent generations, particularly the third, demonstrated no sympathies for National Socialism, and horror in relation to the Holocaust, they are often inclined to believe that their grandparents did not play an integral role in genocidal Nazism. The family romances that emerged were more likely to figure the perpetrator generation as victims. That anti-Semites and perpetrators are not recalled leads Niven to argue that "the memory of German perpetration, guilt, and the suffering of Nazi victims" cultivated in the public sphere in the 1980s and 1990s has not "percolated down to the level of family memory." That family memory is thereby cleared for memories of suffering, which will go unchecked because of the current tendency toward "emotion over enlightenment" and "uncritical empathy over pedagogy," leads Niven to conclude that private memory has now invaded the public realm, particularly through the proliferation of literary, documentary, and historical narratives based on private memories and given exposure and distribution by the mass media.[14]

Perhaps, though, the public and the private are too neatly divided here. Fuchs and Mary Cosgrove point out that studies such as Welzer's, which are the cause of so much academic concern, pay more attention to what is said, and neglect the significance of what remains unsaid. "The unsaid . . . can function as a powerful transmitter of the unmastered inheritance that is silently passed down the generational line."[15] Fuchs adds: the "emphatic assertion that 'Grandpa wasn't a Nazi' may mean exactly the opposite." Similarly, in the repeated assertions on the international stage that Germany is a normal democracy — spectacularly expressed by a national Holocaust memorial — may be ghosted by an "anxiety of influence."[16]

The separation of public and private in the practice of memory allows for the isolation of the act of perpetration and its displacement through the uncritical reconfiguration of perpetrators as victims. A similar isolation of perpetrators accompanied the institutionalization of Holocaust memory in the 1990s (the normative framework advocated by Assmann). Thus the 1990s were marked by the increasing national ownership of the memory of the Nazi past.[17] Markers of ownership included the public development of plans for the National Memorial for the Murdered Jews of Europe, the debates surrounding the touring Crimes of the *Wehrmacht* exhibition (1995–99 and 2001), and the publication in German of Daniel Jonah Goldhagen's *Hitler's Willing Executioners* (1996).[18] The *Wehrmacht* exhibition dispelled notions that the regular army had fought a clean war that had nothing to do with genocidal activities in the east and made the externalization of responsibility for the Holocaust difficult. The perpetrators were ordinary Germans (in this case ordinary soldiers), not an élite, inner circle of Nazi militarists, politicians, bureaucrats, and industrialists.

In a similar vein, Goldhagen's thesis claimed that anti-Semitism has been endogenous to German society for centuries and that Nazi ideology and policy were simply catalysts for ordinary Germans to commit genocidal acts. The clumsy ventriloquism of Goldhagen's book that attempted to represent the perpetrator's perspective — a phenomenology of murder — allowed young Germans to note that the perpetrators were supposed to be "ordinary" but also enabled them to distance themselves from the crimes and caricatured perpetrators of the past.[19] As for the exhibition, Niven argues it staged a cathartic reconciliation rather than confrontation with the perpetrator generation.[20]

Schmitz comments on the ownership of memory thus: "The turning point here is the issue of guilt."[21] The shift from the second to the third generations since the war has meant liberation from the guilt and repression experienced by the first generation. Members of the third generation, in particular, have been able to assume historical responsibility for the Nazi past, confessing vicariously for their ancestors. It is the shift in the burden of responsibility or, rather, the alleviation of the burden by the institutionalization of Holocaust memory that has led to the increasing formation of German historical identity around "Germans as victims" rather than Holocaust remembrance.[22] Although not all of the texts that remember German suffering are by definition revisionist, the institutionalization of Holocaust memory creates cultural conditions that may facilitate revisionism. Institutionally unburdened of a collective historical responsibility for the Nazi past, there is less impediment to Germans identifying with victims rather than perpetrators — and this does not mean empathizing with the victims of the Holocaust but rather with those subsuming their place. It seems that the practices of public Holocaust memorialization are too rigid, generating a series of oppositions — authentic/inauthentic, private/public, victim/perpetrator — that are all too invertible.

Bernhard Schlink's novel *Der Vorleser,* contrary to the critical consensus, stages an attempted identification with the perpetrator generation that seeks to overcome this binarism of German cultural memory. The work of Gillian Rose suggests a framework for how *Der Vorleser* might be read against the critical consensus. Rose's critique of postmodern, post-Holocaust philosophy centers on postmodernism's delegitimization of Holocaust narratives, as if all representation is contaminated by the violent logic of the master narratives that rationalized Auschwitz. For Rose, the argument for the overcoming of representation, in its aesthetic, philosophical, and political versions, "converges with the *inner tendency* of Fascism itself." For example, placing Jews beyond representation surely echoes Nazism's abstraction of Jewish identity. Only through an "always contestable and fallible representation" can we know where the representation of fascism converges with the fascism of representation. Otherwise, in our "Holocaust piety," we render the event ineffable, which is *"to mystify something we dare not understand,* because we fear it may it may be all too understandable, all too continuous with what we are — human, all too human."[23] In effect, Rose imagines something akin to Primo Levi's concept of the "grey zone."[24]

A strategic identification with a perpetrator, made possible by admitting such a common ground of humanity, would allow us to see where the representation of fascism and the fascism of representation converge. Only by inhabiting, rather than lapsing into, the perpetrator's perspective could we see where the limits and boundaries of that perspective lie. However, how can one identify and empathize with a perpetrator without displacing knowledge of his or her crimes? Rose imagines the possibility of something like a Nazi Bildungsroman in which the future allegiances of the protagonist are unknown to the reader, and by the time they are known, the reader has already empathized.[25] A crisis of identification in the reader would signify that empathetic bond. Schlink's novel attempts to operate in a similar way, in which the narrator–protagonist suffers a crisis of identity for having desired a perpetrator before he knew her true identity, vicariously establishing for the reader potential bonds of empathy.

If *The Reader* is to inhabit the perspective of the perpetrator to scrutinize rather than disavow it, as in Rose's model of the representation of fascism, then the figure of the perpetrator needs to be available to the narrator (and by this proxy to the reader). Hanna's age (indicating she was not too young to have played an active part in the war) and the narrator's recollection of feeling oblivious and forgetful of the outside world when embracing her (*R* 14) raise suspicions about her. If the teenage Michael was not suspicious of her past, Schlink makes sure that we are when Michael narrates retrospectively. The suspicion concerning Hanna's past grows with descriptions of her scrupulous hygiene (*R* 30) and her fondness for uniforms, which attracted her to her current job as a tram conductor (*R* 37). These hints of (stereotypical) Nazi leanings are compounded by the suspicious lack of detail about her past, or her unwillingness to reveal very much about it (*R* 37). Michael informs us that he had, by the time the affair was in full swing, caught up with his studies since falling ill, including the history of the Third Reich (*R* 39). Given the context, the casual mention of this subject of study is just too conspicuous not to draw the reader's attention. Hints of a stereotyped sadism come with the power games Hanna plays with Michael (*R* 46–47), and her proclivity for violence — she strikes him when she thought she had been abandoned on a holiday they take together (*R* 52–53).

The novel's stereotypical hints of Nazism (sadism, hygiene) do not, at first glance, seem to fit Rose's model. How can Michael desire such a stereotype, and hints of what is to be revealed surely preclude our vicarious identification with her? However, the stereotypical and the proleptical do suggest the revisionary workings of memory. The narrator is self-conscious and explicit about the revision of the past:

> Why does it make me sad when I think back to that time? Is it a yearning for past happiness — for I was happy in the weeks that followed, in which I really did work like a lunatic and passed the class, and we made love as if nothing else in the world mattered. Is it the knowledge of what came later, and that what came out afterwards had been there all along? (*R* 35)

Part of the revisionary process is the isolation of certain moments, the mental images that are, as Siegfried Kracauer might put it, "monogramatic."[26] This is an unchanging image into which is distilled all that is valued about the subject. A highly subjective image that attempts to withstand the passage of time, it can be used to screen out other memories. For Michael, the sight of Hanna in his father's study forms one such memory-image: "It is one of the pictures of Hanna that has stayed with me. I have them stored away, I can project them on a mental screen and watch them, unchanged, unconsumed" (*R* 60). Proleptic, stereotypical, or suspended above time, these images do not make Hanna less available. Rather, they suggest that an identification with her has already been made, announcing a consequent crisis of identity on the part of the narrator. The combination of images points to a desire for the Hanna he knew before her trial and renounces that desire through a desperate attempt to "other" her with cliché and stereotype.

Signs of this crisis of identity are evident in the narration of her trial (in 1965–1966), in which the narrator continues in his attempt to distance himself from her:

> I realized that I had assumed it was both natural and right that Hanna should be in custody. Not because of the charges, the gravity of the allegations, or the force of evidence, of which I had no real knowledge, but because in a cell she was out of my world, out of my life. I wanted her far away from me, so unattainable that she could continue as the mere memory she had become and remained all these years. (*R* 95–96)

Although his disavowel cannot be taken at face value, his personal dissociation from her is informed by a wider cultural dissociation. The numbness that Michael feels at court is observable in other participants, as the "intrusion of horror into daily life" — the atrocities detailed and testified to — has an "anesthetic" effect (*R* 99–101). The narrator adds that "survivor literature talks about this numbness, in which life's functions are reduced to a minimum, behavior becomes completely selfish and indifferent to others, and gassing and burning are everyday occurrences" (*R* 99–101). Perpetrator literature recounts a parallel sensation found in the numbness to mass murder (*R* 99–101). This "general numbness . . . had taken hold not only of the perpetrators and victims, but of all of us, judges and lay members of the court, prosecutors and recorders, who had to deal with these events now" (*R* 99–101).

Michael's fellow seminar students and Schlink's critics voice indignation at an assumed relativism. For example, Ernestine Schlant compares *The Reader* to the attempts at relativizing the Holocaust that sparked the *Historikerstreit* (Historians' Debate). She argues that the "confusion and lack of a moral compass inherent in a comparison of the numbness of the prisoners in the death camp and that of the perpetrators, to say nothing of the courtroom participants, surely needs no comment." The critique Schlant implies is not that self-evident. "How Michael could make such 'linkages' and simultaneously insist that there were differences of 'the greatest, most critical importance' he does not explain."[27] Actually, he does explain. In his general reference to the literature of victims and perpetrators, something akin to Levi's "grey zone" is implied. Schlink's narrator does not advocate a culture of historical relativism, but is, rather, exceptional in his recognition of how such a culture has already been created. It is the grey zone that accommodates both the continuities and fundamental discontinuities between perpetrator and victim. In Levi's conception "in the camp the perpetrators and victims could not be divided into a 'we' inside and the enemy outside, separated by a sharply defined geographic frontier." The system of National Socialism caused the victims to emulate their victimizers. "It is a grey zone with ill-defined outlines which both separate and join the two camps of masters and servants. It possesses an incredibly complicated internal structure, and contains within itself enough to confuse our need to judge." Under such a system, the "deprivation to which they [the victims] were subjected" meant that "the room for choices (especially moral choices) was reduced to zero." The responsibility for blurring the boundaries between victim and perpetrator lies, though, with the "system, the very structure of the totalitarian state."[28] Without a conception of the grey zone, which only the narrator seems to gesture toward and not the culture of Holocaust memory that surrounds him, the Holocaust is reduced to a series of undifferentiated acts of violence and its participants rendered indistinguishable.

Hanna had been a guard, along with four other accused women, at a small satellite camp for Auschwitz, near Cracow. They were indicted with charges for their conduct at the camp, but their main crime was their conduct on a "death" march west. Michael did not remember the details of the first set of charges, but surviving witnesses (camp inmates) did, and they implicated the accused in selections for the gas chambers at Auschwitz (*R* 104–5). Hanna's selections were peculiar in that she had selected "favorites" among the female prisoners, who received special treatment but had to read to her in the evenings (*R* 114–15). These tended to be the "younger," "weaker," and more "delicate" prisoners, who, although saved from work duty, were still sent to the gas chambers (*R* 114–15). The main charge, though, was locking up the female prisoners who were being marched west in a village church one night, during which there was an air raid. The women locked in the church burned to death, all except a mother and daughter (*R* 105–6). The daughter wrote a book of their experiences, which started the criminal investigation that led to the courtroom proceedings (*R* 104). The trial fuels a series of fantasies for Michael:

> Hanna by the burning church, hard-faced, in a black uniform, with a riding whip. . . . [Hanna] being read to. . . . When the hour was over, she told the reader she would be going on the transport to Auschwitz the next morning. The reader, a frail creature with a stubble of black hair and shortsighted eyes, began to cry. Hanna hit the wall with her hand, two women, also prisoners in striped clothing, came in and pulled the reader away. I saw . . . among [her prisoners] . . . her screaming face a mask of ugliness . . . [she] helped things along with her whip. I saw the church steeple crashing into the roof and the sparks flying and the heard the desperation of the women. Alongside these images[:] . . . Hanna pulling on her stockings in the kitchen [. . .] riding her bicycle with skirts flying . . . dancing in front of the mirror [. . .] Hanna listening to me, talking to me, laughing at me, loving me. Hanna loving me with cold eyes and pursed mouth, silently listening to me reading, and at the end banging the wall with her hand, talking to me with her face turning into a mask. The worst were the dreams in which a hard, imperious, cruel Hanna aroused me sexually; I woke from them full of longing and shame and rage. And full of fear about who I really was. (*R* 145–47)

Michael's "clichéd" fantasies that eroticize suffering and in which he plays the role of the sexualized Jewish victim need to be read in the context of the 1960s. The uncertain sense of self that Michael's fantasies leave him with can be read as an indulgent appropriation of Jewish identity, *and* another symptom of his crisis of identity and attempt to distance himself from the object of his desire.

Schmitz, among others, has noted the rigidity of the conceptual framework constructed by members of the second generation in the 1960s by which their parents' generation was identified wholly in terms of perpetration.[29] Michael reports that his university seminar, which followed and analyzed Hanna's trial, was driven by his fellow students' (and their generation's) imputation of collective guilt to the previous generation: "The generation that had been served by the guards and enforcers, or had done nothing to stop them, or had not banished them from its midst as it could have done after 1945, was in the dock, and we explored it, subjected it to trial by daylight, and condemned it to shame" (*R* 89). Although the second generation was alarmed by the legacies of Nazism in German life — Michael cites the Federal Republic's failure to recognize Israel and that old Nazis were still pursuing successful careers in the courts, government, and universities — its homogenization of the previous generation was motivated by shame over their ancestors to whom they were emotionally attached rather than by the shouldering of collective responsibility for the past.[30] The difficult task of displacing the perpetrator generation embodied by Hanna and the narrator's parents — "but the finger I pointed at her turned back to me. I had loved her" (*R* 168) — was the "German fate" of his generation (*R* 169). This task is played out in Michael's fantasies of victimhood, which may represent a desperate attempt to gain critical distance on the previous generation using the available cultural rhetoric of philo-Semitism. Distance from the perpetrator is gained by colonizing the victim's identity.

Michael realizes "that the fantasized images were poor clichés," which "undermined my actual memories of Hanna and merged with the images of the camps that I had in my mind" (*R* 145). Back then the reservoir of images in cultural circulation was limited in scope and was unable to correct his fantasies of Hanna. However, German cultural memory's insistence on these few images also created clichés that detracted from the reality of the camps: "The few images derived from Allied photographs and the testimony of survivors flashed on the mind again and again, until they froze into clichés" (*R* 147). Michael notes, though, that the cultural industry of more recent Holocaust representations from the 1970s to the 1990s — *Holocaust, Sophie's Choice,* and *Schindler's List* — has simply made those clichés or icons more familiar.[31] Michael visits, shortly after the trial, the site of the Stutthof concentration camp in Alsace with iconoclasm in mind: "I wanted reality to drive out the clichés" (*R* 148). Revisiting the site of Stutthof before narrating *The Reader,* Michael realizes that the cultural landscape of memory — in this case the memorial topography of Stutthof — "joined my few already existing images of Auschwitz and Bergen-Belsen, and froze along with them" (*R* 156). It seems, then, that Michael is unable to map out a grey zone of remembrance. The cultural landscape of memory, both in the 1960s and 1990s, resists this kind of ethical cartography. At Stutthof, Michael thinks, "I wanted simultaneously to understand Hanna's crime and to condemn it. . . . But it was impossible to do both" (*R* 156).

His gestures toward a grey zone frustrated, Michael continues in his attempt to lend humanity to Hanna but by transfiguring her into a victim of justice. He does this by means of an interrogation of the judicial system to which she is subject. Observing the trial, Michael points out that a "competent defense would have been able, without attacking the substance of the mother's and daughter's testimony, to cast reasonable doubt on whether these defendants were the actual ones who had done the selections" (*R* 112–13). Michael notes the imprecise nature of witnesses' testimony and its failure to map out accurately a structure of command in the camps and on the march. After pointing out examples of guilt by inductive reasoning (*R* 112–13, 124, 145), Michael notes how, in self-exculpating testimony, the other ex-guards round on Hanna, find in her a scapegoat, and accuse her of submitting a false report to cover up what she (supposedly more than they) had done (*R* 125). At this point in the proceedings, Hanna confesses that she and they had acted out of confusion and then falsely confesses to having written the report (*R* 128).

The judgment of Hanna, as Giorgio Agamben would argue, marks the independence of law from justice and truth, leaving law to be upheld by the force of judgment alone. Agamben contends that such "conceptual confusion" at the trials of Nazis "has made it impossible to think through Auschwitz." For Agamben, this is the "ruination of law."[32] Hanna receives life, the other guards lesser terms in jail, which is indicative of the shortcomings of the justice handed down in the Nazi trials of the 1960s. Unfortunately, as most critics agree, the critique of law here transforms Hanna into a victim, her specific guilt is reduced to a potential guilt, qualified by context of her unproven actions. Nevertheless, it is difficult to separate Michael's attempts at humanizing Hanna from the court's unwillingness to humanize her. Michael notes the judge's indicative refusal to answer Hanna's repeated question: "'What would you have done?'" (*R* 110, 127). The murderous dilemmas Hanna faced and the equally murderous actions that resolve them were all too human.

The question of Hanna's illiteracy, inside and outside the court, though, has caused most critical controversy. Omer Bartov argues that illiteracy motivates Hanna to join the SS before it is discovered by her previous employer and turns her "first into a perpetrator and then into a victim of justice (as Michael ultimately believes)." The consideration of her illiteracy is therefore a confusion of "social or ideological handicap and victim."[33] Schlant finds the illiteracy mystifying: "if illiteracy is not the explanation — and excuse — for Hanna's acts, then what function does it serve in the novel? At the very point where Schlink needs to make a strong case with respect to the Nazi crimes and those who perpetrated them, the novel is weakest."[34] Without an explanation from Hanna, we are left with Michael's speculation on the causal relation between illiteracy and her crimes against humanity: her illiteracy motivated her to leave Siemens for the SS; she did not dispatch prisoners to Auschwitz because they had read to her and had been abused by her, thereby covering her shame; reading to her, their last hours were made more bearable; she did not in court "weigh exposure as an illiterate against exposure as a criminal"; and ultimately, "she accepted that she would be called to account. . . . She was . . . fighting for her own truth, her own justice" (*R* 131–32). Following the advice of his father, who sees no "justification for setting other people's views of what is good for them above their own ideas" (*R* 140–41), Michael does not tell the judge of Hanna's illiteracy. Michael believes that he has enabled her to take responsibility for her own actions, in terms of her own private version of justice rather than in the terms of the legal proceedings to which she is subjected. Michael's law professor argues, "you won't find a single one who really believes he had the dispensation to murder back then" (*R* 89). The professor differentiates between a transcendent or absolute conception of law and a historically contingent law. In the camps and on the march Hanna operated under the auspices of the latter, which she also faces in the courtroom. The implication is that Michael believes he has enabled her to personify the former. This attempt to humanize Hanna is redemptive though. As Dominick LaCapra argues, illiteracy turns her first into scapegoat, which is then transfigured into a sacrificial act — a sacrifice to collective guilt — that redeems her past actions.[35]

The problem remains that Michael does not reveal the crimes of which she is guilty. We never find out exactly what happened that night on the forced march, nor the extent of her activities in the satellite camp. Taberner and Donahue argue that Michael's concern over Hanna's victimization by the legal system, and his dilemma over whether to inform the judge of her illiteracy, distracts from the specifics of her atrocities.[36] If illiteracy does make Hanna a victim of circumstance (in joining the SS) rather than a motivated killer, Schlant is right to ask, then, what does motivate the individual's participation in mass murder? Donahue asserts that the stories Michael hears on his way to Stutthof for the first time, about the *Einsatzgruppen* (task force groups), who kill out of "indifference" to humanity (*R* 150), shed no light on Hanna's motivation and make her more opaque by comparison.[37] Although Michael is "guilty" of loving a perpetrator, he has failed to explain her humanity in light of her actions (*R* 133). His attempts to do so become exculpatory and revisionist, ultimately constructing her in the terms of a redemptive victimhood, which just compounds her mystification.

Most critics contend that Michael's continued practice of reading to her also functions as a failed form of moral instruction by means of the classics of German literature that Michael chooses for their inscriptions of Enlightenment thinking.[38] In tandem, Hanna attains literacy and is able to read the canon of Holocaust (survivor) literature. The last scene, though, in which we (and Michael) see Hanna alive is full of allusions to a child-like innocence on her part rather than a moral maturity.[39] In other words, Michael's continued redemption of her fails, and only leads to a more opaque version of Hanna, who claims mysteriously that only the "dead" (her victims and those she reads about) can "understand" her (*R* 196) — a mystification sealed by her suicide.

As Taberner notes, "Michael was never a very good reader of Hanna anyway."[40] What is more, Michael admits to the selective and subjective nature of his memory that constitutes the narrative: the "right one is the written one [not the other versions]. . . . The written version wanted to be written" (*R* 215). He reads and remembers Hanna poorly, but he does so in cultures of remembrance that are unable to admit the humanity of the perpetrator, to condemn and understand her, in other words, to construct a grey zone of remembrance. Even though he still suffers from a crisis of identity after the trial — "All the questions and fears, accusations and self-accusations, all the horror and pain that had erupted during the trial and been immediately deadened were back, and back for good" (*R* 166) — he cannot transcend the conditions of German memory. We should not conflate Michael and Schlink, and, as Bartov has it, Michael's failure to judge Hanna "leads us to assume that the author's views are more complex than his protagonist's, or more ready to compromise, come to terms, relent."[41] Donahue reads Michael's interpretive failures and the indeterminacy of Hanna as part of Schlink's staging of a general and unethical postmodernist ambiguity.[42] In conclusion, in this chapter I have argued that, through his narrator, Schlink draws attention to the binaries that govern Holocaust memory both in the 1960s and in the 1990s. Michael's ultimate failure to humanize the perpetrator in nonredemptive terms demonstrates the cultural conditions of memory from the 1960s to the 1990s that facilitate a slippage between categories of victim and perpetrator typical of the victim discourse against which Schlink writes.

Notes

[1] Bernhard Schlink, *The Reader*, trans. Carol Brown Janeway (London: Phoenix, 1997). Further references to this work are cited in the text using the abbreviation *R* and page number.

[2] See Ernestine Schlant, *The Language of Silence: West German Literature and the Holocaust* (New York: Routledge, 1999); Omer Bartov, *Mirrors of Destruction: War, Genocide, and Modern Identity* (Oxford: OUP, 2000); Dominick LaCapra, *Writing History, Writing Trauma* (Baltimore: Johns Hopkins UP, 2001).

[3] Aleida Assmann, "On the (In)compatibility of Guilt and Suffering in German Memory," trans. Linda Shortt, *German Life and Letters* 59, no. 2 (2006): 197–98.

[4] Ibid.

[5] See Helmut Schmitz, "The Birth of the Collective from The Spirit of Empathy: From the 'Historians' Dispute' to German Suffering," in *Germans as Victims: Remembering the Past in Contemporary Germany,* ed. Bill Niven (Basingstoke, UK: Palgrave Macmillan, 2006), 103, 104.

[6] "German Government Approves Expellees Museum," *Spiegel Online,* http://www.spiegel.de/international/germany/0,1518,542503,00.html (accessed 15 September 2008).

[7] Helmut Schmitz, "Introduction: The Return of Wartime Suffering in Contemporary German Memory Culture, Literature and Film," in *A Nation of Victims? Representation of Wartime Suffering from 1945 to the Present,* ed. Helmut Schmitz (Amsterdam: Rodopi, 2007), 15.

[8] Anne Fuchs, *Phantoms of War in Contemporary German Literature, Films and Discourse: The Politics of Memory* (New York: Palgrave Macmillan, 2008), 3; Stuart Taberner, "Representations of German Wartime Suffering in Recent Fiction," in Niven, *Germans as Victims,* 167.

[9] Bill Niven, "Introduction: German Victimhood at the Turn of the Millennium," in Niven, *Germans as Victims,* 10, 11.

[10] Schmitz, "Birth of the Collective," 101–2.

[11] Fuchs, *Phantoms of War,* 4.

[12] Harald Welzer, Sabine Moller, and Karoline Tschugnall, *Opa war kein Nazi: Nationalsozialismus und Holocaust im Familiengedächtnis* (Frankfurt am Main: Fischer, 2002).

[13] See Anne Fuchs and Mary Cosgrove, "Introduction: Germany's Memory Contests and the Management of the Past," in *German Memory Contests: The Quest for Identity in Literature, Film and Discourse since 1990,* ed. Anne Fuchs, Mary Cosgrove, and Georg Grote (Rochester, NY: Camden House, 2006), 7; Ruth Wittlinger, "Taboo or Tradition? The 'Germans as Victims' Theme in West Germany until the early 1990s," in Niven, *Germans as Victims,* 75.

[14] Niven, "German Victimhood," 20.

[15] Fuchs and Cosgrove, "Germany's Memory Contests," 7.

[16] Fuchs, *Phantoms of War,* 7.

[17] Schmitz, "Birth of the Collective," 93.

[18] See Karen E. Till, *The New Berlin: Memory, Politics, Place* (Minneapolis: U of Minnesota P, 2005).

[19] See Nancy Wood, *Vectors of Memory: Legacies of Trauma in Postwar Europe* (Oxford: Berg, 1999), 81–82; Bill Niven, *Facing the Nazi Past: United Germany and the Legacy of the Third Reich* (London: Routledge, 2002), 130; Omer Bartov, *Germany's War and the Holocaust: Disputed Histories* (Ithaca, NY: Cornell UP, 2003), 153.

[20] Niven, *Facing the Nazi Past,* 143–74.

[21] Schmitz, "Birth of the Collective," 106.

[22] Ibid., 106; Schmitz, "Return of Wartime Suffering," 4.

[23] Gillian Rose, *Mourning Becomes the Law* (Cambridge: CUP, 1996), 41, 43. Italics in the original.

[24] Primo Levi, *The Drowned and the Saved,* trans. Raymond Rosenthal (London: Abacus, 1988).

[25] Rose, *Mourning Becomes the Law,* 50.

[26] Siegfried Kracaeur, "Photography," in *The Mass Ornament: Weimar Essays,* ed. and trans. Thomas Levin (Cambridge, MA: Harvard UP, 1995), 51.

[27] Schlant, *Language of Silence,* 214.

[28] Levi, *Drowned and the Saved,* 23, 25, 33, 28.

[29] Schmitz, "Birth of the Collective," 105.

[30] William Collins Donahue, "Illusions of Subtlety: Bernhard Schlink's *Der Vorleser* and the Moral Limits of Holocaust Fiction," *German Life and Letters* 54, no. 1 (2001): 70.

[31] See Cornelia Brink, "Secular Icons: Looking at Photographs from the Nazi Concentration Camps," *History and Memory* 12, no. 1 (2000): 135–50.

[32] Giorgio Agamben, *Remnants of Auschwitz: The Witness and the Archive,* trans. Daniel Heller-Roazen (New York: Zone Books, 1999), 18–19, 20.

[33] Bartov, *Mirrors of Destruction,* 214.

[34] Schlant, *Language of Silence,* 214.

[35] LaCapra, *Writing History, Writing Trauma,* 20.

[36] Stuart Taberner, introduction to *Der Vorleser,* by Bernhard Schlink (London: Bristol Classical Press, 2003), 28; Donahue, "Illusions of Subtlety," 79.

[37] Donahue, "Illusions of Subtlety," 67.

[38] See, e.g., Bill Niven, "Bernhard Schlink's *Der Vorleser* and the Problem of Shame," *Modern Language Review* 98, no. 2 (2003): 393.

[39] Ibid.

[40] Taberner, "Introduction to *Der Vorleser,*" 24.

[41] Bartov, *Mirrors of Destruction,* 222.

[42] Donahue, "Illusions of Subtlety," 77.

11: Narrating German Suffering in the Shadow of Holocaust Victimology: W. G. Sebald, Contemporary Trauma Theory, and Dieter Forte's Air Raids Epic

Mary Cosgrove

Imagining Abjection: The Missing Bodies of the Bombed

SINCE W. G. SEBALD RAILED IN HIS Zurich lectures of 1997 against what he described as postwar German writers' lily-livered, even calculated evasion of the experience and consequences of the Allied bombing campaigns of German cities, the literary representation of this phase of the Second World War has been the subject of some debate.[1] The argument, now more than ten years old and modified by others, centered on the repression and taboo of the memory of the bombings. Sebald claimed that the writers of the immediate postwar period chose not to focus on the devastation that, leaving aside the traumatization of German civilians, in environmental terms remained rudely palpable and, one would think, impossible to ignore for many years to come (*LL* 8).[2] Using Alexander and Margarete Mitscherlichs' thesis regarding the German inability to mourn, Sebald argued that the energy of the new West German nation had been invested in the task of frenzied rebuilding and material gain.[3] Distracted thus, the majority gaze could avoid the obviously morbid foundations on which the pristine edifice of economic success rested: the rank, warmly malodorous, vermin-infested, steadily liquefying putrefaction of the dissolving dead (*LL* 12–13). Almost Baudelairean in his invocation of, in Julia Kristeva's sense, the abject human corpse, Sebald appeared to be saying that even those writers who did engage with the bombings failed to capture this vital level of the experience: the intimate proximity to all civilian survivors of rotting, stinking bodies.[4] For him the literary representation of the bombing atrocities would have been more convincing, concrete, and authentic, had these writers simply engaged their noses (*LL* 18). In his grand vision of repression the cellars full of corpses start to look like the national dirty secret, the sepulchral vault of a depersonalized German unconscious, while the exemplary industry above ground is a parody of the reality principle gone into manic overdrive (*LL* 21).

As Robert G. Moeller and others have pointed out, however, the story of German suffering during the bombings was anything but a secret in the immediate postwar period.[5] Indeed, the very corpses that Sebald complained were so absent from the literature of the 1950s provided important grist to the mill of German victimization discourses at the social, political, and cultural levels in both German states. Add to this the significant number of literary works, overlooked by Sebald, that did attempt to engage with the impact of the bombings on Germans and their cities, and his argument starts to sound like the tendentiously vicarious reconstruction of someone who through accident of birth was absent from the events but who felt that the bombings shaped them profoundly. Andreas Huyssen contends that Sebald's essay on the air war is a correction of the gap left by the generation of postwar writers.[6] From this viewpoint Sebald's essay travels back in time to do properly the job of representing this particular aspect of German suffering: righting the mnemonic wrongs of his literary forefathers by filling the gap left by the missing bodies of the bombed.

Particularly striking about the organization of Sebald's argument is thus the central position attributed to the literary rendering of "up close and personal" sensory experience for the purposes of, as Eric L. Santner terms it, the recuperation of affect long after traumatic events: remembering or, in Sebald's case, imagining the trauma by imagining abjection, that is, straining back from the present moment to inhale the once fetid stench of others' decay.[7] His focus on the absence of the local sights and smells of dead bodies from most accounts of the bombings he mentions can be understood as an attempt retrospectively to correct the olfactory malfunction and selective myopia of the writers of this generation. He puts himself in their shoes among the war ruins and raises the abject into a marker for the authentic recuperation of traumatized feelings. Only through imaginative engagement with the sensory impact of the dead on the living in the open graveyards of the destroyed cities can we — those born later — start to get an inkling of what the area bombings must have been like.

A further explanation for Sebald's fixation on the disgusting dimension to processes of decay lies in his overarching repression argument. From this angle, the corpse rhetorically supports his taboo hypothesis, as if the shock factor of reconstructing rot is tantamount finally to "getting real" in 1997, thereby blowing apart the supposed taboos of the past. Getting one up on the slipshod German writers of this generation is also icing on the cake for someone like Sebald who rarely approved of the literary ef-

forts produced by this cohort.[8] As Volker Hage points out, it was ultimately impossible to know what it was that Sebald imagined as the right
literary representation for any kind of trauma: he did not seem to know it
himself.[9] But, as I elaborate shortly, this does not make Sebald into an
extraordinary problem case in what Moeller terms the "long history of
memory" of German victimization. His was simply a loud and timely voice
on a topic that needed airing in the new "normalized" context of postunification Germany.[10] And he is not alone with his exacting standards for
representing the pain of others. For it seems that very few writers or the-
orists can agree on what constitutes the appropriate representative mode
for articulating trauma and historical catastrophe, even while the terms
and conditions for a fitting language of trauma, as I will show later, have
become increasingly formulaic. Indeed, Sebald's high aesthetic standards
for the literary representation of trauma provide an excellent foil for my
analysis, in my last section, of writer Dieter Forte's epic depiction of the
German childhood experience of being bombed.[11] For Forte's narrative
style that has been rightly accused of a rather naive portrayal of "Germans
as victims" departs from the narrative norms of trauma discourse that
Sebald's literary work in many ways exemplifies.[12] Thus a comparison of
these two different perspectives reveals much about our expectations of
what should constitute a trauma narrative. Such reflection, moreover, inevitably asks how the notion of trauma and its now special connection to
Holocaust victims transfers to the narrative field of Germans as victims.[13]

Things have moved on since 1997. Bill Niven's recent edited volume
shows that there was never a taboo on the topic of German suffering in
either German state.[14] Certainly, geopolitical allegiances made it more difficult to address some forms of suffering than others, but to speak of a
blanket prohibition on Germans as victims is not accurate. In 2002, Günter
Grass and Jörg Friedrich both published works dealing with the taboo on
German victimization.[15] Friedrich's controversial study, which focused on
the creaturely suffering of German civilians in the bombings at the expense of historical contextualization, provoked especially heated debate.
His emotive work filled the gap that Sebald had identified in 1997:
bombed bodies took center stage in the book. While Friedrich's work was
criticized for its neglect of the greater context of German responsibility
for the Second World War and for its questionable borrowing from the language of Holocaust "victimology,"[16] it was agreed that there was now a
need to address German suffering in a manner that went beyond the
taboo discussion to recognize that the topic of Germans as victims was a
legitimate discourse alongside, but emphatically not at the expense of,
other discourses of suffering and perpetration. This insistence on balance
pointed to a careful inclusiveness, as Niven terms it, in the parameters of
these debates.[17]

Yet even this problematic borrowing from the language of Holocaust victimhood resulted in some productive clarification of trauma terminology. Assmann notes in her analysis of the German term *Opfer* (victim), that there are different "kinds" of victims. On the one hand, those who willingly sacrifice themselves for a greater cause, that is, heroes or martyrs, may be termed *Opfer*. Yet, confusingly, *Opfer* may also refer to defenseless victims, that is, to those who are victimized by others and can do nothing to prevent their demise within an asymmetrical power relationship. The former group controls their fate, even if their end is tragic. By contrast, Jewish Holocaust victims provide the paradigm for the second kind of "victimology." As Assmann observes, this particular version of the victim has gained international currency in recent years: in our post-Holocaust age being recognized as having been an absolute victim has now become a positive marker of identity.[18]

On the point of keeping victim and perpetrator collectives clearly demarcated, Assmann makes a strong case for not applying to the perpetrator collective the concept of trauma as a general descriptor. While trauma can be part of individual perpetrator biographies, trauma and victimization should not become identity norms for a German collective that is obliged on the national and international stage to acknowledge the norm of guilt and responsibility for the crimes of the Holocaust.[19] The transference of the special aura of the Holocaust victim to German bombing victims is most certainly not what Sebald desired when he complained about the lack of abjection in postwar German literature. His objection is more fundamentally a reflection on the evasion of confrontation with guilt and shame, as if on closer inspection the many German corpses would reveal themselves in truth to be signifiers of the genocide of Europe's Jews. To conceive of Germans as victims of "total war" and to begin to mourn for traumas endured can happen in an ethical manner only if the greater context of what preceded the bombings also is remembered. The imperative to position German victimization within the context of German perpetration demonstrates just how tricky it is to write about German suffering in an ethical manner that is also aesthetically convincing. It should therefore come as no surprise that while Forte's representation of Germans as victims has been criticized for its naïveté, like Sebald he insists on the importance of Auschwitz as the general context where all commemorative acts concerning the German experience of bombing should take place.[20]

Signifying Suffering: The Postmodern Placebo Effect

The polemicizing use of abject imagery that we encounter in Sebald and Friedrich points to a more general problem in the signification of suffering that goes beyond the particular difficulties in the depiction of the German experience. Leaving aside the divisive issue of historical contextualization, common to both is an interest in the abject on the point of representing German suffering, as if trauma and catastrophe can be communicated most effectively in the description of physical processes of decay.

Behind this preference for the body is a sneaking regard for the power of the signification of the literal. I emphasize the term "signification" here because it is conceptually impossible to speak with intellectual rigor about the presence of the literal in any representative form. This is not to endorse the idea that we live in a world of simulacra that is somehow cut off from lived experience because the arbitrary nature of signification means that the essence of reality can never be captured in representation. To paraphrase Susan Sontag: it is a breathtaking provincialism to speak of reality only as a signifying spectacle, especially when it comes to the issue of other people's anguish, for this position suggests that there is no real suffering in the world.[21] It is undeniable, however, that on the issue of pain and trauma this basic problem of the relationship between signification and reality is pushed to the extreme. In the postwar context the discussion begins with Theodor W. Adorno's claim that there can be no poetry after Auschwitz — language cannot hope to communicate the breakdown in civilization that occurred during the Holocaust.[22] Instead, language will always encounter a lack in its signifying prowess, a gap or an emptiness where the catastrophe, in representational terms, should be but cannot ever be because as an extreme case of reality it is beyond signification. Thus the problem of how to represent the "unrepresentable" accompanies many reflective studies of the Holocaust.[23] As Santner shows, moreover, this problem of representation has also been an issue for Germans who are trying to come to terms with the past. Using the problem case of Paul de Man whose wartime writings gave voice to a refined kind of anti-Semitism that cast the ethical engagement of his subsequent work in a questionable light, Santner suggests that in signification terms the idea of the postmodern is inseparable from the post-Holocaust. The implication here is that Adorno's claim is a constitutive part of all postmodern theories of signification. In this regard Santner mentions Derrida's concept of the structurally elegiac dimension of every linguistic utterance, the idea that any signification is inconceivable without acknowledging its redundancy and signifying emptiness.[24]

As Santner points out, the problem with insisting on the elegiac quality of the signifier — as did de Man — is that any recuperation of traumatic affect that one, as a member of the post-Holocaust perpetrator collective, might be interested in doing is destined to fail. This is because the emptiness that is inscribed in the basic makeup of the signifier hinders subjective expression. In other words, if representation can only ever evoke

loss because the structural limitations of signification mean that it functions through the evocation of gaps and silence, then the question becomes
one of how to convey a sense of trauma that pierces the universal ano-
nymity of emptiness — the signifying norm — to articulate an authentic
sense of loss. To put it another way: if a writer is interested in conveying a
personal sense of loss, guilt, and responsibility, how do they get around
the placebo effect of a signifying system that can only ever convey lack
anyway? From this angle, the subjective expression of loss can only ever
be a kind of mute tautology, for how can individual mourning work take
place in the indifferent structure of language?

This might sound improbable; however, the kinds of judgments that
different German writers and thinkers make about each other's efforts to
document the experiences of the Second World War expose just how
emotive the perceived poles of meaningless abstraction and concrete authenticity can be. Although nobody really credits Adorno's proclamation
anymore, insisting instead that somehow we can and must talk about the
trauma of the past, individuals are very picky about what they consider to
be the appropriate way to address these matters.[25] A random sample of
some voices will suffice to show what I mean. Sebald concludes that Grass's
and Alfred Andersch's mechanical attempts to represent the Jewish experience of Nazi persecution do not work.[26] And while Hermann Kasack and
Hans Erich Nossack at least made the effort to write about the bombings,
in the end even their accounts are too abstract for Sebald (*LL* 61). By
contrast, Alexander Kluge's documentary style with its focus on concrete
details is deemed most effective (*LL* 80). Forte remarks that Sebald's
approach to reconstructing the experience of the bombings, while worth-
while, does not convince because he did not witness the event; no amount
of academic research will be able to cover up that biographical deficit (*SS*
33–34). By the same token, Sebald comments that Forte's novel on the
bombing of Düsseldorf, while most assuredly based on authentic memories, equally fails to convince because it is not documentary enough in
style; it lacks a certain literary sophistication that complicates representation, one of trauma discourse's criteria. Further, Walter Kempowski's
multivolume collection of documents that show how Germans and Jews
experienced the everyday reality of the Third Reich is also not convincing
for Sebald, for here we encounter an excess of documentation in the absence of any literary input.[27]

All comments are concerned with the particular bugbear of post-
Holocaust representation debates: authentic versus inauthentic representation. And while there have been differences of opinion concerning just
this matter from the perspective of Holocaust victims — Primo Levi versus Jean Améry, the issues raised by the Wilkomirski scandal — in the
context of Germans as victims, the indelible mark of perpetration compli-

cates the discussion.[28] Being a member of a guilty collective seems to push writers into a state of constant dissatisfaction with the efforts of their group, as if nothing anybody ever writes can do the work of mourning in the right way — whatever that might be. Moreover, performing mourning work in the right way seems to be connected increasingly to an idea of subjectivity (as opposed to impersonal, cold abstraction) that centers on specific details. In Sebald's essay on the air war and also in Friedrich's work, the bombed body is revived with just this authenticity claim in mind: it occupies the ethically invested discursive position of mediator between the *langue* and *parole* of trauma: the abstraction of total destruction and the concrete moment of organic decay. To put it another way, the central idea behind Sebald's invective is the distinction between trauma as an abstract and therefore rather suspect concept and the individual moment of traumatization that due to its focus on detail is somehow more authentic. And with this distinction we have arrived at what is so interesting about Sebald's air war essay — the fear as a German of falling into the wrong kind of trauma discourse and yet the need to find an adequate subjective language for the expression of German suffering. As Nicholas Stargardt observes, trauma, "like its cultural neighbour, victimhood [. . .] is often treated as a psychological — and moral — absolute. They foreclose the past, telling us what we will find before we have looked."[29] In other words, trauma can very rapidly become a cliché. For the ethically minded writer who is interested in representing the German experience of the air war the danger of cliché is compounded by membership in a guilty collective. It is against this backdrop of the fear of cliché, its aesthetic stasis, and its lack of ethical engagement that we should assess Sebald's rejection of conventional narrative and his demand that an authentic trauma discourse requires the ever more sophisticated mixing of documentary and fictional elements.[30]

Yet not even Sebald is immune to the pitfalls and problems that accompany any attempt to represent suffering. While his prose writing mixes documentary with fictional material, this considered approach has not prevented critics from observing a certain dubious sentimentality in his representation of Holocaust victims.[31] His demands of the catastrophe signifier, the bombed body — that it should display metonymical and metaphorical competence simultaneously, as indecipherable fragment and overarching whole — nevertheless remain high. For how can the focus on individual details really protect against the ethical dangers of extrapolation, abstraction, and the inadvertent slide into the lie of representation? His expectations resonate with the findings of recent American trauma theory, the subject of my next section. For American trauma theory also assigns a special place to the Holocaust victim as a paradigm of traumatized subjectivity that for the lucid writer complicates the aesthetic choices for conveying the experience of German suffering.

The Terms and Conditions of Trauma Theory

One of the central tenets of current trauma discourse, best exemplified in Cathy Caruth's work, is that trauma refuses narrative representation and thereby exposes the feebleness of signification and human reason in the face of a reality so horrific that it cannot be adequately captured in language. According to this line of reasoning, if the trauma can be put into some kind of rational language that attempts to make sense of it, it is somehow robbed of its traumatic authenticity and no longer qualifies as trauma. It follows then that trauma, to be authentic, must remain in a mysterious extralinguistic realm of nonsignification. Thus two contradictory demands are simultaneously placed on the idea of trauma: that it should speak at the same time that it remains silent.[32]

Ruth Leys observes that this conundrum is embedded in the genealogy of the concept since its inception just over a century ago.[33] She describes this paradox as the conflict between the mimetic or representative conceptualization of trauma and its definition as a veridical or literal event independent of signification. On the one hand, the understanding of trauma as a form of mimesis, which has its origins in the early therapeutic practice of hypnosis, holds that traumatic experience can be narrativized (*TG* 50). On the other, the veridical approach that originates in more recent empirical neuroscience refutes the symbolic or narrative dimension to trauma, insisting instead that the traumatic event is baldly external to the cognitive human subject, like a physical wound (*TG* 82). Therefore, the trauma can never be incorporated into a narrative that makes sense of it. With reference in particular to Caruth's work Leys points out that current trauma theory in the humanities has been particularly susceptible to this latter neurobiological insight, expanding it to bolster the claim that in trauma — and especially in the case of Holocaust trauma — we encounter the crisis of historical representation. Sebald's recuperation of the bombed body provides a good example of the illogical expectation that some special signifiers can assume the contradictory dual role of symbolization and literalness.

There is little way of making sense of Caruth's claim except to agree with Leys that here we have a marriage of disciplines that coexist in an unhappy but compelling relationship. It suffices to say that the criterion that trauma should be a literal event outside language and narrative (and therefore outside historical time) derives just as much from a preconceived idea of what trauma should look like as does the idea that trauma can be evoked indirectly through gaps, silences, and deferrals. Both positions — on the one hand antinarrative literal, on the other pronarrative mimesis — are equally formulaic and feed off each other. Common to both positions is the view that conventional declarative narrative simply cannot communicate trauma. However, not every writer chooses to communicate a traumatic experience using these criteria. In my discussion of Dieter Forte's epic narrative of the bombing of Düsseldorf during the Second World War I thus wish to question theory's demand for the foundational incompatibility of language and trauma.

Storytellers and Angels

Der Junge mit den blutigen Schuhen (The Boy with the Bloody Shoes, 1995) is the second installment of Dieter Forte's family trilogy *Das Haus auf meinen Schultern* (The House on My Shoulders, 2003). Beginning with *Das Muster* (The Pattern, 1992) and ending with *In der Erinnerung* (In Memory, 1998), the trilogy is narrated in an epic style that takes a panoramic perspective on the history of the boy's family on both the Polish maternal (the Lucacz) and Italian paternal (the Fontana) sides.[34] While the first installment covers several centuries of family history from 1133 to 1933 — tracking the family's origins in Italy and Poland and the meandering migratory path to Düsseldorf — the second and third volumes, written in the third person from the perspective of the nameless "boy," are based on Forte's life story. These latter installments narrate the experience and memory of the bombing of the district Düsseldorf-Oberbilk. Over the course of the three volumes the narrative moves back and forth between a wide perspective that takes in the historical *longue durée* and the more confined perspective of a child who witnessed the air war.

Der Junge mit den blutigen Schuhen coincides with recent historical scholarship that deals for the first time with the experience of children under National Socialism.[35] It is also part of a trend that has seen the emergence since the mid-nineties of several German narratives on the bombings, for some commentators the sign in unified Germany of a changed reception, as opposed to production context since the end of the war.[36] Forte, however, prefers to explain the creation of his trilogy by invoking the model of traumatic repression to explain the fifty-year incubation period between his childhood experiences and their belated transformation into literary prose (*SS* 42, 59). The act of writing takes on an almost sacred status in this vision. Forte emphasizes the moment of epiphany that accompanied the magical emergence of crystal-clear memories; by insisting on their vivid empirical accuracy he makes a clear case for the close correspondence of signifying totality to signified reality (*SS* 46). In this description of the sudden emergence of a miraculously intact totality of memories that, provided enough time has passed, can form part of a sensible narrative, there is little interest in the gaps and silences of standard trauma discourse (*SS* 65). Indeed, one could say that Forte's trilogy refutes trauma discourse's terms and conditions. There is never any sense, to borrow from Walter Benjamin, even in the sequences describing the worst of the bombings, that the Angelus Novus will appear in the heavens en route into a dire future. Instead, the key conceptual figure for this trilogy is Benjamin's epic storyteller, the ideal figure of premodern cultures who was able to tell stories to a receptive audience (*HS* 513–14). Benjamin's essay on this figure is an acknowledgment that the time of epic storytelling has passed; it is obsolete for the modern world because what it conveys — an ability to make sense of life and death through narrative as well as a sense of belonging — simply does not tally with the alienation of modern experience.[37]

As an epic narrative that tells the story of trauma, Forte's trilogy is thus a contradiction in terms. First, there is never any sense of spatial confusion, even in the scenes where Forte, his mother, and his younger brother are crawling through the cellars of different buildings in an attempt to escape the rapid spread of fire (*HS* 463, 469–70). In these scenes, it is Maria, the boy's mother, who is the focus of the narrative: to call her a character or a protagonist would be doing her an injustice. She is quite simply a force of nature who originates from a dynasty of similar characters that we are told about in detail in *Das Muster*. Second, the descriptions of the boy's neighborhood are also a tribute to roots, origins, firm points of orientation, no matter what devastation is wrought on the area by the bombing campaigns (*HS* 443–46, 455, 497–98, 500, 513). Third, the characters that populate this neighborhood reinforce the same kind of narrative logic: they have clear identities, for the main part they are robust folk, opposed to the National Socialist regime, who display a heartfelt solidarity with the Jews of the neighborhood (*HS* 448, 484–86, 494–98). As Helmut Schmitz points out, the narrative is questionable on these points, but not entirely compromised either, for there is no national subtext and therefore no real interest in presenting the Germans writ large as victims of Hitler and of the bombings.[38] If anything, what we encounter in these descriptions of Düsseldorf-Oberbilk is a personal attempt to retrieve the childhood neighborhood *Heimat* with its unique ethnic mix of inhabitants and its leftist labor traditions.[39] In Forte's case, the slide into sentimentality no doubt originates because this is the reconstruction of his life story and the commemoration of persons dear to him, and not from any questionable attempt to whitewash the collective past through focus on German victimization.

Compared to Uwe Timm's account of his childhood memories of the bombing of Hamburg in *Am Beispiel meines Bruders* (In My Brother's Shadow, 2003) this narrative lacks a certain sophistication that, given the often judgmental monitoring in literary criticism that German victim narratives are subjected to, can skew the nevertheless worthy intentions of this trilogy.[40] It was never conceptualized as the narrative of a sequence of horrors; for Forte, his work was justified only if it contained a positive message of survival and historical contextualization beyond the twentieth century and the air war. If he had not had the message of *Lebensmut* (life courage) to impart, he would not have written the trilogy in the first place (*SS* 63, 66). This is an interesting position, for it places a prohibition on narratives of pure negativity. In other words, negative experiences unavoidably feature in the story of the bombings; however, this negativity does not determine the overall interpretative and conceptual framework of the book. Instead, the positive desire to salvage in writing something from the wreck of one's life can help to explain why Forte opted for a narrative of continuity as opposed to a narrative featuring gaps and interruptions that are designed on the one hand to prompt ethical reflection in the reader's mind and, on the other, to suggest the idea of the traumatic wound as literally inscribed in the body of writing (*SS* 48). Consistent with the sense of a seamless sweep of events from the start to the end of a millennium is the grand message of endurance and survival despite suffering and trauma (*HS* 475). This positive message is continually thematized through a metacommentary on the power of storytelling itself. Books have an important symbolic function in this regard (*HS* 535, 556, 561). Indeed, one of the most cherished family relics is an ancient book that is buried for safekeeping during the bombings (*HS* 539). Beyond the symbolic function of books, however, the narrative often zooms out from the boy's point of view to the epic perspective in order to reflect on the life-giving sustenance of the power of stories (HS 427–29, 504, 542, 615–16). Making sense and attributing meaning is the purpose of this trilogy — as readers we are never really allowed to conclude that war, not even the Second World War, is a phenomenon that cannot be included in the greater chronology of the world. Indeed, Forte's ethical position on the task of narration after Auschwitz is in stark opposition to Adorno's prohibition. Against the idea that history's traumas cannot be rendered in poetic language, horror and trauma are integrated into the organic whole of the narrative that is constructed around the life and death cycles of generations of plucky characters. The narrative thus presents trauma as a phenomenon that is part of life; trauma is not radically Other, it does not exist in an extrahistorical vacuum of burgeoning mystery, power, and silence. This epic inclusiveness can be likened to a further feature of Benjamin's epic narrative: the integration, as opposed to separation from each other, of death and life, a perspective that contrasts with the modern compartmentalization of death safely away from the eyes of the living.[41]

The construction of trauma in contemporary theoretical reflection as an event in history, like the Holocaust, that is beyond the realm of signification, corresponds to this modern compartmentalizing tendency and thus places a question mark over the usefulness of trauma theory for understanding history, and over its influence on the ethics of memory in postwar literature. For it is one-sided: when applied to the analysis of literary accounts of victim experience (whether Jewish, German, or other) trauma theory becomes a theory of secrecy and the historically exceptional. It thus tends to support so-called uniqueness positions in historiography that have their strongest ideological articulation in the specific case of the Holocaust.[42] Bearing this in mind, it is refreshing that Forte chooses a narrative scheme that avoids all secrecy for his representation of the German child as victim of the Allied air war. In so doing he does not fall into the trap of borrowing from the discourse of Holocaust victimology that often intersects with trauma theory and that implies that the Holocaust is entirely unique in history. It cannot be said that Forte's focus on the German victim experience, for all its naïveté in places, is making a uniqueness claim that, like Friedrich's provocative study, implies a problematic equivalence between the victimization of victims and the victimization of the perpetrator nation. This may be deduced from his rejection of the aesthetics of trauma and the rhetoric of mourning. The elegiac loop of signification is absent from this work; in delivering a traditional story Forte circumvents the kind of abstraction Santner identified in de Man's writings. Whatever might be his sentimental lapses, on the level of signifying rhetoric this writer is not looking for exculpation. And we should not forget that accounts of German childhood experience of the war can be uncomfortable for the purist observer, for, as Nicholas Stargardt remarks, the childhood perspective tends to dissolve the barrier between perpetrators and victims: German children belong to neither group entirely.[43]

In response to Sebald's rather dismissive assessment of Forte's story: bearing in mind the inherent contradictions of trauma theory outlined above, it is of secondary importance whether the epic apparatus is a more suitable vessel for conveying subjective trauma than a narrative structure conceived around the montage of fragments and gaps. As I implied earlier, why should a fragmentary narrative (or indeed a deconstructionist theory of trauma) be any better equipped to communicate a negative experience than the rather more old-fashioned chronicle? In the final analysis both are carefully considered constructs and neither is entirely capable of revealing the "authentic" past.

Notes

[1] W. G. Sebald, *Luftkrieg und Literatur: Mit einem Essay zu Alfred Andersch* (Munich: Carl Hanser, 1999). Subsequent references to this work are cited in the text using the abbreviation *LL* and page number.

[2] Andreas Huyssen, "On Rewritings and New Beginnings: W. G. Sebald and the Literature about the Luftkrieg," *Zeitschrift für Literatur und Linguistik* 31 (2001): 72–90; Winfried Wilms, "Taboo and Repression in W. G. Sebald's *On the Natural History of Destruction*," in *W. G. Sebald — A Critical Companion*, ed. J. J. Long and Anne Whitehead (Seattle: U of Washington P, 2004), 175–89; Christian Schulte, "'Die Naturgeschichte der Zerstörung': W. G. Sebalds Thesen zu 'Luftkrieg und Literatur,'" *Text und Kritik* 158 (2003): 82–94.

[3] Andreas and Margarete Mitscherlich, *Die Unfähigkeit zu trauern: Grundlagen kollektiven Verhaltens* (Munich: Piper, 2007).

[4] Kristeva, *Powers of Horror: An Essay on Abjection*, trans. Leon S. Roudiez (New York: Columbia UP, 1982).

[5] Robert G. Moeller, "The Politics of the Past in the 1950s: Rhetorics of Victimisation in East and West Germany," in *Germans as Victims: Remembering the Past in Contemporary Germany*, ed. Bill Niven (Basingstoke, UK: Palgrave Macmillan, 2006), 26–42; in the same book, Niven, "Introduction: German Victimhood at the Turn of the Millennium," 1–25.

[6] Huyssen, "W. G. Sebald," 82–84; Volker Hage, *Zeugen der Zerstörung: Die Literaten und der Luftkrieg: Essays und Gespräche* (Frankfurt am Main: Suhrkamp, 2003), 28, 33–34, 113–31.

[7] Eric L. Santner, *Stranded Objects: Mourning, Memory and Film in Postwar Germany* (Ithaca, NY: Cornell UP, 1990), 155.

[8] See my "Melancholy Competitions: W. G. Sebald reads Günter Grass and Wolfgang Hildesheimer," *German Life and Letters* 59, no. 2 (2006): 217–32 and "The Anxiety of German Influence: Affiliation, Rejection, and Jewish Identity in W. G. Sebald's Work," in *German Memory Contests: The Quest for Identity in Literature, Film and Discourse*, ed. Anne Fuchs, Mary Cosgrove, and Georg Grote (Rochester, NY: Camden House, 2006), 229–52.

[9] Hage, *Zeugen der Zerstörung*, 123–24.

[10] Moeller, "Politics of the Past," in Niven, *Germans as Victims*, 28. Stuart Taberner, *German Literature of the 1990s and Beyond: Normalization and the Berlin Republic* (Rochester, NY: Camden House, 2005); also *German Culture, Politics and Literature into the Twenty-First Century: Beyond Normalization*, ed. Stuart Taberner and Paul Cooke (Rochester, NY: Camden House, 2006).

[11] Dieter Forte, *Das Haus auf meinen Schultern* (Frankfurt am Main: Fischer, 2002).

[12] Taberner, "Representations of German Wartime Suffering in Recent Fiction," in Niven, *Germans as Victims*, 173–75; Bill Niven, "German Victimhood," in ibid., 13; Helmut Schmitz, *On Their Own Terms: The Legacy of National Socialism in Post-1990 German Fiction* (Birmingham, UK: U of Birmingham P, 2004), 247; Stephan

Braese, "Bombenkrieg und literarische Gegenwart: Zu W. G. Sebald und Dieter Forte," *Mittelweg* 36 (2002): 12–19.

[13] Ruth Leys, *Trauma: A Genealogy* (Chicago: U of Chicago P, 2000), 33.

[14] Niven, *Germans as Victims.*

[15] Günter Grass, *Im Krebsgang: Eine Novelle* (Göttingen: Steidl, 2002); Jörg Friedrich, *Der Brand: Deutschland im Bombenkrieg 1940–1945* (Munich: Propyläen, 2002).

[16] Lothar Kettenacker, ed., *Ein Volk von Opfern? Die neue Debatte um den Bombenkrieg 1940–45* (Berlin: Rowohlt, 2003); Aleida Assmann, *Der lange Schatten der Vergangenheit: Erinnerungskultur und Geschichtspolitik* (Munich: Beck, 2006), 76.

[17] Niven, "German Victimhood," in his *Germans as Victims,* 24.

[18] Assmann, *Der lange Schatten,* 80–81.

[19] Ibid., 189.

[20] Hage, *Zeugen der Zerstörung,* 262. Forte, *Schweigen oder Sprechen,* ed. Volker Hage (Frankfurt am Main: Fischer, 2002), 41. Subsequent references to this work are cited in the text using the abbreviation *SS* and page number.

[21] Susan Sontag, *Regarding the Pain of Others* (London: Penguin, 2003), 98–99.

[22] Theodor W. Adorno, *Noten zur Literatur I* (Frankfurt am Main: Suhrkamp, 1973), 61.

[23] Dominick LaCapra, *Writing History, Writing Trauma* (Baltimore: Johns Hopkins UP, 2001); Saul Friedländer, ed., *Probing the Limits of Representation: Nazism and the "Final Solution"* (Cambridge, MA: Harvard UP, 1992); Wolfgang Benz and Dan Diner, eds., *Ist der Nationalsozialismus Geschichte? Zu Historisierung und Historikerstreit* (Frankfurt am Main: Fischer, 1987).

[24] Santner, *Stranded Objects,* 10, 15.

[25] Petra Kiedaisch, ed., *Lyrik nach Auschwitz? Adorno und die Dichter* (Stuttgart: Reclam, 1995).

[26] "Konstruktionen der Trauer: Günter Grass and Wolfgang Hildesheimer," in *Campo Santo,* ed. Sven Meyer (Munich: Carl Hanser, 2003), 101–27; "Der Schriftsteller Alfred Andersch," in *Luftkrieg und Literatur,* 121–60.

[27] Hage, *Zeugen der Zerstörung,* 266 and 274. Kempowski, *Das Echelot: Ein kollektives Tagebuch. Januar und Februar 1943* (Munich: Knaus, 1993) and *Das Echelot: Fuga Furiosa. Ein kollektives Tagebuch. Winter 1945* (Munich: Knaus, 1999).

[28] Irene Heidelberger-Leonard, *Jean Améry: Revolte in der Resignation* (Stuttgart: Klett-Cotta, 2004), 93–103. On the Wilkomirski affair in which it was discovered that Swiss writer Bruno Grosjean had adopted the false Jewish identity of Binjamin Wilkomirski, see Daniel Ganzfried and Sebastian Hefti, eds., *Alias Wilkomirski: Die Holocaust Travestie. Enthüllung und Dokumentation eines literarischen Skandals* (Berlin: Jüdischer, 2002).

[29] Nicholas Stargardt, *Witnesses of War: Children's Lives under the Nazis* (London: Jonathan Cape, 2005), 9.

[30] Hage, *Zeugen der Zerstörung,* 265 and 268–69.

[31] Cosgrove, "Anxiety of German Influence," in Fuchs et al., *German Memory Contests*, 229–52; Stuart Taberner, "German Nostalgia? Remembering German-Jewish Life in W. G. Sebald's *Die Ausgewanderten* and *Austerlitz*," *Germanic Review* 3 (2004): 181–202.

[32] Cathy Caruth, *Unclaimed Experience: Trauma, Narrative, and History* (Baltimore: Johns Hopkins UP, 1996), introd., chap. 1 and 3.

[33] Leys, *Trauma: A Genealogy*. Subsequent references to this work are cited in the text using the abbreviation *TG* and page number.

[34] *Das Muster* (Frankfurt am Main: Fischer, 1992); *Der Junge mit den blutigen Schuhen* (Frankfurt am Main: Fischer, 1995); *In der Erinnerung* (Frankfurt am Main: Fischer, 1998). I use the compilation *Das Haus auf meinen Schultern*.

[35] Stargardt, *Witnesses of War*; Wolfgang and Ute Benz, *Sozialisation und Traumatisierung: Kinder in der Zeit des Nationalsozialismus* (Frankfurt am Main: Fischer, 1998). See also Debbie Pinfold, *The Child's View of the Third Reich in German Literature* (Oxford: OUP, 2001).

[36] Hage, *Zeugen der Zerstörung*, 119–20.

[37] Benjamin, *Illuminationen: Ausgewählte Schriften* (Frankfurt am Main: Suhrkamp, 1961), 272–73.

[38] Schmitz, *On Their Own Terms*, 257.

[39] Stargardt, *Witnesses of War*, 14.

[40] See Braese, "Bombenkrieg und literarische Gegenwart," 19–20.

[41] Benjamin, *Illuminationen*, 421–22.

[42] A. Dirk Moses, "The Holocaust and Genocide," in *The Historiography of the Holocaust*, ed. Dan Stone (Basingstoke, UK: Palgrave Macmillan, 2004), 533–55; Sigrid Weigel, "Télescopage im Unbewssten: Zum Verhältnis von Trauma, Geschichtsbegriff und Literatur," in *Trauma: Zwischen Psychoalayse und kulturellem Deutungsmuster*, ed. Elisabeth Bronfen, Birgit Erdle, and Sigrid Weigel (Cologne: Böhlau, 1999), 51–76.

[43] Stargardt, *Witnesses of War*, 14.

12: Günter Grass's Account of German Wartime Suffering in *Beim Häuten der Zwiebel:* Mind in Mourning or Boy Adventurer?

Helen Finch

"WHAT DO I RETAIN FROM THE WAR and my camp experience besides episodes that have been bound together into anecdotes or wish to remain variable as true stories?" Günter Grass's narrator asks this question at the end of the wartime section of his 2006 autobiography, *Beim Häuten der Zwiebel* (Peeling the Onion).[1] He concludes that the ability to create a literary feast out of the stuff of his imagination, to invite invisible guests to a dazzlingly heterogeneous dinner table, is the most lasting element of his wartime and immediate postwar experiences. Grass tells us, then, that this period has provided the material for his subsequent literary production, as a brief glance over his extensive back catalogue would readily show. How, then, does Grass blend together the two categories of "anecdotes" and "variable true stories" to "have the last word" on the representation of his life in the literary sphere (*PO* 2)? Is *Beim Häuten der Zwiebel* an ethically probing account of his youthful self, or an anecdotal romp?

In this chapter, I examine those aesthetic and ethical pitfalls of the anecdotal approach that conflict with Grass's scrutiny of German wartime suffering and wartime culpability. I address Grass's ethics of representation through close readings of two moments in particular in the wartime and camp sections of his autobiography that throw up disturbing questions about Grass's self-representation — not so much about his own youthful self — he constantly calls his articulation of his identity and ethical choices into question — but rather more about the cast of characters who surround him. These problematic moments call to mind criticisms that fellow writer, literary critic, and academic W. G. Sebald made of Grass's work twenty-three years earlier. In his essay "Constructs of Mourning: Günter Grass and Wolfgang Hildesheimer,"[2] Sebald claims that Grass's ethics of representation, and hence his mourning work on behalf of the victims of National Socialism, are inadequate. According to Sebald, Grass pays lip service to the smell of corpses in the cellar and attempts to include concrete details of the sufferings of the Jews of Danzig in his narrative but mixes so many "picturesque details and brave figures"[3] with his account of the crimes of National Socialism, that his aesthetics only serve as another form of repression of his, and his nation's, culpability in these crimes. Although Sebald is discussing Grass's much earlier work, *Aus dem Tagebuch einer Schnecke* (From the Diary of a Snail, 1972), the questioning of Grass's ethics that has emerged since the publication of his autobiography casts doubts on his aesthetics of representation anew.

The controversy surrounding Grass's confession of service in the *Waffen SS* has struck at the heart of his artistic credibility, and in the German public sphere has overshadowed the literary and ethical import of the autobiography itself. This chapter does not concern itself with the finger-wagging arguments about the rights and wrongs of Grass's SS service, his curious forty-year silence (as Klaus Wagenbach noted in *Die Zeit,* Grass had been relatively open about his SS membership until the mid-1960s),[4] or his eve-of-publication confession, which not only relieved critics of the necessity of actually reading the book, but also made — of a long and reasonably complex narrative — a single, easily digestible moment in Germany's ongoing debate on German wartime guilt and German wartime suffering.[5] Instead, I question the ethics of Grass's representation of German wartime suffering.

Despite Grass's very public intervention in the debate surrounding cultural memory, in the form of his confessional interview in the *Frankfurter Allgemeine Zeitung,*[6] his autobiography is focused on the search for his elusive, often incomprehensible, continuously fictionalized childhood self. Grass is less explicitly concerned with wider questions of twenty-first-century cultural concern than with constructing a subjective account of his wartime experiences. In contrast to *Aus dem Tagebuch einer Schnecke,* this account is in constant dialogue, not with the German discourse of *Vergangenheitsbewältigung* (coming to terms with the past) per se, but with the intertextual relationship of his life to his literary works. Grass is not trying to uncover narratives of hitherto untold wartime suffering, but rather to unearth his own self-in-the-past and the traces of his future authorial selves. Indeed, with a nod to the Bildungsroman tradition, he divides his autobiography into two parts: his *Lehrjahre* (artistic apprenticeship) and his *Wanderjahre* (journeyman years), leaving off at the age of thirty and his arrival as a mature artist. This, then, is an aesthetic project that takes ethics into account, rather than a text about *Vergangenheitsbewältigung.*

Beim Häuten der Zwiebel is a form of autobiography that, to follow Philippe Lejeune's terminology, is not merely "autodiagetic"[7] but that contains a diagetic relationship to a multitude of Grass's authorial selves over the course of fifty years, or, as Stuart Taberner names it, to his "exemplary" life story.[8] *Beim Häuten der Zwiebel* occupies an unstable space between literary autobiography, living history, exemplary memory work, self-exculpation, and intertextual game. As Fuchs notes, the narrative constitutes the self by means of the "fruitful traffic between biography and fiction."[9] Thus, while at all times Grass acknowledges how hard it is to recapture his lost youthful self, the breaks and fissures in his memory, and the "screen memory" that his later literary reworkings of historical events provide for his personal memories, the text is nonetheless presented as a seamless narrative whole. It is a chronological narrative that acknowledges the difficulties inherent in its own construction, but without deliberate authorial inconsistencies or radical aesthetic innovations. Grass attempts to maintain this balance between narrative consistency and subjective dissolution throughout, but his authorial control begins to become disrupted in those sections of the autobiography where he describes his own wartime traumas.

Grass embarks on his endeavor with great panache. If the early sections of the biography are reflective and descriptive — "true stories" (*PO* 2) [wahre Geschichten] — the anecdotal wartime sections of the autobiography provide some of its most disturbing and unexpected images, from the deserters hanging from trees at the roadside as the young Grass stumbles from front to front, to the stolen jam that Grass smuggles in his gas mask container, which explodes when hit by a grenade, cursing him with a jammy bottom for the rest of his wartime experiences. Grass's anecdotal narrative flings the reader as directly as possible into the ripped film of his own memories. At the same time, he constantly wraps these stories in warnings that they have been told and retold so often that their original traces are all but irretrievable.

To describe the ruptures of his self, Grass operates with three interrelated models of memory in the autobiography. First, there is the title model of the onion, that must be peeled to access truth hidden in its layers within. The onion skin is, Grass tells us, inscribed like paper; to peel it is at once to read it and (though this aspect of peeling is nowhere made explicit) destroy it. (The connotation of crocodile tears, which features in the "onion cellar" episode in *The Tin Drum*, is not mentioned here either). Grass complements the model of the onion with the metaphor of the prehistoric fly preserved in amber, presumably Baltic amber. The fly can be surveyed complete and unchanged by the passage of time, but is radically decontextualized, contributing little either to the narrative coherence of the self or to the narrator's understanding of his memories.

During the wartime sections of the novel, neither the amber nor the onion are of much use to Grass:

> Everything that has been preserved as danger survived in the war must
> be doubted, even if it boasts of concrete detail in stories claiming to be
> true and as tangible as the mosquito in my amber. (*PO* 127)

Instead, he compares his wartime memories to a damaged film, run both
backward and forward, with gaps, discontinuities, and obscurities. (Indeed, earlier, Grass writes that memories of Nazi stereotypes in films had
overlaid his own memories; the film that is being ripped is not even
original archive footage in itself). By advertising the danger of inaccuracy,
and the concomitant danger that these few surviving stories have been
retold so frequently that the retelling has taken the place of the original
memory trace, the historical accuracy of Grass's testimony becomes of less
significance than its poetic structures. Significantly, Grass constantly uses
Hans Christoffel Grimmelshausen's baroque novel *Der abentheurliche Simplicissimus Teutsch* (1668) as an intertext through which he mediates his
own horrific experiences when rational recall becomes impossible. Indeed,
even as he was stumbling around the front, Grass writes that he could only
understand his suffering at that time by calling up his memories of this
early German text (*PO* 145).

The deployment of *Simplicissimus Teutsch* points toward the most
problematic moment in Grass's narrative strategy. On the one hand, Grass's
accounts of his aesthetic education offer some of the most rich and self-aware moments in the text, pointing to the faults and ironies in his self-formation. Grass thus records his teenage, self-righteous outrage on reading about the injustices perpetrated against the Germans in the sixteenth
century — this, he transformed into the stuff of his adolescent fiction
while remaining oblivious to the egregious crimes against humanity being
perpetrated outside his living room window in Danzig. Indeed, it is just
as well that he was not able to enter a literary competition in the Nazi
children's newspaper *Hilf mit!*, because

> the premature debut of my literary career would have been Nazi-tarnished; it would have been tantamount to handing the evidence —
> complete with chapter and verse — to the always ravenous journalists
> on a silver platter. (*PO* 35)

This is a richly ironic reflection, at once an attack on the feuilleton culture
that has made Grass famous and notorious for fifty years and a condemnation of his own adolescent misappropriation of German baroque literature for National Socialist fantasy. Here, Grass also implicitly reserves the
right to criticize his youthful Nazi tendencies for himself alone.

On the other hand, however, by marshaling *Simplicissimus Teutsch* later
in the autobiography as an intertextual directory of the wartime horrors
that he views, Grass implicitly forces a parallel between his war text and
that of Grimmelshausen:

> I had already read everything I write here. I had read it in Remarque
> or Céline, who — like Grimmelshausen before them in his description
> of the Battle of Wittstock, when the Swedes hacked the Kaiser's troops
> to pieces — were merely quoting the scenes of horror handed down to
> them. . . . (*PO* 125)

Grass's baroque literary program has often been examined in Grass scholarship,[10] and the wartime intertextual references to Grimmelshausen in *Beim Häuten der Zwiebel* reflect baroque influences that Grass had long incorporated in other works. Nonetheless, the two texts are generically quite different. Thus *Simplicissimus Teutsch* is fictional and fantastic, even as it contains elements of reportage. Similarly, although it is intended, like Grass's text, to provide an account of the protagonist's interior development, such as it is, *Simplicissimus Teutsch* is also a satirical text attacking the Thirty Years' War as a tragedy for the people of Germany, a pointless and circular system of self-destruction that feeds off the oppressed peasants and aggrandizes the powerful. *Simplicissimus* is rich in pointed political critique of war profiteering, human rights abuses, and attacks on contemporary power structures that, although the novel was written twenty years after the Thirty Years' War, certainly still retained topical relevance at the time. By transposing certain tropes of *Simplicissimus* to the front in 1945, Grass dehistoricizes their critical bite, losing Grimmelshausen's contemporary satire in favor of a generalized reaction of horror to the timeless injustices of war. This move elides the crucial difference between a civil war in the premodern German territories and Germany's war of National Socialist aggression against its European neighbors. Moreover, by invoking Grimmelshausen as his mentor on the front, Grass implicitly links his experiences of suffering to his earlier adolescent fantasies about the outrages perpetrated on the German people centuries ago. (Thus Grass is pleased that the SS unit he is assigned to is named after the hero of the sixteenth-century peasant uprising, Jörg von Frundsberg, as the title helps him to see the SS as a European group of vigilantes fighting against the communist enemy). Such a dehistoricizing account of wartime suffering also skirts close to the existentialist reaction to the war that was modish in the early 1950s and that Grass trenchantly criticizes elsewhere in the text.

The remainder of *Beim Häuten der Zwiebel* deploys what Fuchs has correctly identified as a "dialectical process in which each act of self-accusation triggers moments of self-exoneration."[11] The wartime sections of the autobiography, which depart from the otherwise chronological narration of memory in favor of these discontinuous filmic and baroque techniques, are dialectically reflected on throughout the rest of the text, which, at least in its first half, is intensely concerned with an attempt to understand and come to ethical terms with Grass's SS membership. The recourse to an intertextual model, which also firmly sites the autobiography within a lineage of a lifetime's literary production, might be viewed as a necessary strategy to record horrors that would otherwise find no adequate literary expression, as well as recording a significant stage in Grass's aesthetic education.

A closer reading of the wartime passages, however, suggests that Grass's usage of *Simplicissimus Teutsch* coincides with a dehistoricizing, indeed neo-Romantic approach to the events narrated, and consequently allows Grass's self in the past to evade certain confrontations with the specific guilt of his wartime SS membership, even as the framing narrative claims scrupulously to accept responsibility for that guilt. Grass names his sins as sins of omission that can be dialectically redeemed elsewhere in the text of his life. This frequently occurs, in keeping with his Catholic upbringing, for example, when Grass receives absolution from a victim of Nazi tyranny after the war such as his anti-Nazi Latin teacher.

Grass does acknowledge his structural guilt as a member of a war machine that committed human rights violations, as well as indicting the bullying by veterans of the front that formed an inherent part of his SS training. Such institutionalized bullying — Grass need not spell out this point — was intended to produce brutalized recruits who would carry out atrocities without excessive hesitation. When Grass carries out the prank of urinating in his superior's coffee, it is in necessary self-defense against this regime — another recruit suffering the same conditions hanged himself. Equally, when his military superiors attempt to groom Grass for recruitment into the officer class, his protestation that he wants to become an artist after the war saves him from an elite SS training school, and thereby greater culpability in wartime guilt. Thus, boy-scoutish pranks and an emergent understanding of an aesthetic self prove to be essential strategies by which the teenaged Grass resists the totalizing construction of his subjectivity by the National Socialist order.

The picaresque self-image borrowed from Grimmelshausen emerges when Grass's previous delusional self-image as "picture-book hero" (*PO* 125) is destroyed by the realities of war. From this point in the narrative onward, Grass uses the autobiographical self-in-the-past as a naïve mirror of the horrors and absurdities around him. Less felicitously, the picaresque form also encourages the reader to identify with his activities on the front to a problematic degree. The dangers that may be inherent in such identification are intimated at the point when Grass becomes detached from his regiment and stumbles around alone in a wood on the front. (He is escaping an attack by "Ivans": reflecting Nazi stereotypes of mindless eastern hordes, the Russian soldiers Grass encounters are never personalized in any way in his narrative). Thus removed from the National Socialist order, and playing dead "as if he could escape the march of history" (*PO* 136), the teenage Grass constructs a compensatory literary order to map his way through this ahistorical territory. Once the logics of history and memory have broken down, Grass turns to internalized literary models: he compares his weeping, lost, self-in-the-past to a figure who has escaped from a Grimm's fairy tale, and to Simplicius Teutsch himself, who invokes the power of words to help him survive the war.

The woodland scene moves from this intertextual prologue to a filmic buildup of narrative tension: "I heard steps or something that could be construed as steps. An animal of some kind? A boar? Maybe even a unicorn" (*PO* 138). The sombre, metatextual scene of the previous pages is abandoned in favor of a suspenseful narrative characterized by short sentences, swift switching between present and past tense, "an idea for a ballet or movie scene. Like the scene that sets up the climax in every classic Western: the ritual dance before the final shoot-out" (*PO* 138). Lost and terrified, Grass does not know whether the approaching being is friend or enemy. To master his fear, he decides to sing, rejecting contemporary hits and marching songs in favor of the German children's song of loss and homecoming, "Hans left home, on his own." The tension is finally broken when the stranger in the wood responds, "Went into the world alone" (*PO* 139). This deftly constructed scene is indeed worthy of a classic Western, yet provides a strange point of narrative resolution: German wartime suffering is mitigated when, through the power of German folk culture, an older German soldier finds a lost SS member and henceforth takes him under his wing. Returning to his literary intertexts, Grass tells us:

> He became my guardian angel, the soulmate I had seen at work in Grimmelshausen, my Heartbrother: he led me out of the woods and over the fields and across the Russian front line. (*PO* 140)

This touching vignette hovers uncomfortably between the vividness of eyewitness testimony and an ethically dubious mythologization of clichés of German cultural identity: "Two native speakers of German are wandering through the pitch-dark woods" (*PO* 139) [Hier irren zwei menschliche Wesen deutscher Zunge durch den nachtdunklen Wald], two "brothers in song," who address each other in "German soldierspeak" (*PO* 139). Such quasi-existentialist language — language that, as I have noted, Grass sharply critiques at several other points in the autobiography — elides the ethically compromised position of the two German soldiers who are contributing to Hitler's war of aggression. It also elides Grass's personal memory work in favor of a disquieting ahistorical picture of German nobility and brotherhood in the face of nameless suffering. Even if it is intended to be read as a playful or ironic Romantic fairytale, the ethically compromised point in the narrative in which it is inserted is in extremely questionable taste.

Here, it is useful to return to the accusations that Sebald made in relation to *Aus dem Tagebuch einer Schnecke,* Grass's reflections on the *Sozialdemokratische Partei Deutschlands* (SPD, Social Democratic Party of Germany) election campaign of 1967. Sebald argued that Grass's work shows insufficient evidence of mourning for Nazi crimes. He claims that the author creates the hoary old wish-figure of the "Good German" to ward off this mourning and guilt that a real engagement with German culpability in war crimes would cause to his self. (In *Aus dem Tagebuch einer Schnecke* the "Good German" is Hermann Ott alias Zwiefel, a fabulist who, like Scheherazade, spins an endlessly digressive narrative to protect himself from falling victim to the SS). The creation of such figures, Sebald writes, leads German postwar writers to ignore the "grave and lasting deformations in the emotional life of those who let themselves be integrated into the system without questioning it."[12] Sebald further charges Grass with merely copying research about the persecution of the Jewish community of Danzig into his book, without personally engaging with the concrete extent of the atrocities committed. The figure of Hermann Ott thus functions as an alibi that saves Grass from fulfilling his writer's melancholy vocation of true engagement with German crimes. *Aus dem Tagebuch einer Schnecke,* Sebald concludes, is proof that literature alone is no longer adequate to record the truth and is detrimental to the truth.

Mary Cosgrove has mounted a very successful defense of Grass against these charges.[13] She argues that Sebald misunderstands Grass's literary project of *Vergegenkunft* (the merging of past, present, and future into one aesthetic mode), which aims not to foreground guilt and melancholia in a timeless metaphysical space, but rather to make the past irrupt into the present, and to teach the present about the past. For her, *Aus dem Tagebuch einer Schnecke* is primarily a pedagogical and intergenerational project. In turn, she imputes to Sebald a generational *ressentiment,* founded in a compulsively backward-looking melancholy that delegitimizes the time following the Second World War as a "timeless, futureless vacuum."[14] Nonetheless, Sebald's criticisms do point to just those ethically problematic moments of representation of German guilt and German wartime suffering in *Beim Häuten der Zwiebel.* On the one hand, Grass's account is saturated with reflections on personal and national guilt and shame. While the text details certain instances of German wartime suffering that Grass personally witnessed, such as Berlin in flames, Dresden smouldering, columns of refugees attacked by Russian tanks, and the bodies of shot deserters from the German armed forces, it in no way sets out to advocate any kind of moral equivalence between German suffering and the crimes perpetrated by Germans on others. On the other hand, close readings of *Beim Häuten der Zwiebel* reveal traces of just those questionable aesthetic strategies that Sebald diagnosed fifteen years earlier in his work.

For instance, the idealized and improbable figure of the "Good German" is certainly revived in the figure of "Hans," the soldier who saves Grass's Gretel in the woods, and who miraculously preserves Grass's life and his own throughout a series of attacks by "Ivan." Significantly, it is Hans who advises Grass that he should discard the SS runes on his collar if he wants to survive, a tactic that, indeed, Grass seems to have followed until September 2006. Hans, Grass tells us, never aspired to higher than the rank of lance corporal; he only wanted to fulfill the duties of an obedient soldier without in any way subscribing to Nazi ideology. This historically illegitimate contrast between good soldier and bad Nazi is brought out when Grass and Hans are challenged to present their marching orders at a roadblock, and subsequently imprisoned under threat of court-martial.[15] The roadblock is run by a comically sinister Austrian SS officer, who not only takes a sadistic delight in applying the letter of military law that Hans supposedly scorns in favor of brotherly solidarity, but also sports a bejeweled lapdog like a Bond villain. By contrast, Hans's insistence on maintaining the military forms of address between himself and Grass is regarded as a benign maintenance of order in the baroque world of wartime chaos. Once he has escaped the wartime horrors, Grass says that, as a burned child who had lost all belief in God or *Führer,* the lance corporal was the only authority, other than the man who taught him cooking in the prisoner of war camp, whom he still respected. Thus, despite his copious self-scrutiny and self-dissection throughout the text, at no point does Grass place this figure of the "good soldier" under scrutiny. Although he acknowledges that he himself is culpable in German war crimes merely by virtue of having participated in the war machine, without personally having committed any atrocity, the same qualifier is not applied to Hans. In Hans, his "Heartbrother" from Grimmelshausen, Grass preserves German military virtue intact (*PO* 140).

Sebald further accuses Grass, in relation to *Aus dem Tagebuch einer Schnecke,* of paying only perfunctory lip service to the sufferings of the Jews at the hands of the Germans. Now, during the filmic wartime sections of *Beim Häuten der Zwiebel,* Grass writes that he does not try to capture anything that was not in his direct field of vision. Earlier in the autobiography, he does detail the gradual persecution and deportation of the Jews of Danzig as it happened before his curious but indifferent child's eye. The mature Grass expresses horror at his childish lack of anger at the injustices happening before his gaze. Thus the function of Grass's memoir is categorically different to that of his other writings, even such autobiographical texts as *Aus dem Tagebuch einer Schnecke:* it is to bear witness to his own experience, not to expose the "stink of corpses in the cellar" to the reading public. Grass avoids the grand metaphorical set pieces that form part of his fictional works, restricting his record of the end of the war to those images and emotions that he can retrieve from his own experience. It was not until a year after the end of the war, he says, that he truly admitted that he had "unknowingly — or more precisely, unwilling to know — taken part in a crime that did not diminish over the years" (*PO* 196).

Conscious guilt and shame do not form part of his film of German wartime suffering. While describing the gradual awakening of his conscience, Grass describes another perturbing incident when he is detailed, as a POW, to work in a United States Army canteen along with a group of Jewish concentration camp survivors. The canteen is a significant location: along with terror, hunger is the strongest aspect of German wartime suffering throughout the autobiography.

> Much as my hunger gnawed away at me, it was nothing compared to what I later learned had been the prescribed variety in the concentration camps or our camps for Russian prisoners of war, which caused hundreds of thousands to starve, starve to death. But the only hunger I can put into words is my own. . . . (*PO* 160)

This seemingly humble statement, though, swiftly becomes dialectically transformed into resentment regarding German suffering at the hands of the American occupiers. Grass was convinced that his hunger in the POW camp was as a direct result of the policies of the (in the event never implemented) American Morgenthau plan for the reduction of postwar Germany to an agricultural colony. In this depiction of the POW camp, hunger is not presented as a widespread condition throughout Europe after 1945, the consequence of Hitler's war, but specifically experienced as an unfair weapon used by the victorious Americans against the defeated Germans.

When Grass manages to get assigned to work in the United States Army canteen, then, he is shocked by the amount of food that the American soldiers wastefully throw away. This ongoing *ressentiment* informs his entire account of his interaction with his coworkers, the "DPs" (displaced persons, frequently Jewish survivors of German camps). While the two groups of workers initially hurl insults at each other, Grass claims that the group's adolescent rivalry over their relative status as victims and perpetrators is not only semijocular, but also soon subsumed in a collective disgust for the racism of their (white) American masters. Interpunctuating this narrative, Grass narrates his initial exposure to the reality of the mass murder of Jews. He tells how at first he did not know about and then refused to believe the full horror of the camps, even when his American captors provided visual evidence of the genocide. Shame, like hunger, only came later, Grass claims. After completing this guilt-ridden account of his shared culpability, he returns to his anecdotes about the pubescent mud-slinging between the group of child soldiers and the group of concentration camp survivors in the kitchen. The adolescents, he claim, bond over their shared fantasies of girls — "first calling them whores, then putting them on a pedestal" — fantasies that the adolescents consider to be qualitatively different to the "laughable" pinups that the American GIs post (*PO* 197). They also collaborate on stealing food from the kitchen.

Grass ends this account by talking about how he fictionalized the story of one of these Jewish survivors in the speech, "A Talk about Accommodation," that he gave in Tel Aviv in 1967. He completes the stories of his Jewish canteen workers by saying that he presumes that they remained in the canteen before they "probably" found a way to Palestine where "the promise of Israel as a sovereign state and war upon war stood ahead of them" (*PO* 198). Grass's boy-scout anecdote deftly and worryingly transforms the victims into, at the very least, antagonists and, by implication, future perpetrators. In "A Talk about Accommodation," Grass also told the tale of the prisoners of war and the displaced persons. Here, however, Grass's intention is avowedly pedagogical. The two opposing groups of adolescents are personified as "Ben," a survivor, and "Dieter," a German who is "only a part" of Grass (*PO* 198): Ben and Dieter aggressively attack each other in the kitchen, and an Austrian-American United States officer, Mautler, attempts to use the fight as a pedagogical opportunity for explaining the National Socialist system of brutalization. "Strange successes were accounted to the man of reason: Ben and Dieter didn't beat each other up any more: they united against Mautler."[16] In "A Talk about Accommodation," Ben's and Dieter's adolescent antagonism and subsequent refusal to become enlightened about their shared past becomes a parable for relations between Israel and Germany, for complacency about Germany's criminal past and the conservative friendship between Ben Gurion and Konrad Adenauer. In this speech, Grass rhetorically identifies with Mautler, the American enlightener: "Two men in the treadmill of reason were an example for me. For I only want to advocate for reason. She stands, weak, among growing accommodation."[17]

As in *Aus dem Tagebuch einer Schnecke,* published in the same year, Grass here deploys a fictionalization of his past with an avowedly educational, enlightening, and controversial aim. "Ben" and "Dieter," like "Ott alias Zwiefel" become ciphers in Grass's political campaigns. Wartime anecdote, in 1967, becomes transformed into moral allegory.

In *Beim Häuten der Zwiebel,* forty years later, German guilt and Jewish suffering become a side note in a camp narrative otherwise filled with tales of plucky survival tactics and lively black-market deals. It is precisely this boy-scout atmosphere that Sebald in an interview picked out as particularly objectionable in his father's photographs of the early years of the war. The generation of Sebald's father, to which Grass belongs, Sebald suggests, was one that painted participation in the Nazi war as a welcome escape from petit bourgeois existence, and which did not make any meaningful attempt to integrate the "corpses in the cellar" into this jovial picture.[18] For Sebald, the ethics of representation remain paramount in any discussion of German wartime suffering.

Does the particular poetic status of *Beim Häuten der Zwiebel,* which is aesthetically and ethically different from that of Grass's fictional texts, imply that its ethics of representation must also be different? The autobiography is an attempt to retrieve his fifteen-year-old self, who appears as an alien being to him, and an attempt to understand the decisions that he made and the context that he lived in. If in the 1960s Grass deployed anecdotes from his youth as elaborate political allegory, in *Beim Häuten der Zwiebel* the anecdotes reappear stripped of allegory, as a picaresque series of grotesque and engaging adventures. *Beim Häuten der Zwiebel,* it seems, departs from the project of *Vergegenkunft,* and becomes entirely self-reflexive autobiography: not the instruction of ethical selves, but the sentimental education of the aesthetic self is paramount here. The one repeated allegory that appears throughout the text is the one that annoys both Grass's critics and his own sister: that of himself and a fellow teenage POW, Joseph, who repeatedly dice for the meaning of the future together in camp in Bad Aibling. Both youths are Catholic, both have poetic aspirations. But whereas Joseph is passionately ascetic and ambitious, Grass is incorrigibly skeptical, and can only believe in many truths, not Joseph's one. Joseph "swallowed his anti-doubt pills like a good boy" (*PO* 289), whereas Grass remains addicted to his "second hunger" of the flesh, and to undogmatic art. This allegory is not only an entertainingly topical dig at the present "German Pope," Joseph Ratzinger, but also a rejection of universalizing allegory. It is furthermore a rejection of the role of the moralizing Grand Inquisitor that Ratzinger notoriously performed for decades, in favor of picaresque, ambiguous anecdote. By departing from his erstwhile role as the voice of conscience for his nation, Grass can construct an entirely aesthetic self in his memoir, his artistic *Lehrjahre* (apprentice years).

The anecdotal approach has, then, both advantages and pitfalls. If the moralizing self is intolerant, the anecdotal one is resolutely impure, both ethically and sexually. Indeed, Grass's insistence on representing his "second hunger" of sexual desire mirrors the ethical quandaries caused by his boy-scout narration of wartime suffering. The language that Grass gleefully uses to recount his pubescent sexual adventures is priapic, indeed phallocentric: his adolescent penis is relentlessly manly, it tried to penetrate whatever bore penetration [. . .] it lacks reason and intends to remain without reason to the bitter end. (*PO* 56)

His penis is, in fact, more important to the teenaged Grass than the Eastern front: it does not merely penetrate his accounts of wartime suffering, but often displaces them. Thus Grass's memories of the first refugees to arrive in Danzig are juxtaposed against his adolescent fumblings with his cousin in the back of the cinema, and his first sight of columns of East German refugees on the front is entangled with an encounter with a refugee girl who "lets me hold her hand, though nothing more" (*PO* 122). While this priapic narrative is classic Grass bawdiness and classic Grass structural irony — the pleasures of narrative take over from politically correct reflection — the tales of his picaresque "pursuit" of girls are at the same time a clichéd set of adolescent male fantasies that display little engagement with the more nuanced and feminist discourses of gender that have evolved since Grass's adolescence.

Grass's adolescent anecdotes in no way disqualify Grass from exemplary status as moral arbiter, nor do they pollute his entire opus, never mind this autobiography. Yet, they perhaps draw attention to the different ethical considerations attached to life and to literature. Grass's anecdotes are entertaining, memorable, and have their own literary truth, but may fail at a thoroughly ethical representation that does justice to the more complex cultural and political discourses in which the artist has endlessly been embroiled since the end of his *Lehrjahre*. And while the Bildungsroman narrative structure can legitimately focus on the unfolding of the autonomous aesthetic subject, by using this form in his autobiography Grass frequently reduces his surrounding cast of characters to stock figures: good Germans, bellicose Israelis, sadistic Nazis, and willing girls, that is, stock figures that are inadequate to represent the sociohistorical reality that Grass also claims to narrate. Narcissistically scrupulous and eagerly anecdotal in narrating the self, Grass's autobiography fails to ethically reflect on the other figures that he describes. As Grass writes himself, about the writer Erich Maria Remarque, "Over and over, author and book remind me of how little I understood as a youth and how limited an effect literature may have" (*PO* 97).

Notes

[1] Günter Grass, *Beim Häuten der Zwiebel* (Göttingen: Steidl, 2006). Citations here are from the English translation, *Peeling the Onion,* trans. Michael Henry Heim (London: Harvill, 2007), 199. Subsequent references to this work are cited in the text using the abbreviaton *PO* and page number.

[2] W. G. Sebald, "Konstruktionen der Trauer: Über Günter Grass und Wolfgang Hildesheimer," *Deutschunterricht* 35 (1983): 5, 32–46. Citations here are taken from the English translation, "Constructs of Mourning: Günter Grass and Wolfgang Hildesheimer," in *Campo Santo,* ed. Sven Meyer, trans. Anthea Bell (London: Penguin, 2006), 102–29.

[3] Ibid., 118.

[4] Klaus Wagenbach, "Grass hat nichts verschwiegen," *Die Zeit,* 26 April 2007, 18.

[5] See Anne Fuchs, "'Ehrlich, du lügst wie gedruckt': Günter Grass's Autobiographical Confession and the Changing Territory of Germany's Memory Culture," *German Life and Letters* 60, no. 2 (2007): 261–75.

[6] Günter Grass, "Warum ich nach sechzig Jahren mein Schweigen breche," *Frankfurter Allgemeine Zeitung,* 12 August 2006, 33.

[7] Philippe Lejeune, *Le pacte autobiographique* (Paris: Éditions de Seuil, 1975), 16.

[8] Stuart Taberner, "Private Failings and Public Virtues: Günter Grass's *Beim Häuten der Zwiebel* and the Exemplary Use of Authorial Biography," *Modern Language Review* 103 (2008): 166–78.

[9] Fuchs, "'Ehrlich, du lügst wie gedruckt,'" 262.

[10] See Alexander Weber, *Günter Grass's Use of Baroque Literature* (Leeds, UK: W. S. Maney for the Modern Humanities Research Association and the Institute of Germanic Studies, University of London, 1995).

[11] Fuchs, "'Ehrlich, du lügst wie gedruckt,'" 269.

[12] Sebald, "Constructs of Mourning," 116.

[13] Mary Cosgrove, "Melancholy Competitions: W. G. Sebald Reads Günter Grass and Wolfgang Hildesheimer," *German Life and Letters* 59, no. 2 (2006): 217–32.

[14] Cosgrove, "Melancholy Competitions," 220.

[15] See Bill Niven, *Facing The Nazi Past: United Germany and the Legacy of the Third Reich* (London: Routledge, 2002), 153–57.

[16] Günter Grass, *Rede von der Gewöhnung,* in his *Essays und Reden 1955–1969,* ed. Daniela Hermes (Göttingen: Steidl, 1993), 228. Translation mine.

[17] Grass, *Rede von der Gewöhnung,* 233.

[18] Maya Jaggi, "Recovered Memories," interview with W. G. Sebald, *The Guardian,* 22 September 2001. http://www.guardian.co.uk/saturday_review/story/0,3605,555861,00.html (accessed 15 September 2008).

13: Jackboots and Jeans: The Private and the Political in Uwe Timm's *Am Beispiel meines Bruders*

Frank Finlay

Introduction

AS THIS VOLUME AMPLY DEMONSTRATES, the explosion of recent inter-est in "German wartime suffering" is but the latest manifestation of contemporary Germany's often tortuous attempts since 1945 to define its relationship to National Socialism along a continuum that has German perpetration at its opposite pole. A recent feature of this multifaceted "memory work" has been a particularly intense preoccupation across a wide range of cultural and historical texts with the everyday fate and the choices faced by the German population at large in the Third Reich.

The literary arena since 1989–90 has witnessed a burgeoning trend in "life-writing," that is, biographies, memoirs, and diaries, many of which have been published posthumously.[1] Since the turn of the millennium, in particular, there has been a renaissance in "family" or "generational narratives"[2] (either "straight" or "fictionalized" reconstructions of family genealogies) dealing with the problematic heritage of the Nazi past and its transgenerational transmission, precisely at a time when the cohort of eyewitnesses is passing away. In certain cases, of which Timm's *Am Beispiel meines Bruders* (In My Brother's Shadow, 2003)[3] and Ulla Hahn's *Unscharfe Bilder* (Blurred Images, 2003) are good examples, the relationship is between the wartime generation and their children, many of whom have a history of political activism in the 1960s, on which they also reflect. Other texts focus on experience across three generations, such as Stephan Wackwitz's *Ein unsichtbares Land* (An Invisible Country, 2003) or Tanja Dücker's *Himmelskörper* (Heavenly Bodies, 2003).[4] Broadly viewed, some generational narratives have offered more nuanced, less condemnatory and empathetic portrayals of perpetrators than was the case in arguably the quintessential literary genre of the generation of 1968, the so-called "Father Books." Others stand charged with blurring or even obscuring the causal relationship between the suffering meted out by Germans and that which they endured.[5]

The often ferocious debates sparked by a number of these texts have been widely commented on by scholars and have received a great deal of attention in the cultural pages of the European and American serious press. While some commentators have viewed them as essentially positive, as a new, more inclusive and mature stage of "coming-to-terms" with the past, taking a unified nation ever closer to becoming a fully fledged democracy and "normalized nation," others have warned of dangerously exculpatory and vulgar revisionism.[6] As far as the critical discussion of literary representations is concerned, Jan and Aleida Assmann's paradigm of collective memory and cultural identity has exerted considerable normative force as a hermeneutic tool. Scholars in social psychology have also provided a useful critical vocabulary, such as Harald Welzer, for whom the simultaneous publication of Timm's text and those by Hahn, Dückers, and Wackwitz provided evidence of a wider trend.[7]

Lifting the Lid

The key area Timm interrogates is the admixture of personality traits, and familial, societal, ideological, and political factors that propel his eighteen-year-old brother to volunteer to serve as a sapper in the feared Death Head Division of the *Waffen SS*, formed from guard units of the Dachau concentration camp and linked to many mass murders on the battlefield and among occupied civilian populations. The trigger for these investigations is a family heirloom: quite literally a "memory box" containing his brother's field journal, letters home from the Eastern front, and scant personal belongings.[8] Some sixteen years his senior, Karl-Heinz Timm saw action on the Ukrainian front in 1943 and was fatally mutilated during the tank battle of Kursk, the largest in history. Timm's family gave their younger son Uwe the documents to read as a teenager,[9] presumably as a way to access the family's traumatic history, which he was too young to remember. Subsequent attempts to research his brother's life were abandoned for fear that participation in the behind-the-lines political and racial mass murders, which were the defining aspects of Hitler's *Vernichtungskrieg* (war of extermination) against the Soviet Union, might lurk behind the journal's many cryptic references. This was combined with a natural revulsion at its entirely dispassionate and pitiless tone, particularly his brother's professional satisfaction at the gratuitous killing of a Russian soldier who chanced into his gun sights (19), which becomes a leitmotif in Timm's text. This long-standing reluctance to cross the threshold into a potentially murky family past of perpetration, likened to his childhood aversion to the gruesome ending of a fairy tale (11), echoes previous references to the specter of the brother in dream sequences in Timm's essayistic volume *Vogel, friß die Feige nicht* (Bird, Don't Eat the Fig, 1989) and his 1996 novel *Johannisnacht* (Midsummer Night, 1998).[10] The inference is clear; the brother will remain a repressed phenomenon, a taboo that will continue to haunt Timm's subconscious until the lid of the "memory box" is finally lifted (12). The last constraint, an understandable sensitivity to kinship relations, fell away following the death of Timm's mother and sister, leaving him "free to ask all questions, to not have to take anything or anyone into consideration" (12).

Timm thus enters the same terrain of German perpetration as Hannes Heer's itinerant exhibition (and accompanying book) on the Crimes of the *Wehrmacht*,[11] which under the auspices of the Hamburg Institute for Social Research was seen in two incarnations by over a million Germans and Austrians. It rubbished the myth that the German regular army had fought a "clean war" and placed its institutional collusion and the perpetration of individual members in a genocidal conflict at the forefront of social, political, and cultural discourse in Germany.[12] Moreover, Timm makes frequent reference to Christopher R. Browning's *Ordinary Men: Reserve Police Batalion 101 and the Final Solution in Poland*.[13] With its focus on the unrelenting killing spree of middle-aged German reservists from Timm's native Hamburg in the wake of Hitler's rampaging armies, Browning's study is free of the reductionism and monocausal conclusions that Daniel Jonah Goldhagen drew from his later examination of the same data in his headline-grabbing *Hitler's Willing Executioners* (1996). Timm endorses Browning's account that "mass murder and routine had become one. Normality had become exceedingly abnormal." His attempts to understand his brother's private and political selves also share Browning's method and perspective, namely of starkly juxtaposing "the monstrous deeds of the Holocaust . . . with the human faces of the killers," which, by definition, requires a degree of empathy with the perpetrators.[14] This even extends to questioning how he might have behaved in the same situation. It is in this "what if" sense that the brother acts as Timm's own doppelgänger, which his ghostly presence only heightens. Moreover, it is precisely empathy that is singularly absent from the diary's entirely "normal view of every day war" (95), with compassion blanked out in the face of human suffering. This led Karl-Heinz to a kind of moral schizophrenia in which there is no causal connection between the Allied bombing of his native Hamburg, which he deems "not human" (93), and the devastation of the Russian civilian population, exemplified by his division's dismantling of homes to provide matériel to aid the army's motorized advance.

Timm's quest shows that identity is relational, developed collaboratively with others, and that a key conduit for the transmission of values is a family in which the father loomed largest of all — as the conjunction of his forename with that of the older male sibling's in his own underscores (21). Other influences are, of course, external, and it is the intersections of the family's entirely unexceptional vita with German history in the first, tumultuous half of the twentieth century that the personal memoir takes on the more general, "exemplary" significance that its title conveys. This allows it to engage with both the apparently polar opposites of victimhood and perpetration that dominate the present-day discursive context.[15] The exploits of the eponymous brother (and, to a lesser extent, of the father in the Air Force) denote German perpetration; the conflagration of the family's native city and almost simultaneous loss of a son denote German suffering. Timm's historical contextualization also embraces the traumatic aftermath of the First World War and the turmoil of Weimar, as well as the stifling social conservatism of the 1950s and West Germany's dubious and morally evasive engagement with its recent past.

In this absence of any personal memory of his own, save the essentially meaningless fragment that opens the memoir, the brother's "*recorded* memory" (italics in original, 35), the sole articulation of his voice in laconic documents "devoted exclusively to the war" (31), is also of little use. It raises far more questions than it answers, offering virtually no clues to his nature, identity, and behavior (145). Timm's attempts to understand and therefore empathize must rely on assembling the family's oral and photographic memory. Thus the mother's reminiscences of a fearful, sickly, and dreamy Karl-Heinz, with a propensity to slip away to a hidden den only to appear as if from nowhere (presaging his ghostly presence after his death), and who was bullied in the Hitler Youth, are apparently at odds with the overriding family portrait of an idealized war hero, yet they, too, foreground his bravery. The many photographs of the father and son together (and the dearth of those with Timm's sister) confirm their close relationship. Timm presents Karl-Heinz as a "victim" of learned behavior, which inculcated masculinity, obedience, duty, bravery, loyalty, and discipline. This "private" education dovetailed with the political indoctrination of the Hitler Youth, the Labor Service, and ultimately the *Waffen SS* — Karl-Heinz "told no lies . . . was always upright, shed no tears, was brave and obedient. A fine example" (21) — and cast a long shadow over the self-identity of the brother, the "afterthought," submerging him in adulation and hero worship. Timm concludes that his brother did indeed volunteer of his own free will, a tacit act of compliance with what the father, obeying the dictates of society, wanted him to do (59).

In every case Timm's family anecdotes are more revealing of their respective narrator and, by implication, reflective of a "general" attitude, than of the object of the narration, as the following example illustrates. An early and oft-recited family story rationalizes the brother's enlisting in the *Waffen SS* "as if what happened could have been averted" (13), with

Karl-Heinz led astray by a madman — clearly a rendition of the "demonic thesis" of Germany's descent into hell under Hitler's evil leadership, which was popular in the first two decades after the war and which enabled Germans to position themselves as victims of Nazism. For the mother, Karl-Heinz was motivated by an unwillingness to "shirk his duty" and an idealism that was "abused," by the "criminals . . . the others, the . . . task force groups. Especially the men at the top, the leaders" (20). When an alternative to Karl-Heinz's course of action is contemplated, the likelihood that he might have been deputed to a death camp and, therefore, that the *Waffen SS* was not the regular army unit of family legend simply does not occur to the family (22) — hence the repeated reminders that he wore the same uniforms and Death Head insignia as concentration camp guards (15, 102). Thus the mother's wish for her son is restricted merely to his joining a branch of the military less likely to be exposed to frontline combat (63). The family construct is, therefore, of a regular soldier and passive victim of a cabal of National Socialists, with not a single thought given to the moral and ethical implications of his individual choices, the extent to which family upbringing might have actively encouraged them, or to the victims of his actions on the Russian front. This squares with Welzer's seminal and appropriately titled study *Opa war kein Nazi* (Grandpa Wasn't a Nazi, 2005), which shows how the main trope in German family memory construction, based often on the vaguest of facts, is one of victimhood arising not least from an unwillingness to countenance a close relative as a perpetrator.[16]

The family's private remembering, therefore, is every bit as retouched as the picture of a lion ostensibly drawn by the brother but embellished by the father (145). In an effort to drill deeper from the very outset, Timm sets his base texts (the brother's documents and family oral history), what Welzer calls the "album," in the context of the "encyclopedia," that is, recent historical studies of National Socialism. Moreover, Timm alternates his account, frequently from one paragraph to another, with primary documents that fill the gaping holes in private memory; these are co-texts that provide both German perpetrator and Russian and Jewish victim perspectives. For example, General Heinrici's letter and diary entry are adduced to support the contention that the brother simply could not have failed to encounter the horrendous suffering of Russian noncombatants (27–28). A speech and operational directives by perpetrators under whose direct chain of command his brother was eventually to come (SS Chief Himmler, army generals von Manstein, the military supremo at Kursk, where Karl-Heinz perished, and von Reichenau) are stark reminders of the Nazis' ideological conflation of anti-Semitism and anti-Communism. They underscore the regular German army's collusion in mandating, fomenting, and unleashing a racist and genocidal war. We are also reminded that a "normal" good education and academic background were no barrier to the inhuman acts of the commanders of the *Einsatzgruppen* (task force groups), which are juxtaposed with the Holocaust survivor Jean Améry's experience (in *At the Mind's Limits*) to show that learning and culture offered the victims no comfort either (62).

Immediately after citing von Reichenau, a number of isolated examples of German soldiers who followed their own moral compass to show solidarity with their Jewish compatriots, documented by historian Wolfgang Wette, are introduced into the text to refute the exculpatory discourse of acting under orders which was heard so often after the war (135).[17] The section concludes with a direct quote from Søren Kierkegaard (unsourced, but from *Either-Or*), which points intertextually to an ethical code of behavior (147) in which honor and obedience are given a very different meaning to the one they typically possess within the "Prussian" tradition.

Timm notes that von Manstein's past was no barrier to his becoming the unrepentant advisor (1953–60) after the war to the West German government as it set about forming the *Bundeswehr* (West German army). His best-selling, self-justificatory memoirs were an important contribution to the postwar myth of honorable armed forces betrayed by an incompetent Nazi leadership. Wette's book also documents how the American Historical Division allowed *Wehrmacht* generals to record the first version of their history, giving them access to primary documents, which often subsequently went missing or were destroyed. Indeed, Timm was unable to find the *Waffen SS* logbook in German military archives when he embarked on his project (11). Thus the Allies, who needed a West German contribution to NATO with the onset of the Cold War, colluded in the legend of an innocent *Wehrmacht*. As von Manstein's 664-page tome was one of the generals' memoirs read avidly by Timm's father (96), the private family narrative of victimhood is linked intertextually to public discourses in the 1950s that, in full knowledge of the "*extermination*" (Timm's italics) of the Jews, are scarcely imaginable today (99). Moreover, the pointed evocation of the hypocrisy, moral evasions, and linguistic and political continuities from the Third Reich into the 1950s, which allowed criminals back into public life and which the generation of '68 found so reprehensible, provides the moral basis and rationale for Timm's own political rebellion in the late 1960s. Unlike some of his fellow '68ers in recent years, he sees no reason to recant his youthful stance. Moreover, the political rebellion was preceded by a private rebellion when he refuses to continue in the family furrier business, in which, like his brother, he was apprenticed to pursue his literary ambitions.

Another feature of the public debate about the status of German suffering in the cultural memory of the Federal Republic, which is of direct relevance to an understanding of *Am Beipsiel meines Bruders,* has been the propagation by popular historians and the mass media of the notion that until very recently this suffering and loss had somehow gone unspoken. There had been a willful forgetting in the early decades after 1945, it has often been argued, which had then given way to moral fundamentalism; a fanatical, self-righteous insistence on German complicity by the generation of 1968, whose repression of empathy allegedly mirrored their parents' repression of perpetration.[18] This has led in recent years to a proliferation of documentaries, press features, cinema movies, and TV mini-series purporting to raise the taboo on inter alia the bombing war, mass expulsions and rapes, and the fate of POWs in the Soviet Union.[19] Indeed, the stubborn tenacity with which the collective taboo thesis has cemented itself in the face of a wealth of strongly contradictory historical and literary research has already attracted the interest of scholars.[20] When set in this context, Timm's portrayal of his family's remembrance of their wartime involvement acts as an important corrective.

Timm equates the dynamic at work in the family's construction of its positive memory of the brother with its repeated invocation of the carpet bombing of Hamburg; in the same way that the sole fragment of memory of his brother acquired *post facto* contours of meaning in the narratives of the family, so too does his nanomemory of the firestorm become all-important.[21] Timm positions the family's incessant retelling of the events after the war in the context of the eyewitness testimony of the father's letter to Karl-Heinz (37), the latter's response, and his own restrained and empathetic descriptions. The focus of family memory is on heroic, iconic details that strip away the original horror to leave ultimately entertaining and formulaic yarns (38–42), betokening a failure to fully come to terms with them. Timm's counternarrative in no way seeks to minimize the scale and horrific nature of destruction, or the shocking details of the deaths that befell the victims (39), thereby challenging the family's interpretation of events. Thus a letter from Karl-Heinz, at last moved to tears and communicating his incomprehension at the bombing, is sandwiched between a local manifestation of anti-Semitism and information that Jews were not permitted entry to air raid shelters (40).

Timm's intertextual allusion to narratives of Jewish suffering in the Holocaust (Jorge Semprun and Imre Kertész, among others) or direct co-textual insertion of survivor testimony function in a similar way. They not only set German perpetration in sharp relief, as we have already seen with the Jean Améry reference, but also German suffering. Accordingly, Karl-Heinz's letters of gratitude at the regular epistolary contact to home are the contrastive bookends to Primo Levi's testimony, in *The Drowned and the Saved,* to the absolute human desolation, isolation, and "silence," which was the experience of millions of Jews in the concentration camps. It is this German silence on the fate of Jews both during and after the Holocaust that Levi sees as their deepest guilt (105–6). Thus the categorical, a priori differences in the nature and magnitude of Jewish suffering, the recognition of which is absent in many recent works, is evoked simultaneously with German complicity and guilt.[22]

If the oral history of the bombing was part of the soundtrack of Timm's childhood and adolescence in the 1940s and 1950s, so were the wartime reminiscences of the menfolk, particularly of the motley crew of his father's former comrades with their bibulous and exculpatory discussions of how the war might have been won that echo the published memoirs of army generals, only with full-blown anti-Semitic conspiracy theories (99). The highly popular *Landserhefte* (soldiers' tales) replicated in the public domain this private table talk of the mutilated yet morally incorrigible veterans. They peddled in the same army slang and Nazi jargon (highlighted by Timm in italics) images of the "Wehrmacht as a travel agent" (100), and the crudest stereotypes and clichés of enemy nations. Timm's alternative co-texts set the record straight; following a tale of the Kiev buildings booby-trapped by the Russians, a document from Soviet archives and detailed descriptions of German photographic reconnaissance evoke one of the worst single atrocities of the war near the same Ukrainian city, the massacre at Babij Jar (140). Timm as a young man also encountered tales of German war crimes when one particularly unsavory workmate quite freely and shamelessly boasted of the approval his commander bestowed on him when he gratuitously murdered two Russian POWs. Moreover, it is made plain that such communicative events were neither isolated nor restricted to the private family home; they were "everyday stories told after the war, at work, in bars, at home, in dialect or in educated High German" (130–31).

Timm's acute ear for the "whispering of the generations" and "speaking situations" — notions he identified as central to his poetological mission in his Paderborn Lectures — is deployed to good effect to destroy the myth that there was an embargo on expressions of suffering. He rescues for posterity the "communicative memory," to use the Assmanns' term, of a generation now passed, which gives the lie to many of the slogans of current discourse.[23] Furthermore, he finds an adequate formal solution to do so, as I now briefly elaborate.

The intertextuality and montage (and collage when one considers the referencing of photographic images)[24] of *Am Beispiel meines Bruders* are established devices in literature and have generated a wealth of scholarship, with, for example, theories by Mikhail Bakhtin or Julia Kristeva enjoying wide popularity. Common theoretical conclusions are that placing one text alongside another generates a productive dialogue (extending, therefore, also to the "listener"/reader) with results that can be acutely revealing, irrespective of whether parallel, counter, or alternative meanings to the base text(s) are deployed. Here, Bakhtin's notion of "polyphony" may be broadly applicable to Timm's memoir.[25] Thus a plurality of independent and unmerged consciousnesses each with its own world, what Bakhtin calls "voices," which include linguistic matters as well as those relating to ideology of power, are orchestrated. This dialogue of multiple voices is reminiscent to a degree of Peter Weiss's treatment of the Holocaust in his 1965 play *Die Ermittlung* (The Investigation), which was conceived as an oratorio of perpetrator and victim voices. It can operate, as we have seen, at a number of different levels, even extending, for example on page 91, to an individual paragraph. In this episode, the family's "voice" of private victimhood, the twist of fate that deprived them of their son and home (highlighted in italics) is interpenetrated by Timm's interpretative "voice," which draws attention to its political, that is, exculpatory inferences. This echoes the earlier dialogue between "texts" that sets Himmler's racist rant against the family's litany of suffering (37). It should be clear that this "polyphony" is the formal solution to Timm's desire for a coexistence of egalitarian empathy with political critique, with the form of the memoir, therefore, reflecting its "content" in a way far more radical than in conventional histories. Unlike Bakhtin, however, who posited characters/voices entirely free of the controlling hand of an authorial worldview, the organizing structure of Timm's text not only proposes the simultaneity and interconnectedness of German suffering and complicity but also insists on the a priori centrality of German perpetration.[26]

In the Name of the Father

Am Beispiel meines Bruders has much in common with the autobiographical "Father Books," which developed from isolated beginnings, such as Günter Anders' *Wir Eichmannssöhne* (We, Eichmann's Sons) of 1964, to become a veritable flood in the 1970s and 1980s in which a "generation damaged by its fathers" — many politically active '68ers — put their parents on trial and condemned them for their grim silence over involvement in National Socialism.[27] From the scant documentary material available to him, Timm pieces together a snapshot of the private and political factors that determined his father's actions, casting familiar light on the way ideological consent with National Socialism was manufactured. Thus the older Timm is an ardent nationalist and militarist, well versed in the history of Germany's martial glories (24), who volunteered for active service in the First World War and, at that conflict's end, continued fighting in the Baltic states where he acquired the racial and political prejudices as well as the inflated social aspirations of the Prussian officers with whom he served in a private paramilitary *Freikorps* (22; Free Corps). Feeling thwarted in the political turmoil of Weimar Germany, he became close to the ultra right-wing *Organisation Consul* (44), which was responsible for the political assassinations of leading democrats. Having married into a wealthy Hamburg milliner's family and finding the Nazi party too vulgar to actually join (78), this officer manqué welcomed Hitler's vision of national renewal and fantasies of hegemonic power, enthusiastically attaining the officer status he coveted in the Air Force. The father is thus the very incarnation of the authoritarian German masculinity and militarism typical of the "Father Books." Little wonder that Timm's earliest and abiding memory of him is of the aroma of masculine sweat on leather jackboots and military belts, or that he can recollect performing military drill as a party piece as a three-year-old (25–26). As with the "exemplary" brother, there is a clear attempt to universalize the father as a member of the "generation of the guilty" (102), which dominated the German family in the postwar period as a means of compensating for their lost control over the public sphere (69). Timm's pained memories of psychological terror and physical violence point up the continuity of postfascist authoritarianism and latent violence, *"normal"* in the streets and the schools of the 1940s and 1950s (149; italics in the original), echoing the attitudes that made Browning's "normal men" possible.

Timm senior is a typical "father" figure in many other respects. Existential insecurity caused by war, defeat, humiliation, and imprisonment combines with the inability to find a sustainable postwar orientation. The deferral of an honest engagement with his complicity and suffering leads to a transfer of guilt, including to the Allies, for the Holocaust (134). It also leaves him incapable of affective communication. Writing of his younger self in the third person and hence with considerable hindsight, Timm sees his earliest literary experiments as a reaction to this silence (134–35). The father's frustrated antagonistic energies are channeled after 1945 into a "new war against the culture of the victors" (69, 71), which sets him on a collision course with his teenage son, who prefers blue jeans to his father's jackboots (which his brother craved), the libertine charms of American popular films, fashion, and jazz — and those more locally accessible in Hamburg's red-light district (30) — to the social and moral conservatism of 1950s West Germany. Significantly and equally typically, the political and private is linked in the ultimate failure in the role of father; Hans Timm is unable to speak honestly with his son, to tolerate his own needs and desire for autonomy and independence. Moreover, the father's entire value system, with its blind subservience to authority, is at odds with an antiauthoritarianism of the kind advocated by the generation of '68, precisely because it promoted dissent in the face of social and collective pressure. It was this courage to say "no" which Timm's intertexts proved were the rarest exceptions under National Socialism and which are absent in his third-person recollections of his upbringing (72). Finally, his empathetic understanding of conflicts of loyalty, which he experienced in the German Communist Party (151), proves no barrier to the unequivocal indictment of his relatives as proxies for a general German ethical failure to at the very least bear witness to German crimes (147), rather than either maintaining, in Primo Levi's terms, a "criminal" silence or endlessly babbling about their own suffering.

In crucial aspects, however, Timm's portrayal of his father differs from the "Father Books" genre of the 1970s and 1980s. These tended to judge the parents primarily as political beings, with little understanding for private motivations. Similarly, there was an emphasis on perpetration to the exclusion of empathy with suffering.[28] Conversely, Timm's text is a measured attempt to keep wishful thinking in check (79) and to avoid "pinning labels too hastily on him" (134). For example, his father's difficult childhood in Coburg is recorded. There is also admiration for his professional skill at taxidermy, which offered the chance of professional advancement overseas (63), and of the postwar improvisatory get-up-and-go, which brought brief prosperity to his furrier business, trappings of affluence, and acclaim in Hamburg's commercial circles (82). Other details, often genuinely pathetic, recognize a fundamentally inflated image at the core of his father's character, probably traceable to his feckless experience in the *Freikorps*. It led him to ignore his real talents, poor career decisions and, ultimately, a deep-seated melancholia when the gap between his ideal and real self became unbridgeable (45). In a moving section, Timm describes the one time he saw his father cry, not only at the death of his beloved son and heir in whom his future plans were vested, but at the whole gamut of repressed memories that, judging by the one disturbing incident in the camp for Russian POWs which he did relate, exceptionally (103), were very likely traumatic.

A final departure from the Father Books is perhaps the most obvious one: *Am Beispiel meines Bruders* avoids a single-gender perspective by incorporating sympathetic accounts of Timm's sister, whom the father marginalized, including of her belated achievement of personal happiness, and, most prominently, of his mother. While her quietism during National Socialism is not ignored, or the limits of her political insights thereafter, there is understanding for her genuine attempts to mourn her son's loss in her old age, as well as the positively connoted inscription as the humorous progenitor of this "mummy's boy's" literary talents.

Conclusion

Uwe Timm's *Am Beispiel meines Bruders* is an important contribution to the recent flood of family narratives of German memories of the war. The diary of his brother provides Timm with a framework for his own self-discovery; the factors that helped shape his identity leading to a private and political rebellion. The text also intervenes directly in recent discourses surrounding German perpetration and German suffering. The meditations on the brother provide a case study to complement the insights of recent historical findings, while the portrayal of the father offers a close-up of a generation that involved itself in, and then denied responsibility for, National Socialism. Timm applies the empathetic perspective brought to bear on the brother to the exploration of the father and thereby, while having much in common with the "Father Books" of the 1970s and rehearsing a similar critique, he achieves a more measured understanding, also contributing to the reinvigoration of an otherwise moribund genre. Moreover, Timm's seismographic record of private oral history and public discourse of the 1950s compellingly refutes a widely propagated thesis that there has been a taboo on German suffering until relatively recently. His retrieval and storage of a "private" communicative memory is thus a major "political" contribution to German cultural memory. Timm's short memoir stands out on two major counts. While a less accusatory tone can be found in other recent literary works, he is unflinching in still finding the wartime generation guilty for failing to bear witness to their own complicity, irrespective of how this might have varied in practice. Perhaps most significantly, because it is a potential template for future literary treatments, Timm finds a "polyphonic" form adequate to his empathetic yet critical aims; the interplay of heterogeneous memory-voices that he is able to orchestrate is an innovative structuring principle of the book. It makes evident at the level of form and content his insistence on the temporal and causal precedence of German perpetration, integrating the "normative frame of generally accepted validity," which Aleida Assmann has proposed as a way to transcend the impasse of the polarized recent debates.[29]

Notes

[1] Owen Evans, *Mapping the Contours of Oppression: Subjectivity, Truth and Fiction in Recent German Autobiographical Treatments of Totalitarianism* (Amsterdam: Rodopi, 2006). See also Stuart Taberner, "Representations of German Wartime Suffering in Recent Fiction," in *Germans as Victims: Remembering the Past in Contemporary Germany,* ed. Bill Niven (Basingstoke, UK: Palgrave Macmillan, 2006), 164–80.

[2] See Friederike Eigler, *Gedächtnis und Geschichte in Generationenromanen seit der Wende* (Berlin: Erich Schmidt, 2005) and Silke Horstkotte, "'Ich bin ins Reich der Toten geraten': Stephan Wackwitz and the New German Family Novel," in *New German Literature: Life-Writing and Dialogue with the Arts,* ed. Julian Preece, Frank Finlay, and Ruth J. Owen (Oxford: Peter Lang, 2007), 325–42.

[3] Uwe Timm, *Am Beispiel meines Bruders* (Cologne: Kiepenheuer and Witsch, 2003). All subsequent page references to this work are cited parenthetically in the text.

[4] See Mila Ganeva, "From West-German *Väterliteratur* to Post-Wall *Enkelliteratur:* The End of the Generation Conflict in Marcel Beyer's *Spione* and Tanja Dückers's *Himmelskörper,*" *Seminar* 43, no. 2 (2007): 149–62.

[5] See Stuart Taberner, *German Literature of the 1990s and Beyond: Normalization and the Berlin Republic* (Rochester, NY: Camden House 2005), 106–64. See also Helmut Schmitz, *On Their Own Terms: The Legacy of National Socialism in Post-1990 German Fiction* (Birmingham, UK: U of Birmingham P, 2004) and the contributions by Schmitz and Bill Niven in Stuart Taberner, ed., *Contemporary German Fiction: Writing in the Berlin Republic* (Cambridge: CUP, 2007), 125–58.

[6] See *German Culture, Politics and Literature into the Twenty-First Century: Beyond Normalization,* ed. Stuart Taberner and Paul Cooke (Rochester, NY: Camden House, 2006). The parameters of the "suffering" debate are dealt with in Bill Niven's "Introduction: German Victimhood at the Turn of the Millennium," in *Germans as Victims,* 1–25. See also Aleida Assmann, "On the (In)Compatibility of Guilt and Suffering in German Memory," *German Life and Letters* 59, no. 2 (2006): 187–200; Graham Jackman, "Introduction," *German Life and Letters* 57, no. 4 (2004): 343–56; and *A Nation of Victims? Representations of German Wartime Suffering from 1945 to the Present,* ed. Helmut Schmitz (Amsterdam: Rodopi, 2007).

[7] Harald Welzer, "Im Gedächtniswohnzimmer: Warum sind Bücher über die eigene Familiengeschichte so erfolgreich? Ein ZEIT — Gespräch mit dem Sozialpsychologen Harald Welzer über das private Erinnern," *Die Zeit,* 25 March 2004, 43–46.

[8] Anne Fuchs uses the term "affective memory icon" in her "From *Vergangenheitsbewältigung* to Generational Memory Contests in Günter Grass, Monika Maron and Uwe Timm," *German Life and Letters* 59, no. 2 (2006): 169–86, 184.

[9] "'Ich wollte das in aller Härte.' Ein TAZ, Interview mit Uwe Timm über sein Buch 'Am Beispiel meines Bruders,'" http://www.taz.de/pt/2003/09/13/a0245.nf/text (accessed 15 September 2008).

[10] See Rhys Williams, "'Eine ganz normale Kindheit': Uwe Timms *Am Beispiel meines Bruders,*" in *"(Un-)erfüllte Wirklichkeit": Neue Studien zu Uwe Timms Werk,* ed. Frank Finlay and Ingo Cornils (Würzburg: Königshausen and Neumann, 2006), 173–75.

[11] Hannes Heer and Klaus Naumann, eds., *Vernichtungskrieg: Verbrechen der Wehrmacht 1941–1944* (Hamburg: Zweitausendeins, 1997).

[12] For a detailed discussion, see Bill Niven's *Facing the Nazi Past: United Germany and the Legacy of the Nazi Past* (London: Routledge, 2002), chap. 6.

204 ♦ Frank Finlay

[13] Christopher R. Browning, *Ordinary Men: Reserve Police Batalion 101 and the Final Solution in Poland* (New York: Harper Collins, 1992). References here are to the Penguin edition, 2001.

[14] Ibid., xiv.

[15] See Assmann, "German Memory," 195.

[16] Quoted from Ruth Wittlinger, "Taboo or Tradition? The 'Germans as Victims' Theme in the West Germany until the mid-1990s," in Niven, *Germans as Victims,* 64.

[17] Wolfram Wette, *The Wehrmacht: History, Myth, Reality* (Cambridge, MA: Harvard UP, 2006).

[18] See Helmut Schmitz, "Representations of the Nazi Past II: German Wartime Suffering," in *Contemporary German Fiction: Writing in the Berlin Republic,* ed. Stuart Taberner (Cambridge, MA: CUP, 2007), 144.

[19] See Paul Cooke, "*Dresden* (2006), Teamworx and *Titanic* (1997): German Wartime Suffering as Hollywood Disaster Movie," *German Life and Letters* 61, no. 2 (2008): 279–94.

[20] See Stefan Berger, "On Taboos, Traumas and Other Myths: Why the Debate about German Victims of the Second World War Is Not a Historians Controversy," in Niven, *Germans as Victims,* 210–24. As an example of relevant literary scholarship, see Volker Hage's anthology, *Hamburg 1943: Literarische Zeugnisse des Feuersturms* (Frankfurt am Main: Fischer, 2003).

[21] This found an earlier literary transposition in Uwe Timm, *Die Entdeckung der Currywurst (The Discovery of the Curried Sausage)* (Cologne: Kiepenheuer and Witsch, 1993). The citation here is from the paperback edition (Munich: DTV, 2002), 24.

[22] See also Schmitz, "Nazi Past II," 154.

[23] Uwe Timm, *Erzählen und kein Ende* (Cologne: Kiepenheuer and Witsch, 1993). See also Matteo Galli, "Vom Denkmal zum Mahnmal: Kommunikatives Gedächtnis bei Uwe Timm," in Finlay and Cornils, *"(Un-)erfüllte Wirklichkeit,"* 162–63.

[24] On montage, see Peter Hutchinson, *Games Authors Play* (London: Methuen, 1983), 69–72.

[25] See Simon Dentith, *Bakhtinian Thought: An Introductory Reader* (London: Routledge, 1995), 41–64.

[26] See Schmitz, "Nazi Past II," 154.

[27] For an excellent typology of the genre, see Jochen Vogt, "Er fehlt, er fehlte, er hat gefehlt . . . Ein Rückblick auf die sogenannten Väterbücher," in *Deutsche Nachkriegsliteratur und der Holocaust,* ed. Stephan Braese, et al. (Frankfurt am Main: Campus, 1998), 385–412.

[28] Michael Schneider, "Fathers and Sons, Retrospectively: The Damaged Relationship between Two Generations," *New German Critique* 31 (1984): 4.

[29] Assmann, "German Memory," 200.

14: Memory-Work in Recent German Novels: What (if Any) Limits Remain on Empathy with the "German Experience" of the Second World War?

Stuart Taberner

IN HIS EXCELLENT DISCUSSION OF "historicism, sentimentality and the problem of empathy," Helmut Schmitz argues that "an uncritical representation of Germans as victims is [. . .] frequently in danger of reproducing collective notions of identity based on ethnically dubious concepts."[1] In a second piece, Schmitz argues more forcefully that the ultimate aim of "discursive attempts to 'contain' the Holocaust within a nationalised memory discourse" — the attempt to refocus contemporary perspectives onto "Germans as victims" — is to "relegitimise a German perspective on National Socialism from the vantage point of empathy."[2] Empathy, in Schmitz's view, may be all too easily misappropriated for the purpose of rebuilding a German national consciousness and excluding the primary victims of Nazism — Jews, Sinti, and Roma, homosexuals, the mentally and physically disabled, slave laborers, and dissidents persecuted by the regime and the millions who sustained it.

Yet it may be that *all* attempts in contemporary German writing to depict the life stories of so-called ordinary Germans empathetically, and not just those that offer an uncritical representation of German suffering, reproduce collective notions of identity and "relegitimise a German perspective on National Socialism," to use Schmitz's formulation. They do this almost by definition insofar as the attempt to create empathy, of whatever kind, already presumes a collective. At the most general level, this may be "humankind." Within the context of German authors writing on "German" themes for German readers, however, it quickly comes to imply a "German" collective — the degree of exclusivity will vary, of course, and this is certainly worth examining. What is of interest here, then, is the struggle *within* this collective memory to define the *boundaries* of empathetic identification.

In this chapter, I examine three literary texts dealing with the experiences of "ordinary Germans" during the war years: Walter Kempowski's

Alles umsonst (All in Vain, 2006); Günter Grass's *Beim Häuten der Zwiebel* (Peeling the Onion, 2006), and Thomas Medicus's *In den Augen meines Großvaters* (In My Grandfather's Eyes, 2004). The first of these novels allows for a relatively "easy" gesture of sympathy with a child separated from his mother, who had been arrested for harboring a Jew, and subsequently forced to embark on one of the treks from the east by the advancing Red Army. Precisely this choice of "absolute" victims, however, may disguise the novel's problematic aspects. The second and third novels are part of the recent interest in the more complex story to be told about those (far more numerous) individuals who were both complicit to a greater or lesser degree but also in some way victims of the ferocious campaign waged against Germany by its enemies, of the regime, or, more broadly, of "events." Grass's and Medicus's texts, therefore, explore the limits of empathy. Rather than viewing the current focus on Germans as victims as a sure sign of a disavowal of historical responsibility, I argue, it may be more useful to examine contemporary literary texts on the Nazi past as engaging in a refreshingly honest debate on collective memory, more specifically on what kinds of actions — that is, which forms of complicity — may be seen as "understandable" and which remain nonintegrable into a "universal narrative" of the inescapable collusion of ordinary people in historical circumstances.

Walter Kempowski's *Alles umsonst:* Empathy with Ordinary Germans

Walter Kempowski's *Alles umsonst* strives to recreate a "lost world."[3] The novel invites its reader to journey back to East Prussia, a region of small commercial towns, minor country estates, agriculture and livestock, and ethnically diverse populations living in close proximity, and back to the closing months of the Second World War. We are transported to the Georgenhof, residence of the von Globig family: Eberhard, whose father was promoted to the Wilhelmine nobility in 1905 — not "true" nobility, then — and who is presently away serving in the supply corps in Italy; Katharina, his wife, originally from Berlin and scarcely at home in rural East Prussia; and their son, Peter, a boy of twelve years and a sensitive child dimly aware of his mother's sense of dislocation and muted mourning for his sister Elfie, who had died two years previously and who is now buried in the woods nearby. Sharing the residence, and, as she sees it, running the entire household, is "Tantchen" (little aunt), a relative originally from Silesia but driven from her home after the First World War. The von Globigs are visited regularly by Dr. Wagner, the local teacher, who is secretly in love with Katharina but too conscious of the privilege extended to him by the family in allowing him to come to the house to ever act. In addition, Katharina is plagued by Drygalski, epitome of the lower middle-class social climbers who supported the Nazi revolution in such great numbers. Drygalski rules over the only recently established "model" settlement near to the estate and has taken it on himself to investigate his genteel neighbors' less than enthusiastic embrace of the Party's social and political program. In particular, he objects to Katharina's unduly sympathetic, in his view, at least, treatment of the foreign laborers who work on the estate — Wladimir, a Pole, and the two Ukrainian women, Vera and Sonja, who have came voluntarily from their homeland to work as domestic servants; no doubt he would be equally disapproving of her fraternization with the French and Italian POWs held locally (*AU* 60). Finally, Katharina dreams, just occasionally, of Sarkander, the local mayor, with whom, it is implied, she had a brief affair while her husband was in Berlin in 1936 for the Olympics, a liaison that may have produced Elfie.

These relationships hint at the complex social, political, and historical interactions that shape the context within which the particular events of early 1945 will play out: the accumulation of ancient injustices and resentments weighing on the present, the decline of the landed elite and the rise of the lower middle classes, the clash between a traditional culture of deference and the revolutionary energy of Nazism, the enforced (occasionally, unforced) intimacy between different ranks and ethnic groups, and the changing position of individuals in relation to family, social networks, and new economic realities. The series of "guests" who come into the house more or less uninvited and impose on Katharina's hospitality — *Der Ökonom* (economist), the woman violinist, the painter, the Baltic baron and his wife, the first refugees from further east — serve to locate the narrative more specifically in the historical moment of early 1945: they utter dark intimations of the Soviet advance, allude to Katharina's lack of preparedness, and give human faces to a population busily divesting itself of all obvious links between it and National Socialism.

Kempowski's novel clearly incorporates a historicizing mode vis-à-vis its subject matter. "Thick description" of the tangle of social and ethnic ties, historical rivalries, and the uneasy simultaneity of tradition and modernity made all the more acute by rapid and revolutionary change thus underpins the narrative's psychologizing presentation of the text's key characters. Their actions are marked as understandable, perhaps even predictable, responses to the manner in which they are situated in relation to the dense accretion of historical events, social relationships, and shifting political realities. Certainly, most of those we encounter are broadly, if rather superficially, pro-Nazi, or if not pro-Nazi then at least unthinkingly accepting of the anti-Semitism, racism, and "Hitler cult" that pervade contemporary society. Even Katharina, who, as an unwordly devotee of an elite culture of aesthetic sensibility, is instinctively repulsed by the brute — and lower-class — Nazis, admires Ina Seidel (1885–1974), the composer of the infamous poems written as tributes to Adolf Hitler, and enjoys the 1942 film *Rembrandt,* a notorious piece of Nazi anti-Semitic propaganda (*AU* 91). Yet it is clear that Katharina is drawn to Seidel not on account of her Nazi connections but because she speaks to her own flight into interiority at times of turmoil in the "real" world, to her sense of loss for a child that died of scarlet fever, and to her melancholia and dislocation, with works such as *Das Wunschkind* (Planned Child) (1930), *Tröstliche Begegnung* (Comforting Meeting, 1932–1933), and *Lennacker: Das Buch einer Heimkehr* (The Book of Return, 1938). Katharina also devours Eckart von Naso and Konrad Muschler (correct spelling: Reinhold Conrad Muschler), two novelists, along with Seidel, known for syrupy historical fiction with clear but generally unthreatening nationalistic undertones. Such reading, it is implied, by no means indicates an embrace of Nazi ideology but points to a sentimental love of her country. Above all, she enjoys "die 'Blauen Bücher'" (Blue Books), sets of images of the German lands designed for melancholic indulgence (*AU* 89).[4]

Even Drygalski, the petty Nazi bureaucrat who harasses Katharina, may be understood as a product of his time. Ruined by the global economic crisis of 1929, he is helped back to his feet by the Party and experiences the Nazi seizure of power as a chance for a new beginning (*AU* 136). Katharina's husband Eberhard, a logistics officer who had "nothing to do with weapons" (*AU* 11), is just as much a creation of the world he inhabits. He shows kindness to the Ukranian servants Vera and Sonja but delivers swift corporal punishment when required (*AU* 182). Nor does he discern that in maximizing the economic exploitation of the conquered territories (*AU* 31) he is complicit in the crimes that he has witnessed in the east but which appear to him to take place in parallel to his own honorable work (*AU* 158). For Eberhard, his military service follows from his civilian life as an agriculturalist; his blindness to the suffering of the Slav population reflects the norms of the period in which he lives.

The novel's characters act as they do, it is intimated, because they can act no differently — the weight of the past, their place within the social order, ties of race and nation, and historical circumstances predetermine the responses available to them, responses that are inflected by the accidental composition of their individual personalities. This applies as much to "positive" as to "negative" deeds. Katharina harbors a Jew in flight from the Gestapo, and yet she does this not because she sets herself heroically against the prejudices of her time — she expresses no outrage when she hears rumors of atrocities (*AU* 232) — but because her pastor asked her to, or because she is paralyzed by characteristic indecision, or, she speculates, because she wants to prove to herself that she dares take a risk (*AU*

164). Of Jews, in fact, she is more or less entirely ignorant, beyond the clichéd bigotry of her age. The literary works of Stefan Zweig and Jakob Wassermann sit on her bookselves, presumably alongside Seidel, von Naso, and Muschler, but she does not even know that these two authors were Jewish. More broadly, individual deeds, whether good or bad, are simply contingent within the endlessly cyclical motions of human history.

War, occupation, and expulsion — these are the structuring devices of a story in which there are no clear victims and no clear perpetrators, only successive generations of intimately intertwined individuals who inflict suffering (or suffer themselves), depending on which group they happen to belong to at any given time. Georgenhof is only a part of an older estate that was reduced to ashes by the French in 1807 during Napoleon's Russian campaign (*AU* 86). In 1919, it is reported, the Russians had murdered and pillaged their way through the German estates in the Baltic region, and in 1941, the Germans did the same in the Soviet Union. The table in a church listing the names of the fallen soldiers of 1870–71 and 1914–18 (*AU* 329) points ahead to the dead of 1939–45, and the Tantchen's expulsion from Silesia, of course, stands in for the successive waves of expulsions since time immemorial. The very prevalence of mutual suspicion, prejudice, and even atrocity appears to exculpate all concerned. Wladimir, for example, witnessed the murder of comrades by the Red Army but is himself "against Jews" (*AU* 165), perhaps genocidally so, and certainly to a greater extent than the Germans Katharina and Eberhard von Globig for whom he works. Whether an individual is a perpetrator or a victim is simply a matter of timing. And, in the end, fate is indifferent to ethnicity, class, or guilt or innocence. During the trek related in the second half of the text, Vera is strung up, Tantchen is killed by a strafing fighter plane, and Dr. Wagner is crushed beneath a wagon.

At the close of *Alles umsonst* Peter is dragged onto one of the last refugee ships to depart by none other than Drygalski, who gives up his own place to save the boy. The Nazi bureaucrat sacrifices himself for the sake of the son of a family that he had long despised as insufficiently committed to the cause. As always, however, interpersonal dynamics are more important in determining individual acts of kindness or cruelty than any agency characters may exercise in relation to the larger events that shape their environment: Drygalski saves Peter, it is implied, to make up for his earlier resentment of the family's social status. In this text, motives are complex, outcomes unpredictable, and clear-cut judgments impossible. All that literary fiction can achieve, it seems, is to tell the stories of those ordinary Germans caught up in world history with sympathy and a degree of understanding.

Günter Grass's *Beim Häuten der Zwiebel:*
Empathy with the Waffen SS Recruit

In an interview published on 12 August 2006 in advance of his new book, *Beim Häuten der Zwiebel,*[5] Günter Grass divulged that he had served with the *Waffen SS* from late 1944 until his capture by American forces on 8 May 1945. In the weeks that followed, writers, literary critics, historians, and politicians disagreed on whether this belated confession had enhanced the author's moral authority or rather undermined his insistence for over almost sixty years on the need to confront the Nazi past.

Similar to Kempowski's *Alles Umsonst, Beim Häuten der Zwiebel* focuses on the "life-world" of its protagonist, the author as an adolescent and young man between the outbreak of war in September 1939 and the publication of *Die Blechtrommel* (The Tin Drum) in 1959. The reader is presented, for example, with the narrator's account of his adolescence, relationship with his parents, growing obsession with the opposite sex, and experiences at school. Later, we are told of his compulsory labor service, time spent manning an antiaircraft battery, attempt to volunteer for the submarine corps, induction into the military, and eventual deployment as a member of the *Waffen SS* 10th Tank Division Frundsberg, and of how he was wounded during shelling by Red Army artillery, managed to return to his own lines, and was captured by the American army in a military hospital in Marienbad. In the aftermath of the German defeat, we read, Grass was interned in POW camps in Bavaria, where he took a cookery course using ingredients available only in the imagination of the participants, and, after his release, he began a career as a sculptor working on tombstones. He lost his virginity, traveled to Italy, met his future wife Anna, moved to Berlin, and then to Paris, where he completed *Die Blechtrommel.*

In *Beim Häuten der Zwiebel,* we learn little about the author that we did not already know — with one obvious exception — and those aspects of his unique experience to which we are given access are almost invariably immediately aligned with the social, political, philosophical, and cultural conflicts of the day. The story that might have been told of the author's early years will be subordinated to the chronicle of how a young German from Danzig, an irrelevance in himself, came to be swept up by global upheavals and epoch-making conflicts and be fashioned by a series of dates that, for his readers in the present, resonate with worldwide historical importance: the pogrom of 9 November 1938, the outbreak of war on 1 September 1939, the defeat at Stalingrad in February 1943, the end of the Second World War on 8 May 1945, the currency reform of 20 June 1948, and the East Berlin uprising of 17 June 1953. In short, Grass's narrative is for the most part representative rather than revelatory. The only installment that does not appear as already situated as "typical" of the experience of the millions of ordinary Germans is his service with the *Waffen SS*. This is the sole moment of disruption within the text, the one episode that requires the author to explore and examine the particular, subjective motives of his seventeen-year-old self. It is this episode that, as evidenced by the heated debate it provoked,[6] tests the new limits of empathetic identification: is it now possible to "understand" the motives and historical "situatedness" even of individuals whose combat jackets had displayed the feared SS insignia?

The answer provided by Grass's text to this question is that it may be permissible, more than sixty years after the defeat of the Nazi dictatorship, to begin to acknowledge the folly of a young man motivated by adolescent arrogance, teenage testosterone and misplaced pride. "Serious" perpetration, however, remains beyond the pale, and the reality of broad German culpability must always be restated. The young Grass's unquestioning acquiescence and his blind belief in the *Führer* are thus contextualized as a consequence of his petit-bourgeois formation and his schoolboy susceptibility to propagandistic tales of the heroism of the German armed forces. The narrator speaks, then, of how the prospect of military service promised escape from the claustrophobia (*BH* 77) of his parents' household and success with girls, and refers to "foolish pride of my early years" (*BH* 127). In this way, the particular circumstances of Grass's adolescence are universalized to the extent that the specific, initially disruptive fact of his *Waffen SS* service can be posited as merely one of many possible paths that fate might have chosen for a seventeen-year-old German boy in 1944. Simple membership of this infamous organization no longer appears as an egregious crime in itself, as proof positive of murderous intent. For the old man that the *Waffen SS* recruit has become sixty years later, a degree of historical responsibility remains but this is a generalized liability, what the narrator describes as a "*Mit*verantwortung" (*collective* responsibility, *BH* 127), rather than individual guilt.

What is interesting with respect to our attempt to identify the limits of empathetic understanding in the contemporary period is the rhetorical investment the narrator makes to maneuver his readership into accepting, indeed embracing, the notion that even a *Waffen SS* recruit might be only *relatively* complicit and, moreover, deserving of our compassion. While a more nuanced view has been taken in recent years of individuals' actions during the Hitler years — Bill Niven's positing of a new willingness to address the past "in all of its contradictoriness"[7] — the intensity of this rhetorical investment suggests that the narrator, acting as proxy for the author Günter Grass, is conscious of pushing up against a taboo. Thus an elaborate ritual is devised in which a series of insistently self-critical questions relating to the adolescent Grass's failure to interrogate the broader circumstances of his youth anticipate, and exceed, any cross-examination of the author's testimony that the reader might otherwise initiate. Why did he not ask about the German assault on Poland in September 1939 (*BH* 16)? Why did he not ask about the fate of a classmate who was suddenly absent (*BH* 22–23)? Why did he not ask what happened to the Latin teacher who "disappeared"? And why did he not wonder whether the young fellow recruit who refused to take up his weapon during training, comically named by his peers "Wirtunsowasnicht" (Wedontdothat) on account of his repetition of this mantra, might provide an example for *him* of the possibility of at least passive resistance? (*BH* 103). Suitably impressed by the narrator's willingness to address his juvenile omissions, the reader is primed to move from the particular to the universal, that is, from the specific issue of the young Grass's unwillingness to question the regime and his subsequent admission to the *Waffen SS* to the more general issue of just how many boys of his age might reasonably be expected to have demonstrated greater insight — "Wirtunsowasnicht" was exceptional, Grass the representative "norm." It seems unlikely that the reader, aware that so many ordinary Germans neglected to ask the "right" questions, would rush to condemn this one individual.

The limits of empathetic understanding, therefore, appear to have expanded: the large majority of "ordinary Germans" may now be forgiven their susceptibility to Hitler's charismatic leadership and even a degree of complicity in the Nazi system. The key condition, Grass's text implies, is that such folly be made available as a salutary tale and as a model for a democratic engagement with the past. Throughout *Beim Häuten der Zwiebel,* accordingly, the narrator time and again balances his youthful omissions against the exemplary sacrifice made by the public figure who offers up his own biography as an object lesson in self-deception and a guide to personal and political rehabilitation. In Grass's reading of his public's mood, at least, people are entitled to their past mistakes, but their errors must be acknowledged and effectively integrated into a strategy of recuperative enlightenment.

Thomas Medicus's *In den Augen meines Großvaters:* The Limits of Empathy

In recent years, as has been widely noted, much of German writing on the Nazi past has focused on the transgenerational dynamic between the wartime generation, their sons and daughters, the '68ers now often reviewing their own previous automatic condemnation of their parents, and the grandchildren of the last, fading witnesses to Hitler's regime.[8] Günter

Grass's *Im Krebsgang* (Crabwalk, 2003), for example, is structured as a trialogue involving all three generations, whereas other well-known texts such as Uwe Timm's *Am Beispiel meines Bruders* (In My Brother's Shadow, 2003), Ulla Hahn's *Unscharfe Bilder* (Blurred Images, 2003),[9] or Dagmar Leupold's *Nach den Kriegen: Roman eines Lebens* (After the Wars: Novel of a Life, 2004), restrict themselves to those who directly experienced Nazism (including, in Timm's case, a brother who served in the *Waffen SS* and was killed on the Eastern front) and the '68ers who transformed the fledgling Federal Republic with their protests and who, in the present, are turning to reflection on their role in shaping its "culture of contrition."[10] Novels by younger authors, notably Marcel Beyer's *Spione* (Spies, 2000) and Tanja Dückers's *Himmelskörper* (Heavenly Bodies, 2003), focus on the grandchildren and their efforts to come to know the wartime fates of their grandparents.

Thomas Medicus's *In den Augen meines Großvaters* (2004) traces the author's attempts to access the psychology of his grandfather, Wilhelm Crisolli, a general in the *Wehrmacht,* and to reconstruct the circumstances of his assassination in Italy in the closing months of the war. What is important for our discussion of the new limits of empathy is the manner in which the novel explores the grandson's inner conflict as he wrestles with his often ambivalent desire to "understand" his grandfather while striving to arrive at a definition of "acceptable" conduct, that is, both comprehensible within the historical context and pardonable sixty years later, which does not offend his firm belief in the criminality of the Hitler regime and of those who sustained it. Medicus's grandfather, then, offers an interesting case of a senior participant in the Nazi system who remained relatively "clean" and whose identifiable criminal acts — "criminal" in today's terms — cannot be straightforwardly categorized as examples of Nazi prejudice or Nazi brutality but may rather derive from an "acting-out" of the norms of an East Prussian social universe structured by values such as honor, obedience, order, and consequentiality. The grandfather is clearly complicit in Nazism, as is the world from which he hails, and yet the fact that his motives appear more "noble," however misguided his service to the regime may be, raises, in the mind of his grandson at least, a moment of profound doubt as to whether he might rather be worthy of empathetic understanding than be automatically condemned.

The first forty pages or so of *In den Augen meines Großvaters* concern not the grandfather but the grandson, presenting a psychological profile of an individual and, by implication, an entire postwar generation, traumatized by loss and intimations of an inherited guilt. The narrator, therefore, is plagued by a sense of dispossession, both physical, in relation to the lost homelands in the East, and psychic, concerning the "German heroes" of past wars that may not be remembered or mourned. (The contrast here is with Granchester in which he witnesses how the English are permitted to idealize Rupert Brooke). At the same time, he is also susceptible to a form of escapist melancholia — in which twentieth-century crimes, particularly the Holocaust, are subsumed into a narrative without human agency — and of modernity and its handmaidens: mechanized slaughter, genocide, ethnic conflict, and expulsion. On crossing the Polish-Belorussian-Lithuanian-Soviet border zone in 1990 — a peculiarly post–Cold War anthropological pessimism is characteristic of the narrator's stance[11] — he thus imagines the entire history of the region's conflicts filing past him "like one long procession of ghosts."[12] The fate of his own parents and grandparents, driven from eastern reaches that, previously unfamiliar, he now longs to visit, appear to him to be part of this never-ending cycle of violence, retribution, and brutal expulsion.[13]

The narrator's sudden and unexpected fascination with the fates of his parents and grandparents mirrors the contemporary shift of focus away from broad, structural analyses of the "Nazi system" toward individual life stories. This shift, it is implied, is provoked by direct confrontation with the "authentic sites" of history after forty years of Cold-War hiatus: in the east, he senses how the master narrative of the twentieth century — of states, war, defeat, and division — is giving way to a multitude of smaller, local stories (*AG* 24). What follows, accordingly, is a detailed reconstruction of his grandparents' social and historical formation, their indirect experience of the First World War and the humiliation of the defeat of 1918, their skepticism toward the Weimar Republic, Annemarie's love of music and dancing, and Wilhelm's aristocratic respect for tradition, ties of loyalty, and respect for the state. Medicus's grandfather, in particular, is to be understood within his own time, and as a product of his background, that is, of Lutheranism, Prussian values, and the soldier's codex (*AG* 141).

This attempt at a historicist reconstruction of his grandfather's life — the life of a man now remembered first and foremost as a servant of Hitler — is presented as a deliberate smashing of a taboo (*AG* 62). More specifically, it is an attempt to move beyond his implication in the Nazi system to reveal the "real" man who was a husband to his grandmother and a father to his own mother. On viewing a photograph of his grandfather's funeral, then, the narrator comments: "I was fixated on the Hitler salute" (*AG* 57). To get to know the individual whose coffin is concealed by the flag with its Nazi swastika, he will need to follow the invitation to enter into this photograph, and into the others showing his grandfather alive, huddled with his fellow officers (*AG* 62). Telling the story of his grandfather will require a conscious, and controversial, effort of empathetic identification with the man in Nazi uniform.

Thus far, Medicus's text might appear as a potentially revisionist work, imbued, perhaps, with neoconservative cultural pessimism, scarcely sublimated revanchism, historical evasiveness, and nostalgia for "Prussian" values. Alternatively, it might seem to replicate the somewhat "easy" identification with the fate of ordinary Germans detectable in Kempowski's *Alles umsonst*. Yet *In den Augen meines Großvaters*, as suggested by the title with its hint that the universe as seen through his grandfather's eyes may not be the same as the one viewed through his own, is more concerned with the grandson's traumatic (and always doomed) striving to establish historical truth (and the epistemological uncertainty he experiences with respect to his own position vis-à-vis his grandfather's culpability) than it is with any straightforward rehabilitation of a "misguided" generation of Nazi functionaries or an (imaginative) reappropriation of a lost "German" world in the East. The bulk of the novel, as such, relates the narrator's obsessive journeying to Tuscany, to the locations of his grandfather's story, his struggle to reconcile the bewilderingly divergent accounts he assembles, and his efforts, overwhelmingly unsuccessful, to distill from these and the few documents he can find a bare minimum of historical fact.

Wilhelm Crisolli was certainly no fantatical Nazi. All witnesses agree that the German general was, for the most part, reasonable in his dealings with the local population and especially friendly toward the women in whose villa he had been billeted (*AG* 197). Beyond this, however, it is almost impossible for the narrator to establish the extent of his responsibility for some of the sterner measures reported by eyewitnesses or, indeed, to verify the degree to which he intervened to prevent excesses. Three episodes in particular remain shrouded in mystery. First, whether he disobeyed Hitler's order to fight to the last during the Russian campaign, as the narrator's aunt claims (*AG* 213–14). Second, the circumstances surrounding his authorization of the execution of an Italian priest and two women suspected of collaborating with partisans. Third, following the ambush in which he was mortally wounded, whether he asked that there be no reprisals against civilians.

With respect to the first and third questions — his supposed insubordination and his dying plea for mercy toward local civilians — the narrator finds it impossible to establish any clarity. He is presented with wildly conflicting accounts from a variety of sources, some of whom may have an interest in presenting a particular "truth." The encouraging prospect that the grandfather's Prussian values, even as they predisposed him to obedience toward the state, may also have made possible some distance between him and the regime to the extent that loyalty to those under his command and respect for the conventions of warfare (he may have believed his ambushers to have been clothed in regular army uniforms and therefore legitimate combatants) counted for more than his oath to Hitler thus cannot be confirmed one way or another. In and of themselves, however, these episodes, in spite of, or perhaps precisely on account of their ambiguous implications, may have created enough doubt about the motives for the general's wartime record to allow for an empathetic reading of his entanglement in the Nazi system. What is damning is his part in the execution of the priest and the two women. Here too, a rigid Prussian adherence to procedure might have been available as a mitigating circumstance: perhaps Crisolli was not directly involved in the sentencing but simply signed it off as a "bureaucratic procedure" (*AG* 239). Yet it becomes apparent to the narrator that his grandfather's resolve to permit these executions — three days after the failure of the July plot — represented a clear choice, an unambiguous decision to demonstrate his loyalty to the regime and to suppress his instinctive aversion to its leaders: "Nothing seemed more wrong to him than to be divided within himself at this most critical moment" (*AG* 194).

In a novel in which the impossibility of arriving at any complete or acceptably accurate version of the past is repeatedly thematized, the grandson's fixation on the absoluteness of his grandfather's guilt concerning the execution of three individuals is surely significant. It may well be the case that this episode was hardly noteworthy against the backdrop of the massacres being concurrently carried out by elements of the SS, for example (*AG* 195), but that it happened, and that his grandfather was instrumental in making it happen, forever blocks any possible progression from a sensitive exploration of his Prussian background and the way this predicted his involvement as an army officer under Hitler to an uncritical rehabilitation. In this text, empathetic understanding may create a more nuanced impression of the context within which individuals acted, but its limits are defined by a resolute awareness that, even within the terms of their cultural conditioning and their age, those same individuals had the opportunity, and indeed the responsibility, to make choices.

Conclusion

So what limits, if any, remain on empathy with the German experience of the Second World War? First and foremost, the recent shift in the focus of interest away from the abstract structures of Nazi ideology and violence toward the "lived experience" of ordinary Germans, encouraged by diverse factors including the imminent passing of the wartime generation but also, for example, the massacres of longtime neighbors by "ordinary" Serbs, Bosnians, and Croats in the early 1990s and in Kosovo toward the end of the decade, has fostered a more textured view of the lives of individual Germans between 1939 and 1945. Certainly, their crimes both of commission and omission can seem less unique and thereby less damning, the product perhaps of the fatal fallibility of human beings seemingly caught up in an endless cycle of aggression and counteraggression; at the same time, their suffering may be invoked by present-day photographs of expellees or of towns destroyed by NATO bombing. Without doubt, then, the postunification period, and particularly the period since the mid-1990s, has witnessed the emergence of a "German perspective on National Socialism from the vantage point of empathy," to cite Helmut Schmitz once again.[14]

Yet this need not always be a negative development. In the place of a rather black-and-white condemnation of an entire population, recent literary representations of ordinary Germans, for the most part at least, may reflect a new willingness to engage with "real" individuals on a case-by-case basis, balancing an empathetic understanding of historical context with a contemporary perspective on the evil to which the actions of these individuals contributed and on the extent of their contribution. This produces, of course, a "messier" picture: the naïve, even ignorant Katharina featured in Kempowski's *Alles umsonst,* misguided perhaps, probably passively tolerant of the regime but not directly complicit; the youthful Günter Grass, seduced by Nazi rhetoric and let down by his craving to boast of heroic exploits, but lucky enough, viewed retrospectively, that his war did not last long enough for him to participate in atrocities; the German general, relatively "clean" but incapable of reflecting critically on the abuse of his Prussian values by the Nazi regime he served. "Real" people emerge in these stories, demanding a more differentiated response from the reader, an awareness of the complexity of human nature and of the obscurity of events distant in time, and an acknowledgment of the difficulties involved in judging people in the past. This may be unnerving, but it most likely enriches historical understanding, and it certainly makes for better fiction.

At the close of Medicus's *In den Augen meines Großvaters,* the question of historical responsibility is raised once again. The narrator's conclusion is perhaps surprisingly definitive for a novel in which very little can be known for sure. The narrator insists there is no escape from family history or family culpability; there can only be acceptance of ambivalence (*AG* 243). And only the latter, that is, an empathetic understanding of the historical actors' circumstances, choices, and constraints — *and* an awareness that individuals nonetheless bear responsibility for their deeds as much as for their omissions — makes possible a more nuanced remembering and thus a less suspect form of forgetting.

Notes

[1] Helmut Schmitz, "Historicism, Sentimentality and the Problem of Empathy: Uwe Timm's *Am Beispiel meines Bruders* in the Context of Recent Representations of German Suffering," in *A Nation of Victims? Representations of German Wartime Suffering from 1945 to the Present,* ed. Helmut Schmitz (Amsterdam: Rodopi, 2007), 205.

[2] Helmut Schmitz, "The Birth of the Collective from the Spirit of Empathy: From the 'Historians' Dispute' to German Suffering," in *Germans as Victims: Remembering the Past in Contemporary Germany,* ed. Bill Niven (Basingstoke, UK: Palgrave Macmillan, 2006), 95.

[3] Walter Kempowski, *Alles umsonst* (Munich: Albrecht Knaus, 2006), 10. Subsequent references to this work are cited in the text using the abbreviation *AU* and page number.

[4] Kempowski's references to these authors (correct spelling for Muschler's first name is Reinhold Conrad), and later to Gotthardt Freiherr von Erztum-Lohmeyer, a minor author honored by Hitler (ibid., 362), may indicate a desire to rescue these and other authors discredited by their appropriation by the Nazis.

[5] Günter Grass, *Beim Häuten der Zwiebel* (Göttingen: Steidl, 2006). Subsequent references to this work are cited in the text using the abbreviation *BH* and page number.

[6] For a useful discussion of the debate and an analysis of the novel, see Anne Fuchs's "'Ehrlich, du lügst wie gedruckt': Günter Grass's Autobiogaphical Confession and the Changing Territory of Germany's Memory Culture," *German Life and Letters* 60, no. 2 (2007): 261–75.

[7] See Bill Niven, *Facing the Nazi Past: United Germany and the Legacy of the Third Reich* (London: Routledge, 2002), 5.

[8] See, e.g., Anne Fuchs, *Phantoms of War in Contemporary German Literature, Films and Discourse: The Politics of Memory* (New York: Palgrave Macmillan, 2008).

[9] See Helmut Schmitz, "Representations of the Nazi Past II: German Wartime Suffering," in *Contemporary German Fiction: Writing in the Berlin Republic,* ed. Stuart Taberner (Cambridge: CUP, 2007), 142–58.

[10] Karl Wilds, "Identity Creation and the Culture of Contrition: Recasting 'Normality' in the Berlin Republic," *German Politics* 9, no. 1 (2000): 83–102.

[11] There are similarities both in tone and message with Hans Magnus Enzensberger's *Die große Wanderung* (1992) and *Aussichten auf den Bürgerkrieg* (1993).

[12] Thomas Medicus, *In den Augen meines Großvaters* (Munich: DVA, 2004), 24. Subsequent references to this work are cited in the text using the abbreviation *AG* and page number.

[13] There are echoes here of the fiction of W. G. Sebald, particularly *Die Ausgewanderten* (1992) and *Austerlitz* (2001). See my "German Nostalgia? Remembering German-Jewish Life in W. G. Sebald's *Die Ausgewanderten* and *Austerlitz,*" *Germanic Review* 79, no. 3 (2004): 181–202.

[14] Schmitz, "Birth of the Collective," 95.

15: "Secondary Suffering" and Victimhood: The "Other" of German Identity in Bernhard Schlink's "Die Beschneidung" and Maxim Biller's "Harlem Holocaust"

Kathrin Schödel

IT HAS OFTEN BEEN CLAIMED THAT until the 1990s there had existed a taboo, or at least strict discursive rules in German public discourse, regarding depictions of "Germans as victims," which made it difficult for Germans to remember and mourn their own wartime suffering. According to this interpretation of the history of German *Vergangenheitsbewältigung* (coming to terms with the past), the taboo was finally lifted in the years following German unification, allowing for the slow emergence of a long-neglected, more differentiated account of the experiences of "normal" Germans during the Nazi period, which is still in need of elaboration today. In this chapter, I examine this version of the history of German public memory as a construct that is closely linked to contemporary discourses of German identity but which also relies on complementary constructions of its "Other." The obvious counterpart to the apparent new openness of the memory of National Socialism are other forms of public memory, especially the seemingly simplistic and moralistic memory of the Holocaust associated with the generation of '68. Yet I argue that the complementary Other created in recent debates about the need for greater differentiation in German memory discourse is often a particular construction of Jewish identity. To explore the connection between German "secondary suffering" — that is, the notion of a struggle with the memory of German guilt, and calls for a more complex approach to remembering National Socialismand a problematic view of Jewish identity, I examine two very different short stories: Bernhard Schlink's "Die Beschneidung" (The Circumcision, 2000) and Maxim Biller's "Harlem Holocaust" (1990).

The famously provocative German-Jewish writer Henryk M. Broder seems to have been outraged by his invitation to talk at a conference entitled "After the Shoah: Is there a Jewish identity in Germany?"[1] On his homepage entitled "selber schuld, wenn Sie mir schreiben" (it's your own fault if you write to me), he complains: "Every schmuck who goes shopping at Aldi with a jute bag wants to know whether at least Jewish identity has survived if all the Jews had to bite the dust." On the one hand, Broder is referring here to German philo-Semitism, that is, the exaggerated "love" for Jews that functions as a displacement of feelings of guilt and discomfort and can even be seen as a dangerous continuation of anti-Semitic thought in its undifferentiated view of "the Jews."[2] Yet there is also something more subtle at stake here. Heinz Peter Preußer, who wrote to Broder to invite him to give the talk in question, is clearly not a naïve philo-Semite. He explains, for instance, that the conference is intended to "offer possible alternatives to substantialist, not to say racist definitions of Jewishness or Jewish thought" (cited on Broder's homepage; see note 1). Broder's outrage, then, seems to be directed at the need for a definition of Jewish identity at all and at the use of Jewish identity as the Other that helps define Germanness. Thus he asks, reversing the topic of the talk he was meant to give: "Is there a German identity in Germany? And if there is: why does it express itself mainly through the search for a Jewish identity?" (see note 1).

Aspects of this problematic interdependence of constructions of a German identity conceived of as burdened by the past and of a Jewish identity as its Other may be found in Bernhard Schlink's short story "Die Beschneidung" from the collection *Liebesfluchten* (Flights of Love, 2000). In this story about the relationship between Andi, a member of the "second generation" of Germans after the Nazi period, and Sarah, an American Jew, both in their twenties, the protagonist asks his girlfriend:

> "Do you love me?"
> She sat up and laid a hand on his chest. "Yes."
> "Why?"
> "Because you're sweet and clever, honest, generous. Because you're such a trouper and make life so difficult for yourself. You want to make everything right for everybody, and although you manage a lot of things, you can't do it all, how could you, but you try all the same, and that touches my heart."[3]

Sarah's description of the protagonist corresponds to the way he is depicted throughout the story: as a young man who is so worried about how he appears to others that he hardly manages to develop his own identity. In the German original it is obvious that it is not just the protagonist's obsession with how he is perceived by others that makes his life difficult, but also their actual image of him. The others, who in this story — significantly — are almost exclusively Jewish Americans, look at the young German and see the Nazi past. In the German version of the story, then, Sarah addresses Andi as "mein treuer kleiner Soldat" (my loyal little soldier).[4] Even in a declaration of love she thus makes a clear link to the image of the militaristic German of the past. The word "Soldat" (soldier) also refers back to Andi's account of his father's role in the Second World War (*B* 203). The English translation, "you're such a trouper," misses the allusion to the German context, perhaps subconsciously working against the problematic grain of Schlink's story and thereby perhaps making it more palatable for British and especially American readers.

With Andi, Schlink creates a German of the second generation, whose difficulties in finding his own identity can be seen as a literal as well as, perhaps, an allegoric depiction of what has been referred to as secondary suffering, the predicament allegedly caused by omnipresent references to German guilt. Indeed, the character who constantly encounters stereotypical notions of Germanness and the Nazi past may be a fictionalized embodiment of, for instance, Martin Walser's complaint that Germans were still not allowed to refer to themselves as "ein normales Volk" (a normal people), which was voiced just two years before the publication of Schlink's volume.[5] Several reviews of Schlink's *Liebesfluchten* also made this connection.[6] The "suffering" in question here is an ostensible psychological problem, that is, the struggle to come to terms with the past and to find a German identity in the face of perceived accusations and discursive restrictions. In this view, German national identity appears as "beschnitten" (circumcised or curtailed). That Schlink's story is supposed to be read as a representative depiction in this way is rather obvious. His protagonist suffers because he is treated by non-Germans as a "typical" German, not as an individual. It is also evident that his musings echo contemporary discussions regarding representations of National Socialism and German identity. For instance, Andi contemplates his experiences when watching "American and English war films": "he had known that Germans were justifiably presented as the villains, but had felt torn all the same" (*C* 215). In this way, the story invites generalizations — it is never simply about the love between one man and one woman but about the relationship between two characters standing in for their respective backgrounds. There is also not a single figure in the story who might counterbalance the frequent anti-German remarks uttered by non-German characters, who are almost all explicitly identified as Jews. Thus, in Schlink's story, more directly than in many other expressions of such secondary suffering, those who impose discursive rules and make life difficult for Germans by thwarting German "normality" are Jewish. Unlike in Walser's speech, which works by implication rather than by explicit statements, in Schlink's story there is a direct connection between the supposed secondary suffering endured by Germans and what has been called "secondary anti-Semitism," that is, anti-Semitism "because of Auschwitz."[7] Jews and *their* memory of the Holocaust — rather than the Nazi past itself — appear as the primary obstacles to the development of a less burdened German identity and a more nuanced view of the past.

Matthias Lorenz has analyzed the connection in "Die Beschneidung" between anti-Semitism and the rejection of so-called political correctness imagined as all-powerful in relation to the discourse about the German past.[8] Thus Lorenz demonstrates in detail how the Jews in Schlink's text impose discursive restrictions on the German protagonist. Andi, then, struggles because he tries to conform to their often-exaggerated demands and loses his own identity. In the case of Schlink's story, a critical depiction of undifferentiated philo-Semitism, which culminates in Andi's decision to get circumcized as a first step to conversion, turns into anti-Jewish resentment — in the character certainly, but also within the story as a whole. Obviously, in these circumstances, the relationship between Andi and Sarah — which can be read as Schlink's allegory for German-Jewish relations in the second generation after the Holocaust — cannot work: the German is obsessed with feelings of guilt, which are fueled by the Jewish characters in the story, mainly Sarah, who is shown to be insensitive at best and racist at worst.[9] She, for instance, talks about "deutsche Wesenart" (German nature, *B* 230) — in the English version this again appears toned down as "something essentially German" (*C* 229) — and its relation to National Socialism. Despite its problematic depiction of Jews, "Die Beschneidung" did not create a notable scandal when it first appeared in Germany, nor, indeed, with its publication in the United States and Britain, perhaps due to the slightly less provocative tenor of the translated version. The positive review of *Flights of Love* in the *Times Literary Supplement,* which mentions "The Circumcision" as the most controversial of the stories because of its superficial treatment of Holocaust memory,[10] did, however, spark a renewed, and heated, discussion of Schlink's 1995 best-selling novel *Der Vorleser* (The Reader, 1997).[11] This debate and the largely positive reception of the new collection very likely influenced the marketing of subsequent editions of *Der Vorleser* for English readers: the 2004 paperback edition of *The Reader* introduces Bernhard Schlink on its cover as the "author of *Flights of Love*."[12] That "Die Beschneidung" has not received greater attention may be on account of the story simply not having been read as widely as *Der Vorleser.* Yet there might also be another, more disconcerting, reason for the lack of a critical assessment of Schlink's depiction of Jews in this short story: the choice of American rather than German-Jewish characters may make it easier to get away with clichés. Indeed, anti-American stereotypes may be less taboo than anti-Jewish ones in German discourse. Schlink's story could also be read as a reaction to the debate on Daniel Goldhagen's *Hitler's Willing Executioners,* which was published in German in 1996. Sander Gilman has shown how a specific stereotype of Goldhagen as an example of the "vindictive American Jew" — a version of the "prototypical vengeful Jew" — was to be found in several reviews of Goldhagen's book.[13] Schlink's American Jews thus correspond to a stereotype not uncommon in German public discourse. While the opposition between Germans and Jews remains the central theme of Schlink's story, it is also one between Germans and Americans, with the result that Schlink is able to avoid making any direct statements about German Jews. That would, indeed, have made his construction of Jews as the Other of Germans much more difficult as he would have had to admit that there are Jewish Germans.

I now focus on an aspect of the construction of Jews in German discourse that is less obviously negative but which nonetheless leads to a generalizing, stereotyped image of a collective Other, and which is to be found not only in Schlink's problematic story but also in other, less crude expressions of secondary suffering. To return to the scene quoted above, in which the couple discuss their love for one another, Andi explains his passion for Sarah as follows: "You know who you are, where you come from, where you're going and what you need to make life work. I love you for the firm footing you have in the world" (C 216). In Andi's view, then, his girlfriend has a stable identity, rooted not least in her knowledge of her origins — the implied contrast to the speaker is obvious.[14] Again, the English translation changes the emphasis of this passage slightly. In German, Andi talks about "den festen Ort, den du in der Welt hast" (the firm place you have in the world, B 218). The metaphor of place together with the verb "herkommen" (to come from, B 217) in the previous sentence, which relates to "Herkunft" (origins) make it clear that Andi is talking about Sarah's cultural background. The story as a whole also supports Andi's interpretation of the strong and stable identity of the American-Jewish woman in contrast to the weak sense of self and belonging of the German. In the following, I hope to demonstrate the problematic side of Schlink's fictional construction of such a difference, aspects of which might at first seem rather innocuous.

In keeping with Andi's description of her, Sarah is shown to be well integrated into an extended family with a lively practice of religious traditions, from which Andi feels excluded even though he is invited to take part: "in the rituals of her family and faith she had a world, a treasure, that would always remain closed to him" (C 205). At this stage in the story, Andi's observations, rendered in free indirect speech, seem rather harmless, and they could be seen as a depiction of feelings of exclusion characteristic of any jealous lover. In the passage just cited he also regrets that he did not receive Sarah's "first kiss, her first embrace" (C 205). Yet the story does not undermine its central character's point of view in relation to his description of Jewish figures. Andi's feeling of exclusion from a close-knit religious community is proved right, and with a vengeance, when

Sarah's sister, Rachel, declares that the worst thing that could possibly happen to her sons would be for them to marry a non-Jewish woman (*C* 208). She also makes negative remarks about "mixed marriages" (*C* 209) in general. Lorenz points out that the German word Rachel uses, "Mischehe" (*B* 211), was also Nazi vocabulary; the text might thus draw an implicit comparison between Jewish religious law and National Socialism.[15] In a later passage, Andi explicitly makes a similar comparison: he likens the act of circumcizing to the Nazi practice of tattooing members of the SS and seems to give preference to the latter because "tattoos can be removed" (*C* 245). Comparisons between Jews and Nazis are one of the typical strategies of anti-Semitism after the Holocaust as they serve to relativize German guilt and to undercut the position of Jewish victims as morally superior to German perpetrators.[16] With regard to this particular passage concerned with circumcision, it might be argued that Schlink is not condoning such anti-Semitic tendencies, but rather showing their development in his central character. However, the author does not employ any narrative strategies that might encourage the reader to view Andi in such a negative light. It is only the protagonist's exaggerated and failed attempt at "changing over" (*C* 246) into Sarah's world by getting circumcized that — mainly through the perspective of the doctor, who performs the operation (*C* 246–49) — is portrayed in an unambiguously critical fashion.

To return to my focus on the stereotypical image of Jews, which is situated, as it were, before the threshold of such blatant anti-Semitism: Sarah's Jewish family is shown to cultivate a rich, communicative memory dating back as far as the eighteenth century; her "Uncle Aaron was a spirited, witty storyteller" (*C* 199). I quote as well the German original — "erzählte mit Lust und Witz" (*B* 200) — because, as we shall see, it may be read as an intertextual reference, be it a conscious one or a coincidence of phrasing. "Erzählen" (to narrate, to tell stories) is a key term in discussions about remembering the German past. In Uncle Aaron's narrative, pogroms and exile become part of, and are more or less subsumed within, stories of economic success, love, marriage, and having children.[17] This forms a marked contrast to Andi's family, where storytelling is not practiced in the same way. Andi talks about a scarcity of stories — "erzählen" — in his family with reference to the war (*B* 203), and when Sarah meets his parents, talk of their origins relates almost entirely to his father's role in the Second World War (*C* 219–20), thus cutting short a narrative stretching further back in time. At the beginning of the story, Andi complains to Sarah that her relatives did not want to know anything about him, other than that he was German, which seemed to make all other information "irrelevant" (*C* 204). The motif of telling — or not being able to tell — stories about the German past can be related to arguments within public discourse on German memory. In the mid-1980s' debate on historicizing National Socialism, for instance, the historian Martin Broszat complained that in writing about German history, the "Lust am [. . .] Erzählen" (the pleasure in storytelling) had been lost.[18] It appeared that there were only clear-cut moralizing accounts of the past, rather than stories doing justice to individual experience. Broszat's phrase is echoed in Schlink's characterization of Sarah's uncle. His "Lust" in narrating their family history stands in opposition to the apparent lack of storytelling by Germans about the German past. It has also often been claimed that in German memory culture it is almost impossible to look beyond the caesura of the Nazi past and talk about previous eras of German history without relating them to the rise of National Socialism.[19] The family memory dating back to life in the shtetl (C 199) is not only the complementary Other of such assertions, but with its rather casual in-clusion of individual stories of persecution and suffering it is also a coun-terpart to more recent claims that there are no narratives about German suffering within family as well as cultural memories.

In accordance with the male protagonist's perception of her, Schlink's character Sarah finds it easy to identify with a collective "we" stretching beyond her own lifetime and experience.[20] When Andi, trying to question her prejudices against Germans, asks her, "'So how many Germans do you know?,'" Sarah replies, "'Enough, and along with those that we've been happy to get to know, there are the one's we'd have rather not got to know, but got to know anyway'" (C 235–36). Even though Sarah is talking about a traumatic past, it appears throughout the story that her identification with a Jewish collective gives her strength as well as power over her German boyfriend when she deploys her victim identity to si-lence his arguments. Achieving this kind of collective identity is seen to be difficult for Germans in the face of partly internalized accusations of guilt. In relation to the Nazi past, Andi describes his own position, in an only ostensibly self-critical remark, as follows: "I differentiate complicated things into an 'on the one hand' and 'on the other'" (C 227), or in Schlink's more poetic original, "daß ich differenziert im Einerseits und Andererseits die Komplikationen sehe" (B 228). Sarah's response to such differenti-ation is dismissive: "It's not complicated. What's right is simple" (C 226). Throughout "Die Beschneidung" Jewish identity and the memory of the Holocaust appear as both stronger and "einfacher" (i.e., simpler, easier), than the German memory of Nazism and hence German identity.

Schlink's fictional text brings out what is implicit in other construc-tions of the difficulties of developing a German identity today. In at least some versions of the recent discourse of German suffering the memory of the Holocaust appears as somehow completed. It is now apparently only the story of the *non*-Jewish-German victims that has not been told. So, for instance, in Günter Grass's novella *Im Krebsgang,* it seems to be above all the neglect of the history of Germans as victims that makes troubled youngsters in search of a German identity turn to neo-Nazism. That Grass's protagonist commits an anti-Semitic murder is not associated with a failure to overcome anti-Semitic tendencies and a failing sense of empathy with the Jewish victims of Nazism — and thus a failure of public and individual memory of the Holocaust — but rather is attributed to the lack of a German identity and to the absence of a non-right-wing discourse incorporating Germans as victims.[21] Grass's narrator, a fictionalized version of the author, blames his own generation for not telling the story of the expulsions in the East.[22] The memory of German suffering, therefore, is lacking while the memory of the Holocaust seems to be complete. Framing a narrative about German history that includes both suffering and guilt is understood to be ethically difficult and complicated, while the memory of the Holocaust, by contrast, seems clear-cut: good and evil, victim and perpetrator are easy to identify. Only if other memories, seen as not directly related to the Holocaust, such as the bombings of German cities or the expulsions, become part of the memory of the Nazi past, does differentiation apparently become necessary. This means that it is now often no longer the Holocaust that is seen as defying representation but rather the complexity of German everyday life under Nazism. An identity based on victimhood — even if it is traumatic — seems "easy" and "simple," as demonstrated by Schlink's Sarah, and therefore desirable. Hence Andi tries to obtain such a simple identity himself by having a circumcision, or, more generally, imagery and metaphors from the memory of the victims of the Holocaust are transferred onto German memory discourse. Such attempts at rewriting German history in terms of German victimhood function as a displacement of German guilt and strive to gain influence and legitimacy by becoming part of a victim-centered memory perceived as dominant. And it seems that these attempts are often informed by a particular construction of the memory of the Jewish victims of the Holocaust: the notion of "Jewish memory" as simple, straightforward, and a solid foundation for a strong collective identity. Because of this construction, victim-centered memory of the Holocaust — seen as exclusively Jewish — is simultaneously looked down on. This is demonstrated by Schlink's choice of metaphor: attaining such a simple identity means "circumcizing" or "curtailing" German identity. In this view, victim-centered memory lacks the differentiation now defined as typically "German."

It cannot be denied that it is ethically challenging to talk about suffering among non-Jewish Germans, and that there is still a certain need to do so, a need to find ways of narrating different wartime experiences, and hence a need for differentiation. It is also true that there exist simplistic versions of Holocaust memory, especially the kind of officious philo-Semitic identification of non-Jewish Germans with the victims, criticized by Broder in the passage cited near the beginning of this chapter. However, if the stereotype of a simple and easy *Jewish* memory of the Holocaust is established as the Other of a complex and burdened German identity within the search for new forms of memory, the idea of differentiation becomes a means of creating difference and exclusion, thus leading to its very opposite: one-sided and resentful discourses of identity and memory. To further analyze and deconstruct this phenomenon, and by way of conclusion, I now briefly turn to Maxim Biller's 1990 short story "Harlem Holocaust."

While Schlink's text reproduces and fabricates stereotypes without introducing any elements into his narrative that might serve to undermine these clichés, Biller's satire "Harlem Holocaust" does just that: in an often shocking and provocative way, it explores stereotypes and projections of Germans and Jews, and through its grotesque exaggerations and its complex narrative strategy makes the reader question his or her own assumptions.[23] Biller uses the figure of an unreliable first-person narrator, whose early confession of suffering from "Schwindelanfälle und Zerrbilder" (dizziness and distorted pictures) warns the reader not to take all of his observations at face value.[24] But it is only at the very end of the story that he or she finds out to what a large extent the narrator, and the reader with him, had been deluded.[25] In a postscript, a fictional editor reveals details about the fictional author of the story, that is, the narrator, and about its main character, which contradict some of the narrator's assertions. Moreover, the fictional editor describes the entire text as a "document [. . .] of the great German disease" (*HH* 61). Yet even this postscript does not create an unambiguous reading of what has gone before: it remains up to the reader to speculate on which parts of the story might be adequate representations of a realistic fictional world and which parts are solely to be attributed to the narrator's sick fantasies. It does not provide an easy answer to the question of what exactly consitutes the "great German disease."[26]

Biller's narrator refers to himself as "a suffering German perpetrator's son" (*HH* 12), and there are many ways in which it could be shown that the German-Jewish author Biller satirizes the same phenomenon that Schlink's text enacts. Biller's suffering second-generation German narrator feels weak and impotent in comparison to the central character of his story, Gerhard Warszawski, an American Jew of German descent who writes novels and short stories, which are successful in Germany, and whom the narrator imagines as powerful and erotically attractive because of his victim status. The narrator's fantasies of Warszawski's easy identification with a seemingly straighforward American-Jewish identity (*HH* 15–18) are very similar to Schlink's stereotypical notions, for instance, when Warszawski declares "'In contrast to you, I always know what's good and what's bad. We do not know any degenerate abysses, no obstinacies, no hesitations'" (*HH* 15–16).[27] Similar to Schlink's character Andi, the narrator feels excluded from a Jewish "world" (*HH* 18 and *C* 205), which he admires but ultimately resents. While Schlink's text underscores such notions, Biller calls them into question by revealing them as the narrator's distorted projections and allowing for different points of view. Warszawski's difficulties with his own identity are, for instance, also shown (*HH* 33). Here, however, I conclude my brief look at Biller's "Harlem Holocaust" in a slightly odd place, that is, the "Nachwort" (Afterword) of the 1998 paperback edition by the critic Gustav Seibt.

In his afterword, Seibt develops a version of the construct of an easy Jewish versus a "burdened" German identity. He writes:

> Since the murder of the Jews, the Germans have felt uncomfortable with themselves, whether they admit it or not. They have good reasons for not trusting one another anymore. They find themselves disagreeable, and constantly nag about something in themselves. The Holocaust cast a concrete-like joylessness over German existence. All traits of tormented thinking, excessive piousness, desires for punishment, justification, and purity in our culture have been intensified to a pathological degree, and have at the same time been made aesthetically almost totally fruitless. We have thus lost our sense of ease.
>
> But all forms of story telling ['Erzählen'] presuppose ease, some degree of naivety and a feeling of security [. . .]. A good story [. . .] can only be written on the basis of familiarity or even accordance with the world [. . .]. Such a short story [. . .] requires a world shared by authors and readers. [. . .]
>
> Despite the background of the Jewish catastrophe, Maxim Billler's stories have these prerequisites of good ways of living and expressing emotions; very often pure empathy for the generation of the parents and grandparents, which a Jew can feel naturally, and a German only with hesitation and doubt.[28]

In this critical attitude toward German identity and memory, which is a version of the discourse of secondary suffering, as well as in the well-meaning appreciation of Biller's short stories, the stereotype of the "easier" Jewish identity surfaces, along with the assertion that "Erzählen" is easier for Jews than for Germans: somehow the Holocaust ruined German literature but proves to have been fruitful for "Jewish" literature, in this case, and most fortunately, written in German. Seibt's distinction between "German" and "Jewish" writing corresponds to a general hesitancy to read texts written by Jewish Germans as part of German literature.[29] Without much exaggeration, the critic's expositions could have been taken straight from Biller's satire of German attitudes of philo-Semitism and "Opferneid" (victim envy). It thus provides a further — unintentional? — ironic twist to the story. Seibt reproduces a simplistic distinction between Jewish and German.[30] He also employs the stereotype of the "easier" Jewish identity even when it is in clear contradiction to the story in question. "Harlem Holocaust," as he goes on to say himself (*HH* 68), is by no means a straightforward short story. Rather than presuming any kind of naïveté or "accordance with the world," it radically calls into question the reliability of interpretations of "the world," and it can remind its readers of the difficulties of remembering the Holocaust — for Jews and non-Jews, Germans and non-Germans in different ways. To give just one example, Biller's narrator describes a scene that recurs in Warszawski's writings: it is the memory of a survivor of the Holocaust who hides in a wardrobe while his family is deported by the Nazis and who, after they have all been dragged away, masturbates while fantasizing about his sister (*HH* 38–39). Because this memory is not told directly, but embedded in the narrator's reflections on Warszawski's style, it serves to problematize the possibilities of narrating. The scene itself hints at the voyeuristic, possibly tasteless aspects of Holocaust memory, as well as at feelings of guilt in the survivors and their descendants (*HH* 39–40), but it is at the same time a powerful, shocking reminder of the reality of the suffering of the victims of Nazi Germany.

Schlink's story "Die Beschneidung" and, to a much lesser degree, Seibt's afterword to Biller's "Harlem Holocaust," have been presented in this chapter as examples of the construction of a burdened German identity and a "differentiated" relationship to the German past placed in opposition to a Jewish identity and memory conceived of as easy and simple. When the memory of the Holocaust is criticized for not allowing enough room for differentiation in narratives of National Socialism, to the extent, for instance, that it precludes the memory of Germans as victims, this critique is often explicitly directed against the German generation of '68 and its insistence on an undivided focus on German guilt. Yet a problematic transference of the claim that there exists a moralistic and over-simple memory of the Holocaust in German discourse to the claim that *Jewish* memory and identity are representative of such a simple memory might suggest itself as a frighteningly convenient construction of the Other of a new, more "complex" German memory. Schlink's story provides an example of this connection between the complaint about secondary suffering caused by the insistence on German guilt, a demand for more differentiation, and a derogatory view of an easy Jewish identity. In reflections on German memory discourse it has become relatively common to view the memory of Germans as victims critically, asking whether it does justice to the memory of Germans as perpetrators, and to the memory of the victims of Germans. At the same time the inclusion of

German wartime suffering into public memory is often applauded as a recent development toward more differentiation. If we refer to a more refined discourse of German victimhood and suffering, however, there might be a danger that the implied Other of this discourse is the clichéd image of Jewish memory I have tried to identify in the two texts by Schlink and Seibt. There may also be a danger that notions of complexity and difficulties in remembering become ever more associated with an exclusively "German" memory that appears as superior to its Other.

Notes

[1] Letter from Heinz Peter Preußer (22 May 2000) quoted on Henryk M. Broder's website, in his diary under the title "Deutsche Identität? (Maxim Biller), 15 June 2000," http://www.henryk-broder.de/html/tb_biller.html (accessed 15 September 2008). All translations mine.

[2] See Lars Rensmann, *Demokratie und Judenbild: Antisemitismus in der politischen Kultur der Bundesrepublik Deutschland* (Wiesbaden: VS Verlag für Sozialwissenschaften, 2005), 86–87.

[3] The English translation of *Liebesfluchten* was first published in 2001; I quote from the paperback edition. Bernhard Schlink, "The Circumcision," in *Flights of Love,* trans. John E. Woods (London: Phoenix, 2002), 215–16. Subsequent references are cited in the text using the abbreviation *C* and page number.

[4] Bernhard Schlink, "Die Beschneidung," in *Liebesfluchten* (Zürich: Diogenes, 2000), 217. Subsequent references are cited in the text using the abbreviation *B* and page number.

[5] Martin Walser, "Die Banalität des Guten: Erfahrungen beim Verfassen einer Sonntagsrede aus Anlaß der Verleihung des Friedenspreises des Deutschen Buchhandels," *Frankfurter Allgemeine Zeitung,* 12 December 1998, 15.

[6] See, e.g., Tilman Krause, "Schwierigkeiten beim Dachausbau: Bernhard Schlink legt nach dem sensationellen Erfolg von 'Der Vorleser' seinen ersten Erzählband vor," *Welt Online,* 29 January 2000, http://www.welt.de/print-welt/article 499765/Schwierigkeiten_beim_Dachausbau.html (accessed 15 September 2008).

[7] Rensmann, *Demokratie und Judenbild,* 90–91.

[8] Matthias N. Lorenz, "'Political Correctness' als Phantasma: Zu Bernhard Schlinks 'Die Beschneidung,'" in *Literarischer Antisemitismus nach Auschwitz,* ed. Klaus-Michael Bogdal, Klaus Holz, Matthias N. Lorenz (Stuttgart: J. B. Metzler, 2007), 222–27.

[9] Ibid., 231–33.

[10] Kathleen Bogan, "Pressures of Peace," *Times Literary Supplement,* 15 February 2002.

[11] See Frederic Raphael, letter to the editor, *Times Literary Supplement,* 8 March 2002; Jeremy Adler, letter to the editor, *Times Literary Supplement,* 21 March 2002; in Germany, e.g., see Volker Hage, "Unter Generalverdacht. Kulturkritiker

rüsten zu einer bizarren Literaturdebatte: Verharmlosen erfolgreiche Bücher wie Günter Grass' Novelle 'Im Krebsgang' oder Bernhard Schlinks Roman 'Der Vorleser' die Schuld der Deutschen an Holocaust und Zweitem Weltkrieg?," *Der Spiegel* 15 (2002): 177–81.

[12] Bernhard Schlink, *The Reader,* trans. Carol Brown Janeway (London: Phoenix, 2004).

[13] Sander L. Gilman, "Who Is Jewish? The Newest Jewish Writing in German and Daniel Goldhagen," in his *Love + Marriage = Death: And Other Essays on Representing Difference* (Stanford, CA: Stanford UP, 1998), 192.

[14] See Lorenz, "'Political Correctness' als Phantasma," 234.

[15] Ibid., 233.

[16] Such comparisons often occur in statements criticizing Israel (see Rensmann, *Demokratie und Judenbild,* 174–75).

[17] See Lorenz, "'Political Correctness' als Phantasma," on the anti-Semitic structure of this invented family history (235–36).

[18] Martin Broszat, "Plädoyer für eine Historisierung des Nationalsozialismus," *Merkur* 39, no. 5 (1985): 375.

[19] See Lorenz, "'Political Correctness' als Phantasma," 234.

[20] See ibid., 232, in which Lorenz describes the passage as depicting Sarah's negative habit of assuming the "Status eines Holocaustopfers" (status of a Holocaust victim).

[21] See Helmut Schmitz, who writes on *Im Krebsgang:* "empathy with *German* suffering is seen as necessary in order to pre-empt German revanchism," in "Representations of the Nazi Past II: German Wartime Suffering," in *Contemporary German Fiction: Writing in the Berlin Republic,* ed. Stuart Taberner (Cambridge: CUP, 2007), 151.

[22] See Günter Grass, *Im Krebsgang: Eine Novelle* (Göttingen: Steidl, 2002), 99.

[23] See Barbara Beßlich, "Unzuverlässiges Erzählen im Dienst der Erinnerung: Perspektiven auf den Nationalsozialismus bei Maxim Biller, Marcel Beyer und Martin Walser," in *Wende des Erinnerns? Geschichtskonstruktionen in der deutschen Literatur nach 1989,* ed. Barbara Beßlich, Katharina Grätz, and Olaf Hildebrand (Berlin: Erich Schmidt, 2006), 43.

[24] In the German, the notion of a distortion of reality is also underlined by the second meaning of the word for dizziness "Schwindel," which is "swindel." Maxim Biller, *Harlem Holocaust* (Cologne: Kiepenheuer and Witsch, 1998), 9. Subsequent references are cited in the text using the abbreviation *HH* and page number. *Harlem Holocaust* was first published as part of the collection of stories *Wenn ich einmal reich und tot bin* (1990) (When I Am Finally Rich and Dead). All translations mine.

[25] See Rita Bashaw, "Comic Vision and 'Negative Symbiosis' in Maxim Biller's *Harlem Holocaust* and Rafael Seligmann's *Der Musterjude,*" in *Unlikely History: The Changing German-Jewish Symbiosis, 1945–2000,* ed. Leslie Morris and Jack Zipes (New York: Palgrave, 2002), 267.

[26] See Thomas Kniesche, "Das deutsch-jüdisch-amerikanische Dreieck: 'Amerika' als anderer Schauplatz in der zeitgenössischen deutsch-jüdischen Literatur," in *Das*

Amerika der Autoren: Von Kafka bis 09/11, ed. Jochen Vogt and Alexander Stephan (Munich: Wilhelm Fink, 2006), 355.

[27] See Bashaw for a discussion of Biller's depiction of anti-Semitism and anti-Americanism ("Comic Vision," 268).

[28] Gustav Seibt, "Der letzte Augenblick der Unschuld: Ein Nachwort von Gustav Seibt," in Biller, *Harlem Holocaust,* 67–68, my translation.

[29] See Erin McGlothlin, "Writing by Germany's Jewish Minority," in Taberner, *Contemporary German Fiction,* 231.

[30] Jefferson Chase points out a similar problem in readings of "German-Jewish literature": "If they read texts in search of identities, even hybrid ones, critics set up a reductive situation akin to that of Jews in Germany in Biller's fiction. The individual becomes a cipher for the group and little else" ("Shoah Business: Maxim Biller and the Problem of Contemporary German-Jewish Literature," *German Quarterly* 74, no. 2 [2001]: 113).

Works Cited

Abraham, Nicholas. "Notes on the Phantom: A Complement to Freud's Meta-psychology." In *The Shell and the Kernel*, by Nicholas Abraham and Maria Torok, 171–76. Chicago: U of Chicago P, 1994.

Adler, Jeremy. "Letter to the Editor." *Times Literary Supplement*, 21 March 2002.

Adorno, Theodor W. *Noten zur Literatur I*. Frankfurt am Main: Suhrkamp, 1973.

Adorno, Theodor W., and Max Horkheimer. *Dialectic of Enlightenment: Philosophical Fragments*. Stanford, CA: Stanford UP, 2002.

Allgemeine Wochenzeitung der Juden in Deutschland, 27 December 1963.

Assmann, Aleida. *Der lange Schatten der Vergangenheit: Erinnerungskultur und Geschichtspolitik*. Munich: Beck, 2006.

———. "On the (In)Compatibility of Guilt and Suffering in German Memory." Translated by Linda Shortt. *German Life and Letters* 59, no. 2 (2006): 187–200.

———. "Stabilisatoren der Erinnerung — Affekt, Symbol, Trauma." In *Die dunkle Spur der Vergangenheit: Psychoanalytische Zugänge zum Geschichtsbewusstsein*, edited by Jörn Rüsen and Jürgen Straub, 31–52. Frankfurt am Main: Suhrkamp, 1998.

Assmann, Jan. *Das kulturelle Gedächtnis: Schrift, Erinnerung und politische Identität in frühen Hochkulturen*. Munich: Beck, 1992.

Bachelard, Gaston. *The Poetics of Space*. Translated by Maria Jolas. Boston: Beacon Press, 1994.

Bance, Alan. "Heinrich Böll's 'Wo Warst Du, Adam?': National Identity and German War Writing — Reunification as the Return of the Repressed." *Forum for Modern Language Studies* 29, no. 4 (1993): 311–22.

Barthes, Roland. *La chambre claire*. Paris: Éditions du Seuil, 1980.

Bartov, Omer. *The Eastern Front 1941–1945, German Troops and the Barbarisation of Warfare*, 2nd ed. Basingstoke, UK: Palgrave, 2001.

———. "Germany as Victim." *New German Critique* 80 (2000): 29–40.

———. *Germany's War and the Holocaust: Disputed Histories*. Ithaca, NY: Cornell UP, 2003.

———. *Mirrors of Destruction: War, Genocide, and Modern Identity*. Oxford: OUP, 2000.

Bashaw, Rita. "Comic Vision and 'Negative Symbiosis' in Maxim Biller's *Harlem Holocaust* and Rafael Seligmann's *Der Musterjude*." In *Unlikely History: The Changing German-Jewish Symbiosis, 1945–2000*, edited by Leslie Morris and Jack Zipes, 263–76. New York: Palgrave, 2002.

Benjamin, Walter. *Illuminationen: Ausgewählte Schriften*. Frankfurt am Main: Suhrkamp, 1961.

———. *Illuminations: Essays and Reflections*. Edited by Hannah Arendt. New York: Schocken, 1968.

———. "Theses on the Philosophy of History." In *Illuminations*, 245–55. London: Random House, 1999.

Benz, Wolfgang, and Ute Benz. *Sozialisation und Traumatisierung: Kinder in der Zeit des Nationalsozialismus*. Frankfurt am Main: Fischer, 1998.

Benz, Wolfgang, and Dan Diner, eds. *Ist der Nationalsozialismus Geschichte? Zu Historisierung und Historikerstreit*. Frankfurt am Main: Fischer, 1987.

Berger, Stefan. "On Taboos, Traumas and Other Myths: Why the Debate about German Victims of the Second World War Is Not a Historians Controversy." In Niven, *Germans as Victims*, 210–24.

Beßlich, Barbara. "Unzuverlässiges Erzählen im Dienst der Erinnerung: Perspektiven auf den Nationalsozialismus bei Maxim Biller, Marcel Beyer und Martin Walser." In *Wende des Erinnerns? Geschichtskonstruktionen in der deutschen Literatur nach 1989, 1989*, edited by Barbara Beßlich, Katharina Grätz, and Olaf Hildebrand, 35–52. Berlin: Erich Schmidt, 2006.

Biller, Maxim. *Harlem Holocaust*. Cologne: Kiepenheuer and Witsch, 1998.

Bisky, Jens. "Wenn Jungen Weltgeschichte spielen, haben Mädchen stumme Rollen. Vielfach verändert, mehrfach überarbeitet, ohne Beweis der Echtheit: Das Buch der Anonyma. Wer war die Anonyma in Berlin?" *Süddeutsche Zeitung*, 3 September 2003.

Boa, Elizabeth. "Telling It How It Wasn't: Familial Allegories of Wish-Fulfillment in Postunification Germany." In Fuchs et al., *German Memory Contests*, 67–86.

Bogan, Kathleen. "Pressures of Peace." *Times Literary Supplement*, 15 February 2002.

Bohrer, Karl Heinz. "Die permanente Theodizee: Über das verfehlte Böse im deutschen Bewußtsein." In Bohrer, *Nach der Natur: Über Politik und Ästhetik*, 131–61. Munich: Carl Hanser, 1988.

Böll, Heinrich. "An einen Bischof, einen General und einen Minister des Jahrgangs 1917." In *Essayistische Schriften und Reden 2*, edited by Bernd Balzer, 234. Cologne: Kiepenheuer and Witsch, 1977.

———. "Die Botschaft." In *Werke Band 3*, edited by Frank Finlay and Jochen Schubart, 156. Cologne: Kiepenheuer and Witsch, 2003.

———. *Briefe aus dem Krieg 1939–1945*. Mit einem Vorwort von Annemarie Böll und einem Nachwort von Hamish Reid, Herausgegeben und kommentiert von Jochen Schubert. Cologne: Kiepenheuer and Witsch, 2001.

———. *Die Fähigkeit zu trauern*. Munich: DTV, 1985.

———. *Interviews I*. Edited by Bernd Balzer. Cologne: Kiepenheuer and Witsch, n.d. [1979].

———. *Rom auf den ersten Blick: Lanschaften Städte Reisen*. Bornheim-Merten: Lamuv, 1987.

Bourdieu, Pierre. *Photography: A Middle-brow Art*. Translated by Shaun Whiteside. Cambridge: Polity, 1990.

Braese, Stephan. "Bombenkrieg und literarische Gegenwart: Zu W. G. Sebald und Dieter Forte." *Mittelweg* 36 (2002): 4–24.

———. "Tote zahlen keine Steuern: Flucht und Vertreibung in Günter Grass' *Im Krebsgang* und Hans-Ulrich Treichels *Der Verlorene*." *Gegenwartsliteratur* 2 (2003): 171–96.

Braun, Christina von. *Stille Post: Eine andere Familiengeschichte*. Berlin: Propyläen, 2007.

Brink, Cornelia. "Secular Icons: Looking at Photographs from the Nazi Concentration Camps." *History and Memory* 12, no. 1 (2000): 135–50.

Brockmann, Stephen. *German Literary Culture at the Zero Hour*. Rochester, NY: Camden House, 2004.

———. *Literature and German Reunification*. Cambridge: CUP, 1999.

Broder, Henryk. "Deutsche Identität? (Maxim Biller), 15 June 2000." http://www.henryk-broder.de/html/tb_biller.html (accessed 15 September 2008).

Broszat, Martin. "Plädoyer für eine Historisierung des Nationalsozialismus." *Merkur* 39, no. 5 (1985): 373–85.

Browning, Christopher R. *Ordinary Men: Reserve Police Battalion 101 and the Final Solution in Poland*. New York: Harper Collins, 1992.

Bruhns, Wibke. *Meines Vaters Land: Geschichte einer deutschen Familie*. Munich: Econ, 2004.

Bullivant, Keith. *Beyond 1989: Re-reading German Literary History since 1945*. Providence, RI: Berghahn Books, 1997.

Butler, Michael. "Wir wollen abschwören allem Irrsinn vergangener Jahre . . .": The Early Letters of Heinrich Böll." *University of Dayton Review* 24, no. 3 (Summer 1997), 7–15.

Caruth, Cathy. *Unclaimed Experience: Trauma, Narrative, and History*. Baltimore: Johns Hopkins UP, 1996.

Chase, Jefferson. "Shoah Business: Maxim Biller and the Problem of Contemporary German-Jewish Literature." *German Quarterly* 74, no. 2 (2001): 111–31.

Clarke, David. "Guilt and Shame in Hans-Ulrich Treichel's *Der Verlorene.*" In *Hans-Ulrich Treichel,* edited by David Basker, 61–78. Cardiff, UK: U of Wales P, 2004.

Clarke, David, and Arne De Winde. *Reinhard Jirgl: Perspektiven, Lesarten, Kontexte.* Amsterdam: Rodopi, 2007.

Connerton, Paul. *The Tragedy of Enlightenment: An Essay on the Frankfurt School.* Cambridge: CUP, 1980.

Cooke, Paul. "*Dresden* (2006), Teamworx and *Titanic* (1997): German Wartime Suffering as Hollywood Disaster Movie." *German Life and Letters* 61, no. 2 (2008): 279–94.

———. "*Der Untergang* (2004): Victims, Perpetrators and the Continuing Fascination of Fascism." In Schmitz, *A Nation of Victims?,* 247–61.

Cosgrove, Mary. "The Anxiety of German Influence: Affiliation, Rejection, and Jewish Identity in W. G. Sebald's Work." in Fuchs et al., *German Memory Contests,* 229–52.

———. "Melancholy Competitions: W. G. Sebald Reads Günter Grass and Wolfgang Hildesheimer." *German Life and Letters* 59, no. 2 (2006): 217–32.

Crownshaw, Rick. "German Suffering or 'Narrative Fetishism'?: W. G. Sebald's 'Air War and Literature: Zurich Lectures.'" In *Searching for Sebald: Photography after W. G. Sebald,* edited by Lise Patt, 558–83. Los Angeles: ICI Press, 2007.

Dentith, Simon. *Bakhtinian Thought: An Introductory Reader.* London: Routledge, 1995.

Derrida, Jacques. *Specters of Marx.* London: Routledge, 1994.

Die Welt, 7 May 1992, 106.

Dische, Irene. *Großmama packt aus.* Translated by Reinhard Kaiser. Munich: DTV, 2006.

Dokumentation der Vertreibung der Deutschen aus Ost-Mitteleuropa, Gesamtausgabe in 8 Bänden. Munich: DTV, 2004.

Donahue, William Collins. "Illusions of Subtlety: Bernhard Schlink's *Der Vorleser* and the Moral Limits of Holocaust Fiction." *German Life and Letters* 54, no. 1 (2001): 60–81.

Dye, Elizabeth. "Painful Memories: The Literary Representation of German Wartime Suffering." PhD diss., University of Nottingham, 2006.

Eco, Umberto. *The Role of the Reader: Explorations in the Semiotics of Texts.* Bloomington: U of Indiana P, 1979.

Eigler, Friederike. *Gedächtnis und Geschichte in Generationsromanen seit der Wende.* Berlin: Erich Schmidt, 2005.

Evan, Richard J. Review of *Hitlers Volksstaat* (*Hitler's Beneficiaries*) by Götz Aly. *The Nation,* 8 January 2007.

Evans, Owen. *Mapping the Contours of Oppression: Subjectivity, Truth and Fiction in Recent German Autobiographical Treatments of Totalitarianism.* Amsterdam: Rodopi, 2006.

Finlay, Frank, and Ingo Cornils, eds. *"(Un-)erfüllte Wirklichkeit": Neue Studien zu Uwe Timms Werk.* Würzburg: Königshausen and Neumann, 2006.

Fischer, Eva-Elisabeth. "Vom Krieg der Männer gegen die Frauen: Helke Sanders Film *BeFreier und Befreite.*" *Süddeutsche Zeitung,* 11 December 1992.

Flucht Vertreibung Integration. Edited by Petra Rösgen. Published by Stiftung Haus der Geschichte der Bunderrepublik Deutschland. Bielefeld: Kerber, 2006.

Forte, Dieter. *Das Haus auf meinen Schultern.* Frankfurt am Main: Fischer, 2002.

———. *In der Erinnerung.* Frankfurt am Main: Fischer, 1998.

———. *Der Junge mit den blutigen Schuhen.* Frankfurt am Main: Fischer, 1995.

———. *Das Muster.* Frankfurt am Main: Fischer, 1992.

———. *Schweigen oder Sprechen.* Edited by Volker Hage. Frankfurt am Main: Fischer, 2002.

Franzen, Günter. "Der alte Mann und sein Meer." *Die Zeit.* http://www.zeit.de/2002/07/200207_l-grass_xml?page=all (accessed 22 February 2008).

Freud, Sigmund. *Beyond the Pleasure Principle.* In *The Complete Psychological Works of Sigmund Freud.* Vol. 18. London: Hogarth Press, 1953.

———. *The Interpretation of Dreams.* In *The Complete Psychological Works of Sigmund Freud.* Vols. 4–5. London: Hogarth Press, 1953.

Friedländer, Saul, ed. *Probing the Limits of Representation: Nazism and the "Final Solution."* Cambridge, MA: Harvard UP, 1992.

Friedrich, Jörg. *Der Brand: Deutschland im Bombenkrieg 1940–1945.* Munich: Propyläen, 2002.

Fuchs, Anne. "After-Images of History: Thomas Medicus's *In den Augen meines Großvaters.*" In *Jahrbuch Gegenwartsliteratur,* edited by Paul Michael Lützeler, 252–71. Tübingen: Stauffenburg, 2006.

———. "A *Heimat* in Ruins and the Ruins as *Heimat:* W. G. Sebald's *Luftkrieg und Literatur.*" In Fuchs et al., *German Memory Contests,* 287–302. Rochester, NY: Camden House, 2006.

―――. "'Ehrlich, du lügst wie gedruckt': Günter Grass's Autobiographical Confession and the Changing Territory of Germany's Memory Culture." *German Life and Letters* 60, no. 2 (2007): 261–75.

―――. *Family Narratives and the Politics of Memory in German Literature, Film and Discourse since Unification: Phantoms of War.* Houndsmills, UK: Palgrave Macmillan, 2008.

―――. "From *Vergangenheitsbewältigung* to Generational Memory Contests in Günter Grass, Monika Maron and Uwe Timm." *German Life and Letters* 59, no. 2 (2006): 169–86.

―――. *Phantoms of War in Contemporary German Literature, Films and Discourse: The Politics of Memory.* New York: Palgrave Macmillan, 2008.

―――. *Die Schmerzensspuren der Geschichte: Zur Poetik der Erinnerung in W. G. Sebalds Prosa.* Cologne: Bohlau, 2004.

―――. "The Tinderbox of Memory: Generation and Masculinity in *Väterliteratur* by Christoph Meckel, Uwe Timm, Ulla Hahn and Dagmar Leupold." In Fuchs et al., *German Memory Contests,* 41–66.

Fuchs, Anne, and Mary Cosgrove, eds. *German Memory Contests: The Quest for Identity in Literature, Film and Discourse since 1990.* Edited by Anne Fuchs, Mary Cosgrove, and Georg Grote. Rochester, NY: Camden House, 2006.

―――. "Introduction: Germany's Memory Contests and the Management of the Past." In Fuchs et al., *German Memory Contests,* 6.

―――. *Memory Contests.* Special issue of *German Life and Letters* 59, no. 2 (2006): 163–68.

Fussenegger, Gertrud. *Das verschüttete Antlitz.* Darmstadt: DVA, 1957.

Galli, Matteo. "Vom Denkmal zum Mahnmal: Kommunikatives Gedächtnis bei Uwe Timm." In Finlay and Cornils, *"(Un-)erfüllte Wirklichkeit,"* 162–63.

Ganeva, Mila. "From West-German *Väterliteratur* to Post-Wall *Enkelliteratur:* The End of the Generation Conflict in Marcel Beyer's *Spione* and Tanja Dückers's *Himmelskörper.*" *Seminar* 43, no. 2 (2007): 149–62.

Ganzfried, Daniel, and Sebastian Hefti, eds. *Alias Wilkomirski: Die Holocaust Travestie. Enthüllung und Dokumentation eines literarischen Skandals.* Berlin: Jüdischer, 2002.

Gehrmann, Karl Heinz. "Versuche der literarischen Bewältigung." In *Die Vertriebenen in Westdeutschland: Ihre Eingliederung und ihr Einfluss auf Gesellschaft, Wirtschaft, Politik und Geistesleben,* edited by Eugen Lemberg and Friedrich Edding, 276. Kiel: Ferdinand Hirt, 1959.

Geiger, Arno. *Es geht uns gut.* Munich: DTV, 2007.

"German Government Approves Expellees Museum." *Spiegel Online.* http://www.spiegel.de/international/germany/0,1518,542503,00.html (accessed September 2008).

Gilman, Sander L. "Who Is Jewish? The Newest Jewish Writing in German and Daniel Goldhagen." In Gilman, *Love + Marriage = Death: And Other Essays on Representing Difference*, 184–202. Stanford, CA: Stanford UP, 1998.

Grass, Günter. *Beim Häuten der Zwiebel.* Göttingen: Steidl, 2006.

———. *Crabwalk.* Translated by Krishna Winston. London: Faber and Faber, 2003.

———. "Ich erinnere mich." Talk given at the Future of Memory conference, Vilnius, 2000. http://www.steidl.de/grass/a2_5_vilnius.html (accessed 15 September 2008).

———. *Im Krebsgang: Eine Novelle* Göttingen: Steidl, 2002.

———. "Nie Wieder Schweigen." http://www.radiobremen.de/online/grass/reden/schweigen.shtml.

———. *Peeling the Onion.* Translated by Michael Henry Heim. London: Harvill, 2007.

———. *Rede von der Gewöhnung,* in Günter Grass, *Essays und Reden 1955–1969.* Edited by Daniela Hermes, 220–33. Göttingen: Steidl, 1993.

———. "Warum ich nach sechzig Jahren mein Schweigen breche." *Frankfurter Allgemeine Zeitung,* 12 August 2006, 33.

———. "Writing after Auschwitz." In *Two States, One Nation?* Translated by Krishna Winston and Arthur S. Wensinger, 94–123. London: Secker and Warburg, 1990.

Greiner, Ulrich. "Die deutsche Gesinnungsästhetik." *Die Zeit,* 9 November 1990. Reprinted in *"Es geht nicht nur um Christa Wolf": Der Literaturstreit im vereinten Deutschland,* edited by Thomas Anz, 208–16. Munich: Spangenberg, 1991.

Grimm, Erk. "Die Lebensläufe Reinhard Jirgls: Techniken der melotraumatischen Inszenierungen." In *Reinhard Jirgl: Perspektiven, Lesarten, Kontexte,* edited by David Clarke and Arne De Winde, 197–226. Amsterdam: Rodopi, 2007.

Hage, Voker. *Hamburg 1943: Literarische Zeugnisse des Feuersturms.* Frankfurt am Main: Fischer, 2003.

———. "Unter Generalverdacht. Kulturkritiker rüsten zu einer bizarren Literaturdebatte: Verharmlosen erfolgreiche Bücher wie Günter Grass' Novelle 'Im Krebsgang' oder Bernhard Schlinks Roman 'Der Vorleser' die Schuld der Deutschen an Holocaust und Zweitem Weltkrieg?" *Der Spiegel* 15 (2002): 177–81.

———. *Zeugen der Zerstörung: Die Literaten und der Luftkrieg: Essays und Gespräche.* Frankfurt am Main: Suhrkamp, 2003.

Hage, Volker, Rainer Moritz, and Hubert Winkels, eds. *Deutsche Literatur 1998: Jahresüberblick.* Ditzingen: Reklam, 1999.

Hahn, Ulla. *Unscharfe Bilder*. Munich: DVA, 2003.

Hall, Katharina. Günter Grass's "Danzig Quintet": Explorations in the Memory and History of the Nazi Era from *Die Blechtrommel* to *Im Krebsgang*. Oxford: Peter Lang, 2007.

Hamburger, Michael. *String of Beginnings: Intermittent Memoirs 1924–1954*. London: Skoob Books, 1991. Originally published as *A Mug's Game: Intermittent Memoirs 1924–1954*. London: Carcanet Press, 1973.

Heer, Hannes, and Klaus Naumann, eds. *Vernichtungskrieg: Verbrechen der Wehrmacht 1941–1944*. Hamburg: Zweitausendeins, 1997.

Heidelberger-Leonard, Irene. *Jean Améry: Revolte in der Resignation*. Stuttgart: Klett-Cotta, 2004.

Hein, Christoph. *Landnahme*. Frankfurt am Main: Suhrkamp, 2005.

Helbig, Louis F. *Der Ungeheure Verlust: Flucht und Vertreibung in der deutschsprachigen Belletristik der Nachkriegszeit*. Wiesbaden: Harrassowitz, 1996.

Hermand, Jost. "Darstellungen des Zweiten Weltkrieges." In *Literatur nach 1945 (I): Politische und Regionale Aspekte*, edited by Jost Hermand, 32. Wiesbaden: Athenaion, 1979.

Hirsch, Marianne. *Family Frames, Photography, Narrative, and Postmemory*. Cambridge, MA: Harvard UP, 1997.

———. "Surviving Images: Holocaust Photographs and the Work of Postmemory." *Yale Journal of Criticism* 14, no. 1 (2001): 5–37.

Hoffmann, Gabriele. *Heinrich Böll, erweiterte Ausgabe*. Bornheim-Merten: Lamuv, 1985.

Hoffmann, Ruth. *Die schlesische Barmherzigkeit*. Munich: Aufstieg, 1974. First edition published 1950.

Horstkotte, Silke. "'Ich bin ins Reich der Toten geraten': Stephan Wackwitz and the New German Family Novel." In *New German Literature: Life-Writing and Dialogue with the Arts*, edited by Julian Preece, Frank Finlay, and Ruth J. Owen, 325–42. Oxford: Peter Lang, 2007.

Hutchinson, Peter. *Games Authors Play*. London: Methuen, 1983.

Huyssen, Andreas. "On Rewritings and New Beginnings: W. G. Sebald and the Literature about the Luftkrieg." *Zeitschrift für Literatur und Linguistik* 31 (2001): 72–90.

"'Ich wollte das in aller Härte.' Ein TAZ, Interview mit Uwe Timm über sein Buch 'Am Beispiel meines Bruders.'" http://www.taz.de/pt/2003/09/13/a0245.nf/text (accessed September 2008).

Ihlenfeld, Kurt. *Wintergewitter*. Berlin: Eckart, 1951.

"Interview mit Günter Grass." *Steidl*. http://www.steidl.de/grass/ (accessed 23 February 2008).

Jackman, Graham. "Gebranntes Kind? W. G. Sebald's 'Metaphysik der Geschichte.'" *German Life and Letters* 57, no. 4 (2004): 456–71.

———. "Introduction." *German Life and Letters* 57, no. 4 (2004): 343–56.

Jaggi, Maya. "Recovered Memories." Interview with W. G. Sebald. *The Guardian*, 22 September 2001.

Jarvis, Siehe Brian. *Postmodern Cartography: The Geographical Imagination in Contemporary American Culture.* London: Pluto Press, 1998.

Jarvis, Simon. *Adorno: A Critical Introduction.* Cambridge: CUP, 1998.

Jirgl, Reinhard. *Die Unvollendeten.* Munich: Hanser, 2003.

Kafka, Franz. "Eine kaiserliche Botschaft." In *Gesammelte Werke in zwölf Bänden,* vol. 1, 221. Frankfurt am Main: Fischer, 1994.

———. "A Little Fable." In *The Collected Short Stories of Franz Kafka,* edited by Nahum N. Glatzer, 445. Harmondsworth, UK: Penguin, 1988.

Kammler, Clemens. "Unschärferelationen: Anmerkungen zu zwei problematischen Lesarten von Reinhard Jirgls Familienroman *Die Unvollendeten.*" In *Reinhard Jirgl: Perspektiven, Lesarten, Kontexte,* edited by David Clarke and Arne De Winde, 227–35. Amsterdam: Rodopi, 2007.

Kammler, Clemens, and Matthias Krallmann. "'Ich wollte niemandem ähnlich sein . . .': Hans-Ulrich Treichel's Erzählung *Der Verlorene* als Beitrag zur inneren Geschichtsschreibung der Nachkriegsgeneration." *Deutschunterricht* 51, no. 4 (1999): 99–102.

Kempowski, Walter. *Alles umsonst.* Munich: Albrecht Knaus, 2006.

———. *Das Echelot: Ein kollektives Tagebuch. Januar und Februar 1943.* Munich: Knaus, 1993.

———. *Das Echelot: Fuga Furiosa. Ein kollektives Tagebuch. Winter 1945.* Munich: Knaus, 1999.

Kettenacker, Lothar, ed. *Ein Volk von Opfern? Die neue Debatte um den Bombenkrieg 1940–1945.* Berlin: Rowolth, 2003.

Kiedaisch, Petra, ed. *Lyrik nach Auschwitz? Adorno und die Dichter.* Stuttgart: Reclam, 1995.

Kluger, Ruth. *Still Alive: A Holocaust Girlhood Remembered.* New York: Feminist Press, 2001.

Kniesche, Thomas. "Das deutsch-jüdisch-amerikanische Dreieck: 'Amerika' als anderer Schauplatz in der zeitgenössischen deutsch-jüdischen Literatur." In *Das Amerika der Autoren: Von Kafka bis 09/11,* edited by Jochen Vogt and Alexander Stephan, 337–64. Munich: Wilhelm Fink, 2006.

Koepnick, Lutz. "Photographs and Memories." *South Central Review* 21, no. 1 (Spring 2004): 94–129.

Kracaur, Siegfried. "Photography." In *The Mass Ornament: Weimar Essays,* edited and translated by Thomas Levin, 47–63. Cambridge, MA: Harvard UP, 1995.

Krause, Tilman. "Schwierigkeiten beim Dachausbau: Bernhard Schlink legt nach dem sensationellen Erfolg von 'Der Vorleser' seinen ersten Erzählband vor." *Welt Online,* 29 January 2000. http://www.welt.de/print-welt/article499765/Schwierigkeiten_beim_Dachausbau.html (accessed 15 September 2008).

Kristeva, Julia. *Powers of Horror: An Essay on Abjection.* Translated by Leon S. Roudiez. New York: Columbia UP, 1982.

Kroll, Frank-Lothar, ed. *Flucht und Vertreibung in der Literatur nach 1945.* Berlin: Gebr. Mann, 1977.

LaCapra, Dominick. *Writing History, Writing Trauma.* Baltimore: Johns Hopkins UP, 2001.

Ledig, Gert. *Die Stalinorgel.* Frankfurt am Main: Suhrkamp, 2003.

———. *Vergeltung.* Frankfurt am Main: Suhrkamp, 1999. Translated by Shaun Whiteside as *Payback.* (London: Granta, 2003).

Lejeune, Philippe. *Le pacte autobiographique.* Paris: Éditions de Seuil, 1975.

Lethen, Helmut. *Verhaltenslehren der Kälte: Lebensversuche zwischen den Kriegen.* Frankfurt am Main: Suhrkamp, 1994.

Leupold, Dagmar. *Nach den Kriegen.* Munich: Beck, 2004.

Levi, Primo. *The Drowned and the Saved.* Translated by Raymond Rosenthal. London: Abacus, 1988.

Leys, Ruth. *Trauma: A Genealogy.* Chicago: U of Chicago P, 2000.

Long, J. J. "Monika Maron's *Pawels Briefe:* Photography, Narrative and the Claims of Postmemory." in Fuchs et al., *German Memory Contests,* 147–65.

Lorenz, Matthias N. "'Political Correctness' als Phantasma: Zu Bernhard Schlinks 'Die Beschneidung.'" In *Literarischer Antisemitismus nach Auschwitz,* edited by Klaus-Michael Bogdal, Klaus Holz, Matthias N. Lorenz, 219–242. Stuttgart: J. B. Metzler, 2007.

Löwy, Michael. *Fire Alarm: Reading Walter Benjamin's "On the Concept of History,"* Translated by Chris Turner. London: Verso, 2005.

Marx, Friedhelm, ed. *Erinnern, Vergessen, Erzählen.* Göttingen: Wallstein, 2007.

McGlothlin, Erin. "Writing by Germany's Jewish Minority." In Taberner, *Contemporary German Fiction,* 231.

Medicus, Thomas. "Im Archiv der Gefühle: Tätertöchter, der aktuelle 'Familienroman' und die deutsche Vergangenheit." *Mittelweg* 36 (2006): 2–15.

———. *In den Augen meines Großvaters.* Munich: DVA, 2004.

Meyer, Sven. *Campo Santo*. Translated by Anthea Bell. Munich: Carl Hanser, 2003.

Middlebrook, Martin, and Chris Everitt. *The Bomber Command War Diaries: An Operational Reference Book 1939–1945*. London: Penguin, 1990.

Mitscherlich, Andreas and Margarete. *Die Unfähigkeit zu trauern: Grundlagen kollektiven Verhaltens*. Munich: Piper, 2007.

Moeller, Robert G. "Germans as Victims? Thoughts on a Post-Cold War History of World War II's Legacies." *History and Memory* 17, no. 1 (2005): 147–94.

———. "The Politics of the Past in the 1950s: Rhetorics of Victimisation in East and West Germany." In Niven, *Germans as Victims*, 26–42.

———. "Remembering the War in a Nation of Victims: West German Pasts in the 1950s." In *The Miracle Years: A Cultural History of West Germany, 1949–1968*, edited by Hanna Schissler, 83–109. Princeton, NJ: Princeton UP, 2001.

———. "Sinking Ships, the Lost *Heimat* and Broken Taboos: Günter Grass and the Politics of Memory in Contemporary Germany." *Contemporary European History* 12, no. 2 (2003): 147–81.

———. *War Stories: The Search for a Useable Past in the Federal Republic of Germany*. Berkeley: U of California P, 2001.

Moran, Dermot. *Introduction to Phenomenology*. London: Routledge, 2000.

Moses, A. Dirk. *German Intellectuals and the Nazi Past*. Cambridge: CUP, 2007.

———. "The Holocaust and Genocide." In *The Historiography of the Holocaust*, edited by Dan Stone, 533–55. Basingstoke, UK: Palgrave Macmillan, 2004.

Neufeld, Michael J. *Von Braun: Dreamer of Space, Engineer of War*. New York: Knopf, 2007.

Neumann, Erich. *Die Große Mutter: Die weiblichen Gestaltungen des Unbewussten*. Düsseldorf: Patmos, 2003.

Niethammer, Lutz. *Kollektive Identität: Heimliche Quellen einer unheimlichen Konjunktur*. Reinbek bei Hamburg: Rowohlt, 2000.

Nietzsche, Friedrich. "On the Uses and Disadvantages of History for Life." In *Untimely Meditations*, edited by Daniel Breazeale, translated by R. J. Hollingdale, 57–124. Cambridge: CUP, 1997.

Niven, Bill. "Bernhard Schlink's *Der Vorleser* and the Problem of Shame." *Modern Language Review* 98, no. 2 (2003): 380–96.

———. *Facing the Nazi Past: United Germany and the Legacy of the Third Reich*. London: Routledge, 2002.

————, ed. *Germans as Victims: Remembering the Past in Contemporary Germany*. Basingstoke, UK: Palgrave Macmillan, 2006.

————. "Implicit Equations in Constructions of German Suffering." In Schmitz, *A Nation of Victims?*, 105–23.

————. "Introduction: German Victimhood at the Turn of the Millennium." In Niven, *Germans as Victims*, 1–25.

Ölke, Martina. "'Flucht und Vertreibung' in Hans-Ulrich-Treichels *Der Verlorene* und *Menschenflug* und in Günter Grass' *Im Krebsgang*." *Seminar* 43, no. 2 (2007): 115–33.

Ortheil, Hanns-Josef. *Abschied von den Kriegsteilnehmern*. Munich: Piper, 1992.

Overath, Angelika. *Nahe Tage: Roman in einer Nacht*. Göttingen: Wallstein, 2005.

Pinfold, Debbie. *The Child's View of the Third Reich in German Literature*. Oxford: OUP, 2001.

Radvan, Florian. "Religiöse Bildlichkeit und transtextuelle Bezüge in Gert Ledigs Luftkriegsroman *Vergeltung*." In *Bombs Away! Representing the Airwar over Europe and Japan*, edited by Wilfried Wilms and William Rasch, 165–79. Amsterdam: Rodopi, 2006.

Raphael, Frederic. "Letter to the Editor." *Times Literary Supplement*, 8 March 2002.

Reid, J. H. "From 'Bekenntnis zur Trümmerliteratur' to *Frauen vor Flußlandschaft*: Art, Power and the Aesthetics of Ruins." *University of Dayton Review* 24, no. 3 (1997): 35–45.

Rensmann, Lars. *Demokratie und Judenbild. Antisemitismus in der politischen Kultur der Bundesrepublik Deutschland*. Wiesbaden: VS Verlag für Sozialwissenschaften, 2005.

Rose, Gillian. *Mourning Becomes the Law*. Cambridge: CUP, 1996.

Rüsen, Jörn, and Jürgen Straub, eds. *Die dunkle Spur der Vergangenheit: Psychoanalytische Zugänge zum Geschichtsbewusstsein*. Frankfurt am Main: Suhrkamp, 1998.

Ryan, Judith. *The Uncompleted Past: Postwar German Novels and the Third Reich*. Detroit, MI: Wayne State UP, 1983.

Santner, Eric L. *Stranded Objects: Mourning, Memory and Film in Postwar Germany*. Ithaca, NY: Cornell UP, 1990.

Scheub, Ute. *Das falsche Leben: Eine Vatersuche*. Munich: Piper, 2006.

Schlant, Ernestine. *The Language of Silence: West German Literature and the Holocaust*. New York: Routledge, 1999.

Schlink, Bernhard. "Die Beschneidung." In Schlink, *Liebesfluchten*, 199–255. Zürich: Diogenes, 2000.

————. "The Circumcision." In *Flights of Love*, translated by John E. Woods, 197–255. London: Phoenix, 2002.

————. *The Reader*. Translated by Carol Brown Janeway. London: Phoenix, 1997.

Schmitz, Helmut. "The Birth of the Collective from the Spirit of Empathy: From the 'Historians' Dispute' to German Suffering." In Niven, *Germans as Victims*, 93–108.

————. "Historicism, Sentimentality and the Problem of Empathy: Uwe Timm's *Am Beispiel meines Bruders* in the Context of Recent Representations of German Suffering." In Schmitz, *A Nation of Victims?*, 197–221.

————. "Introduction: The Return of Wartime Suffering in Contemporary German Memory Culture, Literature and Film." In Schmitz, *A Nation of Victims?*, 1–30.

————, ed. *A Nation of Victims? Representation of Wartime Suffering from 1945 to the Present*. Amsterdam: Rodopi, 2007.

————. *On Their Own Terms: The Legacy of National Socialism in Post-1990 German Fiction*. Birmingham, UK: U of Birmingham P, 2004.

————. "Reconciliation between the Generations: The Normalization of the Image of the Ordinary German Soldier in Dieter Wellershoff's *Der Ernstfall* and Ulla Hahn's *Unscharfe Bilder*." In Taberner and Cooke, *German Culture*, 151–65.

————. "Representations of the Nazi Past II: German Wartime Suffering." In Taberner, *Contemporary German Fiction*, 142–58.

————. "Zweierlei Allegorie: W. G. Sebald's *Austerlitz* und Stephan Wackwitz's *Ein unsichtbares Land*." In *W. G. Sebald and Expatriate Writing*, edited by Gerhard Fischer. Amsterdam: Rodopi, forthcoming 2009.

Schneider, Michael. "Fathers and Sons, Retrospectively: The Damaged Relationship between Two Generations." *New German Critique* 31 (winter 1984): 3–52.

Schneiß, Wolfgang. *Flucht, Vertreibung und verlorene Heimat im früheren Ostdeutschland: Beispiele literarischer Bearbeitung*. Frankfurt am Main: Peter Lang, 1996.

Schulte, Christian. "'Die Naturgeschichte der Zerstörung': W. G. Sebalds Thesen zu 'Luftkrieg und Literatur.'" *Text und Kritik* 158 (2003): 82–94.

Sebald, W. G. *After Nature*. Translated by Michael Hamburger. New York: Random House, 2002.

————. "Air War and Literature: Zürich Lectures." In Sebald, *Natural History of Destruction*, 1–104.

————. *Austerlitz*. Translated by Anthea Bell. New York: Random House, 2001.

———. "Constructs of Mourning: Günter Grass and Wolfgang Hildesheimer." In Meyer, *Campo Santo,* edited by Sven Meyer, 102–29. London: Penguin, 2006.

———. *The Emigrants.* Translated by Michael Hulse. New York: New Directions, 1997.

———. "Konstruktionen der Trauer: Über Günter Grass und Wolfgang Hildesheimer." *Deutschunterricht* 35 (1983): 32–46.

———. *Luftkrieg und Literatur: Mit einem Essay zu Alfred Andersch.* Munich: Carl Hanser, 1999. Translated by Anthea Bell as *On the Natural History of Destruction* (New York: Random House, 2003).

———. *On the Natural History of Destruction.* Translated by Anthea Bell. London: Penguin, 2004.

———. *Die Ringe des Saturn.* Frankfurt: Fischer, 1997.

———. *The Rings of Saturn.* Translated by Michael Hulse. New York: New Directions, 1998.

———. "Der Schriftsteller Alfred Andersch." In Sebald, *Luftkrieg und Literatur,* 121–60.

———. *Vertigo.* Translated by Michael Hulse. New York: New Directions, 1999.

———. "Zwischen Geschichte und Naturgeschichte: Versuch über die literarische Beschreibung totaler Zerstörung mit Anmerkungen zu Kasack, Nossack und Kluge." In Meyer, *Campo Santo,* 69–100. First published in *Orbis Litterarum* 37 (1982): 345–66.

Sebald, W. G., and Gordon Turner. "Introduction and Transcript of an Interview given by Max Sebald (Interviewer: Michael Zeeman)." In *W. G. Sebald: History-Memory-Trauma,* edited by Scott Denham, 21–33. Berlin and New York: Walter de Gruyter, 2006.

Seibt, Gustav. "Der letzte Augenblick der Unschuld: Ein Nachwort von Gustav Seibt." In Biller, *Harlem Holocaust,* 67–68.

Slugocka, Ludmila. *Die deutsche Polenliteratur auf dem Gebiet der Deutschen Demokratischen Republik in der Zeit von 1945–1960.* Poznan, Poland: PWN, 1964.

"So ein Buch kann nur eine Frau schreiben." Television interview with Wibke Bruhns. *Schümer und Dorn: Der Büchertalk.* 17 April 2004.

Sokolowski, Robert. *Introduction to Phenomenology.* Cambridge: CUP, 2000.

Sontag, Susan. *Regarding the Pain of Others.* London: Penguin, 2003.

———. *Under the Sign of Saturn.* New York: Farrar, Straus and Giroux.

Stargardt, Nicholas. *Witnesses of War: Children's Lives under the Nazis.* London: Jonathan Cape, 2005.

Stierlin, Helm. "The Dialogue between the Generations about the Nazi Era." In *The Collective Silence: German Identity and the Legacy of Shame,* edited by Barbara Heimannsberg and Christoph J. Schmidt, 143–61. San Francisco: Jossey-Bass, 1993.

Streim, Gregor. "Der Bombenkrieg als Sensation und als Dokumentation: Gert Ledigs Roman *Vergeltung* und die Debatte um W. G. Sebalds *Luftkrieg und Literatur.*" In *Krieg in den Medien,* edited by Heinz-Peter Preusser, 293–312. Amsterdam: Rodopi, 2005.

Taberner, Stuart, ed. *Contemporary German Fiction: Writing in the Berlin Republic.* Cambridge: CUP, 2007.

———. *German Literature of the 1990s and Beyond: Normalization and the Berlin Republic.* Rochester, NY: Camden House, 2005.

———. "German Nostalgia? Remembering German-Jewish Life in W. G. Sebald's *Die Ausgewanderten* and *Austerlitz.*" *Germanic Review* 3 (2004): 181–202.

———. "Hans-Ulrich Treichel's *Der Verlorene* and the Problem of German Wartime Suffering." *Modern Language Review* 97, no. 1 (2002): 123–34.

———. Introduction to *Der Vorleser,* by Bernhard Schlink, 7–38. London: Bristol Classical Press, 2003.

———. "Literary Debates since Unification." In Taberner, *German Literature,* 1–32.

———. "Literary Representations in Contemporary German Fiction of the Expulsions of Germans from the East." In Schmitz, *A Nation of Victims?,* 223–46.

———. "Philo-Semitism in Recent German Film: *Aimee and Jaguar, Rosenstraße,* and *Das Wunder von Bern.*" *German Life and Letters* 58, no. 3 (2005): 357–72.

———. "Private Failings and Public Virtues: Günter Grass's *Beim Häuten der Zwiebel* and the Exemplary Use of Authorial Biography." *Modern Language Review* 103 (2008): 166–78.

———. "Representations of German Wartime Suffering in Recent Fiction." In Niven, *Germans as Victims,* 164–80.

Taberner, Stuart, and Paul Cooke, eds. *German Culture, Politics, and Literature into the Twenty-First Century: Beyond Normalization.* Rochester, NY: Camden House, 2006.

Tar, Zoltan. *The Frankfurt School: The Critical Theories of Max Horkheimer and Theodor W. Adorno.* London: John Wiley, 1977.

Till, Karen E. *The New Berlin: Memory, Politics, Place.* Minneapolis: U of Minnesota P, 2005.

Timm, Uwe. *Am Beispiel meines Bruders.* Cologne: Kiepenheuer and Witsch, 2003.

———. *Die Entdeckung der Currywurst (The Discovery of the Curried Sausage).* Munich: DTV, 2002.

———. *Erzählen und kein Ende.* Cologne: Kiepenheuer and Witsch, 1993.

Tooze, Adam. "Einfach verkalkuliert." *Zeit Online.* http://www.taz.de/index.php?id=archivseite&dig=2005/03/12/a0289 (accessed 1 March 2008).

———. *The Wages of Destruction: The Making and Breaking of the Nazi Economy.* London: Allen Lane, 2006.

Treichel, Hans-Ulrich. *Anatolin.* Frankfurt am Main: Suhrkamp, 2008.

———. *Der Entwurf des Autors: Frankfurter Poetikvorlesungen.* Frankfurt am Main: Suhrkamp, 2000.

———. *Heimatkunde oder Alles ist heiter und edel.* Frankfurt am Main: Suhrkamp Taschenbuch, 2000.

———. *Leib und Seele: Berichte.* Frankfurt am Main: Suhrkamp, 1998.

———. *Lost.* Translated by Carol Brown Janeway. London: Picador, 1999.

———. *Menschenflug.* Frankfurt am Main: Suhrkamp, 2005.

Vees-Gulani, Susanne. *Trauma and Guilt: Literature of Wartime Bombing in Germany.* Berlin: Walter de Gruyter, 2003.

Vogt, Jochen. "Er fehlt, er fehlte, er hat gefehlt . . . Ein Rückblick auf die soge-nannten Väterbücher." In *Deutsche Nachkriegsliteratur und der Holocaust,* edited by Stephan Braese, et al., 385–412. Frankfurt am Main: Campus, 1998.

Wackwitz, Stephan. *Ein unsichtbares Land: Familienroman.* Frankfurt am Main: Fischer, 2003.

Wagenbach, Klaus. "Grass hat nichts verschwiegen." *Die Zeit,* 26 April 2007, 18.

Walser, Martin. "Die Banalität des Guten: Erfahrungen beim Verfassen einer Sonntagsrede aus Anlaß der Verleihung des Friedenspreises des Deutschen Buchhandels." *Frankfurter Allgemeine Zeitung,* 12 December 1998, 15.

———. "Erfahrungen beim Verfassen einer Sonntagsrede." In *Die Walser-Bubis-Debatte,* edited by Frank Schirrmacher, 7–17. Frankfurt am Main: Suhrkamp, 1999.

Weber, Alexander. *Günter Grass's Use of Baroque Literature.* Leeds, UK: W. S. Maney for the Modern Humanities Research Association and the Institute of Germanic Studies, University of London, 1995.

Weigel, Sigrid. "Families, Phantoms and the Discourse of 'Generations' as Pol-itics of the Past: Rejection and Desire for Origins." Unpublished manuscript.

————. *Genea-Logik: Generation, Tradition und Evolution zwischen Kultur-und Naturwissenschaften*. Munich: Wilhelm Fink, 2006.

————. "'Generation' as Symbolic Form: On the Genealogical Discourse of Memory since 1945." *Germanic Review* 77 (2002): 264–77.

————. "Télescopage im Unbewussten: Zum Verhältnis von Trauma, Geschichtsbegriff und Literatur." In *Trauma: Zwischen Psychoanalyse and kulturellem Deutungsmuster*, edited by Elisabeth Bronfen, Birgit R. Erdle, and Sigrid Weigel, 51–76. Cologne: Böhlau, 1999.

Welzer, Harald. "Im Gedächtniswohnzimmer: Warum sind Bücher über die eigene Familiengeschichte so effolgreich? Ein ZEIT — Gespräch mit dem Sozialpsychologen Harald Welzer über das private Erinnern." *Die Zeit*, 25 March 2004, 43–46.

————. "Schön unscharf: Über die Konjunktur der Familien- und Generationenromane." *Mittelweg* 36 (2004): 53–64.

Welzer, Harald, Sabine Moller, and Karoline Tschuggnall. *Opa war kein Nazi: Nationalsozialismus und Holocaust im Familiengedächtnis*. Frankfurt am Main: Fischer, 2002.

Wette, Wolfram. *The Wehrmacht: History, Myth, Reality*. Cambridge, MA: Harvard UP, 2006.

Wilds, Karl. "Identity Creation and the Culture of Contrition: Recasting 'Normality' in the Berlin Republic." *German Politics* 9, no. 1 (2000): 83–102.

Williams, Rhys. "'Eine ganz normale Kindheit': Uwe Timms *Am Beispiel meines Bruders*." In Finaly and Cornils, *"(Un-)erfüllte Wirklichkeit,"* 173–84.

————. "'Mein Unbewusstes kannte . . . den Fall der Mauer und die deutsche Wiedervereinigung nicht": The Writer Hans-Ulrich Treichel." *German Life and Letters* 52, no. 2 (2002): 208–18.

Wilms, Wilfried. "Taboo and Repression in W. G. Sebald's *On the Natural History of Destruction*." In *W. G. Sebald — A Critical Companion*, edited by J. J. Long and Anne Whitehead, 175–89. Seattle: U of Washington P, 2004.

Wittlinger, Ruth. "Taboo or Tradition? The 'Germans as Victims' Theme in West Germany until the early 1990s." In Niven, *Germans as Victims*, 62–75.

Wollschläger, Hans. "Nur eines Menschen Stimme, gewaltig zu hören." *Frankfurter Allgemeine Zeitung*, 9 October 2001.

Wood, Nancy. *Vectors of Memory: Legacies of Trauma in Postwar Europe*. Oxford: Berg, 1999.

Žižek, Slavoj. *The Ticklish Subject: The Absent Centre of Political Ontology*. London: Verso, 2000.

Contributors

KARINA BERGER is a PhD student at the University of Leeds. Her thesis examines the trajectory of literary representations of the expulsion of ethnic Germans from the eastern territories from the 1950s to the current day.

ELIZABETH BOA is Emeritus Professor of German at the University of Nottingham. She has published books on the German novel (coauthor J. H. Reid), on Wedekind, on Kafka, and is coauthor with Rachel Palfreyman of *Heimat — A German Dream: Regional Loyalties and National Identity in German Culture 1890–1990* (Oxford, 2000). She was also coeditor with Janet Wharton of *Women and the Wende* (German Monitor 31, 1994) and with Heike Bartel of *Anne Duden: A Revolution of Words* (German Monitor 56, 2003) and of *Pushing at Boundaries: Approaches to Contemporary German Women Writers from Karen Duve to Jenny Erpenbeck* (German Monitor 64, 2006).

STEPHEN BROCKMANN is Professor of German at Carnegie Mellon University in Pittsburgh, Pennsylvania. He is the author of *Literature and German Reunification* (1999), *German Literary Culture at the Zero Hour* (2004), and *Nuremberg: The Imaginary Capital* (2006). From 2002 to 2007 he was the managing editor of the *Brecht Yearbook*. In the autumn term of 2007 he was Visiting Leverhulme Professor at the University of Leeds.

DAVID CLARKE is Lecturer in German at the University of Bath. His research interests include the literature of the German Democratic Republic, contemporary German literature, and German film. He is the author of *"Diese merkwürdige Kleinigkeit einer Vision": Christoph Hein's Social Critique in Transition* (Rodopi, 2002) and has recently coedited, with Arne De Winde., *Reinhard Jirgl: Perspektiven, Lesarten, Kontexte* (Rodopi, 2007).

MARY COSGROVE is Lecturer in German at the University of Edinburgh. She has published on contemporary German and German-Jewish literature, including Albert Drach, Wolfgang Hildesheimer, Günter Grass, and more recently W. G. Sebald. She coedited a prize-winning book on German memory culture since unification, published by Camden House in 2006 (*Choice* Outstanding Academic Title Award 2007). She also coedited a special issue of *German Life and Letters* in 2006 on German memory contests. Her monograph on Austro-Jewish writer Albert Drach was published in 2004 by Niemeyer (Conditio Judaica). She is currently working on a monograph on melancholy in German literature since 1960.

RICK CROWNSHAW is a lecturer in the Department of English and Comparative Literature at Goldsmiths, University of London. He has published essays on Holocaust literature, museums, monuments, and memorials. With Jane Kilby and Antony Rowland, he is coeditor of *The Future of Memory* (Berghahn Books, forthcoming). He is currently finishing a monograph, *The Afterlife of Holocaust Memory in Contemporary Literature and Culture* (to be published by Palgrave Macmillan).

HELEN FINCH is a lecturer in German at the University of Liverpool. She has published articles on W. G. Sebald and Günter Grass, and is currently working on a monograph comparing the works of W. G. Sebald with those of Peter Handke and Botho Strauß.

FRANK FINLAY is Professor of German at the University of Leeds and currently President of the Conference of University Teachers of German in Great Britain and Ireland. His publications include books and articles on literature, culture, and aesthetics in postwar Germany and Austria, with a recent focus on writing since the *Wende*. He is a member of the editorial team nearing completion of the 27-volume *Kölner Ausgabe der Werke Heinrich Bölls* and is Joint Director of the Leeds-Swansea Colloquia on Contemporary German-Language Literature.

KATHARINA HALL is Senior Lecturer in German at the University of Swansea. She has published widely on contemporary German literature, history, and culture, including articles on the work of W. G. Sebald, Bernhard Schlink, and Zafer Şenocak. Her monograph, *Günter Grass's 'Danzig Quintet': Explorations in the Memory and History of the Nazi Era from* Die Blechtrommel *to* Im Krebsgang (Peter Lang), and an edited volume, *Esther Dischereit* (University of Wales Press), appeared in 2007. She is currently the principal investigator on the major research project Detecting the Past: Representations of National Socialism in English- and German-Language Crime Fiction, Television and Film and is coeditor, with David Basker, of the forthcoming volume *German Crime Fiction* (European Crime Fiction Series, University of Wales Press, 2010).

COLETTE LAWSON is a PhD student at Nottingham Trent University and holds a studentship with the AHRC-funded project Germans as Victims based at Leeds University. Her thesis examines the debate surrounding W. G. Sebald's *Luftkrieg und Literatur* and analyzes literary representations of the Allied bombings in the postwar and postunification periods.

CAROLINE SCHAUMANN is Assistant Professor of German Studies at Emory University in Atlanta, Georgia. Her teaching and research interests include postwar and postwall German literature and culture, German-Jewish literature, and nature writing. Schaumann recently published *Memory Matters: Generational Responses to Germany's Nazi Past in Recent Women's Literature* (Walter de Gruyter, 2008). In addition, she has published research articles, teaching materials, and given numerous presentations on the changing discourses on the Nazi past in the 1990s and 2000s. Schaumann is currently working on a book-length study that examines the cultural shifts in the perception, written text, and imagery of mountains from the mid-1800s to the present.

HELMUT SCHMITZ is Associate Professor of German at the University of Warwick. He has published widely on contemporary German literature, especially on memory of National Socialism and the war. He is the author of a monograph on Hanns-Josef Ortheil (Heinz, 1997) and of the book *On Their Own Terms: The Legacy of National Socialism in Post-1990 German Fiction* (University of Birmingham Press, 2004). He has coedited, with Georgina Paul, *Entgegenkommen: Dialogues with Barbara Köhler* (Rodopi, 2000), *German Culture and the Uncomfortable Past* (Ashgate, 2001), and *A Nation of Victims? Representations of German Wartime Suffering from 1945 to the Present* (Rodopi, 2007). An edited collection, *Von der nationalen zur internationalen Literatur: Transkulturelle deutschsprachige Literatur und Kultur im Zeitalter globaler Migration* is forthcoming with Rodopi in 2009.

KATHRIN SCHÖDEL has just completed her PhD thesis on *Literarisches versus politisches Gedächtnis? Martin Walsers Friedenspreisrede und sein Roman Ein springender Brunnen* at the University of Erlangen, Germany. She has published several articles on remembering the National Socialist period in German literature, for instance, "'Narrative Normalization' and Günter Grass's *Im Krebsgang*" in *German Culture, Politics, and Literature into the Twenty-First Century: Beyond Normalization* (2006), and is coeditor with Susanne Kollmann of the volume *PostModerne De/Konstruktionen: Ethik, Politik und Kultur am Ende einer Epoche* (Lit Verlag, 2004).

STUART TABERNER is Professor of Contemporary German Literature, Culture, and Society at the University of Leeds. He has written widely on postwar literature, society, and culture. His most recent monograph *German Literature of the 1990s and Beyond* appeared in 2005. He is editor of a number of collections, including *Recasting German Identity* (2002, with Frank Finlay); *German Literature in the Age of Globalisation* (University of Birmingham Press, 2004); *German Culture, Politics, and Literature into the Twenty-First Century: Beyond Normalization* (2006, with Paul Cooke); and *Contemporary German Fiction: Writing in the Berlin Republic* (Cambridge University Press, 2007).

Index

Lightning Source UK Ltd.
Milton Keynes UK
UKOW052325180412

190985UK00001B/35/P